Lecture Notes in Computer Science 4420

Commenced Publication in 1973
Founding and Former Series Editors:
Gerhard Goos, Juris Hartmanis, and Jan van Leeuwen

Shriram Krishnamurthi   Martin Odersky (Eds.)

Compiler Construction

16th International Conference, CC 2007
Held as Part of the Joint European Conferences
on Theory and Practice of Software, ETAPS 2007
Braga, Portugal, March 26-30, 2007
Proceedings

 Springer

Volume Editors

Shriram Krishnamurthi
Brown University
Computer Science Department
Providence, RI, USA
E-mail: sk@cs.brown.edu

Martin Odersky
EPFL
School of Computer and Communication Sciences
Institute of Core Computing
Lausanne, Switzerland
E-mail: martin.odersky@epfl.ch

Library of Congress Control Number: 2007921957

CR Subject Classification (1998): D.3.4, D.3.1, F.4.2, D.2.6, F.3, I.2.2

LNCS Sublibrary: SL 1 – Theoretical Computer Science and General Issues

ISSN   0302-9743
ISBN-10   3-540-71228-3 Springer Berlin Heidelberg New York
ISBN-13   978-3-540-71228-2 Springer Berlin Heidelberg New York

Springer is a part of Springer Science+Business Media

springer.com

© Springer-Verlag Berlin Heidelberg 2007
Printed in Germany

Typesetting: Camera-ready by author, data conversion by Scientific Publishing Services, Chennai, India
Printed on acid-free paper   SPIN: 12029303   06/3142   5 4 3 2 1 0

Foreword

ETAPS 2007 is the tenth instance of the European Joint Conferences on Theory and Practice of Software, and thus a cause for celebration.

The events that comprise ETAPS address various aspects of the system development process, including specification, design, implementation, analysis and improvement. The languages, methodologies and tools which support these activities are all well within its scope. Different blends of theory and practice are represented, with an inclination towards theory with a practical motivation on the one hand and soundly based practice on the other. Many of the issues involved in software design apply to systems in general, including hardware systems, and the emphasis on software is not intended to be exclusive.

History and Prehistory of ETAPS

ETAPS as we know it is an annual federated conference that was established in 1998 by combining five conferences [Compiler Construction (CC), European Symposium on Programming (ESOP), Fundamental Approaches to Software Engineering (FASE), Foundations of Software Science and Computation Structures (FOSSACS), Tools and Algorithms for Construction and Analysis of Systems (TACAS)] with satellite events.

All five conferences had previously existed in some form and in various colocated combinations: accordingly, the prehistory of ETAPS is complex. FOSSACS was earlier known as the Colloquium on Trees in Algebra and Programming (CAAP), being renamed for inclusion in ETAPS as its historical name no longer reflected its contents. Indeed CAAP's history goes back a long way; prior to 1981, it was known as the Colleque de Lille sur les Arbres en Algebre et en Programmation. FASE was the indirect successor of a 1985 event known as Colloquium on Software Engineering (CSE), which together with CAAP formed a joint event called TAPSOFT in odd-numbered years. Instances of TAPSOFT, all including CAAP plus at least one software engineering event, took place every two years from 1985 to 1997 inclusive. In the alternate years, CAAP took place separately from TAPSOFT.

Meanwhile, ESOP and CC were each taking place every two years from 1986. From 1988, CAAP was colocated with ESOP in even years. In 1994, CC became a "conference" rather than a "workshop" and CAAP, CC and ESOP were thereafter all colocated in even years.

TACAS, the youngest of the ETAPS conferences, was founded as an international workshop in 1995; in its first year, it was colocated with TAPSOFT. It took place each year, and became a "conference" when it formed part of ETAPS 1998. It is a telling indication of the importance of tools in the modern field of informatics that TACAS today is the largest of the ETAPS conferences.

The coming together of these five conferences was due to the vision of a small group of people who saw the potential of a combined event to be more than the sum of its parts. Under the leadership of Don Sannella, who became the first ETAPS steering committee chair, they included: Andre Arnold, Egidio Astesiano, Hartmut Ehrig, Peter Fritzson, Marie-Claude Gaudel, Tibor Gyimothy, Paul Klint, Kim Guldstrand Larsen, Peter Mosses, Alan Mycroft, Hanne Riis Nielson, Maurice Nivat, Fernando Orejas, Bernhard Steffen, Wolfgang Thomas and (alphabetically last but in fact one of the ringleaders) Reinhard Wilhelm.

ETAPS today is a loose confederation in which each event retains its own identity, with a separate programme committee and proceedings. Its format is open-ended, allowing it to grow and evolve as time goes by. Contributed talks and system demonstrations are in synchronized parallel sessions, with invited lectures in plenary sessions. Two of the invited lectures are reserved for "unifying" talks on topics of interest to the whole range of ETAPS attendees. The aim of cramming all this activity into a single one-week meeting is to create a strong magnet for academic and industrial researchers working on topics within its scope, giving them the opportunity to learn about research in related areas, and thereby to foster new and existing links between work in areas that were formerly addressed in separate meetings.

ETAPS 1998–2006

The first ETAPS took place in Lisbon in 1998. Subsequently it visited Amsterdam, Berlin, Genova, Grenoble, Warsaw, Barcelona, Edinburgh and Vienna before arriving in Braga this year. During that time it has become established as the major conference in its field, attracting participants and authors from all over the world. The number of submissions has more than doubled, and the numbers of satellite events and attendees have also increased dramatically.

ETAPS 2007

ETAPS 2007 comprises five conferences (CC, ESOP, FASE, FOSSACS, TACAS), 18 satellite workshops (ACCAT, AVIS, Bytecode, COCV, FESCA, FinCo, GT-VMT, HAV, HFL, LDTA, MBT, MOMPES, OpenCert, QAPL, SC, SLA++P, TERMGRAPH and WITS), three tutorials, and seven invited lectures (not including those that were specific to the satellite events). We received around 630 submissions to the five conferences this year, giving an overall acceptance rate of 25%. To accommodate the unprecedented quantity and quality of submissions, we have four-way parallelism between the main conferences on Wednesday for the first time. Congratulations to all the authors who made it to the final programme! I hope that most of the other authors still found a way of participating in this exciting event and I hope you will continue submitting.

ETAPS 2007 was organized by the Departamento de Informática of the Universidade do Minho, in cooperation with

- European Association for Theoretical Computer Science (EATCS)
- European Association for Programming Languages and Systems (EAPLS)
- European Association of Software Science and Technology (EASST)
- The Computer Science and Technology Center (CCTC, Universidade do Minho)
- Camara Municipal de Braga
- CeSIUM/GEMCC (Student Groups)

The organizing team comprised:

- João Saraiva (Chair)
- José Bacelar Almeida (Web site)
- José João Almeida (Publicity)
- Luís Soares Barbosa (Satellite Events, Finances)
- Victor Francisco Fonte (Web site)
- Pedro Henriques (Local Arrangements)
- José Nuno Oliveira (Industrial Liaison)
- Jorge Sousa Pinto (Publicity)
- António Nestor Ribeiro (Fundraising)
- Joost Visser (Satellite Events)

ETAPS 2007 received generous sponsorship from Fundação para a Ciência e a Tecnologia (FCT), Enabler (a Wipro Company), Cisco and TAP Air Portugal.

Overall planning for ETAPS conferences is the responsibility of its Steering Committee, whose current membership is:

Perdita Stevens (Edinburgh, Chair), Roberto Amadio (Paris), Luciano Baresi (Milan), Sophia Drossopoulou (London), Matt Dwyer (Nebraska), Hartmut Ehrig (Berlin), José Fiadeiro (Leicester), Chris Hankin (London), Laurie Hendren (McGill), Mike Hinchey (NASA Goddard), Michael Huth (London), Anna Ingólfs-dóttir (Aalborg), Paola Inverardi (L'Aquila), Joost-Pieter Katoen (Aachen), Paul Klint (Amsterdam), Jens Knoop (Vienna), Shriram Krishnamurthi (Brown), Kim Larsen (Aalborg), Tiziana Margaria (Göttingen), Ugo Montanari (Pisa), Rocco de Nicola (Florence), Jakob Rehof (Dortmund), Don Sannella (Edinburgh), João Saraiva (Minho), Vladimiro Sassone (Southampton), Helmut Seidl (Munich), Daniel Varro (Budapest), Andreas Zeller (Saarbrücken).

I would like to express my sincere gratitude to all of these people and organizations, the programme committee chairs and PC members of the ETAPS conferences, the organizers of the satellite events, the speakers themselves, the many reviewers, and Springer for agreeing to publish the ETAPS proceedings. Finally, I would like to thank the organizing chair of ETAPS 2007, João Saraiva, for arranging for us to have ETAPS in the ancient city of Braga.

Edinburgh, January 2007   Perdita Stevens
                                      ETAPS Steering Committee Chair

Preface

This volume constitutes the proceedings of the 2007 Compiler Construction (CC) conference, held March 26–27, 2007 in Braga, Portugal as part of the ETAPS umbrella.

In keeping with tradition, CC solicited both research descriptions and tool papers, though most submissions were in the former category. We accepted 14 out of 60 submissions, all in the research paper category. Each submission was reviewed by at least three PC members, with papers co-authored by PC members receiving at least one additional reviewer. Forty-two papers had at least some support, and thus warranted deliberation. (Only one paper was entirely outside the scope of the conference.) The papers were discussed at a (lively!) live PC meeting held in Lausanne, Switzerland, on December 4, 2006. Almost all PC members attended the meeting, with the remainder participating by telephone.

CC had, in a few instances, to contend with the growing problem of defining what constitutes a prior publication in an era when workshops are now published in the ACM's Digital Library (and other such formal on-line repositories). As we have observed on the PCs of other venues, PC members in CC had mixed views on this matter. In a few years we therefore expect to see standardized policy to cover such cases.

We thank the many people who eased the administration of CC 2007. Foremost, the PC (and their subreviewers) did a thorough and conscientious job. Perdita Stevens invested enormous effort into the smooth running of ETAPS. Jay McCarthy offered round-the-clock support for the CONTINUE software that handled our papers. Yvette Dubuis (of EPFL) and Dawn Reed (of Brown) provided stellar administrative support to the Chairs, with Mme. Dubuis also organizing the PC meeting. EPFL helped sponsor the PC meeting. Philipp Haller provided valuable help in preparing the proceedings. Finally, the ETAPS and CC Steering Committees ensured the smooth passage of many matters.

January 2007

Shriram Krishnamurthi
Martin Odersky

Organization

Program Committee

Chairs: Shriram Krishnamurthi, Brown University, Providence
Martin Odersky, EPFL, Lausanne

Eric Allen, Sun Microsystems, Inc.
Emery Berger, University of Massachusetts Amherst
Rastislav Bodik, University of California, Berkeley
William Cook, University of Texas at Austin
Chen Ding, University of Rochester
Sabine Glesner, Technical University of Berlin
Dan Grossman, University of Washington
Rajiv Gupta, University of Arizona
Andrew Kennedy, Microsoft Research Cambridge
Christian Lengauer, University of Passau
Cristina Videira Lopes, University of California, Irvine
Todd Millstein, University of California, Los Angeles
G. Ramalingam, Microsoft Research India
Vijay Saraswat, IBM TJ Watson Research Center
Zhong Shao, Yale University
Yannis Smaragdakis, University of Oregon
Gregor Snelting, University of Passau
Joost Visser, Universidade do Minho
Reinhard Wilhelm, Saarland University

Reviewers

Arnold, Gilad
Arnold, Matthew
Barik, Raj
Bastoul, Cedric
Bierman, Gavin
Bond, Michael
Brandes, Thomas
Chilimbi, Trishul
Cohen, Albert
Felleisen, Matthias
Größlinger, Armin
Griebl, Martin
Grund, Daniel

Lin, Calvin
Lucas, Philipp
Marlow, Simon
Merz, Peter
Naeem, Nomair
Nagarajan, Vijay
Palsberg, Jens
Penso, Lucia Draque
Pierce, Benjamin
Pister, Markus
Rabbah, Rodric
Reineke, Jan
Reppy, John

Herrmann, Christoph A.
Hind, Mike
Ibrahim, Ali
Joyner, Mackale
Jump, Maria
Kelsey, Kirk
Kitchin, David
Kulkarni, Prasad
Lhotak, Ondrej

Shankar, AJ
Solar-Lezama, Armando
Sridharan, Manu
Tallam, Sriraman
Vouillon, Jerome
Whalley, David
Wiedermann, Benjamin
Ylvisaker, Benjamin
von Praun, Christoph

Table of Contents

Program Analysis

New Algorithms for SIMD Alignment*

Liza Fireman[1], Erez Petrank[2,**], and Ayal Zaks[3]

[1] Dept. of Computer Science, Technion, Haifa 32000, Israel
liza@cs.technion.ac.il
[2] Microsoft Research, One Microsoft Way, Redmond, WA 98052, USA
erez@cs.technion.ac.il
[3] IBM Haifa Research Laboratory, Mount Carmel, Haifa 31905, Israel
zaks@il.ibm.com

Abstract. Optimizing programs for modern multiprocessor or vector platforms is a major important challenge for compilers today. In this work, we focus on one challenging aspect: the SIMD ALIGNMENT problem. Previously, only heuristics were used to solve this problem, without guarantees on the number of shifts in the obtained solution. We study two interesting and realistic special cases of the SIMD ALIGNMENT problem and present two novel and efficient algorithms that provide *optimal* solutions for these two cases. The new algorithms employ dynamic programming and a MIN-CUT/MAX-FLOW algorithm as subroutines. We also discuss the relation between the SIMD ALIGNMENT problem and the MULTIWAY CUT and NODE MULTIWAY CUT problems; and we show how to derive an approximated solution to the SIMD ALIGNMENT problem based on approximation algorithms to these two known problems.

1 Introduction

Designing effective optimizations for modern architectures is an important goal for compiler designers today. This general task is composed of many non-trivial problems, the solution to which is not always known. In this paper we study one such problem — the SIMD ALIGNMENT problem, which emerges when optimizing for multimedia extensions. Previously only heuristics were studied for this problem [25,30,14]. In this paper we present two novel algorithms that obtain optimal solutions for two special cases. These special cases are actually broad enough to cover many practical instances of the SIMD ALIGNMENT problem.

Multimedia extensions have become one of the most popular additions to general-purpose microprocessors. Existing multimedia extensions are characterized as Single Instruction Multiple Data (SIMD) units that support packed, fixed-length vectors, such as MMX and SSE for Intel and AltiVec for IBM, Apple and Motorola. Producing SIMD codes is sometimes done manually for important specific application, but is often produced automatically by compilers (referred to as auto-vectorization or simdization). Explicit vector programming is time consuming and error prone. A promising alternative is to exploit vectorization technology to automatically generate SIMD codes from

---

* This research was supported by THE ISRAEL SCIENCE FOUNDATION (grant No. 845/06).
** On sabbatical leave from the Computer Science Department, Technion, Haifa 32000, Israel.

S. Krishnamurthi and M. Odersky (Eds.): CC 2007, LNCS 4420, pp. 1–15, 2007.

programs written in standard high-level languages. However, simdization is not trivial. Some of the difficulties in optimizing code for SIMD architectures stem from hardware constraints imposed by today's SIMD architectures [25].

One restrictive hardware feature that can significantly impact the effectiveness of simdization is the alignment constraint of memory units. In AltiVec [10], for example, a load instruction loads 16-byte contiguous memory from 16-byte aligned memory address (by ignoring the least significant 4 bits of the given memory address). The same applies to store instructions. Now consider a stream: given a stride-one memory reference in a loop, a *memory stream* corresponds to all the contiguous locations in memory accessed by that memory reference over the lifetime of the loop. The alignment constraint of SIMD memory units requires that streams involved in the same SIMD operation must have matching offsets.

Consider the following code fragment, where integer arrays a, b, and c start at 16-byte aligned addresses.

```
for (i = 0; i < 1000; i++) do
    a[i] = b[i+1] + c[i+2];
end for
```

The above code includes a loop with misaligned references. It requires additional realignment operations to allow vectorization on SIMD architectures with alignment constraints. In particular, unless special care is taken, data involved in the same computation, i.e., $a[i]$, $b[i+1]$, $c[i+2]$, will be relatively misaligned after being loaded to machine registers. To produce correct results, this data must be reorganized to reside in the same slots of their corresponding registers prior to performing any arithmetic computation.

The realigning of data in registers is achieved by explicit shift instructions that execute inside the loop and therefore affect performance significantly. The problem is to automatically reorganize data streams in registers to satisfy the alignment requirements imposed by the hardware using a minimum number of shift executions. Prior research has focused primarily on vectorizing loops where all memory references are properly aligned. An important aspect of this problem, namely, the problem of minimizing the number of shifts for aligning a given expression has been studied only recently.

An alternative to performing shift operations at runtime is to modify the layout of the data in memory. This alternative suffers from several obvious limitations. In this paper the initial data alignment is assumed to be predetermined.

1.1   This Work

In this work we investigate the computational complexity of the SIMD ALIGNMENT problem. A formal definition of the problem, motivation, and examples from current modern platforms appear in Section 2. The main contribution of this paper is the presentation of two new algorithms that provide *optimal* solutions for two special cases. These special cases are quite general and cover many practical instances.

A polynomial-time algorithm for expressions with two alignments. For expressions that contain two distinct predetermined alignments, an efficient algorithm based on solving a MINIMUM NODE S-T CUT problem can compute an optimal solution to the SIMD ALIGNMENT problem.

A polynomial-time algorithm for a single-appearance tree expression. For expressions that contain no common sub-expressions (i.e. form a tree) and where each array appears only once in the expression, an efficient algorithm based on dynamic programming can compute an optimal solution to the SIMD ALIGNMENT problem.

We stress that both cases are realistic and are common in practice. Also, the two cases do not supersede one another: one case is broader in the sense that it works on any expression, not necessarily a tree, and the other case is broader in the sense that it applies to an arbitrary number of alignments.

The SIMD ALIGNMENT problem can be mapped to the MULTIWAY CUT problem, and known algorithms for MULTIWAY CUT [11] can be used to solve the SIMD ALIGNMENT problem. However, known hardness results [12,5] do not hold for the SIMD ALIGNMENT problem if a shifted stream may be used in both its original form and its shifted form (see Section 9). Furthermore, the mapping to the MULTIWAY CUT problem is more involved in this case (see Section 7).

1.2 Organization

In Section 2 we formally define the SIMD ALIGNMENT problem. In Section 3 we list useful heuristics proposed in the literature so far.In Section 4 we propose a graph representation of the SIMD ALIGNMENT problem, which will be used by the algorithms. In Sections 6 and 5 we present the efficient algorithms for the special case of expressions with only two alignments and for single-appearance tree expressions, respectively, and in Section 8 we present the effectiveness of these algorithms. Section 7 relates the SIMD ALIGNMENT problem to MULTIWAY CUT problems. Relevant prior art is described in Section 9 and Section 10 concludes.

2   An Overview of the SIMD ALIGNMENT Problem

We begin by defining the SIMD ALIGNMENT problem.

Definition 1. The SIMD ALIGNMENT problem
Input: *An expression containing input operands, sub-expressions (operations) and output operands, with an alignment value assigned to every input and output operand.*
Solution: *A specification of shifts for some input operands and operations, such that the inputs to each operation all have the same alignment values and the inputs to output operands have the desired alignment values.*
Cost: *The number of shifts in the solution.*

Note that for each operation of the given expression, the solution may specify several shifts if the result of the operation is needed in different alignments, or it may specify no shifts at all if the result is needed only in the same alignment as its inputs. This applies to input operands as well. However, a solution is feasible only if the inputs of *each* operation and output operand are properly aligned. An elaborate description of how the shift operation is used with real platforms and a detailed example may be found in the thesis [15].

Shifting of data from one alignment value to another requires one shift operation but typically may require preliminary preparation of pre-loading and setting shift amount [23]. This preliminary work can often be placed before the loop where it is tolerable, whereas the shift operations themselves are part of the expression and must remain inside the loop. That is why our objective is to minimize the number of shifts.

3   Previous Heuristics

Previous work concentrated on identifying operations that can be vectorized assuming all operands are aligned. Several simple heuristics have been proposed to solve the alignment problem. In this section we shortly survey these heuristics, originally presented in [14], each of which can be shown to be sub-optimal for simple realistic instances [15].

- *Zero-Shift Policy.* This policy shifts each misaligned load stream to offset zero, and shifts the store stream from offset zero to the alignment of the store address. This simple policy is employed by the widespread GCC compiler [21,24].
- *Eager-Shift Policy.* This policy shifts each load stream to the alignment of the store.
- *Lazy-Shift Policy.* This is a greedy policy of inserting shifts as late as possible in the expression. This policy does not specify how to break ties when different shifts may be used.
- *Majority Policy.* This policy shifts each load stream to the majority of the alignments of the input and output streams, and shifts the store stream from the majority offset to the alignment of the store address.

4   An Abstraction of SIMD Alignment

In what follows, it will be useful to represent instances of the SIMD ALIGNMENT problem using annotated graphs. We provide a graph representation for instances in which an array appears in the expression in one alignment only. The proposed representation may also be used in the general case, but for arrays appearing with multiple alignments the cost of the solution cannot be easily translated from graphs to expressions. This is because a single shift can be used for multiple alignments of the same array (e.g. to align both $a[i]$ to match $b[i+1]$ and $a[i+1]$ to match $c[i+2]$). Note, however, that this does not hold if only two distinct alignments are considered, as is the case in Section 6.

We call an expression in which each array appears with one alignment only a *single-appearance expression*. Most of the techniques employed in this paper relate to the study of graph algorithms. The representation of a single-appearance expression as a directed graph is the standard representation of expressions as graphs, except for two modifications. First, we add alignment labels to the nodes. Second, all appearances of the same array are represented by a single node. The nodes that represent the input and output streams are associated with alignment labels that signify the initial and final alignments, respectively, and the name of the array. Each operation (sub-expression) is also represented by a graph node. The operation nodes are labelled with the operation they carry. The nodes for input streams of an operation are connected to the node of the operation by incoming edges.

Consider the following example:

for $(i = 0; i < 1000; i++)$ **do**
$\quad a[i+3] = b[i+1] * c[i+2] + c[i+2] * d[i+1];$
end for

The corresponding graph representation for the above expression is shown in Figure 1. This graph has three leaves (input nodes) labelled $1(b), 2(c), 1(d)$ and one root (output node) labelled $3(a)$. The labels signify the initial and final alignments and the array names. The operation nodes are labelled with the operation they represent. Note that the graph in this example in not a tree. It is a Directed Acyclic Graph (DAG).

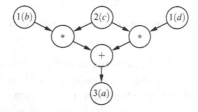

Fig. 1. A graph representation of $a[i+3] = b[i+1] * c[i+2] + c[i+2] * d[i+1]$

4.1   A Solution to a Graph Representation of a Single-Appearance

An important property of the expression execution is that once we shift a stream, we can use the shifted stream repeatedly without paying more shifts. In addition, even if we shift a stream we can still use its original alignment. We consider this property in the solution representation and its cost definition.

A solution to the graph representation of a single-appearance SIMD ALIGNMENT problem is a labelling of the nodes. The cost of a solution for the graph $G(V, E)$ is the sum of the costs $c(v)$ associated with each node $v \in V$, where $c(v)$ is the number of distinct labels of v's successor nodes that are also different from the label of v. We claim that this cost of the graph solution is equal to the cost of the corresponding solution of the expression. We interpret the solution to the graph as shifting specifications for the expression execution as follows. Each operation is executed at the alignment that is the label of its corresponding node in the graph. A stream represented by node v should be shifted from the alignment represented by its label to the alignments of its successors (if different from its own). This specifies a valid execution of the expression because all operations have their input stream shifted to the same alignment. We need to show that the computed cost represents the minimal number of shifts required to execute the operations at the alignment specified by the graph solution. The expression is a single-appearance expression and therefore a shift must be done for a node if its successors do not have the same label. If an array appears with more than one alignment in the expression, shifting it once could save shift to another use of this array. We do not deal with sharing shifts among multiple alignment appearances of input operands or subexpressions. Therefore, the cost of the solution for a graph is exactly the number of shifts that should be executed in order to compute the expression with the alignments specified by the graph solution. In Figure 2 we show an example of a graph with a given solution.

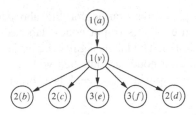

Fig. 2. A graph that exemplifies the cost of SIMD

The labelling shown in Figure 2 costs only two shifts, because the descendants of v have only two distinct shift labels that are also different from its own label (2 and 3). Therefore, v should be shifted from alignment 1 to alignments 2 and 3, enabling the execution of the rest of the computation without any further shift.

We are now ready to define the problem SIMDG.

Definition 2 (The SIMDG Problem)
Input: (G, L) where $G(V, E)$ is a DAG representation of a single-appearance expression and L is a set of predetermined shift labels for the source and sink nodes.
Solution: a labelling c for all nodes, which is an extension of the given labelling L.
Cost function: for a labelling c the cost is:

$$\sum_{v \in V} |\{c(u) \ : \ \exists u \in S(v) \ \ c(u) \neq c(v)\}|$$

where $S(v)$ is the set of successor nodes of v.
Goal: finding a solution with minimum cost.

From this point on we stick to the graph representation and consider the SIMDG problem rather than the original SIMD ALIGNMENT problem.

5 A Polynomial-Time Algorithm for Single-Appearance Tree Expressions

In this section we deal with expressions having an arbitrary number of alignments, but whose graph representations form a tree and any array appears in the expression at most once. We show that the SIMD ALIGNMENT problem can be solved in polynomial-time using dynamic programming in such cases.

In what follows, we consider the SIMD ALIGNMENT problem in its graph representation as defined in Section 4 and denote the input graph by $T = (V, E)$. The graph T
is a directed tree, with edges oriented from leaves to root. We further denote by I the
set of all predetermined alignment labels appearing in the leaves and the root of the
given tree. We consider only solutions that restrict the labelling of the inner nodes to
alignment labels in I. The optimal solution is again among the considered solutions.

A *solution* to the graph representation of a SIMD ALIGNMENT problem is again an
alignment labelling of the operation nodes in the graph, i.e., a complete alignment
labelling of the entire graph. Such a labelling can be translated into a solution for the
SIMD ALIGNMENT associated instance in the following way. For every edge $(u, v) \in E$
connecting nodes of different labels: $c(u) \neq c(v)$, a shift is introduced from alignment
$c(u)$ to alignment $c(v)$. Clearly, any labelling of the graph represents a *feasible* solution
(though not necessarily an optimal one). The cost of a solution is equal to the number
of such shifts, because shifts cannot be reused (the out-degree is 1).

Definition 3. *We say that a graph edge is a* shift edge, *with respect to a given alignment
labelling of a tree, if its two incident nodes have distinct labels.*

The dynamic programming algorithm computes incremental solutions to the problem
by considering larger and larger subtrees. The optimal solution of a subtree is computed
using the values computed for its immediate subtrees. In particular, let v be a node in
the tree T and consider the subtree T_v of T rooted at v. For each possible alignment $i \in I$,
denote by $OPT_T(v, i)$ the minimum number of shift edges required by any labelling of
T_v that assigns label i to node v. Note that the optimal labelling and the corresponding
cost may be different for different i's in I.

The dynamic programming algorithm computes the entries of a matrix *val* with an
entry $val(v, i)$ for each node v and each possible shift $i \in I$. For each node v, the entry
$val(v, i)$ represents a partial solution for T_v such that $val(v, i) = OPT_T(v, i)$. After computing the values $val(v, i)$ for all nodes v and alignments i, the algorithm uses them to
label the tree optimally.

Recall that the tree representing the expression has leaves representing the input
operands and a root representing the output. The edges are directed from the leaves to
the root. The algorithm (see Algorithm 1) iterates over the nodes of the tree in topological order (starting from leaves and reaching the root at the end), filling the rows in the
matrix $val(v, i)$. The base of this computation are the leaves for which a predetermined
alignment label is provided. For each leaf v we set the value of $val(v, i)$ to be 0 if i is
the predetermined alignment of v and ∞ otherwise. Then, the inner nodes of the tree are
traversed in topological order, such that a node is visited after all its predecessors in the
tree have been visited. The value of $val(v, i)$ for a node v with label i is computed by
adding the costs associated with all incoming edges $(u, v) \in E$, where each such cost is
the minimum of $val(u, j) + I_{(i \neq j)}$ taken over all $j \in I$, where $I_{(i \neq j)}$ is 1 if $i \neq j$ and 0
otherwise. Finally, the algorithm considers the entry $val(v, i)$ where v is the root node
and $i = s_v$ is the predetermined alignment of the root as the cost of the solution. It is
shown in the proof that this process computes $val(v, i)$ so that $val(v, i) = OPT_T(v, i)$, for
each node v and $i \in I$.

Next, the tree is traversed from root to leaves in order to label all inner vertices in a consistent manner that matches the minimum number of shift edges. Given that each vertex has only one outgoing edge, its value is determined once, creating no conflicts.

Algorithm 1. Solving a Single-Appearance Tree expression.

Input: a tree $G(V, E)$ with the leaves and root having predetermined labels.
Output: a labelling $s(v)$ for all vertices.

```
 1: for every node v in topological order (from leaves to root) do
 2:     for every i ∈ I do
 3:         if v is a leaf, having predetermined alignment label sᵥ then
```
4:    $\quad\quad\quad val(v,i) = \begin{cases} 0 & i = s_v \\ \infty & i \neq s_v \end{cases}$
```
 5:         else
```
6:    $\quad\quad\quad val(v,i) = \sum_{u:(u \to v) \in E} \min_j \{val(u,j) + I_{(i \neq j)}\}$
```
 7:             where I_{i≠j} equals 1 if i ≠ j and 0 otherwise
 8:         end if
 9:     end for
10: end for
```

```
11: Set s(v) = sᵥ for root and leaf nodes
12: for every node u in reverse topological order from root (excluding) to leaves (excluding) do
13:     Let v be the unique successor of u: (u → v) ∈ E.
14:     s(u) = argmin_j{val(u,j) + I_{s(v)≠j}}
15:     where argmin_j is an index j for which the value val(u,j) + I_{s(v)≠j} is minimal.
16: end for
```

For a rigorous proof of correctness the reader is referred to the thesis [15]. The complexity of Algorithm 1 is governed by line 6 in which the algorithm computes the entries of the matrix val. There are $k|V|$ entries in this matrix where $k = |I|$, and for every node $v \in V$ we add $d^-(v)$ addends each requiring k comparisons, where $d^-(v)$ is the in-degree of v in the tree. Hence the total complexity of the algorithm is $O(k \sum_{v \in V} d^-(v)k) = O(k^2|E|) = O(k^2|V|)$.

6   A Polynomial-Time Algorithm for Expressions with Only Two Alignments

In this section we present a polynomial-time algorithm for a restricted SIMD ALIGN-MENT problem. We restrict the expression to be a SIMDG expression (and in particular, a single-appearance expression) that contains only two distinct predetermined alignments associated with the input and output operands. Note that such restricted cases can appear in practice, when there are only two possible alignment values (0 and 1, e.g. when vectorizing for pairs of elements) or when more than 2 alignment values exist but all input and output operands are confined to two values (not necessarily 0 and 1).

Our algorithm uses a variant of the standard cut problem in graphs. In this variant, the cut is specified by nodes and not by edges. Let us first define a node cut in a graph.

Definition 4. A node s-t cut [1]

Given a connected undirected graph $G = (V,E)$ and two specified vertices $s,t \in V$, for which $(s,t) \notin E$, a node s-t cut is a subset of $V \setminus \{s,t\}$ whose removal from the graph disconnects the vertices s and t from each other.

We now define the MINIMUM NODE S-T CUT problem that we use to solve the variant of the SIMD ALIGNMENT problem restricted to two alignments. An optimal solution to the MINIMUM NODE S-T CUT problem can be constructed in polynomial time using a max-flow algorithm [1,9].

Definition 5. MINIMUM NODE S-T CUT problem

Input: *a connected, undirected graph $G = (V,E)$ and two specified vertices $s,t \in V$, for which $(s,t) \notin E$.*

Problem: *find a node s-t cut with a minimum number of nodes.*

Given an expression as an input to the SIMD ALIGNMENT problem, we represent it as a graph and then use an algorithm for MINIMUM NODE S-T CUT to construct a minimum node s-t cut, which is then used to provide a solution to our original problem in terms of minimum shifts.

Algorithm 2 for handling two alignments proceeds as follows. We start by considering the directed graph $G = (V,E)$ that represents the SIMD ALIGNMENT expression. Denote the two alignments by 0 and 1 for clarity; the algorithm depends neither on the values of the alignments nor on the possible number of alignments. We construct an undirected graph H by performing the following actions to the graph G. First, each pair of nodes u and v that share a common successor node w (that is: $(u,w),(v,w) \in E$) are connected by an edge (u,v), if not already connected[1]. The direction of this (u,v) edge is immaterial, as we will be ignoring the directions of the edges E from now on. We further add two "terminal" nodes s_0 and s_1 that serve as source and target nodes s and t for the MINIMUM NODE S-T CUT problem. An edge is added between s_0 and each node whose alignment label is predetermined to 0, and similarly for s_1. In addition, sink nodes (which do not feed other nodes, but typically store into memory) are not expected to host shifts and should refrain from being cut nodes. This can be accomplished by merging each terminal node with all sink nodes connected to it, or by assigning infinite capacity (for max flow routine below) to sink nodes with predetermined labels[2]. Denote by H the obtained graph.

Next, we find a minimum node s-t cut C in H. Finding a solution to the MINIMUM NODE S-T CUT problem is possible in polynomial time using MAX FLOW algorithms [1,9]. Denote by G' the (undirected) graph obtained by removing the cut C from H. Clearly s_0 and s_1 belong to G' and there is no path connecting s_0 and s_1 in G'. As the cut is in nodes, there may be more than two connected components on G'. All nodes in the component S_0 that contains s_0 are labelled 0 and all nodes in the connected component S_1 that contains s_1 are labelled 1. We now return to the original (directed) graph G to label the remaining nodes. The labelled predecessor nodes (excluding those that belong

---

[1] Graphs with such additional edges are sometimes called *moral*, stressing that the parents of each node are "married". Note however that a parent may have more than one spouse.

[2] If a sink node does not have predetermined alignment, it will not belong to any minimum node-cut due to the "morality" property.

to C) of each yet-unlabelled node must all have the same label, because every pair of such predecessors has been connected by an edge in H. We label each un-labelled node by the label of its predecessors. Source nodes (without predecessors) may belong to C, typically have predetermined labels which they retain. All remaining nodes are labelled 0 (we could label them 1 as well). Finally, a shift is provided for each node of the cut, to be applied to the result of the corresponding operation (i.e. *after* the operation is executed), from the label of the cut node to the "other" label (of one or more successor nodes).

An example. Consider the following code and its corresponding DAG which appears in Figure 3 (a). Two shifts are required to compute this expression.

for $(i = 0; i < 1000; i\text{++})$ **do**
$$f[i] = (a[i+1] * b[i+1] + a[i+1] * c[i+1])$$
$$+ (a[i+1] * d[i] + a[i+1] * e[i]);$$
end for

Algorithm 2 produces the graph H with two additional terminals s_0 and s_1, and parent-connecting edges. It then finds a node-cut as in Figure 3 (b). We mark the cut nodes by encircling them with a bold line. The sets S_0 and S_1 are also marked.

Finally, we interpret the cut nodes as creating shifts in the computation. Array a is shifted from alignment 1 to alignment 0 (this is node v_3 in the cut). As previously stressed, even though the array a is shifted, it may still be used with its original

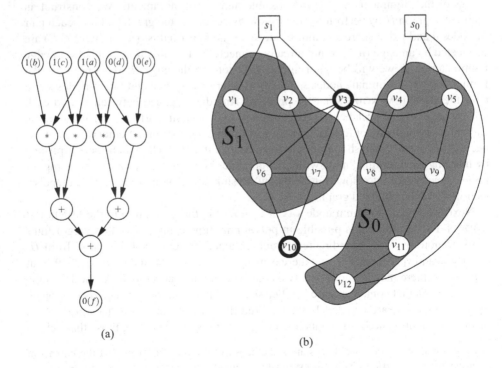

(a)

(b)

Fig. 3. (a) The DAG corresponding to $f[i] = (a[i+1]*b[i+1] + a[i+1]*c[i+1]) + (a[i+1]* d[i] + a[i+1]*e[i])$. (b) A minimum node $s_0 - s_1$ cut for the corresponding graph H.

alignment. Node v_{10} is the other cut node, therefore, the result of the computation $a[i+1] * b[i+1] + a[i+1] * c[i+1]$ is shifted from alignment 1 to alignment 0, enabling the execution of the final computation. Note that node v_8 has two predecessors both with predetermined labels: v_3 and v_4. The label of v_8 is set to the (predetermined) label of v_4, because v_4 is not a cut-node (as opposed to v_3).

For a rigorous proof of correctness the interested reader is referred to the thesis [15]. The complexity of the algorithm is governed by the node cut phase whose complexity is $O((|V|_H)^2 \cdot |E|_H) = O(|V|^2 \cdot |V|^2) = O(|V|^4)$ [9], implying that the complexity of Algorithm 2 is $O(|V|^4)$.

7 The MULTIWAY CUT and the NODE MULTIWAY CUT Problems

We now compare the SIMDG alignment problem to the MULTIWAY CUT and the NODE MULTIWAY CUT problems. We show the relations and the differences between the SIMDG problem and these two known problems.

Definition 6 (Multiway Cut). *Given an undirected graph $G(V,E)$ and a set of terminals $S = \{s_1, s_2, \ldots, s_k\} \subseteq V$, a* multiway cut *is a set of edges whose removal disconnects the k terminals from each other. The Multiway Cut Problem is the problem of finding a multiway cut with minimum weight, where the weight is the sum over the weights of the cut-edges.*

Multiway cuts appear, for example, in the problem of loop fusion for optimal reuse [13,18,16].

Definition 7 (Node Multiway Cut). *Given an undirected connected graph $G(V,E)$ and a set of terminals $S = \{s_1, s_2, \ldots, s_k\} \subseteq V$, a* node multiway cut *is a subset of $V \setminus S$ whose removal disconnects the k terminals from each other. The NODE MULTIWAY CUT Problem is the problem of finding a node multiway cut with minimum weight. Here the weight of the cut is the sum of the weights of the cut-nodes.*

We stress the difference between the above problems using the example in Figure 2. A minimal multiway cut for the undirected graph corresponding to the graph in Figure 2 includes **three** edges — when v is labelled 3. A minimal *node* multiway cut for this graph includes a **single** node — v. An optimal solution to the SIMDG problem for this graph costs **two** shifts — when v is labelled 1, indicating that it should be shifted to label 2 and to label 3. We now state the relations between the problems without proofs and derive approximation algorithms from them. (For more motivation and full proofs see [15].)

Lemma 1. *Every approximation algorithm to the MULTIWAY CUT problem with approximation ratio r provides an approximation algorithm to the SIMDG problem with approximation ratio $\deg(G) \cdot r$ where $\deg(G)$ is the maximum degree of graph G.*

Lemma 2. *Every approximation algorithm to the NODE MULTIWAY CUT problem with approximation ratio r yields an approximation algorithm with approximation ratio $(k-1) \cdot r$ for the SIMDG problem.*

For the MULTIWAY CUT problem there exist a (2-2/k)-approximation algorithm and a 3/2-approximation algorithm. For the NODE MULTIWAY CUT problem there exists a (2-2/k)-approximation [29]. Therefore we can deduce the following.

Corollary 1. *Using the* MULTIWAY CUT *approximation algorithms and Lemma 1 yield approximation algorithms for the SIMDG problem of approximation ratios* $deg(G) \cdot (2 - 2/k)$ *and* $deg(G) \cdot 3/2$.

Corollary 2. *Using the* NODE MULTIWAY CUT *approximation algorithm and Lemma 2, we obtain an approximation ratio of* $(2 - 2/k) \cdot (k - 1)$ *for the* SIMD ALIGNMENT *problem.*

8 Results

In Sections 6 and 5 we provided optimal algorithms for two special cases. In this section we demonstrate the practical advantage of using these algorithms compared to the heuristics mentioned in Section 3.

The effectiveness of Algorithm 1 was tested on complete binary tree expression graphs of various depths. Denote by k the number of possible different alignments in the tree. For each depth d we consider the full binary tree of depth d and randomly generate the alignments (shift labels) of the input vertices (the leaves) and the alignment of the output vertex (the root) in the range of 1 to k. We also let the bound k range from 2 to 7. For the trees randomly obtained as above, we ran Algorithm 1 and each heuristic described in Section 3. Table 1 tells for how many of the random trees (of depth d and k different alignments) none of the heuristics matched the optimal solution obtained by Algorithm 1. Note that as the size of the tree grows, the percentage of trees in which Algorithm 1 outperformed all of the heuristics grows rapidly. For intuition on where the heuristics fail the reader is referred to the thesis [15].

We now turn to examine the case of a general DAG with only two possible shift labels in their input and output vertices. The effectiveness of Algorithm 2 was tested on layer graphs of various depths and widths. Given the depth d and the width w, the vertices are determined and (assuming that operations are binary) two parents are randomly selected for each node. Random shift labels out of the two possible alignments are then assigned

Table 1. The percentage of test-runs in which Algorithm 1 outperformed all heuristics

k	d=3	d=5	d=8
2	24.2%	94.6%	98.5%
3	28.4%	96.7%	98.8%
4	32.7%	95.4%	99.3%
5	27.4%	96.6%	98.1%
6	26.3%	94.7%	99.0%
7	29.2%	95.3%	98.7%
8	30.7%	96.4%	99.0%

Table 2. The percentage of test-runs in which Algorithm 2 outperformed all heuristics

width depth	3	4	5	6	7
3	23.0%	18.8%	30.5%	17.3%	24.3%
4	23.4%	21.5%	26.3%	35.2%	29.6%
5	23.3%	38.4%	28.8%	31.0%	24.7%
6	27.1%	32.2%	24.9%	38.1%	46.4%
7	37.4%	50.3%	32.3%	34.6%	45.4%
8	33.2%	34.3%	53.2%	42.8%	53.8%
9	45.6%	38.8%	40.3%	37.6%	48.9%

to the input and output nodes. Again, Algorithm 2 and all heuristics were run on these randomly generated graphs and Table 2 shows the percentage of test-runs in which the algorithm outperformed all the heuristics. Further discussion and an example on which the heuristics fail appear in the thesis.

Finally, in order to check the shifting overhead on the execution of a program, we ran a program containing a loop that repeatedly computes an expression on the AltiVec platform, with various numbers of iterations. The optimal solution imposes one shift on this expression, whereas the best heuristic imposes two. The percentage of running time difference grows as the number of iterations increases, steadying eventually around 6%. More details appear in the thesis [15].

9 Related Work

There are two general approaches to optimizing code for SIMD architectures: the classical loop-based vectorization scheme [2] and the extraction of parallelism from acyclic code [19,27]. Our scheme applies generally to the simdization of any expression, although due to the overheads associated with shifts it is more relevant to expressions that reside in loops, as in the loop-based scheme.

The work that is most closely related to ours is that of Eichenberger, Wu and O'Brien [14], which presents a set of heuristics for placing shifts in given expressions. These heuristics are described in Section 3. The study there first finds the shift schedule and then generates the relevant code. The shift schedule computed by our algorithms can be used to replace the first part of their study and feed their code generation to obtain more efficient code. A subsequent work [30] extends some of these heuristics to handle runtime alignment and alignment in the presence of length conversion operations.

Several compilers including VAST [28], GCC [21], compilers for SSE2 [3,4] and VIS [8] provide re-alignment support using the Zero-Shift heuristic which shifts all arrays to alignment zero before each operation. Our work can be used to further improve the code generated by such compilers. Some SIMD architectures provide re-alignment capabilities without requiring explicit shift operations [22]. Such architectures do not suffer (or suffer less) from the SIMD ALIGNMENT problem. Additional related work concentrates on detection of misalignment and techniques to increase the number of aligned accesses[20]. Our work deals with minimizing the number of shifts given a set of misaligned accesses, and is complementary to these techniques.

More heuristics for a more general case have been recently proposed by Ren et al. [26]. Typically, an SIMD platform may allow more advanced operations than just shifts. For example, Altivec allows any general projection of elements from two registers into a third register. Ren et al. propose a heuristic method to deal with streams of strides greater than one. This is an important related task that we do not consider here.

In [12,6,17,7] an interesting similar, yet different, problem is considered. They consider the efficient distribution of data to a set of distributed processors so that the communication required to compute the given program expressions is minimized. The distribution of array elements is restricted to affine transformations. There is a cost for communication if during an operation a processor has to access array cells that are not included in the data distributed to this processor. On one hand, this problem generalizes ours as shifts are a special case of general communication, and putting array entries in subsequent locations in memory is a special case of affine transformations on array entries. However, these works assume a severe restriction which makes their case very different than ours in practice. They assume no copies are made, so if data is moved it cannot be used in the original location (unless moved back again). In contrast, we assume that once a shift has been executed the data stream can be used both in its shifted form and in its original form without paying any extra cost. The inability to use streams in this manner is crucial to several positive and negative results, and in particular to NP-Hardness proofs [12]. Furthermore, the ability to parallelize communication and computation costs is crucial to NP-Hardness proofs [5] but is not relevant to our model. Thus, these hardness results do not directly apply to our problem. Another difference which is less crucial but should be noted when comparing the results is that we assume predetermined alignments of the arrays, whereas these papers assume that they can set the alignment of the involved arrays. This assumption always allows a no-shift solution to a single-appearance tree expression. Such a solution does not always exist in our formulation.

10 Conclusion

Various challenging problems stand in the way of effective optimizations for vector platforms. In this paper we focused on the SIMD ALIGNMENT problem. In most previous work simdization was studied assuming the input streams are all aligned. This is not the case in practice. Previous study of the SIMD ALIGNMENT problem offered heuristics, with no guarantees on the quality of the obtained solution. In this paper we present two novel efficient algorithms that solve the SIMD ALIGNMENT problem optimally for two important special cases. For the case in which the input expression has only two distinct alignments we present an algorithm that finds an optimal solution by solving the well known MINIMUM NODE S-T CUT problem. For the case where the input expression is a tree containing each array only once, we presented an algorithm that finds an optimal solution using dynamic programming. These two special cases cover many practical instances of the SIMD ALIGNMENT problem.

References

1. R. K. Ahuja, T. L. Magnanti, and J. B. Orlin. *Network flows*. Prentice Hall, 1993.
2. R. Allen and K. Kennedy. *Optimizing Compilers for Modern Architectures*. Morgan Kaufmann, 2001.
3. A. Bik. *The Software Vectorization Handbook: Applying Multimedia Extensions for Maximum Performance*. Intel Press, June 2004.
4. A. Bik, M. Girkar, P. M. Grey, and X. Tian. Automatic intra-register vectorization for the intel architecture. *International J. of Parallel Programming*, 2:65–98, April 2002.
5. V. Bouchitt'e, P. Boulet, A. Darte, and Y. Robert. Evaluating array expressions on massively parallel machines with communication/computation overlap, 1995.
6. S. Chatterjee, J. R. Gilbert, R. Schreiber, and S.-H. Teng. Automatic array alignment in data-parallel programs. In *Proceedings of POPL*, pages 16–28. ACM Press, 1993.
7. S. Chatterjee, J. R. Gilbert, R. Schreiber, and S.-H. Teng. Optimal evaluation of array expressions on massively parallel machines. *ACM Trans. Program. Lang. Syst.*, 17(1):123–156, 1995.

8. G. Cheong and M. S. Lam. An optimizer formultimedia instruction sets. In *In Second SUIF Compiler Workshop*, August 1997.
9. T. H. Cormen, C. Stein, R. L. Rivest, and C. E. Leiserson. *Introduction to Algorithms*. McGraw-Hill Higher Education, 2001.
10. M. Corporation. Altivec technology programming interface manual. June 1999.
11. E. Dahlhaus, D. S. Johnson, C. H. Papadimitriou, P. D. Seymour, and M. Yannakakis. The complexity of multiway cuts (extended abstract). In *Proceedings of the 24th ACM symposium on Theory of computing*, pages 241–251, New York, NY, USA, 1992. ACM Press.
12. A. Darte and Y. Robert. On the alignment problem. *Parallel Processing Letters*, 4(3):259–270, 1994.
13. C. Ding and K. Kennedy. Improving effective bandwidth through compiler enhancement of global cache reuse. *J. Parallel Distrib. Comput.*, 64:108–134, 2004.
14. A. E. Eichenberger, P. Wu, and K. O'Brien. Vectorization for SIMD architectures with alignment constraints. In *Proceeding of PLDI*, June 2004.
15. L. Fireman. The complexity of SIMD alignment. M.Sc. thesis, Technion — Israel Institute of Technology, Department of Computer Science, June 2006. http://www.cs.technion.ac.il/users/wwwb/cgi-bin/tr-info.cgi/2006/MSC/MSC-2006-17.
16. G. R. Gao, R. Olsen, V. Sarkar, and R. Thekkath. Collective loop fusion for array contraction. In *Workshop on Languages and Compilers for Parallel Computing*, pages 281–295, 1992.
17. J. R. Gilbert and R. Schreiber. Optimal expression evaluation for data parallel architectures. *J. Parallel Distrib. Comput.*, 13(1):58–64, 1991.
18. K. Kennedy and K. S. McKinley. Maximizing loop parallelism and improving data locality via loop fusion and distribution. In *Workshop on Languages and Compilers for Parallel Computing*, pages 301–320, 1993.
19. S. Larsen and S. Amarasinghe. Exploiting superword level parallelism with multimedia instruction sets. In *Proceedings of PLDI*, pages 145–156, 2000.
20. S. Larsen, E. Witchel, and S. Amarasinghe. Increasing and detecting memory address congruence. In *Proceedings of PACT*, 2002.
21. D. Naishlos. Autovectorization in gcc. In *Proceeding of GCC Developers Summit*, pages 105–118, 2004.
22. D. Naishlos, M. Biberstein, S. Ben-David, and A. Zaks. Vectorizing for a SIMdD DSP Architecture. In *Proceedings of CASES*, pages 2–11, 2003.
23. D. Nuzman and R. Henderson. Multi-platform auto-vectorization. In *Proceedings of CGO*, pages 281–294, 2006.
24. D. Nuzman and A. Zaks. Autovectorization in gcc – two years later. In *Proceedings of GCC Developers Summit*, pages 145–158, 2006.
25. G. Ren, P. Wu, and D. Padua. A preliminary study on the vectorization of multimedia applications for multimedia extensions. In *16th International Workshop of Languages and Compilers for Parallel Computing*, October 2003.
26. G. Ren, P. Wu, and D. A. Padua. Optimizing data permutations for simd devices. In *Proceedings of PLDI*, pages 118–131, 2006.
27. J. Shin, M. Hall, and J. Chame. Superword-level parallelism in the presence of control flow. In *Proceedings of CGO*, pages 165–175, Washington, DC, USA, 2005. IEEE Computer Society.
28. C. B. Software. VAST-F/AltiVec: Automatic Fortran Vectorizer for PowerPC Vector Unit. http://www.psrv.com/vast altivec.html, 2004.
29. V. V. Vazirani. *Approximation Algorithms*, pages 38–40,155–160. Springer-Verlag, 1st edition, 2001.
30. P. Wu, A. E. Eichenberger, and A. Wang. Efficient simd code generation for runtime alignment and length conversion. In *Proceedings of CGO*, pages 153–164, Washington, DC, USA, 2005. IEEE Computer Society.

Preprocessing Strategy for Effective Modulo Scheduling on Multi-issue Digital Signal Processors[*]

Doosan Cho[2], Ravi Ayyagari[1], Gang-Ryung Uh[1], and Yunheung Paek[2]

[1] Computer Science Dept., Boise State University
[2] Electrical and Computer Science Dept.,Seoul National University

Abstract. To achieve high resource utilization for multi-issue *Digital Signal Processors* (DSPs), production compilers commonly include variants of the *iterative modulo scheduling* algorithm. However, excessive cyclic data dependences, which exist in communication and media processing loops, often prevent the modulo scheduler from achieving ideal loop initiation intervals. As a result, replicated functional units in multi-issue DSPs are frequently underutilized. In response to this resource underutilization problem, this paper describes a compiler preprocessing strategy that capitalizes on two techniques for effective modulo scheduling, referred to as *cloning1* and *cloning2*. The core of the proposed techniques lies in the direct relaxation of cyclic data dependences by exploiting functional units which are otherwise left unused. Since our preprocessing strategy requires neither code duplication nor additional hardware support, it is relatively easy to implement in DSP compilers. The strategy proposed has been validated by an implementation for a StarCore SC140 optimizing C compiler.

1 Introduction

As communication and media signal processing applications get more complex, system designers seek programmable high performance fixed-point Digital Signal Processors (DSPs). Recent *multi-issue* high performance DSPs[1] are designed to meet such demand by providing (1) multiple functional units, (2) advanced issue logic that allows a variable number of instructions to be dispatched in parallel, and (3) optimizing compilers that automatically tune C algorithms for performance [8,17].

In particular, to exploit the multiple functional units available in multi-issue DSPs, optimizing compilers commonly use a software pipelining strategy. Software pipelining is a global loop scheduling concept which exploits instruction level parallelism across loop iteration boundaries. Optimizing C compilers for multi-issue DSPs commonly adopt variants of the *iterative modulo scheduling* pioneered by Rau and Glaser [2]. Although existing iterative modulo scheduling approaches [7,17] are proven to be effective, excessive cyclic data dependences, which are frequently observed in communication and

---

[*] Research is supported in part by NASA Idaho EPSCoR, Intel Corporation, Korea MIC grant #A1100-0501-0004, Korea MOST grant #M103BY010004-05B2501-00411, Korea IITA grant #IITA-2005-C1090-0502-0031, and NANO IP/SOC Promotion Research Program.
[1] Dominant market players in multi-issue DSPs are ADI/INTEL Blackfin ADSP-BF53x, Motorola StarCore SC140, and Texas Instruments TMS320C64x.

S. Krishnamurthi and M. Odersky (Eds.): CC 2007, LNCS 4420, pp. 16–31, 2007.
© Springer-Verlag Berlin Heidelberg 2007

media processing loops, restrict modulo scheduling quality [13]. As a result, replicated functional units in multi-issue DSPs are often left underutilized.

To address this resource utilization problem, the objective of this paper are twofold: (1) analyzing the nature of the data dependences existing in various signal processing applications, and (2) engineering an effective compiler preprocessing strategy for multi-issue DSPs to help an existing modulo scheduler achieve a high quality loop schedule. For this, the paper describes our preprocessing that directly relaxes excessive cycle data dependences with two techniques, referred to as *cloning1* and *cloning2*. Since these two techniques exploit underutilized functional resources, neither code duplication nor additional hardware support are required, and therefore, it is relatively amenable to implement in DSP compilers. To measure the feasibility and effectiveness of our pre-processing strategy for multi-issue DSPs, the StarCore SC140 DSP processor is used as the representative.

2   Motivation: Excessive RecMII

We formally define the commonly used loop scheduling terms in this paper; for the definitions of other modulo scheduling terms, consult [2].

Definition 1. *A* **candidate loop** *for an iterative modulo scheduler is the loop with the branch-free body that can run in DSP hardware looping mode [10].* [2]

Definition 2. *A* **recurrence circuit** *is a data dependence circuit that exists in a Data Dependence Graph (DDG), which is formed from an instruction to an instance of itself.*

Definition 3. **ExRecMII** *is the difference between RecMII and ResMII, iff RecMII $\geq$ ResMII.*

According to our benchmark for SC140, various signal processing loop kernels manifest that ExRecMII is the dominant limiting factor that either fails candidate loops to be modulo scheduled or modulo schedules with excessively large II.

2.1   Loop-Carried True Dependence

As the first example of ExRecMII, consider the C code fragment shown in Figure 1(a) that implements the *Fast Fourier Transformation* (FFT) algorithm. For the shaded candidate loop body in Figure 1(a), the SC140 optimizing compiler produces highly optimized assembly code as shown in Figure 1(b), which is yet to be modulo scheduled.

For iterative modulo scheduling, II of the candidate loop in Figure 1(b) is initially set equal to MII, which is computed as follows. First, each iteration of the branch-free loop body shown in Figure 1(b) requires 7 units of *Arithmetic and Logic Unit* (ALU) and 6 units of *Address Arithmetic Unit* (AAU), and the SC140 multi-issue DSP can supply at most 4 units of ALU and 2 units of AAU per cycle [3]. Thus, ResMII is 3, which is $\max(\lceil \frac{7}{4} \rceil, \lceil \frac{6}{2} \rceil)$. Second, this candidate loop body contains several data

---

[2] The optimizing C compiler performs if-conversion to allow more loops to be modulo scheduled.

[3] To support high computing needs, StarCore 140 has 4 ALU units and 2 AGU units.[17]

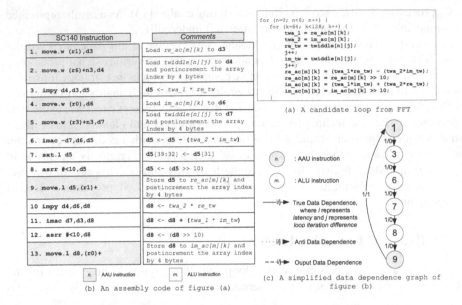

Fig. 1. C Code fragment from FFT and corresponding loop body in SC140

dependence recurrence circuits. `RecMII` is 6 for the FFT and one such circuit is depicted in Figure 1(c).[4] Since `MII` is `max(ResMII,RecMII)`, `II` is initially set to 6 for a modulo schedule.

For analysis, consider the loop-carried data dependence in Figure 1(c). This dependence is **true** since the value of induction variable `r1` in the 9th instruction is referenced by the 1st instruction in the subsequent loop iteration. In addition, the dependence chain from the 1st instruction down to the 9th instruction is transitively **true**. This type of cyclic **true** dependence is often created by the compiler when a source address for a computation is used as the destination address to store the result of the computation, which is a very common pattern in DSP applications. Due to this cyclic **true** dependences, the FFT candidate loop fails to be modulo scheduled since `MII` of 6 is the ratio which can be achieved by local acyclic scheduling.

2.2 Loop-Carried False Dependence

As the second example for `ExRecMII`, consider the C code fragment in Figure 2(a) that implements the half-rate *Global System for Mobile communication (GSM)* algorithm. For the candidate loop body in Figure 2(a), that uses the *European Telecommunications Standards Institute (ETSI)* compliant C macros [6], the optimizing compiler produces highly optimized assembly code as shown in Figure 2(b), which is yet to be modulo scheduled.

---

[4] The other `RecMII` circuit is omitted since the type of loop-carried data dependence is same as that of the circuit in Figure 1(c).

For iterative modulo scheduling, candidate loop `II` is initially set equal to `MII`, which is computed as follows. First, each iteration of the branch-free loop body shown in Figure 2(b) requires 4 units of ALU and 5 units of AAU. Thus, `ResMII` is 3, which is $\max(\lceil\frac{4}{4}\rceil,\lceil\frac{5}{2}\rceil)$. Second, `RecMII` for the half-rate GSM is 5 and the corresponding `RecMII` recurrence circuits are depicted in Figure 2(c). Since `MII` is `max(ResMII, RecMII)`, `II` is initially set to 5 for modulo scheduling.

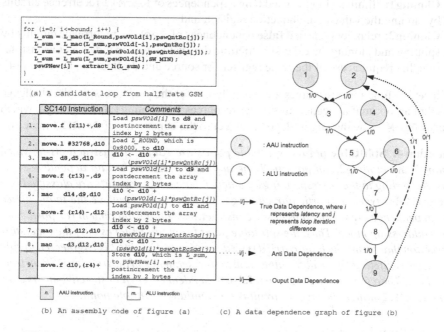

```
...
for (i=0; i<=bound; i++) {
    L_sum = L_mac(L_Round,pswVOld[i],pswQntRc[j]);
    L_sum = L_mac(L_sum,pswVOld[-i],pswQntRc[j]);
    L_sum = L_mac(L_sum,pswPOld[i],pswQntRcSqd[j]);
    L_sum = L_msu(L_sum,pswPOld[i],SW_MIN);
    pswPNew[i] = extract_h(L_sum);
}
...
```

(a) A candidate loop from half rate GSM

	SC140 Instruction	Comments
1.	move.f (r11)+,d8	Load pswVOld[i] to d8 and postincrement the array index by 2 bytes
2.	move.l #32768,d10	Load L_ROUND, which is 0x8000, to d10
3.	mac d8,d5,d10	d10 <- d10 + (pswVOld[i]*pswQntRc[j])
4.	move.f (r13)-,d9	Load pswVOld[-i] to d9 and postdecrement the array index by 2 bytes
5.	mac d14,d9,d10	d10 <- d10 + (pswVOld[-i]*pswQntRc[j])
6.	move.f (r14)-,d12	Load pswPOld[i] to d12 and postdecrement the array index by 2 bytes
7.	mac d3,d12,d10	d10 <- d10 + (pswPOld[i]*pswQntRcSqd[j])
8.	mac -d3,d12,d10	d10 <- d10 - (pswPOld[i]*pswQntRcSqd[j])
9.	move.f d10,(r4)+	Store d10, which is L_sum, to pswPNew[i] and postincrement the array index by 2 bytes

| n. | AAU instruction | m. | ALU instruction |

(b) An assembly code of figure (a)

(c) A data dependence graph of figure (b)

Fig. 2. C Code fragment from half-rate GSM and corresponding loop body in SC140

For analysis, consider the two loop-carried data dependences in Figure 2(c). First, the dependence from the 9th back to the 2nd instructions is **anti** since d10 value claimed from the 9th instruction is generated by the 2nd instruction. Second, the dependence from the 8th back to the 2nd instructions is **output** since both instructions store results to d10. This type of composite loop carried dependences is often observed when DSP specific instructions are selected by the code generator. Due to these two `RecMII=5` recurrence circuits, half-rate GSM candidate loop fails to be modulo scheduled with `II` smaller than 5.

Note that modulo scheduling requires a candidate loop `II` be selected before scheduling is attempted. A smaller `II` corresponds to a shorter execution time. Since the `MII` is a lower bound on the smallest possible value of `II` for which a modulo schedule exists, the candidate loop `II` is initially set equal to the `MII` and increased until a modulo schedule is obtained. Therefore, a preprocessing strategy that lowers the `MII` by reducing `RecMII` can be quite an effective preparation to achieve high loop initiation rate modulo schedules.

3 Problem Formulation

The compiler eases our preprocessing task by putting every candidate loop body such that intra-loop **false** dependences are removed whenever possible. In that setting, our preprocessing reduces ExRecMII by exploiting underutilized functional resources by capitalizing on the following two techniques.

- **Cloning1**: eliminate loop-carried **true** dependences of RecMII recurrence circuits by cloning the value of an induction register, and
- **Cloning2**: relax loop-carried **false** dependences of RecMII recurrence circuits by splitting and cloning the excessive lifetime data value used in a *destructive* instruction that requires use of the same register for source and destination, i.e. mac [14].

Since few functional resources are typically left for the preprocessing, the challenge is to find an optimal allocation of critical resources for cloning1 and cloning2, which reduces RecMII by the largest degree, subject to the constraints of ResMII increase.

Definition 4. Splittable points: *splittable points are candidate instructions to which cloning1 and cloning2 can potentially be applied for RecMII data dependence circuits. According to the corresponding data dependences, these points are classified into* **true** *and* **false** *types. In particular, cloning1 is engineered to remove the loop-carried* **true** *dependence created by a load/store instruction with postincrement (or postdecrement) addressing mode. Thus, the splittable point for cloning1 takes only the load/store instruction that forms the loop-carried* **true** *dependence. Cloning2 is engineered to split the excessive lifetime of the data value created by a sequence of destructive DSP instructions [14]. Therefore, for loop-carried* **false** *dependences, each destructive instruction of the RecMII data dependence circuit is a potentially splittable point.*

3.1 Benefit Estimation

Once splittable points are identified for a set C of RecMII recurrence circuits, these points need to be partially ordered to make the best use of underutilized resources for our preprocessing. First, the potential benefit of the preprocessing for the kth RecMII circuit $\in C$, is estimated by the following equation:

$$B_k = \text{RecMII}_k - \text{RecMII}_k{'} \tag{1}$$

where RecMII$_k{'}$ is the largest dependence length of the dismantled recurrence circuits when cloning1 and cloning2 are applied to the kth RecMII circuit. B_k is used as a metric to estimate the local benefit of the preprocessing. Second, the overall (global) benefit of clonings for C is estimated by the following equation:

$$B_C = \text{RecMII} - \text{MAX}(\text{RecMII}_k{'}) \quad \text{for all RecMII}_k \in C \tag{2}$$

However, Equations 1 and 2 are not sufficient to achieve the desired partial ordering since a splittable point can be shared by multiple RecMII recurrence circuits. For this reason, the benefit estimation can potentially make our preprocessing fail to find the desired partial ordering.

Note that since the preprocessing techniques cloing1 and cloning2 require additional registers and functional resources, the proposed preprocessing is required to check the availability of these resources while estimating benefit.

3.2 Register Constraint and Resource Constraint

The number of architected registers of a processor is denoted as R_T, where T represents a register file type, i.e., data or address, which depends on architecture characteristics. First, to avoid spill code in a candidate loop, our preprocessing applies cloning1 and cloning2 only when the register budget allows. This register budget is the first constraint, which requires that additional register need N for clonings must not exceed the difference between R_T and the number of loop variables kept in registers.

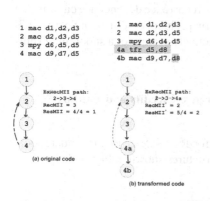

(a) original code

(b) transformed code

Fig. 3. A negative effect of cloning2

Improper application of clonings to a given set of RecMII circuits either makes no improvement on II by simply wasting resources or may even make II worse due to the excessive increase in ResMII. As an illustration, consider the example candidate loop in Figure 3(a), which contains a RecMII= 3 recurrence circuit (2-3-4) and ResMII= 1. When the data register d5 of the 3rd mac instruction is cloned with additional data register d8, MII is reduced by 1 in Figure 3(b).[5] Nevertheless, in case clonings increase ResMII more than the decrease in RecMII, net effect can make MII worse. To prevent such an indiscriminate application of clonings which may require more resources than the architecture can possibly provide, resource budget is additionally considered as the second constraint for our preprocessing. The resource budget is modeled using Rau's reservation table [2], which represents the resource occupation of each loop instruction in a partial schedule.

3.3 Problem Formalization: MAX-MIN

The solution to our resource allocation problem, which searches for an optimal sequence of splittable points, requires the ability to identify the best splittable point I_s from all possible permutations of splittable points. Obviously, a backtracking-based algorithm cannot be a viable approach since the runtime complexity of this combinatorial problem grows exponentially in terms of the number of splittable points. To respond to this intractability,

1. *Max-Min* problem is formulated that requires a solution to maximize the decrease in II while minimizing both register pressure and resource bound, and
2. *Branch and Bound* approach is employed to effectively search for an optimal split point I_s.

---

[5] ExRecMII is reduced from 2 to 0.

In particular, the Max-Min problem for our preprocessing is to seek an I_s that maximizes $profit$ under the register and resource constraints described in Section 3.2.

$$\text{profit}(I_s) = (B_C/N) \tag{3}$$

where B_C is computed by Equations 1 and 2, and N is the number of additional registers required for clonings. Note that, since the benefit estimation with Equations 1 and 2 is not sufficient to find an optimal partial ordering, the branch and bound approach may produce a suboptimal solution.

4   Preprocessing Strategy for Effective Modulo Scheduling

Since a candidate loop can have exponentially many recurrence dependence circuits, the proposed preprocessing strategy sets up the Max-Min problem described in Section 3.3, and exploits a *divide-and-conquer* principle to effectively search for a suboptimal splittable point I_s.

4.1   Divide Step: Detecting ExRecMII Recurrence Circuits and Finding Splittable Points

To identify all recurrence circuits which account for ExRecMII in a candidate loop, we use Tiernan's algorithm [12] with the C data structures shown in Figure 4:

```
/* Elementary Circuit (Recurrence Circuit) */
struct EM_CT {
       unsigned char  head;    // Inst number: head of the circuit
       unsigned char  tail;    // Inst number: tail of the circuit
       unsigned char II_rc;    // Initiation interval of rc
       unsigned char *   P;    /* Elementary Path building array
                                  used in Tiernan's algorithm */
       bvect          circuit; /* Circuit representation
                                  in bit vector */
       struct LIST * i_ecs;    /* Other recurrence circuits that
                                  intersect with this circuit */
       struct LIST * p_ecs;    /* Other recurrence circuits
                                  that are properly contained */
       int            status;  // DRYRUN| DONE| CLONE1| CLONE2
};

/* List of Ex-RecMII Recurrence Circuit */
static struct LIST *ECs;
```

Fig. 4. Elementary Circuit (EC) and EC list C data structures

1. When Tiernan's algorithm confirms a non-trivial [6] recurrence circuit rc=(inst$_1 \rightarrow$ inst$_2 \rightarrow \ldots \rightarrow$inst$_n$), each dependence edge in rc is retrieved from DDG to estimate II_{rc}.

---

[6] A trivial recurrence circuit is a self recurrence circuit whose dependence arc is from an operation to itself.

2. The confirmed rc is added to EC list, which is sorted in descending order using II_{rc} as key. For this step, C data structures in Figure 4 are used; struct EM_CT for a recurrence circuit and struct LIST for EC list.
3. Prior to rc insertion, for each rc_i in EC list, the following two EM_CT fields of rc_i and rc are updated.
   - i_ecs: set of intersecting recurrence circuits, and
   - p_ecs: set of properly contained recurrence circuits.

The i_ecs and p_ecs fields are later exploited to find an optimal splittable point for cloning2. Since the initialization of these two fields for each recurrence circuit potentially requires the algorithm to determine set relationships with all other recurrence circuits, the upper bound for set operations is $O(n^2)$, where n is the number of recurrence circuits of a candidate loop body. Therefore, in order to perform a set operation in constant time, we represent the constituent instructions of a recurrence circuit as a bit vector, which are encoded into the circuit field of EM_CT.

When the circuit confirmation completes, the II_{rc} of the head circuit in the EC list is the RecMII recurrence circuit. If RecMII > ResMII, then all the circuits that share the same value of II_{rc} in the EC list are ExRecMII circuits. For each ExRecMII recurrence circuit, splittable points are determined as a divide step. In particular, starting backward from the loop instruction indexed by tail to the head, splittable points are detected while performing a local reaching definition analysis to estimate the register need N for clonings.

4.2   Conquer Step

PHASE 1: Simplification

Theorem 1. *Unless all loop-carried* **true** *dependences of* ExRecMII *circuits are eliminated by cloning1, the* RecMII *of a candidate loop cannot be reduced by cloning2.*

Proof. For a candidate loop that contains ExRecMII circuits, C=$\{c_1,c_2,\ldots,c_n\}$, assume that c_k and $c_l \in C$ are dependence recurrence circuits which share a splittable point I_s. Without loss of generality, let the loop-carried dependence of c_k be **false** for cloning2 and let the loop-carried dependence of c_l be **true** for cloning1. When cloning2 is first applied to I_s along c_k dependence path, the technique introduces additional data transfer instruction that clones the value of destination operand u to other register v. Since c_l also shares the splittable point I_s, subsequent references to u in c_l must be renamed to v to preserve the original semantic. Therefore, cloning2 cannot reduce RecMII since ExRecMII of c_l remains unchanged.

Theorem 1 implies the following corollaries which simplifies the desired search into three steps.

Corollary 1. *Cloning1 must be applied prior to applying cloning2 to reduce* ExRecMII.

Corollary 2. *The optimality in allocating functional resources is not affected by the order of splittable points selection for cloning1.*

1. Partition the set of ExRecMII recurrence circuits into *c-worklist* for cloning1 and *d-worklist* for cloning2, where *c-worklist* is a set of ExRecMII circuits whose loop-carried dependences are **true** and *d-worklist* is a set of ExRecMII recurrence circuits whose loop-carried dependences are **false**.
2. According to Corollaries 1 and 2, randomly select a sequence of splittable points from c-worklist as long as register and resource constraints can be met.
3. Find an optimal sequence of splittable points from d-worklist using a branch-and-bound search algorithm.

PHASE 2: Search for an optimal solution from a d-worklist

An optimal sequence of splittable points for a d-worklist can be found only when the following side effects are accurately estimated.

1. The number of circuits in the d-worklist whose RecMII can be simultaneously improved when a particular splittable point is cloned.
2. The prediction whether the overall loop schedule gets worse when the particular point is cloned.

As an instance of the first side effect, consider Figure 2(c) that shows two RecMII=5 recurrence circuits. When the 7th mac instruction is cloned, the loop-carried **false** dependences from these two circuits can be simultaneously relaxed with no increase in ResMII.[7]

As an illustration of the second side effect, consider the example candidate loop in Figure 5(a), which contains two RecMII=3 recurrence circuits. When the 3rd mac instruction is accidentally cloned for rc_A, the dependence path of rc_B is increased by 1 as shown in Figure 5(b), and as a result, the overall loop schedule can get worse.

To consider these two side effects in finding an optimal sequence of splittable points from d-worklist, our preprocessing first formulates an instance of Max-Min problem, that has the form (S,p), where S is the set of splittable

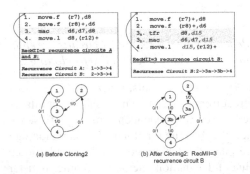

(a) Before Cloning2   (b) After Cloning2: RecMII=3 recurrence circuit B

Fig. 5. An example of indiscriminate cloning2

points $\{I_{S_1}, I_{S_2}, \cdots, I_{S_n}\}$ from d-worklist and p is the profit function that estimates the benefit of a given splittable point in terms of overall number of delisted circuits from d-worklist when the point is cloned. For this profit estimation, the i_ecs and p_ecs fields in EM_CT which are described in Section 4.1 are exploited.[8] Second, the

---

[7] This happens because the resource bound for half-rate GSM is determined by the contention on AAU in SC140 DSP.

[8] When the second side effect is forecasted for a given splittable point, the profit function returns a negative value.

preprocessing exploits the branch and bound search approach [4] and effectively searches for an optimal splittable point $I_{S_x} \in S$ whose $p(I_{S_x}) \geq p(I_{S_y})$ for all y=1,2,$\cdots$,n and y $\neq$ x.

1. **Initialization:** the maximal *Priority Queue*(PQ) [5] as an abstract data type is initialized with a set of splittable points defined in Definition 4, where the priority of each splittable point $I_{S_i} \in S$ is set to $p(I_{S_i})$. PQ has four basic operations: *isEmpty()*, *delMax()*, *validate(I_S)*, and *insert(I_S)*. Second, the branching factor bf, which is the lower bound of the profit function p, will be initialized to 0.

2. **Analyze and Bound:** the *delMax()* returns the current maximum splittable point I_{S_i} together with the EM_CT rc_i. First, the resource and register constraints for I_{S_i} will be checked. Second, if these constraints can be satisfied, the profit $p(I_{S_i})$ will be compared to the current lower bound to determine whether it is beneficial to explore the search space rooted at I_{S_i}. Third, if I_{S_i} is beneficial, the lower bound bf will be reset to $p(I_{S_i})$.

3. **Branch:** If I_{S_i} is not beneficial, then the profit $p(I_{S_i})$ will be adjusted and I_{S_i} will be enqueued with *insert(I_{S_i})*. Otherwise, the current context before the branching will be saved so that remaining search space rooted at other splittable points can be explored.

4. **Iteration:** steps 2 and 3 will be repeated until *isEmpty()* returns true.

PHASE 3: Code Generation with Cloning1 and Cloning2

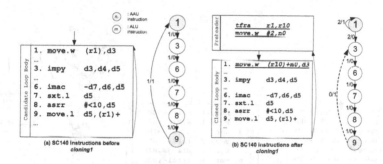

Fig. 6. RecMII=6 recurrence circuit of FFT candidate loop

Phase 3 - Cloning1: The recurrence circuit in Figure 6(a) highlights RecMII=6 of the FFT loop illustrated in Figure 1. Since this circuit is formed with cyclic **true** dependences, the ExRecMII deems irreducible. However, careful analysis on this circuit leads us to observe the following:

1. The loop-carried **true** dependence is an artifact of scheduling insensitive loop optimization, such as induction variable elimination and addressing mode optimization.
2. The loop-carried **true** dependence has no memory (store-load) dependence.

When these two conditions are met, the loop-carried **true** dependence edge can be removed by cloning1, which replicates an original induction register. As an illustration, cloning1 removes the loop-carried **true** dependence in Figure 6(a) as follows.

1. Allocate one additional induction register to clone the value of the original induction register r1, and initialize it at the loop preheader. First, live-variable analysis followed by local reaching definition indicates the availability of additional register r10 to clone the value of r1. Second, a transfer instruction tfra r1,r10, which initializes the cloned register r10, is placed at the loop preheader as shown in Figure 6(b).
2. Prepare one additional operation that clones the induction register r1 used in the 1st instruction, which was selected according to Definition 4. Place this additional operation prior to the update of r1 value. In particular, to minimize resource pressure on AAU units, postincrement addressing mode is exploited at the 1st instruction. Note that, since the memory stride between the 1st and 9th instructions differs by two bytes, indexed postincrement addressing mode is selected as shown in Figure 6(b).
3. Finally, eliminate the original loop-carried **true** dependence by making the cloned operand being referenced. Since the 1st instruction is already amended to reference clone operand r10, no additional change is required.

As a result of this transformation, the original loop-carried **true** dependence is removed. By applying cloning1 to other RecMII=6 recurrence circuit that exists in Figure 1(b), MII is reduced from 6 to 4. Without a single modification to an existing modulo scheduler, a higher loop initiation rate of 4 is effectively achieved and the modified schedule results in a 17% performance improvement.

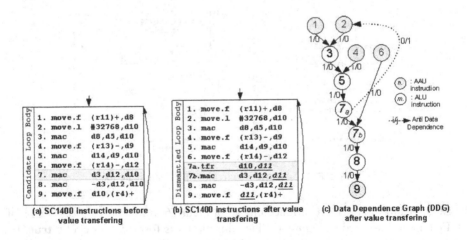

| (a) SC1400 instructions before value transfering | (b) SC1400 instructions after value transfering | (c) Data Dependence Graph (DDG) after value transfering |

Fig. 7. GSM code applied the solution

Phase3 - Cloning2: Figure 7(a) shows the candidate loop body, which contains two RecMII=5 recurrence circuits highlighted in Figure 2(c). To relax the loop-carried **false** dependences from these RecMII recurrence circuits without strip-mining the original loop and unrolling the loop kernel, cloning2 technique is engineered, which splits excessive lifetimes of registers by moving data values around. In particular, cloning2 targets for complex [14] and destructive instructions that requires use of the same register for source and destination. As an illustration, cloning2 relaxes the `RecMII` loop-carried **false** dependences that exist in Figure 7(a) as follows.

1. BB search in phase 2 selects the 7th `mac` instruction as the splittable point.
2. Allocate one additional register to clone the excessive lifetime of $d10$ of the `mac`. For this task, the same live-variable analysis, followed by local reaching definition analysis, tells us the availability of $d11$.
3. Place one additional transfer instruction, the $7_a{}^{th}$ instruction in Figure 7(b), to split the lifetime of $d10$ with the cloned $d11$.

When this modification is made, the loop-carried **anti** dependence from the 9th back to the 2nd instruction and the loop-carried **output** dependence from the 8th back to the 2nd instruction in Figure 7(a) are both relaxed; Figure 7(c) depicts relaxed recurrence circuits. As a result of cloning2, the original `RecMII=5` for half rate GSM candidate loop is effectively lowered to 3 and the modified schedule results in a 4.7% performance improvement.

4.3 Unified Framework: Divide-and-Conquer

For a given candidate loop, the actual cloning1 and cloning2 techniques will be performed only when the analysis from divide-and-conquer steps forecasts the entire recurrence circuits in c-worklist and d-worklist can be simultaneously relaxed. Since this process iterates until there is no further change in `ExRecMII`, most of the search space for an optimal sequence of splittable points, which means an optimal allocation of underutilized functional units in a multi-issue DSP, is typically exhausted.

5 Experimental Results

This section describes results of a set of experiments to illustrate effectiveness of the unified preprocessing strategy described in Section 4.3, which is implemented for the SC140 optimizing C compiler. The experimental input is a set of candidate loops obtained from DSPStone [18], MediaBench [3], half-rate GSM, enhanced full rate GSM, and other industry signal application kernels. Table 1 lists benchmarks used for our experiments.

In order to isolate impacts on performance and code size purely from our preprocessing, two sets of executables for SC140 multi-issue DSP are produced for benchmarks listed in Table 1;

- **ORIG:** fully optimized one with original C compiler, and
- **PRE:** fully optimized one with revised C compiler with our preprocessing proposed.

With these two sets of executables, we measured (1) cycle counts with StarCore *cycle count accurate* simulator `simsc100`, and (2) code size with StarCore utility tool, `sc100-size`. The performance improvements (decrease in cycle counts) and code size increase due to our preprocessing were measured in percent, using formula $((\mathbf{ORIG} - \mathbf{PRE})/\mathbf{ORIG}) * 100$.

Table 1. Benchmarks used in experiments

Acronym	FD	LMS	Conv	ComFFT	FFT	Matrix	FIR
Program	FIR2DIM	LMS	Convolution	complex FFT	FFT	Matrix	FIR
Description	2 dimensional Finite Response Filter	Least mean squared adaptive filters	Convolution	128 point complex FFT	Integer stage scaling FFT	Generic matrix multiply	Finite impulse response filter
Acronym	Mat1x3	Ncomp	BiNsec	IIR	Latsyn	Pcrypto	GSM (sc, af, ut, dec, ad, sy)
Program	Matrix1x3	N_complex_upd ates	Biquad_N_sec tion	IIR	Lattice synthesis	Panama cryptographic module	GSM
Description	1x3 matrix multiply	Complex multiply	One IIR biquad	IIR filter	Typical DSP multiply two vector operation	Panama stream/hash module	V_search, aflatRecursion, utcount, decode, add, syn, fil modules from Global System for Mobile telecommunication

Figure 8(a) reports performance improvements achieved by applying the unified algorithm in Section 4.3, which is based on cloning1 and cloning2 techniques respectively. The overall performance improvement from our preprocessing ranges from 0.3% to 29.5%, and the average performance improvement is 12.9%. Considering there is no modification made to existing iterative modulo scheduler and the performance comparison is made to highly optimized SC140 DSP code, performance gain from our preprocessing was impressive. In particular, the performance improvements on Mat1x3, FIR, FFT and ComFFT benchmarks were brought to our attention, since

1. iterative application of cloning1 followed by cloning2 for an existing modulo scheduler can deliver more performance gain by effectively reducing the ExRecMII of a candidate loop, and
2. the preprocessing strategy described in Section 4.3 can detect and exploit such opportunities for an effective modulo scheduling.

Note that none of benchmarks in Figure 8(a) reports performance degradation. This is not a coincidence, since our algorithm is designed to apply cloning1 and cloning2 only when the additional operations for these techniques can be placed in non-critical recurrence circuits.

Figure 8(b) reports code size increase due to the unified algorithm. Since cloning1 and cloning2 reduces ExRecMII, existing modulo scheduler discovers instruction level parallelism across more loop iteration boundary and as a result, achieves a better modulo schedule. Since the size of the prologue and the epilogue grow proportionally as more loop iterations of a candidate loop get overlapped for a final schedule, code size increase is unavoidable. However, we also observed that existing modulo scheduler can find a better loop schedule for a number of loop iteration boundaries when our preprocessing is applied. This is the reason why our preprocessing to IIR, GSMdec, GSMad and GSMsy benchmarks, reports significant performance improvements with negligible increase in code size.

For benchmarks listed in Figure 8(b), overall code size increase from the proposed preprocessing ranges from 0% to 63.1%, and the average increase is 13.99%. However, note that benchmarks in Table 1 are critical loop kernels which typically account for

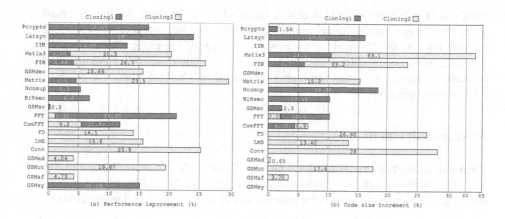

Fig. 8. Percent wise performance improvement (number of cycles reduction) and code size increment compared to the original

5% - 10% of entire application code size. By carefully applying the preprocessing to mission critical loops with profiling, overall code size increase can be hold to a moderate amount.

6 Related Work

To effectively lower this ExRccMII, Lam pioneered a compiler technique, referred to as Modulo Variable Expansion (MVE), that removes loop-carried **anti** and **output** dependencies in recurrence circuits [15]. Since MVE achieves the desired removal with loop unrolling followed by register renaming, a high loop unrolling factor might incur an increase in code size and register pressure. Another drawback of this scheme is that those candidate loops which execute for a multiple number of times the unrolling factor can only be properly accommodated. To overcome this problem, either peeling candidate loops for some number of loop iterations or adding a branch out of the unrolled loop body are required [11].

To duplicate the effect of MVE without loop unrolling, Huff proposed an innovative *rotating register files* as an architectural feature in a hypothetical VLIW processor similar to Cydrome's Cydra 5 [16]. Since the Huff technique still requires a large number of the architected rotating registers to support MVE without code expansion, Tyson and et al. ameliorated Huff technique with *register queues* and *rq-connect* instruction [9]. In their technique, register queues share a common name-space with physical register files. As a consequence, the architected rotating register space is no longer a limiting factor.

7 Conclusion

This paper describes compiler optimizations that preprocess loop kernels of signal processing applications to relax their intrinsic data dependencies and thereby, complementing iterative modulo scheduler. The presented strategy is implemented for the

StarCore SC140 optimizing C compiler backend. As a result of the implementation, a 12.9% average runtime improvement is reported for benchmarks in Table 1; This runtime improvement is made at the expense of a 13.99% average code size increase. Considering that no modification is made to existing modulo scheduler and that the performance comparison is made to highly optimized SC140 DSP code, we believe that this gain is impressive.

Acknowledgement

We thank Bharadwaj Yadavalli, John Griffin, Ramesh Peri, Robert Cohn, and Sanjay Jinturkar for many valuable discussions that improved the quality of this paper. We thank the anonymous reviewers for their constructive comments and suggestions.

References

1. A. Stoutchinin. An Integer Linear Programming Model of Software Pipelining for the MIPS R8000 Processor. In *Proceedings of the 4th International Conference on Parallel Computing Technologies*, 1997.
2. B. Rau. Iterative modulo scheduling. In *HP Laboratories Technical Report, HPL94115*, Nov 1995.
3. C. Lee, M. Potkonjak, and W. Smith. MediaBench: A Tool for Evaluating and Synthesizing Multimedia and Communications Systems. In *Proceedings of the 30th Annual IEEE/ACM International Symposium on Microarchitecture*, Nov 1997.
4. D. Smith. Random trees and the analysis of branch and bound procedures. In *Journal of the Association for Computing Machinery*, Jan 1984.
5. R. Sedgewick. Algorithms in C. Third Edition, Addison-Wesley Pearson Education, 2003.
6. D. Batten, S. Jinturkar, J. Glossner., M. Schulte, and P. D'Arcy. A new approach to DSP intrinsic functions. In *Proceedings of the Hawai International Conference on Systems and Science*, Jan 2000.
7. E. Stotzer and E. Leiss. Modulo Scheduling for the TMS320C6x VLIW DSP Architecture. In *Proceedings of the SIGPLAN'99 Workshop on Languages, Compilers, and Tools for Embedded Systems*, May 1999.
8. E. Tan and W. Heinzelman. DSP architectures: past, present and futures. In *ACM SIGARCH Computer Architecture News*, Vol.31, No.3, pages 6-19, June 2003.
9. G. Tyson, M. Smelyanskiy, and E. Davidson. Evaluating the Use of Register Queues in Software Pipelined Loops. In *IEEE Transactions on Computers*, Vol.50, No.8, pages 769-783, Oct 2001.
10. G. Uh, Y. Wang, D. Whalley, and et al. Compiler Transformations for Effectively Exploiting Zero Overhead Loop Buffer. In *Software-Practice & Experience*, Vol 35, pages 393-412, 2005.
11. H. Allan, B. Jones, M. Lee, J. Allan. Software Pipelining. In *ACM Computing Surveys*, Vol.27, No.3, Sep 1995.
12. J. Tiernan. An efficient search algorithm to find the elementary circuits of a graph. In *Communications of the ACM*, pages 12-35, Dec 1970.
13. J. Sias, H. Hunter, and W. Hwu. Enhancing loop buffering of media and telecommunications applications using low-overhead predication. In *Proceedings of the 34th Annual International Symposium on Microarchitecture*, Dec 2001.

14. R. Leupers and P. Marwedel: Instruction selection for embedded DSPs with complex instructions. In *Proceedings of European Design Automation Conference*, Sep 1996.
15. M. Lam. Software pipelining: an effective scheduling technique for VLIW machines. In *Proceedings of the SIGPLAN'88 Conference on Programming Language Design and Implementation*, June, 1988.
16. R. Huff. Lifetime-Sensitive Modulo Scheduling. In *Proceedings of the SIGPLAN'93 Conference on Programming Language Design and Implementation*, June, 1993.
17. StarCore, Inc. SC140 DSP Core Reference Manual. Atlanta, GA, 2001.
18. V. Zivojnovic, J. Velarde, C. Schager, and H. Meyr. DSPStone - A DSP oriented Benchmarking Methodology. In *Proceedings of International Conference on Signal Processing Applications and Technology*, 1994.

An Array Allocation Scheme
for Energy Reduction in
Partitioned Memory Architectures

K. Shyam[1] and R. Govindarajan[2]

[1] Sasken Comunication Technologies Limited
Bangalore, India
kshyam@sasken.com
[2] SuperComputer Education and Research Center
Indian Institute of Science, Bangalore 560 012, India
govind@serc.iisc.ernet.in

Abstract. This paper presents a compiler technique that reduces the energy consumption of the memory subsystem, for an off-chip partitioned memory architecture having multiple memory banks and various low-power operating modes for each of these banks. More specifically, we propose an efficient array allocation scheme to reduce the number of simultaneously active memory banks, so that the other memory banks that are inactive can be put to low power modes to reduce the energy. We model this problem as a graph partitioning problem, and use well known heuristics to solve the same. We also propose a simple Integer Linear Programming (ILP) formulation for the above problem. Our approach achieves, on an average, 20% energy reduction over the base scheme, and 8% to 10% energy reduction over previously suggested methods. Further, the results obtained using our heuristic are within 1% of optimal results obtained by using our ILP method.

1   Introduction

The use of portable hand-held devices like PDAs mobile phones, laptops, palm-tops, etc., is on the increase. Further, portable devices of today are becoming functionally more and more sophisticated. As the functionalities of these devices increase, it places a huge demand on the power source. Since most of these devices rely on internal sources of power, i.e., batteries and are hand-held, it is impor-tant to make these devices as energy efficient as possible. Reducing the energy consumption is important as it improves the lifetime, and cost of the battery. Further, as it reduces the heat dissipated by the system, it increases the relia-bility of the device.

A majority of embedded applications are data intensive and access a large number of arrays in deeply nested loops. It has been observed that a major por-tion of the energy expended by the programs is in the memory subsystem [3]. In light of these observations, this paper presents a technique to minimize the energy consumed by off chip memory modules, which are divided into banks.

S. Krishnamurthi and M. Odersky (Eds.): CC 2007, LNCS 4420, pp. 32–47, 2007.

Each of these banks can operate at various low-power operating modes. In such an architecture, if the data segments of an application are allocated to memory banks such that, a majority of the memory banks can be placed in a low-power mode, for large parts of the duration of execution of a program, it leads to a reduction in the energy consumed by the memory subsystem. Thus in this paper we try to present a technique for such a data segment (array) placement for energy reduction.

Techniques for allocating arrays to memory banks have been proposed earlier. Earlier approaches [6,7] either model the array allocation problem as a maximum weight path cover problem or use a set of heuristics and certain subgroup ordering. As will be observed in Section 3, neither of these approaches is akin to the array allocation problem and results in inferior solution. We model this problem as a graph partitioning problem which is a natural way of formulating the array allocation problem. The arrays in a single partition are allocated to a single memory bank. During this partitioning process, we try to minimize the sum of the weights of the edges that are being cut. We use existing well-known heuristics to solve the graph partitioning problem. Lastly formulating the array allocation problem as a graph partitioning problem has also led us to develop an Integer Linear Programming formulation(ILP) for it.

Initial experiments on array intensive benchmarks show that, on an average our approach obtains around 21% reduction over energy-unaware allocation and 8% to 10% improvement over the method proposed in [6]. In comparison to the optimal solution obtained from the ILP formulation, our heuristic approach produces near optimal allocation in most of the cases and is within 1% of the energy consumption values obtained by using ILP techniques.

Section 2 presents a brief introduction to partitioned memory architectures and low-power operating modes. Section 3 motivates the problem addressed and the issues involved with earlier approaches using an example. In Section 4, we discuss our problem formulation techniques and heuristics that we have used to solve them. We present experimental results in Section 5. Section 6 compares our work with related work. Finally, we conclude the paper in Section 7.

2   Background

In this section we give a brief background about the partitioned memory architecture and various low-power operating modes. The memory is divided into banks and each of these banks can be placed into one of the following low-power modes, *Standby, Napping, Power-Down* and *Disabled*, depending on the access patterns. A memory bank is in active mode when it is processing read and write requests [14]. Each low-power operating mode is characterized by the energy consumed in that mode and the resynchronization time. Resynchronization time is the time that is needed for the bank to move from the low-power mode it is currently in to the active mode. The resynchronization times (in cycles), and the energy consumption (in nJ), of various low power operating modes are: 9000 cycles and 0.00875 nJ for Power-Down mode, 30 cycles and 0.0206 nJ for Napping mode, 2 cycles and 0.468 nJ for Stand-By mode and zero cycles and 0.718 nJ for Active mode respectively. These memory bank energy values and resynchronization times are obtained from the current values of a 2.5V, 1.25nS cycle time, 4MB memory bank [14]. Since resynchronization times are high for those modes which consume the least energy we must choose a low-power mode carefully.

In our study, initially we assume an oracle memory bank activation, i.e., the memory bank m that would be required at time t, is transitioned exactly at time $(t - r_t)$, where r_t is the resynchronization time from the low-power mode the bank is currently in, to the active mode. We also study the effects of waking up the memory bank at time t, when the actual memory request is made. This incurs a penalty of r_t cycles as the memory bank becomes available only at time $(t + r_t)$. We refer to this scheme as *on-demand activation*.

If a memory bank m is accessed at times t_1 and t_2, for the purpose of our experiments, the low power mode that the bank can be put into for the duration $[t_1 - t_2]$ is calculated as follows. We consider only those low power modes for which the resynchronization time is less than $(t_2 - t_1)$. Let (E_{pd}, R_{pd}), (E_{np}, R_{np}), (E_{sb}, R_{sb}) be the energy consumption and resynchronization times of the memory bank in Power-Down, Napping, Standby modes and E_{act} the energy consumption in the Active mode. If $R_{sb} < (t_2 - t_1)$, then the energy that would have been expended, if a bank is in a particular low-power mode E_{lp} is given by $min((E_{pd} * (t_2 - t_1 - R_{pd}) + E_{act} * R_{pd}), (E_{np} * (t_2 - t_1 - R_{np}) + E_{act} * R_{np}), (E_{sb} * (t_2 - t_1 - R_{sb}) + E_{act} * R_{sb}))$. Thus for the duration $[t_2 - t_1]$ the bank is put into that mode which consumes the minimum energy. This paper, however, does not deal with how the appropriate low-power mode is identified and the memory bank is transitioned into that mode. This requires an estimation of the duration $(t_2 - t_1)$ which can be obtained either through compile time analysis or through profile runs.

3   Motivation

3.1   Motivating Example

In this section we describe the problem formulation with the help of the example. Consider the example code given in Figure 1. In loops L1, L2, L3, L4, and L5, the pairs of arrays accessed are a and d, a and b, c and d, b and c, and b and d. Let us assume loops L1, L2, L3, L4 and L5 take N, $2N$, $4N$, $8N$ and N cycles respectively. Further let us assume that arrays a and d occupy 1 MB each, while arrays b and c each occupy 2 MB. Last, let there be two memory banks in the architecture, each of size 4MB. For simplicity, in this example, we assume that

```
float a[N]; double b[N], c[N]; float d[N];
L1: f or(i = 0; i < N ; i + +)
        {d[i], a[i]}
L2: f or(i = 0; i < N ; i + +)
        {a[i], b[i]}
L3: f or(i = 0; i < N ; i + +)
        {c[i], d[i]}
L4: f or(i = 0; i < N ; i + +)
        {b[i], c[i]}
L5: f or(i = 0; i < N ; i + +)
        {b[i], d[i]}
```

Fig. 1. Motivating Example

the memory bank can be in either active or power-down mode and the resynchronization time is zero.

In an energy unaware allocation, the arrays are allocated in the order in which they are declared. In this example, arrays a and b will reside in memory bank M_1, while array c will partially reside in both banks. Array d will reside in bank M_2. For this allocation, since arrays a and d are accessed in loop L1, both memory banks need to be in the *active* mode during its execution. Since 2 memory banks are active for N cycles, we say that for $2N$ bank-cycles[1] the memory is *active*. Similarly for loops L2, L3, L4, and L5, the memory is *active* for $2N$, $8N$, $16N$ and $2N$ bank-cycles respectively. Table 1 shows that in the energy unaware allocation, the memory banks are active for a total of $30N$ bank-cycles.

Table 1. Memory Banks Active under Various Methods for the Example Code

Loop	No. of Exec.Cycles	Arrays Accessed	Energy-Unaware Banks Active	Energy-Unaware Bank-Cycles	MWPC Method Banks Active	MWPC Method Bank-Cycles	Graph Partitioning Banks Active	Graph Partitioning Bank-Cycles
L1	N	a, d	1, 2	$2N$	1, 2	$2N$	1	N
L2	$2N$	a, b	1	$2N$	1	$2N$	1, 2	$4N$
L3	$4N$	c, d	1, 2	$8N$	2	$4N$	1, 2	$8N$
L4	$8N$	b, c	1, 2	$16N$	1, 2	$16N$	2	$8N$
L5	N	b, d	1, 2	$2N$	1, 2	$2N$	1, 2	$2N$
Total				$30N$		$26N$		$23N$

3.2 Problems with Existing Approaches

The Maximum Weight Path Cover (MWPC) method proposed by Delaluz et.al in [6] uses the Array Relation Graph (ARG). The ARG for our motivating example is shown in Figure 2. The maximum weight cover of a graph is a path which includes all the nodes in the graph (but not necessarily all the edges) such that the sum of the weights of all edges in the path is the maximum among all covers. A MWPC for the ARG is a—b—c—d, which is depicted in the figure using thick edges. The method proposed in [6] suggests that the nodes are traversed in the order in which they appear in the MWPC and are allocated to various memory banks, subject to availability of space in each memory bank. We will assume an array is allocated fully to a single memory bank, whenever the size of the array is less than that of any memory bank. According to the above

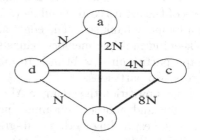

Fig. 2. Array Relation Graph and its Maximum Weight Path Cover

---

[1] We introduce the metric bank-cycle (similar to man-months) to collectively represent the number of memory banks and the cycles for which they remain active.

MWPC, arrays a and b will be allocated to memory bank $M1$ and c and d to memory bank $M2$. For this allocation, the memory banks that are *active* in each loop and the bank-cycles for which the memory is *active* are shown in Table 1. We see that memory is *active* for a total of $26N$ bank-cycles.

Although the MWPC method correctly identifies that edge (b, c) has a large weight, the requirement to allocate arrays to memory banks in the order in which they appear in the MWPC causes the bad decision in this example. Further, MWPC does not take into account the set of nodes that are already allocated to a partition. More specifically, if nodes v_1, v_2, v_3 are already allocated, in that order to partition P_1, and in choosing between v_4 and v_5 that can also be allocated to the same partition P_1, it only considers the weight of edges (v_3, v_4) or (v_3, v_5), and not the cumulative benefits due to edges from v_1 and v_2 to v_4 or v_5. This is a basic limitation of formulating the array allocation problem as a Maximum Weight Path Cover problem.

We now visit the heuristic proposed in [7] and show that it has a few ambiguities. The authors propose the use of compiler-directed clustering, where the objective is to group array variables with similar lifetime access patterns, so that they can be placed in the same memory module. This method uses three heuristics namely *last-use*, *first-use*, and *same-use* pattern to divide the arrays into subgroups and then using the fourth heuristic, reorder the array variables across two neighboring subgroups which have similar access patterns. However the ordering of the subgroups in the first 3 steps (sub-grouping steps) is arbitrary and is not akin to the underlying problem. As a consequence, the heuristic may or may not result in a good partition depending on the subgroup order generated by the implementation. Further, the sub-grouping may result in a degenerated case where each array is in a subgroup by itself. In fact, for our motivating example this degenerated situation arises after applying the *first-use* and *last-use* heuristics. This prevents an efficient allocation of arrays to memory banks.

3.3   Overview of Our Approach

From the discussion in the previous sections, we observe that, given an ARG, we need to partition it into a number of sub-graphs such that the sum of the sizes of the arrays corresponding to the nodes in each sub-graph is less than that of a memory bank size. The edges across the sub-graphs correspond to the cost of keeping multiple memory banks simultaneously active. The objective of the graph partitioning problem is to minimize the sum of the weights of the edges across two partitions.

Let us partition the example ARG into two sub-graphs, one containing nodes a and d and another containing nodes b and c. The sum of the sizes of the array corresponding to these sub-graphs is less than 4MB, the size of a memory bank. The edges that are across the two sub-graphs are: (a, b), (b, d), and (c, d). The sum of the weights of these edges is $7N$. For this allocation, the memory banks that are *active* in each loop and the bank-cycles for which the memory is *active* are shown in Table 1. We see that memory is *active* for a total of $23N$ bank-cycles.

4   Our Approach

In this section we formulate the array allocation problem as a graph partitioning problem, which, in turn, leads to an Integer Linear Programming formulation.

4.1   Graph Partition Formulation

We now give a formal definition of this problem. Let $G = \{V, E, w, c\}$ be the array relation graph which is an undirected graph where each vertex v represents an array. We use the same symbol v to denote the node as well as the array it represents. An edge (u, v) represents that the arrays corresponding to u and v are accessed together in same region of program execution. Associated with each edge (u, v) is a cost $c_{u,v}$, which represents the number of cycles for which arrays u and v are accessed together. Since G is undirected, $c_{u,v} = c_{v,u}$. Finally we associate a weight w_v with each vertex v which corresponds to the size of the array v. Let w be a positive number, such that $0 < w_v \leq w$ for all v. We are given a memory architecture with k memory banks where the size m of each memory bank is greater than w. We can make this assumption without loss of generality since, if for some v, $w_v > m$, then a number of memory banks $l = \lfloor (w_v/m) \rfloor$ can be allocated exclusively for v and the remaining array locations in v can be considered in our array allocation problem.

A *k-way partition* of G is a set of subsets $G_i = \{V_i, E_i, w, c\}$, such that

1. Any pair of subsets G_i and G_j are disjoint.
2. $\bigcup_{i=1}^{k} V_i = V$ and
3. For all $(u, v) \in E$, (u, v) is in E_i iff $u \in V_i$ and $v \in V_i$.

A partition is *admissible* if $\sum_{v \in V_i} w_v \leq m$ for all G_i. An edge $(u, v) \in E$ is said to be an external edge for a partition if $u \in E_i$ and $v \in E_j$ and $i \neq j$. The *cost* of a partition is the summation of weights of all external edges. We refer to this cost as the external cost of the partition. The partitioning problem is thus to find an admissible partition of G with minimal external cost.

The optimal partitioning problem is NP-Complete [11]. There are a number of heuristic approaches to this problem. We used one such heuristic proposed in [11]. The heuristic proposed primarily aims to find a minimal cost partition of a set of $2n$ elements into two sets of n elements each. The heuristic algorithm works by starting with a pair of initial partitions A and B and swapping vertices $a \in A$ and $b \in B$ to the other partition based on External Cost (ECost) and Internal Cost (ICost). We define ECost of a as $E_a = \sum_{y \in B} c_{ay}$. We also define ICost I_a as $I_a = \sum_{x \in A} c_{ax}$. Similarly we define ECost E_b and ICost I_b for each $b \in B$. Let $D_a = E_a - I_a$ for each $a \in A$ be the difference between the ECost and ICost. Now according to a lemma proved in [11], for any $a \in A$ and $b \in B$, if they are interchanged, the reduction in the partitioning cost is given by $R_{ab} = D_a + D_b - 2 * c_{ab}$. The nodes a and b are interchanged to partitions B and A respectively if $R_{ab} > 0$.

Next we generalize the heuristic algorithm for doing a *k-way partition* (refer
to Algorithm 1). In Step 1 the graph is partitioned into a set of k *admissible*
partitions. We then proceed to make sure that they are pairwise optimal. To do
that we consider a pair of such partitions. In Step 5 and Step 7 we calculate the
ICost and ECost. In Step 9 we iterate through the elements of each of the pairs
and calculate the reduction in partitioning costs, if they were to be interchanged.
In Step 14 we choose the pair of nodes a and b, which has the largest positive
R_{ab} value. We move a to partition G_j and b to partition G_i if the resulting
partitions are admissible. We repeat the steps till no more such interchanges are
possible. This process is performed pair-wise on the partitions till no interchange
of elements occurs.

We shall illustrate the heuristic on the example graph in Figure 2. The graph
is split into two sets A, containing the elements $\{a, b\}$, and B, containing the
elements $\{c, d\}$. Now if we consider $a \in A$ and $c \in B$ we have $E_a = N$,
$I_a = 2N$, $E_c = 8N$, $I_c = 4N$, $D_a = -N$ and $D_c = 4N$ The R_{ac}
value is now $3N$. We see that this is the maximum value and hence we need to
interchange a and c. We get the partition (a, d) and (b, c). The algorithm iterates
over step 2 to step 11 and then concludes that no more interchanges are possible
and hence terminates.

Algorithm 1. Algorithm to partition a graph

---
1. Partition the graph G randomly into subsets $G_1, G_2, ..., G_k$ such that $G_i = \{V_i, E_i, w, c\}$ and $\sum_{j \in V_i} w_j \leq m$. (*Admissible* Partitions)
2. Do
3.   Take a pair of partitions G_i and G_j that are not marked as pairwise optimal.
4.   Repeat
5.   For each $a \in G_i$ calculate E_a, I_a, D_a
6.   EndFor
7.   For each $b \in G_j$ calculate E_b, I_b, D_b
8.   EndFor
9.   For each $a \in G_i$ do
10.   For each $b \in G_j$ do
11.   Calculate R_{ab}.
12.   EndFor
13.   EndFor
14.   For the largest R_{ab} value, $R_{ab} > 0$, interchange $a \in G_i$ and $b \in G_j$ if the resulting partitions $G_i\prime$ and $G_j\prime$ are admissible.
15.   Until all $R_{ab} > 0$
16.   Mark G_i and G_j as being optimal with respect to each other
17. While there is no interchange of elements between any two pairs G_i and G_j

There are quite a number of implementations of the graph partitioning algorithm available. We use one such implementation described in [10]. A detailed discussion on the technique used for performing the partitioning can be found in [10].

4.2 Integer Linear Programming Formulation

In this section we formulate the array allocation problem as an Integer Linear Programming problem. We use the Array Relation Graph representation for this formulation too. We use a 0-1 integer variable with $x_{ij} = 1$ to denote that array i is allocated to a memory bank j. Let s_j denote the size of memory bank j. If all memory banks are of size m, then $s_j = m$ for all j. Once again we assume that the size of an array w_v is less than that of a memory bank size s_j. Further, since we assume an array can be allocated to only one memory bank, we have the following constraint:

$$\sum_{j=1}^{k} x_{ij} = 1 \text{ for all } i = 1, n \tag{1}$$

Now the sum of the sizes of arrays allocated to each memory bank must be less than the size of the memory bank. This constraint can be formulated as:

$$\sum_{i=1}^{n} x_{ij} * w_i \leq s_j \text{ for all } j = 1, ..., k \tag{2}$$

Note that in the above equation w_i is a constant. To model whether an edge (i, j) is an external edge, i.e., spans two partitions, we use a 0-1 integer variable e_{ij}. If $x_{ip} = 1$ and $x_{jq} = 1$, where $p \neq q$, indicating that arrays i and j are placed in two different memory banks (viz. p and q), then the edge (i, j) is an external edge and therefore the value of e_{ij} must be one. This is specified by the following logical statement $(x_{ip} \wedge x_{jq}) \implies e_{ij}$. This can be written as a linear constraint as follows:

$$x_{ip} + x_{jq} - e_{ij} < 2 \text{ for all } i, j \in [1, n] \text{ and } p, q \in [1, m] \tag{3}$$

It can be seen that if $x_{ip} = 1$ and $x_{jq} = 1$, then e_{ij} should be equal to 1 to satisfy the above equation. Although the above constraint does not necessarily set the value of e_{ij} to 0 when either of $(x_{ip} = 0)$ or $(x_{jq} = 0)$, the use of e_{ij} in the objective function will ensure this. Thus the objective function of the array allocation problem is to minimize the sum of the weights on the external edges. That is

$$minimize \sum_{i=1}^{n} \sum_{j=i+1}^{n} e_{ij} * c_{ij} \tag{4}$$

subject to Equations 1, 2 and 3. Note that c_{ij}s in the objective function are constants.

5   Experimental Results

5.1   Implementation Details

We have used the SUIF compiler framework [18] to implement our data allocation heuristics. We first compile the given benchmark into a SUIF intermediate file. SUIF provides a framework to analyze this intermediate file on the basis of data dependence framework, live dependence analysis, etc. We use the dependency analysis framework to compute a co-access index matrix, which is the edge weight matrix C_{uv}. That is, for a given array A in the program, this matrix is used to find out those arrays that are accessed together along with this array. The sizes of the arrays, along with co-access index matrix are used to construct the ARG which in turn is used as input to the array allocation heuristic. We have implemented Algorithm 1 for our array allocation heuristic. The output of the heuristic is the partition of arrays into different memory banks. For the Integer Linear Programming problem formulation we have used the commercial solver CPLEX® [5]. From the partition obtained from the heuristic or CPLEX solver, we derive the declaration order of the arrays (with appropriate padding) to enforce the partition to different memory banks. We also make necessary modifications to accommodate arrays whose sizes are greater than the memory banks.

We have used Simple-Scalar[16] to simulate the execution of the benchmark programs. The benchmarks with modified array declaration order, are compiled using the PISA tool-chain compiler provided along with the Simple-Scalar distribution with -O2 optimizations. We have simulated full program execution. The energy consumption of the memory subsystem is estimated by first generating the address trace and determining the active or low-power modes in which the memory banks are in during the different regions of program execution. The energy consumption of the memory subsystem is estimated using the method outlined in Section 2.

5.2   Evaluation Methodology

We have used six *array-dominated* and *data-intensive* benchmarks, four from scientific applications and two applications from the embedded systems domain. *Liv8* is a part of the Livermore[12] kernel, which does 2D ADI Integration and has 6 arrays with a dataset size of 33MB. *tomcatv* having 6 arrays and a dataset of 48MB, is a part of SPEC'95 benchmark suite and is a vectorized mesh generation program. *eflux* is a part of Perfect Club benchmark suite and is widely used in image processing applications. It has 5 arrays and a data set size of 42MB. *vpenta* having 8 arrays and a dataset of size 34MB, is a part of the nasa7 kernel, a program in the SPEC'92 floating-point benchmark suite, and is a routine to invert 3 pentadiagonals. The *MPEG-4 Encoder and Decoder* is a video decoder and encoder, having 12 arrays and a dataset of 54MB. The *AMR Encoder and Decoder* is a speech encoder and decoder. It has 10 arrays and a dataset of size 57MB. These are primarily used in many multimedia applications for portable devices like video capture etc. For the purposes of our experiments, a fifteen minute raw video sample and a fifteen minute raw audio sample were used. These samples were encoded and then decoded back to raw video and raw audio samples.

Many portable devices of today do not provide multiprogramming environment nor have a virtual memory subsystem. Hence, we have assumed a single program environment and all addresses are physical addresses. Further, for most of our experiments, we have assumed a memory system without caches. We have assumed an in-order execution processor having two memory system ports, four integer and floating point ALU's, and one integer and one floating point multiplier/divider.

5.3 Results

First we report the performance comparison of four different array allocation techniques. The *No-allocation* scheme refers to one in which arrays are allocated to memory banks in the order in which they are declared in the program. However, we assume that, whenever possible, inactive memory banks are put into appropriate low power mode even in this *No-Allocation* scheme. The *MWPC* technique refers to Delaluz' scheme [6] which allocates arrays to memory banks based on the Maximum Weight Path Cover approach. The *HGPS* scheme corresponds to the heuristic graph partitioning scheme discussed in Section 4.1. Finally, the *ILPS* scheme refers to the ILP formulation presented in Section 4.2. In this study we assume a memory bank size of 2MB and a memory subsystem having enough memory banks to hold all the arrays. In all these experiments, we assume oracle activation of a memory bank as discussed in Section 2. The oracle activation scheme, assumed equally for all four schemes, gives the upper bound of the energy reduction achievable by each of the schemes. We will

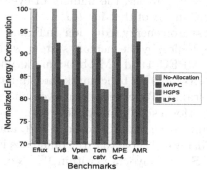

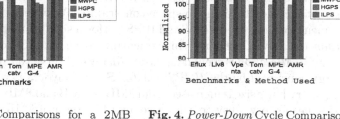

Fig. 3. Energy Comparisons for a 2MB Memory Bank

Fig. 4. *Power-Down* Cycle Comparisons for a 8MB Memory Bank

evaluate our schemes under a more realistic on-demand activation scheme later in this section.

In Figure 3 we plot the energy consumption of the memory subsystem, for all the benchmarks under various allocation schemes normalized to the *No-Allocation* scheme, which is treated as the base case. We observe that the the *MWPC* scheme achieves an energy reduction of 8% to 12% in various benchmarks programs. Whereas, *HGPS* and *ILPS* achieve a reduction of 18% to 20% in comparison to the *No-Allocation* scheme. Thus the *HGPS* and *ILPS* schemes achieve a further reduction in energy of 8% to 10% over MWPC. This clearly demonstrates the limitation of formulating the array allocation problem as a Maximum Weight Path Cover problem and also highlights the benefits of the graph partitioning approach.

Further, we observe that our heuristic graph partitioning method performs as well as the optimal solution given by the ILPS solver. This is encouraging, given that the heuristic approach takes only 0.1 seconds on the average to solve an average graph partitioning problem, while the ILPS solver could take hundreds of seconds for the same problem. However, in many cases, when the number of arrays and/or memory banks is small (less than 20), the ILPS solver was also able to obtain the optimal partition within 2 seconds.

Much of the effectiveness of the heuristic in trying to reduce the energy consumed by the memory subsystem comes from placing a memory bank in the lowest power mode possible viz., *Power-Down* mode for the largest number of cycles. Hence an increase in number of Power-Down cycles would mean that it is able to find large intervals of idle time for a particular memory bank. Figure 4 plots the power-down mode cycles for all the benchmarks running on a system which has memory banks of size 8MB, normalized to the base case i.e., the *No-Allocation* scheme. As can be observed from Figure 4, the *HGPS* heuristic scheme proposed in this paper is able to place a memory bank in Power-Down mode for as much as 25% more cycles when compared to the base case and upto 12% when compared to using *MWPC* heuristic. Further, the number of cycles in the power-down mode for the *HGPS* is within 1% of that for *ILPS*.

Next we study the impact of memory bank size on energy reduction. In Figure 5 we plot the actual energy consumed (in micro-Joules) by the memory system, with memory bank sizes of 2MB, 4MB, or 8MB, for MPEG-4 and AMR benchmarks under various array allocation schemes. The results for other benchmarks are similar and are not included here due to space constraints. We observe that even under various memory bank sizes *HGPS* and ILPS perform significantly better than *No-Allocation* and *MWPC* schemes. An average improvement of 8% over *MWPC* and 18% over *No-Allocation* is seen in all cases. Also we observe that the difference in the energy consumed by the *HGPS* and *ILPS* array layouts is within 1%. Next, as the memory bank size is increased from 2MB to 4MB and 8MB, the energy consumed by the memory subsystem increases by 14% in case of AMR and 105% in case of MPEG-4. However this increase is seen uniformly across all allocation schemes.

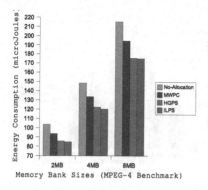 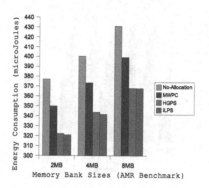

Fig. 5. Energy Comparisons for MPEG-4 and AMR Benchmarks

This is due to fewer memory banks and hence fewer opportunities available for the memory allocation scheme to put them to low power modes.

Next we compare the oracle memory bank activation and *on-demand* memory bank activation schemes. As explained in Section 2, the *on-demand* activation scheme results in increased execution time due to resynchronization time. Further, the low-power mode *(Standby, Napping, Power-down)* to which a memory bank is put into is determined assuming oracle knowledge. Figure 6 plots the energy consumed by *MWPC* and *HGPS* methods with *oracle* and *on-demand* memory bank activation, normalized to *No-Allocation* method. In this graph *MWPC(OD)* and *HGPS(OD)* refer to *MWPC* method and *HGPS* schemes with on-demand memory bank activation, while *MWPC* and *HGPS* refer to the respective schemes with oracle activation. The graphs in Figure 6 clearly shows that HGPS with on-demand activation performs better than *MWPC* and *MWPC(OD)* by 5% to 8%. Further, for *HGPS* method it can be observed that the energy consumption difference is only around 3% between oracle and *on-demand* activation, while this difference is upto 6% for *MWPC* method. This could be due to the fact that *HGPS* method is able to place a large number of memory banks in optimum low-power mode, which reduces the need to perform frequent resynchronization.

Figure 7 plots the execution cycles for *on-demand* memory bank activation for *MWPC* and *HGPS* methods normalized to *No-Allocation* method. We have not plotted the execution cycles for oracle memory bank activation schemes as they remain the same. Here we observe that the increase in execution cycles for *HGPS* method is within 3% while it goes upto 5% for *MWPC* method. Thus we conclude that even when we use an *on-demand* activation scheme, we are still able to obtain sufficient energy reduction with little increase in execution time of the program.

In order to study the effect of our array allocation scheme in the presence of caches, we have performed experiments assuming two different L1 cache configurations, a 4K 2-way set associative cache and a 4k 4-way set associative cache. We assumed a memory bank size of 2MB in this experiment. In all these

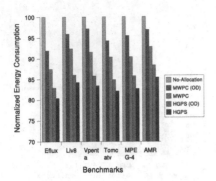

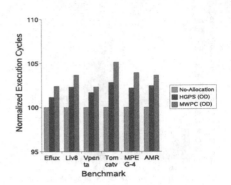

Fig. 6. Energy Comparisons between *oracle* and *on-demand* memory bank activation for a 2MB memory bank

Fig. 7. Execution Cycle Comparisons for *on-demand* memory bank activation for 2MB memory bank

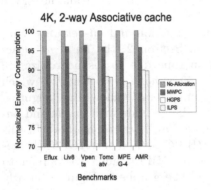

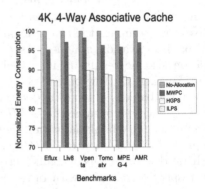

Fig. 8. Energy Comparisons for a 2MB Memory Bank with caches

experiments, we assume oracle activation of a memory bank. Figure 8 gives details of energy consumption of the memory subsystem with caches, for all the benchmarks under various allocation schemes normalized to the *No-Allocation* scheme. We observe that the energy reduction due to various array allocation schemes decreases when the memory subsystem consists of a cache. This is due to the fact that the cache filters many of the memory accesses (due to locality), which, in turn, enables the memory banks to be put into low-power modes for longer duration even in *No-Allocation* scheme. However, we also make an important observation that the *HGPS* and *ILPS* schemes are able to obtain a reduction of about 8% in the energy consumption when compared to *MWPC* scheme, even when a cache is present. The results for remaining memory bank configurations (4MB, 8MB) are along similar lines and have not been included due to space constraints.

6   Related Work

The problem of minimizing the energy consumption of the memory subsystem is dealt with in [6]. They have also proposed loop optimizations such as tiling for reducing the energy consumption which are orthogonal to the array placement technique considered in this paper. Also the loop optimization considered in their paper might introduce control overheads, which may lead to increase in execution time, which in turn may increase the energy consumed by the system. Their work does not model these appropriately.

Array allocation techniques to minimize the energy consumption of the memory subsystem is dealt with in [2]. They have proposed Array-interleaving and memory layout modifications for identifying memory banks which can be transitioned into low power modes. However they focus mainly on optimizations meant for the Java Virtual Machine environment. The array allocation we have proposed however does not limit itself to any particular run-time environment.

A memory bank assignment algorithm for retargetable compilers is proposed in [9]. They profile the program to obtain data access patterns of variables and use this information to place the variables in such a way that the memory banks can be transitioned to a low power mode. However, unlike the various low-power operating modes for memory banks considered in this paper, they assume that each memory bank is either kept in active state or is switched off.

Energy aware variable partitioning along with instruction scheduling for multi-bank architectures has also been dealt with in [17]. An optimal assignment of variables to memory banks is obtained through effective scheduling of memory intensive instructions. The heuristic we have proposed focuses directly on allocating variables to memory banks by making use of the features provided by the underlying hardware.

Assignment of variables to memory banks is also dealt with in [4]. Their work tries to optimize the assignment mainly for Digital Signal Processors. Although they have also reduced the assignment problem to a graph partitioning problem, they use the idea of Maximum Spanning Tree to partition their graph. Array allocation to memory banks that provide various low power operating modes was also done in [15]. The arrays that are accessed together for a large number of times are allocated to a single memory bank by a greedy heuristic which evaluates a trade-off between size of array and access with other arrays currently in the memory banks.

In [1] they consider Page allocation policies, controlled by operating system, that can take advantage of the various low power modes of the memory banks are considered in [1]. They try to reassign frequently used pages to common memory banks, so that the remaining memory banks can be switched to a low power mode without impacting program performance. While their study concentrates on pages and interaction between the operating system and memory banks, our study focuses on arrays and how compilers can make use of the hardware features.

7   Conclusions

In this paper we formulate the array allocation problem as a graph partitioning problem. We observe that this is a more natural formulation for the problem that the earlier approaches [6], [7]. We have used existing heuristic approaches for the graph partitioning problem as a solution to the array allocation problem. We have shown that the array allocation problem can also be formulated as an Integer Linear Programming problem. Our heuristic approaches obtain, on an average, 20% reduction in memory subsystem energy over energy unaware array allocation methods, and 8% to 10% reduction over other competitive methods. Further the heuristic solution performs as well as the optimal solution obtained from the ILP solution, and results in energy consumption that is within 1% of the optimal solution. As future work, we are investigating on methods to determine the appropriate low-power mode for the memory banks.

References

1. A. R. Lebeck, X. Fan, H. Zeng, and C. S. Ellis. Power aware page allocation. In Proc. of the *Ninth International Conference on Architectural support for programming languages and operating systems*. pp.105-116, 2000.
2. R. Athavale, N. Vijaykrishnan, M. Kandemir, M.J. Irwin. Influence of array allocation mechanisms on memory system energy. In Proc. of the *15th International Parallel and Distributed Processing Symposium*, 2001.
3. F. Cathoor, S. Wuytack, E. De Greef, F. Fransen L.Nachtergaele, and H. De Man. System-level transformations for low-power data transfer and storage. *In Low-Power CMOS Design*, R. Chandrakasan and R. Brodersen, Eds. IEEEPress, Piscataway, NJ.
4. Jeonghun Cho, Yunheung Paek, David Whalley, Fast memory bank assignment for fixed-point digital signal processors, *ACM Transactions on Design Automation of Electronic Systems* (TODAES), pp:52-74, 2004
5. CPLEX. http://www.ilog.com/products/cplex/
6. V. Delaluz, M. Kandemir, N. Vijaykrishnan, and M. J. Irwin. Energy-Oriented Compiler Optimizations for Partitioned Memory Architectures. In Proc. of *International conference on Compilers, architecture, and synthesis for embedded systems*, pp.138-147, 2000.
7. V. Delaluz, M. Kandemir, N. Vijaykrishnan, A. Sivasubramniam, and M. J. Irwin. DRAM Energy Management Using Software and Hardware Directed Power Mode Control. In Proc. of *The Seventh International Symposium on High-Performance Computer Architecture* January 2001.
8. L.R. Ford and D.R. Fulkerson, *Flows in networks,* Princeton, New Jersey: Princeton University Press, p.11, 1962.
9. J. D. Hiser and J. W. Davidson. EMBARC: an efficient memory bank assignment algorithm for retargetable compilers. *ACM SIGPLAN Notices*, v.39 n.7, July 2004
10. G. Karypis and V. Kumar. Multilevel k-way hypergraph partitioning. Technical Report TR 98-036, Department of Computer Science , University of Minnesota, 1998.
11. B. W. Kernighan and S. Lin. An efficient heuristic procedure for partitioning graphs. *The Bell System Technical Journal*, 49(2):291-307, 1970.

12. Livermore Kernels. http://www.netlib.org/benchmark/
13. lp_solve. http://groups.yahoo.com/group/lp_solve/
14. Samsung® Electronics - Direct RDRAM DataSheet 2005.
15. V.V.N.S. Sarvani. Compiler Techniques for Code Size and Power Reduction for Embedded Processors, M.Sc[Engg] Thesis, Department of Computer Science and Automation, Indian Institute of Science, Bangalore, India, 2003.
16. D. Burger and T. Austin. The SimpleScalar Tool Set, Version 3.0. Technical report, Department of Computer Science, University of Wisconsin, Madison, 1999.
17. Z. Wang and X. S. Huw Energy-aware variable partitioning and instruction scheduling for multibank memory architectures. *ACM Transactions on Design Automation of Electronic Systems* (TODAES), pp:369-388, 2005.
18. R. Wilson, et al. SUIF: An infrastructure for research on parallelizing and optimizing compilers. *ACM SIGPLAN Notices*, 29(12):31-37, December 1994.

Using Prefetching to Improve Reference-Counting Garbage Collectors*

Harel Paz[1],** and Erez Petrank[2],***

[1] IBM Haifa Research Laboratory, Mount Carmel, Haifa 31905, Israel
paz@il.ibm.com
[2] Microsoft Research, One Microsoft Way, Redmond, WA 98052, USA
erez@cs.technion.ac.il

Abstract. Reference counting is a classical garbage collection method. Recently, a series of papers have extended the basic method to drastically reduce its notorious overhead and extend the basic method to run concurrently and efficiently on a modern computing platform. In this paper we investigate the use of prefetching to further improve the efficiency of the reference-counting collector.

We propose potential prefetching opportunities for the advanced reference-counting collector and report an implementation of a collector that employs such prefetching. The proposed prefetch instructions were inserted into the Jikes reference-counting collector obtaining an average reduction of 8.7% of the memory management overheads.

1 Introduction

The performance gap between memory latency and processors' speed is increasing, causing memory accesses to become a performance bottleneck. Cache hierarchies are used to reduce this gap, but caches are of limited size and usually cannot hold the application's entire working set. Thus, cache misses typically form a performance bottleneck. Data prefetching is a technique for reducing or hiding the memory stalls caused by cache misses. Prefetching data to the cache before being accessed by the program hides the latency of loads that miss the cache, and improves the overall program execution time (as prefetch is a non-blocking memory operation). On the negative side, prefetching increases memory traffic, cache pollution, and the number of executed instructions. In addition, to achieve performance improvement, prefetch scheduling should be done with care. Data prefetched too early may be evicted from the cache before used, while a late prefetch will not mask the system latency.

Compiler-inserted data prefetching have been proposed for predictable access patterns such as accesses to arrays and certain pointer applications (e.g., [1,2,3,4]). Standard platforms usually automatically prefetch data from the memory whose access can be easily predicted.

Boehm [5] was the first to study the use of prefetching for garbage collection. Prefetching turned out to be very effective for a mark-sweep collector, especially since

---

* This research was supported by THE ISRAEL SCIENCE FOUNDATION (grant No. 845/06).
** Work done while the author was at the Computer Science Dept. at the Technion.
*** On sabbatical leave from the Computer Science Department, Technion, Haifa 32000, Israel.

S. Krishnamurthi and M. Odersky (Eds.): CC 2007, LNCS 4420, pp. 48–63, 2007.
© Springer-Verlag Berlin Heidelberg 2007

the collector accesses each object once in an order that may be predicted. Subsequent work [4,6,7] showed that prefetching was able to further reduce the cost of a tracing garbage collection. But all of this work has concentrated on tracing collectors and the potential of prefetching for reference-counting collectors remained open.

In this work we study the use of prefetching for reference counting. Reference counting [8] differs from tracing collectors in the sense that its cost is directly related to the execution of the program, rather than being proportional to the amount of live space. Also, it has better cache behavior, since the objects that are touched during the collection are allocated thereafter and used by the program. Traditionally, it was believed that reference counting had a high overhead and that it required an atomic update for any pointer modification, making it unsuitable for modern parallel platforms. However, it was lately shown [9,10] that the overhead can be dramatically decreased and that the atomicity requirement can be eliminated. Thus, reference counting became a viable option again for modern computing. Subsequent papers [11,12,13,14] have further shown that techniques developed for tracing collectors, can be modified and extended to work with reference-counting collectors as well. This line of work is crucial to making reference counting compete with the efficiency of the thoroughly studied tracing collectors. This paper reports an additional such study, the use of prefetching to improve reference counting efficiency, and show that data accessed by a reference-counting collector can be partially predicted. Thus, prefetching can be used to reduce the cache misses' overhead incurred by a reference-counting collector and improve the collector efficiency.

The representative generic reference-counting algorithm that we use to develop the prefetching techniques in this work uses deferred reference counting [15] and employs the update coalescing write-barrier proposed in [9,10]. The State-of-the-art efficient reference-counting collectors employ these mechanisms to obtain their efficiency.

We consider three main parts of the memory manager: (1) the reference-count increments stage, (2) the reference-count decrements and object deletion stage, and (3) objects' allocation. In accordance with these stages, we identify five major opportunities where data accesses can be predicted in advance, and prefetch instructions may be inserted to improve performance. We study these opportunities and measure the improved performance of each stage, and of the overall garbage collection execution. We do not study prefetch opportunities with a cycle collection algorithm. A cycle collector is based on some sort of tracing, and hence Boehm's work [5] already handles it.

Implementation and measurements. We have implemented the proposed prefetching insertions with the reference-counting collector supplied with the Jikes RVM [16]. We used the SPECjbb2000 benchmark, the SPECjvm98 benchmarks suite [17] and the DaCapo benchmarks suite [18]. We first measure the general behavior of these benchmarks and show that most objects are accessed multiple times by the reference-counting collector. This means that the original collector (without the prefetching) encounters a lot of cache hits, perhaps reducing the potential impact of prefetching on the execution. Moreover, repetitive accesses tend to be close in time. Nevertheless, the implemented prefetch instructions reduce garbage collection overhead by as much as 14.9% and on average by 8.7% when measured across all benchmarks.

Organization. We review the reference-counting collector in Section 2. The prefetch insertion opportunities of the reference-counting collector are presented in Section 3. Results and related work are discussed in Sections 4 and 5. We conclude in Section 6. Due to lack of space, implementation details and more results are provided in [19].

2   The Reference-Counting Collector

We start by reviewing the reference-counting collector and presenting a pseudo code that will be used to explain the prefetch instructions insertions later (in Section 3). Basically, a reference-counting collector maintains a reference-count field for each object signifying the number of pointers that reference the object. A naive reference-counting system updates the reference counts during each pointer update via a *write barrier*. When a pointer is modified from pointing to O_1 into pointing to O_2, the write barrier decrements the count of O_1 and increments the count of O_2. When the counter of an object is decremented to zero, it is reclaimed. At that time, the counts of its children are decremented as well, possibly causing more reclamations recursively.

The reference-counting collector we refer to includes two major improvements, which substantially reduce the computational overhead required to adjust reference counters. First, it employs the deferred reference-counting method of Deutsch and Bobrow [15], which tracks only stores into the heap (ignoring local references stores). The second technique employed is the Levanoni-Petrank update-coalescing write barrier [9,10], which records information on modified objects and uses it to update the reference counts during garbage collection. Consider a pointer slot that, between two garbage collections, is assigned the values $o_0, o_1, o_2, \ldots, o_n$. Instead of executing 2n reference-count updates for these assignments: $RC(o_0)--$, $RC(o_1)++$, $RC(o_1)--$, $RC(o_2)++$, $\ldots$, $RC(o_n)++$, only the two required updates are executed: $RC(o_0)--$ and $RC(o_n)++$.

To implement update coalescing, the collector we investigate employs two buffers: *ModBuffer* and *DecBuffer*. *ModBuffer* contains the addresses of the objects which were created or modified since the previous collection. Reading these addresses during the garbage collection gives us the o_n values, whose RC values should be incremented. The *DecBuffer* contains the addresses of the o_0 objects recorded before the objects in the *ModBuffer* were first modified after the previous collection. The reference counts of these objects should be decremented. Note that in the *DecBuffer* we have objects that were referenced in the previous collection by the objects that are in the *ModBuffer*.

To simplify this work, the collector we have used works in a stop-the-world manner. An involved mechanism is developed in the original paper [9,10] to support collector concurrency and application parallelism.

2.1   Pseudo Code

Next, we present a general pseudo code of a reference-counting collector which employs the coalescing write barrier. The pseudo code assumes the existence of two buffers, *ModBuffer* and *DecBuffer* as explained above.

Mutator cooperation. The mutators need to execute garbage-collection related code on two occasions: when updating an object and when allocating a new object. This is accomplished by the Update (Figure 1) Procedure and the New (Figure 2) Procedure. Procedure Update (Figure 1) describes the write barrier which is activated at each (heap's) pointer assignment[1]. During the first modification of an object after a collection, the write barrier records the modified object in *ModBuffer* and it sets its dirty bit. Next, the modified object's pointers are recorded in the *DecBuffer*. After the logging has occurred, the actual pointer modification happens. Procedure New (Figure 2) is used when allocating an object. Upon the creation of an object, its address is logged onto *ModBuffer*, and the *dirty* bit of the new object is set. There is no need to record its children slot values as they are all null at creation time.

Phases of the collection. The collector's algorithm runs in phases as follows.

- Mark roots: the objects directly reachable from the program roots are marked.
- Process ModBuffer: the collector clears the dirty marks of the objects logged in *ModBuffer*, while incrementing the reference counts of their current descendants.
- Reclaim garbage: the collector decrements the reference counts of the objects logged in *DecBuffer* while (recursively) reclaiming objects which have a zero reference count and which are not referenced by the system roots.
- Prepare next collection: un-marks the objects referenced from the program roots and prepares the buffers for the next collection.

Collector code. The reference-counting collector's code for a collection cycle is presented in Procedure Collection-Cycle (Figure 3). Procedure Process-ModBuffer (Figure 4) handles the objects logged in *ModBuffer*. These are the objects that were modified or created since the previous collection cycle. This procedure first clears the dirty bit of an object logged in *ModBuffer*, and then increments the reference count of the objects it references. Procedure Process-DecBuffer-and-Release (Figure 5) decrements the reference counts of objects logged in *DecBuffer*, and performs the recursive deletion if necessary. Procedure Prepare-Next-Collection (Figure 6) cleans the *Roots*, *ModBuffer* and *DecBuffer* buffers.

2.2 Allocation Using Segregated Free Lists

A garbage collector is accompanied by a memory allocator that serves the application's allocations requests and the collector's reclamations requests. We have built our implementation on the Jikes RVM, which uses the standard segregated free lists allocator [20,21,22] with the reference-counting collector. Since a couple of prefetch insertion opportunities are proposed for the allocator, we review this allocator below.

A segregated free lists allocator holds, for each possible allocation size, a linked list of available memory. Upon an allocation request, a chunk is taken from the free list of the appropriate size. When a chunk is freed, it is returned to the appropriate free list. Jikes RVM implementation uses a *block-oriented* segregated free lists allocator [20]

---

[1] When dealing with multithreading the write barrier must be modified by either using an atomic operation for the pointer assignment or the non-atomic extension proposed by Levanoni and Petrank [9,10]. To simplify the discussion, we consider the simplest form of the write barrier. This treatment handles well atomic operations and does not change much if we adopt the more sophisticated non-atomic write-barrier.

Procedure Update(*o*: **object**, *offset*: **int** , *new*: **object**)
1.   if not *o.dirty* then   // OBJECT NOT DIRTY
2.   add *o* to *ModBuffer*
3.   *o.dirty* :=true   // SET DIRTY
4.   foreach pointer field *ptr* of *o* which is not NULL
5.   add *ptr* to *DecBuffer*
6.   write(*o*, *offset* ,*new*)

Fig. 1. Reference counting: Update Operation

Procedure New(*size*: **Integer**, *obj*: **Object**)
1.   Obtain an object *obj* of size *size* from the allocator.
2.   insert the address of *obj* into *ModBuffer*
3.   *obj.dirty* := true
4.   return *obj*

Fig. 2. Reference counting: Allocation Operation

Procedure Collection-Cycle
1.   accumulate all object directly reference by the program roots onto *Roots*
2.   Process-ModBuffer
3.   Process-DecBuffer-and-Release
4.   Prepare-Next-Collection

Fig. 3. Reference counting- Collection Cycle

Procedure Process-ModBuffer
1.   for each object *obj* whose address is in *ModBuffer* do
2.   *obj*.dirty := false
3.   // INCREMENT CURRENT REFERENT OF THE OBJECT *obj*
4.   for each pointer *ptr* of *obj* do
5.   increment *rc* of object referenced by *ptr*

Fig. 4. Reference counting- Process-ModBuffer

that works as follows. The heap is divided into blocks, partitioned to chunks of a single size. The free list of any given size consists of a chain of blocks. Each block has an associated bit-per-chunk mark array (bitmap), which records the occupancy status of each chunk. When a chunk is allocated the relevant bit is marked. The bit is un-marked

---

Procedure Process-DecBuffer-and-Release
1.   for each object *obj* whose address is in *DecBuffer* do
2.   *obj*.rc−−
3.   if *obj*.rc = 0 ∧ *obj* ∉ *Roots* then
4.   for each pointer *ptr* of *obj* do
5.   push *ptr* onto *DecBuffer*
6.   return *obj* to the general purpose allocator

Fig. 5. Reference counting- Process-DecBuffer-and-Release

Procedure Prepare-Next-Collection
1.   *Roots* := ⊘
2.   *ModBuffer* := ⊘
3.   *DecBuffer* := ⊘

Fig. 6. Reference counting- Prepare-Next-Collection

Procedure Build-Block-Free-List
1.   *markWordAddress* := address of the first word in the block's bitmap
2.   *markWordEnd* := address of the last word in the block's bitmap
3.   *previousFree* := cursor address
4.   while *markWordAddress* ≤ *markWordEnd*
5.   *markWord* := word referenced by *markWordAddress*
6.   foreach *bit* in *markWord*
7.   if *bit* is not set then
8.   *objectRef* := address of chunk relevant to *bit*
9.   write *objectRef* into *previousFree*
10.   *previousFree* := *objectRef*
11.   *markWordAddress* += size of word
12.   write null into *previousFree*

Fig. 7. Reference counting- Build-Block-Free-List

when the object held in this chuck is reclaimed. Unused blocks are kept in a block pool. If, upon an allocation request, the relevant free list is empty, a block is taken from the blocks pool, and the first chunk of this block is returned. An empty block (whose all chunks are free) is returned to the blocks pool, and may be used later with a different object size. The collector is responsible of returning empty blocks to the blocks pool.

In Jikes, each free list employs a cursor pointing to the next available chunk for allocation in the corresponding size. After allocating the chunk referenced by the cursor, the cursor is advanced to the next available chunk. To save scanning the bitmap during each allocation, a linked list, containing all the free chunks of a block, is created when the block is first employed after a collection. The Procedure **Build-Block-Free-List** which builds a block's free list is presented in Figure 7.

3   Prefetching for Reference Counting

We now proceed to describing the prefetch opportunities existing for a reference-counting collector (accompanied by a segregated free lists allocator), and the prefetch insertions that we have applied. We partition the discussion according to the collector phases.

3.1   Process-ModBuffer Stage

Consider the pseudo code of the Process-ModBuffer Procedure presented in Figure 4. In this procedure, the collector clears the dirty marks of the objects logged in *ModBuffer*, while incrementing the reference count of their descendants. For this phase

---

Procedure **Process-ModBuffer**
1.   prefetch the first object whose address is in *ModBuffer*
2.   *previous* := *dummyObject*
3.   for each object *obj* whose address is in *ModBuffer* do
4.   prefetch the next object whose address is in *ModBuffer*
5.   *obj*.dirty := false
6.   // INCREMENT CURRENT REFERENT OF THE OBJECT *obj*
7.   for each pointer *ptr* of *obj* do
8.   prefetch the *rc* field of the object referenced by *ptr*
9.   increment *rc* of object referenced by *previous*
10.   *previous* := *ptr*
11.   increment *rc* of object referenced by *previous*

Fig. 8. Reference counting- Process-ModBuffer with prefetch

Procedure **Process-DecBuffer-and-Release**
1.   prefetch the *rc* field of the first object whose address is in *DecBuffer*
2.   for each object *obj* whose address is in *DecBuffer* do
3.   prefetch the *rc* field of the next object whose address is in *DecBuffer*
4.   *obj*.rc− −
5.   if *obj*.rc = 0 ∧ *obj* ∉ *Roots* then
6.   prefetch the word containing the mark-bit relevant to *obj*
7.   for each pointer *ptr* of *obj* do
8.   push *ptr* onto *DecBuffer*
9.   return *obj* to the general purpose allocator
10.   //UNMARK THE MARK-BIT RELEVANT TO *obj*

Fig. 9. Reference counting- Process-DecBuffer-and-Release with prefetch

we propose two prefetch opportunities. The modified Process-ModBuffer Procedure, including the prefetch instructions, is presented in Figure 8. An explanation follows.

The first prefetch opportunity appears during the traversal of *ModBuffer*. The scan of each object referenced by *ModBuffer* imposes a potential cache miss. Since *ModBuffer* is traversed sequentially, this cache miss can be anticipated and avoided. A prefetching of the object that should be scanned in the next iteration is inserted just before scanning the current object. This follows a standard prefetch strategy for loops, placing prefetches for data accessed by the future loop iteration(s) (e.g., [3]). One can imagine prefetching further ahead, but we have obtained the most significant improvements by prefetching a single address ahead. Lines 1 and 4 in Figure 8 execute the proposed prefetch. We will later refer to this strategy as the *ModBuffer-traversal* strategy.

The second prefetch opportunity appears during the reference-count increments. Each increment accesses a reference-count field. To handle a potential cache miss, we slightly delay the increment of an object's reference count. When an increment to a count is required, the count of the object is prefetched; it is only incremented in the following loop iteration. The location of the count is stored in a temporary variable named *previous*. To avoid a special treatment to the first iteration and the implied 'if' statement, we use a dummy object whose reference count is incremented when the first count is prefetched. This delaying strategy is presented in lines 2 and 8-11 of Figure 8. We will later refer to this strategy as the *delay-increment* strategy.

3.2   Process-DecBuffer-and-Release Stage

Figure 5 describes the Process-DecBuffer-and-Release Procedure, in which the collector decrements the reference counts of the objects logged in *DecBuffer*, and recursively reclaims the dead objects. This phase also offers two prefetch opportunities. The modified Process-DecBuffer-and-Release Procedure, which includes these prefetch modifications, is presented in Figure 9. A description follows.

Similarly to the Process-ModBuffer stage, the first prefetch opportunity for the Process-DecBuffer-and-Release stage occurs with the traversal of *DecBuffer*. The reference-count field is accessed for each decrement. This time, we do not typically touch the referent, unless we reclaim it. So only the reference-count field of the referent need be prefetched. Note that unlike before, the objects for which we modify the counts are directly referenced by the buffer (and not the children of the objects pointed from the buffer, as in the handling of the Process-ModBuffer Procedure). We exploit the loop prefetch strategy described in the previous stage and prefetch the reference-count field of the next object in the buffer before handling the current one. Lines 1 and 3 of Figure 9 present this prefetch strategy. We will later refer to this strategy as the *DecBuffer-traversal* strategy.

The second prefetch opportunity at this stage occurs during the reclamation of an object. Once an unreachable object is discovered (line 3 of Figure 5), the object is first scanned and all its descendants are recorded in the *DecBuffer*; only then the object is reclaimed. As described in Section 2.2, the reclamation of an object sums up to unmarking the mark-bit corresponding to this object. Accessing the mark-bit creates a potential miss and so we prefetch the relevant mark-bit word as soon as we realize that the object should be reclaimed. Namely, the prefetch is performed right after line 3 of

```
Procedure Build-Block-Free-List
1.      markWordAddress := address of the first word in the block's bitmap
2.      markWordEnd := address of the last word in the block's bitmap
3.      previousFree := cursor address
4.      while markWordAddress ≤ markWordEnd
5.          markWord := word referenced by markWordAddress
6.          markWordAddress += size of word
7.          prefetch markWordAddress
8.          foreach bit in markWord
9.              if bit is not set then
10.                 objectRef := address of chunk relevant to bit
11.                 write objectRef into previousFree
12.                 previousFree := objectRef
13.     write null into previousFree
```

Fig. 10. Reference counting- Build-Block-Free-List with prefetch

Figure 5. This way, the miss penalty for unsetting the relevant bit later is reduced or even eliminated. Line 6 in Figure 9 presents this prefetch modification. We will later refer to this strategy as the *object-release* strategy.

3.3   Build-Block-Free-List Stage

The fifth prefetch opportunity occurs with the segregated free lists allocator. While iterating over a block's bitmap words, we've inserted a prefetch to the next mark-bit word, before processing the current one. The Build-Block-Free-List Procedure was modified to exploit this loop prefetching strategy as presented in lines 6-7 of Figure 10.

4   Measurements

Platform and benchmarks. We have run our measurements on a dual Intel's Xeon 1.8GHz processors workstation. These processors have a 16KB sized L1 cache and a 512KB sized L2 cache. We have used the SPECjvm98 benchmark suite, the SPECjbb2000 benchmark[2] (both described in SPEC's web site [17]), and the DaCapo benchmarks [18][3].

The collector. We have inserted the proposed prefetch instructions into the reference-counting collector of Jikes [16]. Next, we have compared the original reference-counting collector of Jikes, against the collector modified to include these prefetch instructions. In both collectors, we have disabled the cycle collection algorithm. The cycle collector has a characteristic behavior that resembles tracing collectors and it may

---

[2] We have slightly modified SPECjbb2000, to run a fixed number of transactions instead of running during a fixed time period.

[3] Measurements of _222_mpegaudio and _201_compress are not presented. _222_mpegaudio does not perform meaningful allocation activity. _201_compress main allocation activity concerns cyclic structures, whose reclamation is not relevant in this work. The DaCapo benchmarks presented are the ones we were able to run with Jikes.

Table 1. Reduction in reference-counting overheads obtained by prefetching

Benchmarks	overhead reduction				overall
	Process ModBuffer	Process DecBuffer and Release	Build Blocks	overall gc	benchmark improvement
jess	-0.1% (36.6%)	-0.9% (51.5%)	-11.9% (11.0%)	-1.8%	-0.9%
db	-11.2% (39.2%)	-6.7% (50.5%)	-8.0% (8.9%)	-8.5%	-0.9%
javac	-12.2% (31.6%)	-8.4% (38.6%)	-18.4% (28.4%)	-12.3%	-3.4%
mtrt	-12.3% (26.8%)	-3.3% (46.4%)	-12.3% (25.2%)	-8.0%	-1.5%
jack	-16.3% (31.3%)	-5.9% (54.5%)	-23.2% (11.6%)	-10.8%	-3.1%
jbb	-8.3% (24.9%)	-6.5% (34.0%)	-26.5% (40.1%)	-14.9%	-4.6%
fop	-12.5% (38.7%)	-8.1% (39.5%)	-11.3% (20.8%)	-10.5%	-2.1%
antlr	-16.1% (30.6%)	-8.4% (42.4%)	-24.3% (25.6%)	-14.6%	-1.3%
pmd	-8.7% (30.8%)	-8.4% (43.8%)	-12.3% (25.3%)	-9.6%	-3.3%
ps	3.0% (38.2%)	-3.7% (52.5%)	-13.0% (7.3%)	-1.7%	-0.6%
hsqldb	-18.8% (30.1%)	-11.0% (41.0%)	-17.6% (26.9%)	-14.9%	-4.6%
jython	-9.4% (32.4%)	-0.5% (50.8%)	-6.6% (15.7%)	-4.4%	-1.7%
xalan	2.4% (43.6%)	-1.2% (51.8%)	-24.4% (4.4%)	-0.6%	-0.6%
average	**-9.3%**	**-5.6%**	**-16.1%**	**-8.7%**	**-2.2%**

interfere with the comparison of the reference-counting collectors. For most applications this means a negligible increase in the heap size [13].

Testing procedure. Each benchmark was run ten times for both the original reference-counting collector and the modified reference-counting collector. We report the average of these runs. To guaranty a fair comparison of the garbage collection characteristics, we included only runs in which each benchmark performs the same amount of garbage collections on both collectors. The benchmarks' heap size, employed in our runs, doubles the minimum heap size required (by the reference-counting collector).

4.1   Prefetch Improvements

Table 1 presents the improvements achieved by using prefetching. A negative percentage represents a performance improvement, while a positive percentage represents deterioration in performance. Columns 2-4 present the improvements achieved for each one of the reference-counting collector stages implemented by the **Process-ModBuffer** Procedure (presented in Figure 4), by the **Process-DecBuffer-and-Release** Procedure (presented in Figure 5), and by the **Build-Block-Free-List** Procedure (presented in Figure 7). These presented improvements are calculated relatively to the corresponding reference-count stages. Hence, for example, a -10.0% appearing on the second column indicates a 10.0% performance improvement of the **Process-ModBuffer** stage. To make the picture complete, the numbers in parenthesis (in columns 2-4) present the distribution of Jikes original reference-counting collector overhead within the three different stages. These do not add up to 100% as stages such as scanning threads' stack are not counted. The fifth column presents the overall reference-counting's performance improvement achieved. The sixth column introduces the benchmark's overall throughput improvement due to prefetching.

Normally, Jikes runs the Build-Block-Free-List Procedure lazily when a new block is selected for allocations. Therefore, while the Process-ModBuffer and the Process-DecBuffer-and-Release Procedures are activated once per a garbage collection cycle, the Build-Block-Free-List Procedure is activated numerous times during the benchmark run (i.e., between the collections). In order to accurately measure the time overhead of this procedure, we have slightly modified Jikes reference-counting collector (in both versions) to activate the Build-Block-Free-List Procedure continuously (non-lazily), for all non-empty blocks, once at the end of each collection.

One can see that the proposed prefetch strategies reduce the overall overhead of reference-counting for all benchmarks. This is emphasized by the last line of Table 1, which presents the average improvement of each column. For most benchmarks, prefetching is able to reduce the overhead imposed by each one of the three stages. Note, however, that the improvements are not steady among the different benchmarks and among the different stages. We study this issue in Section 4.2 below.

4.2 Reference-Counting Objects' Access Behavior

In order to understand the potential of prefetch instruction insertions, we investigate the memory access patterns of the reference-counting collector. Recall that tracing collectors traverse the application's live objects in an arbitrary order (depending on the object's graph). If a mark table is used by a tracing collector, each live object is likely to be read exactly once during a collection, since if it was already traversed, its corresponding mark bit in the mark table would indicate that it should not be touched (read) again. This one-touch behavior creates a high miss rate, highly suitable for prefetching.

The cache-miss behavior of reference counting is not that simple to describe. To analyze the way a reference-counting collector accesses objects, we ran the following profiling on memory accesses. We considered each scan of an object and each update of a reference-count as a single memory access[4]. Each such access may cause a cache miss. We recorded the address of each such access into gc-log files, one log file per collection. Next, each gc-log file was analyzed in the following manner. For a given window size w, we checked for each access, if the same address was accessed during the last w (distinct) accesses, creating a cache hit[5]. For each benchmark, we outputted the fraction of hits, i.e., the fraction of repeating accesses within the window size, as a function of the window size.

The results appear in Table 2. We ran the above measurements with five window sizes (addresses): 100, 1000, 10000, 100000, and 1000000. The smaller windows are more representative of L1 cache-miss behavior, whereas the larger window sizes represent behavior with L2 cache sizes.

The measurement should be read as follows. If a 40% percentage appears in the 100 column of a benchmark's line, it means that 40% of the accesses were to memory locations that have been previously accessed during the last 100 accessed (distinct) addresses. A higher percentage means high cache hit ratio and a low potential for effective

---

[4] In this liberal measurement, we counted an object's scan as a single access, although it may have involved multiple accesses, e.g., because a large object may contain several pointer slots.

[5] We always consider a first access of an object in a collection as a miss.

Table 2. Percentage of repeated object accesses (hit ratios) for the entire collection

	window size				
Benchmarks	100	1000	10000	100000	1000000
jess	58.2%	64.1%	66.9%	68.0%	72.7%
db	15.1%	15.8%	16.8%	68.3%	80.2%
javac	31.3%	37.5%	40.5%	42.8%	50.9%
mtrt	13.6%	17.0%	18.5%	19.8%	22.1%
jack	25.9%	27.9%	29.0%	30.5%	36.3%
jbb	23.5%	30.5%	34.7%	38.2%	46.2%
fop	28.5%	33.4%	35.1%	37.0%	42.0%
antlr	23.2%	26.2%	28.1%	29.1%	33.3%
pmd	28.9%	32.0%	35.4%	39.9%	47.3%
ps	78.2%	79.5%	79.8%	80.2%	90.7%
hsqldb	26.0%	27.9%	29.5%	31.7%	40.0%
jython	54.5%	55.4%	56.1%	56.5%	57.1%
xalan	0.4%	0.6%	2.8%	99.0%	99.5%
average	**31.3%**	**34.4%**	**36.4%**	**49.3%**	**55.3%**

prefetching. For a tracing collector, the corresponding measurement would produce an all zeros table (since an object is not traversed twice during a collection).

It turns out that unlike tracing collectors, the repeated access with reference counting is quite high and the repeated accesses have temporal proximity. Hence, many memory accesses hit the L1 cache, making the prefetch a burden, or hit the L2 cache, making the prefetch less effective. Nevertheless, as seen in Table 1, properly inserted prefetching instructions can improve performance substantially. A further exploration (phases profiling) of this memory accesses behavior is provided in [19] for lack of space.

Usually there is correspondence between benchmark improvement percentages (Table 1) and repeated object accesses behavior (Table 2). However, the correspondence is not perfect as repeated object accesses behavior is not the only parameter influencing prefetch improvements. For example, if many benchmark's objects do not contain pointers, then prefetching an object (in order to read its pointers) is a waste. Hence, even if the repeated object accesses fraction of this benchmark is low, prefetching could not improve performance much in this case.

4.3   Prefetch Strategy Profiling

Table 1 presented the prefetch improvements achieved for the different reference-counting stages. However, two different prefetch strategies were implemented in both the **Process-ModBuffer** stage and the **Process-DecBuffer-and-Release** stage. Table 3 breaks the overall improvement into the shares of each particular strategy.

Columns 2-4 of Table 3 present the **Process-ModBuffer** stage, displaying the effect of the strategies *ModBuffer-traversal* and *delay-increment* (presented in Section 3.1). As can be seen, the *ModBuffer-traversal* strategy is the major cause for the prefetch

Table 3. A break of the prefetching improvement due to the two strategies involved in the Process-ModBuffer stage and the two strategies involved in the Process-DecBuffer-and-Release stage

Benchmarks	ModBuffer traversal improvement	delay increment improvement	Process ModBuffer improvement	DecBuffer traversal improvement	object release improvement	Process DecBuffer and Release improvement
jess	-5.5%	5.3%	-0.1%	-0.9%	-0.1%	-0.9%
db	-7.4%	-3.8%	-11.2%	-6.4%	-0.2%	-6.7%
javac	-9.2%	-3.0%	-12.2%	-6.8%	-1.6%	-8.4%
mtrt	-9.5%	-2.9%	-12.3%	-2.0%	-1.4%	-3.3%
jack	-13.8%	-2.5%	-16.3%	-4.3%	-1.7%	-5.9%
jbb	-7.9%	-0.3%	-8.2%	-5.6%	-0.9%	-6.5%
fop	-10.7%	-1.8%	-12.5%	-6.7%	-1.3%	-8.1%
antlr	-13.2%	-2.8%	-16.1%	-6.9%	-1.4%	-8.4%
pmd	-6.6%	-2.1%	-8.7%	-6.6%	-1.8%	-8.4%
ps	-4.0%	7.1%	3.0%	-3.4%	-0.1%	-3.7%
hsqldb	-12.5%	-6.3%	-18.8%	-10.0%	-1.0%	-11.0%
jython	-10.8%	1.4%	-9.4%	-0.1%	-0.4%	-0.5%
xalan	0.2%	2.1%	2.4%	-0.8%	-0.4%	-1.2%
average	**-8.5%**	**-0.7%**		**-4.7%**	**-0.9%**	

improvement of the **Process-ModBuffer** stage. An investigation into the reasons for these improvement differences is provided in [19], due to lack of space.

Columns 5-7 of Table 3 present the **Process-DecBuffer-and-Release** stage, displaying the effect of the strategies *DecBuffer-traversal* and *object-release* (presented in Section 3.2). Here, the strategy responsible for most of the benefit is the *DecBuffer-traversal* strategy. This may be expected as the other prefetching strategy only applies to objects whose reference counts drops to zero. We have not further analyzed the objects' access behavior of the **Process-DecBuffer-and-Release** stage.

4.4   Hardware Counters Measurements

In order to better understand the effect of the inserted prefetch instructions, we have also measured several relevant hardware counters using PAPI (the Performance API [23]). These counters were measured during the garbage collection work of both versions of the reference-counting collector: with and without prefetching. Table 4 presents the difference of these counters between the versions for the entire garbage collection work. Columns 2-4 present the difference in the number of cycles stalled on any resource, the L2 load misses difference and the data TLB misses difference. Column 5 presents the overall garbage collection improvement (presented in Table 1).

It turns out that the strongest influence of the prefetching had been on the TLB misses rather than on the cache itself. The reason is probably that the prefetches were issued too late and therefore only the TLB managed to gain some performance improvement. An attempt to issue the prefetch instructions earlier did not succeed due to the pay in temporary variables (and register pressure).

Table 4. Hardware counters measurements

Benchmarks	Cycles stalled	L2 cache misses	TLB misses	overall gc
jess	-8.8%	-1.1%	-17.3%	-1.8%
db	-4.3%	-0.7%	10.1%	-8.5%
javac	-17.4%	-1.8%	-6.6%	-12.3%
mtrt	-15.8%	-0.6%	-20.1%	-8.0%
jack	-20.0%	-3.2%	-21.1%	-10.8%
jbb	-14.8%	2.5%	-9.4%	-14.9%
fop	-6.6%	0.1%	-14.0%	-10.5%
antlr	-6.3%	0.1%	-15.1%	-14.6%
pmd	-9.6%	0.2%	-11.2%	-9.6%
ps	-2.0%	0%	-21.6%	-1.7%
hsqldb	-14.1%	-0.8%	-21.8%	-14.9%
jython	-4.8%	0.4%	-1.6%	-4.4%
xalan	-0.7%	0.2%	37.6%	-0.6%
average	**-9.6%**	**-0.4%**	**-8.6%**	

5   Related Work

VanderWiel and Lilja [3] provide a detailed survey examining diverse prefetching strategies, such as hardware prefetching, array prefetching and other software prefetching.

Similarly to our approach, several previous studies proposed adding, by hand, prefetch instructions to specific locations in several garbage collectors. However, they all studied tracing collectors. Boehm [5] proposed prefetching objects that are pushed to the mark stack during the mark phase of a mark-sweep collector. This prefetch makes the first cache line of the object available later when popped from stack to be scanned. This prefetching strategy yields improvements in execution time, although suffering from prefetch timing problems: too early prefetches and too late prefetches. These timing problems were addresses by [6,7]. Both suggested improved prefetching strategies to the mark phase by imposing some sort of FIFO processing over the mark stack, in order to control the time between the data prefetch and its actual access. In another related work, Cahoon [4] employs prefetching to improve the memory performance of a generational copying garbage collector.

Appel [24] emulates a write-allocate policy on a no-write-allocate machine by prefetching garbage before it is written (during its space allocation). Hence, the relevant cache line is allocated and the write (occurring during the object allocation) hits the cache.

6   Conclusions

We have studied prefetch opportunities for a modern reference-counting garbage collector. It turns out that several such opportunities typically exist and an implementation on the Jikes Research JVM demonstrates effectiveness in reducing stall times and improving garbage collection efficiency. In particular, the average garbage collection time was reduced by 8.7%.

Investigating the memory access patterns of the reference-counting collector, we found out that, unlike tracing collectors, objects are accessed repeatedly, reducing the potential benefit due to prefetching. These measurements explain the effectiveness of the various strategies at the various stages. Repetitive accesses to objects increase the hit rate and reduce the efficacy of prefetch insertions.

References

1. Callahan, D., Kennedy, K., Porterfield, A.: Software prefetching. In: ASPLOS-IV: Proceedings of the fourth international conference on Architectural support for programming languages and operating systems, New York, NY, USA, ACM Press (1991) 40–52
2. Luk, C.K., Mowry, T.C.: Compiler-based prefetching for recursive data structures. In: International Conference on Architectural Support for Programming Languages and Operating Systems. (1996) 222–233 SIGLAN Notices 31(9).
3. VanderWiel, S.P., Lilja, D.J.: Data prefetch mechanisms. ACM Computing Surveys **32** (2000) 174–199
4. Cahoon, B.: Effective Compile-Time Analysis for Data Prefetching in Java. PhD thesis (2002)
5. Boehm, H.J.: Reducing garbage collector cache misses. In Hosking, T., ed.: ISMM 2000 Proceedings of the Second International Symposium on Memory Management. Volume 36(1) of ACM SIGPLAN Notices., Minneapolis, MN, ACM Press (2000)
6. Cher, C.Y., Hosking, A.L., Vijaykumar, T.: Software prefetching for mark-sweep garbage collection: Hardware analysis and software redesign. In: Eleventh International Conference on Architectural Support for Programming Languages and Operating Systems, Boston, MA (2004) 199–210
7. van Groningen, J.: Faster garbage collection using prefetching. In C.Grelck, Huch, F., eds.: Proceedings of Sixteenth International WOrkshop on Implementation and Application of Functional Languages (IFL'04), Lübeck, Germany (2004) 142–152
8. Collins, G.E.: A method for overlapping and erasure of lists. Communications of the ACM **3** (1960) 655–657
9. Levanoni, Y., Petrank, E.: An on-the-fly reference counting garbage collector for Java. In: OOPSLA'01 ACM Conference on Object-Oriented Systems, Languages and Applications. Volume 36(10) of ACM SIGPLAN Notices., Tampa, FL, ACM Press (2001)
10. Levanoni, Y., Petrank, E.: An on-the-fly reference-counting garbage collector for java. ACM Transactions on Programming Languages and Systems **28** (2006)
11. Azatchi, H., Levanoni, Y., Paz, H., Petrank, E.: An on-the-fly mark and sweep garbage collector based on sliding view. [25]
12. Blackburn, S.M., McKinley, K.S.: Ulterior reference counting: Fast garbage collection without a long wait. [25]
13. Paz, H., Petrank, E., Bacon, D.F., Rajan, V., Kolodner, E.K.: An efficient on-the-fly cycle collection. [26]
14. Paz, H., Petrank, E., Blackburn, S.M.: Age-oriented garbage collection. [26]
15. Deutsch, L.P., Bobrow, D.G.: An efficient incremental automatic garbage collector. Communications of the ACM **19** (1976) 522–526

16. Alpern, B., Attanasio, C.R., Cocchi, A., Lieber, D., Smith, S., Ngo, T., Barton, J.J., Hummel, S.F., Sheperd, J.C., Mergen, M.: Implementing Jalapeño in Java. In: OOPSLA'99 ACM Conference on Object-Oriented Systems, Languages and Applications. Volume 34(10) of ACM SIGPLAN Notices., Denver, CO, ACM Press (1999) 314–324
17. SPEC Benchmarks: Standard Performance Evaluation Corporation. http://www.spec.org/ (1998,2000)
18. DaCapo benchmark suite: The dacapo benchmark suite - version beta051009. (http://www-ali.cs.umass.edu/DaCapo/)
19. Paz, H.: Efficient Memory Management for Servers. PhD dissertation, Technion, Israel Institute of Technology, Department of Computer Science (2006)
20. Boehm, H.J., Demers, A.J., Shenker, S.: Mostly parallel garbage collection. ACM SIGPLAN Notices **26** (1991) 157–164
21. Wilson, P.R., Johnstone, M.S., Neely, M., Boles, D.: Dynamic storage allocation: A survey and critical review. In Baker, H., ed.: Proceedings of International Workshop on Memory Management. Volume 986 of Lecture Notes in Computer Science., Kinross, Scotland, Springer-Verlag (1995)
22. Jones, R.E.: Garbage Collection: Algorithms for Automatic Dynamic Memory Management. Wiley, Chichester (1996) With a chapter on Distributed Garbage Collection by R. Lins.
23. PAPI: The Performance API. (http://icl.cs.utk.edu/papi/overview/)
24. Appel, A.W.: Emulating write-allocate on a no-write-allocate cache. Technical Report TR-459-94, Department of Computer Science, Princeton University (1994)
25. OOPSLA'03 ACM Conference on Object-Oriented Systems, Languages and Applications. In: OOPSLA'03 ACM Conference on Object-Oriented Systems, Languages and Applications. ACM SIGPLAN Notices, Anaheim, CA, ACM Press (2003)
26. Proceedings of the 14th International Conference on Compiler Construction. In: Proceedings of the 14th International Conference on Compiler Construction, Edinburgh, Springer-Verlag (2005)

Accurate Garbage Collection in Uncooperative Environments with Lazy Pointer Stacks

Jason Baker, Antonio Cunei, Filip Pizlo, and Jan Vitek

Computer Science Department
Purdue University
West Lafayette, IN 47906, USA
{baker29,cunei,filip,jv}@cs.purdue.edu

Abstract. Implementing a new programming language by the means of a translator to an existing language is attractive as it provides portability over all platforms supported by the host language and reduces the development time as many low-level tasks can be delegated to the host compiler. The C and C++ programming languages are popular choices for many language implementations due to the availability of efficient compilers on many platforms, and good portability. For garbage-collected languages, however, they are not a perfect match as they provide no support for accurately discovering pointers to heap-allocated data. We evaluate the published techniques, and propose a new mechanism, lazy pointer stacks, for performing accurate garbage collection in such uncooperative environments. We implemented the new technique in the Ovm Java virtual machine with our own Java-to-C++ compiler and GCC as a back-end, and found that our technique outperforms existing approaches.

1 Introduction

Implementing a high-level programming language involves a large development effort. The need for performance of the resulting environment has to be balanced against portability and extendibility. One popular implementation technique is to use a language translator to transform the code into an existing language, thus leveraging existing technology for part of the implementation. A time tested road has been to use C or C++ as a form of portable assembly language. This approach takes advantage of the portability of C++ and offloads many optimizations to the native compiler.

However, these advantages come at a price. Some control over representation and code generation must be relinquished. One often encountered problem is that a C++ compiler such as GCC[1] will not provide support for automatic memory reclamation. It is up to the language implementer to bridge the semantic mismatch between the features of the high-level language and what is available in the low-level language. In the case of garbage collection, implementers end up programming *around* the C++ compiler to ensure that garbage can be reclaimed.

The most straightforward solution to the problem is to use a *conservative* garbage collection algorithm. A conservative collector does not require cooperation

S. Krishnamurthi and M. Odersky (Eds.): CC 2007, LNCS 4420, pp. 64–79, 2007.

from its environment – it will traverse the stack and heap, and treat every value that could possibly be a pointer as a pointer. Conservative garbage collection algorithms, however, may not be appropriate for the task at hand. For example, in the domain of real-time systems, all application deadlines must be met even in the presence of collector-induced pauses. For this to happen, the garbage collector has to be predictable – a trait not found in conservative collectors. Conservative collectors may also fail to reclaim some unused memory because of non-pointer words that appear to be valid pointers to dead objects.

This paper looks at how to support *accurate* garbage collection, in which all pointers can be correctly identified in an uncooperative environment. Although our work environment is Java, the discussion generalizes to other high-level language translators. We evaluate several approaches to generating idiomatic C++ code that maintains enough information to allow a garbage collector to accurately find and replace pointers. Our goal is to minimize the overheads, bringing the performance of our accurate configuration as close as possible to that of our conservative configuration. The work is being done in the context of the Ovm virtual machine framework. We offer the following contributions:

- **Lazy pointer stack:** We present a class of new techniques for maintaining accurate information on the call stack. It promises lower overheads than previous work because the information is only materialized when needed leaving the native compiler free to perform more optimizations.
- **Catch & thunk stack walking:** We propose an efficient technique for saving and restoring the pointers on a call stack, which extends lazy pointer stacks by exploiting the exception handling features of the C++ language.
- **Implementation:** We implemented our technique in the Ovm framework. We report on our implementation and describe our optimizations.
- **Evaluation:** We compare our technique against an efficient conservative collector and two previously published techniques for accurate collection. The results suggest that our approach incurs less overhead than other techniques.
- **Validation:** We report on the implementation of a real-time garbage collector within Ovm using lazy pointer stacks to obtain accurate stack roots.

2   The Ovm Virtual Machine

Ovm is a framework for building virtual machines with different features. An Ovm *configuration* determines a set of features to be integrated into an executable image. While Ovm supports many configurations, one of the project's topmost goals was to deliver an implementation of the Real-time Specification for Java running at an acceptable level of performance [4]. This section discusses the two most important aspects of the real-time configuration of Ovm with respect to our implementation of the collection algorithms described in this paper. Sources and documentation for Ovm are available from our website [5]. The reader is referred to [6,4,7] for further description of the framework.

The J2c Compiler. The Real-time Ovm configuration relies on ahead-of-time compilation to generate an executable image that can be loaded in an embedded device (such as the UAV application discussed in [4]). The Ovm ahead-of-time compiler called j2c performs whole-program analysis over the user code as well as the Ovm source (the virtual machine framework consists of approximately 250'000 lines of Java code). j2c translates the entire application and virtual machine code into C++, which is then processed by the GCC compiler.

The Ovm Threading subsystem. Ovm uses user-level threading. Multiple Java threads are mapped onto one operating system thread. Threads are implemented by *contexts* which are scheduled and preempted under VM control. Asynchronous event processing, such as timer interrupts and I/O completion is implemented by the means of compiler-inserted *poll checks*. A poll check is simply a function call guarded by a branch on the value of a global variable. Our current poll check insertion strategy leads to less than 2.5% overhead. Studies we have done with a real-time application show that the latency between the arrival of an event and the execution of a poll check tends to be under $6\mu s$. For a detailed description of these results the reader is referred to [4].

We leverage poll checks in our implementation of memory management. Context switches only occur at poll checks and a small well-understood set of scheduler actions. The garbage collector can only run while a thread is blocked at a poll check, calling the memory allocator or invoking a scheduler operation. This makes for a simple definition of garbage collection safe points: in Ovm the only safe points are method calls and poll checks.

3   Previous Work: Accurate Stack Scanning

It is often possible to assume that heap-allocated data structures have accurate type-descriptors, and that information can be used by the garbage collector. Determining the location of pointers in the stack, however, is less easy. While the native C/C++ compiler knows which locations in the call stacks contain pointers and which don't, this knowledge is normally lost once the executable has been produced.

We found two previously used techniques for accurately scanning C call stacks. The simpler of the two uses an explicit stack of live pointers. The other approach, presented by Henderson [8], involves building a linked list of frames that contain pointers. This section describes both techniques in detail.

Explicit Pointer Stacks. While a C compiler is free to lay out local variables however it wants, it has less freedom when dealing with objects in the heap. When generating C code, a language translator can choose to emit code that will store all pointers in an array that is at a known location and has a fixed layout. We call this array an *explicit pointer stack*. Consider Fig. 1(a), where a function allocates an object, stores a pointer to it in a local variable, and then calls a second function passing the pointer as an argument. Fig. 1(b) illustrates the same function using an explicit pointer stack. The code uses a global pointer to the topmost element of the stack, PtrStackTop. The prologue of the function increments the stack top by the number of pointer variables used in the function

```
void Foo(void) {
    void *ptr = AllocObject();
    Bar(ptr);
    ...
}
```

(a) Generated C code

```
static void **PtrStackTop;
void Foo(void) {
    // allocate stack slot for the pointer
    PtrStackTop++;
    PtrStackTop[-1] = AllocObject();
    Bar(PtrStackTop[-1]);
    ...
    // relinquish stack slot
    PtrStackTop--;
}
```

(b) Explicit pointer stack

```
struct PtrFrame {
    PtrFrame *next;
    unsigned len;
}
static PtrFrame *PtrTop;
void Foo(void) {
    // describe this frame
    struct Frame: PtrFrame {
        void *ptr;
    }
    Frame f;
    f.len = 1;
    f.next = PtrTop;
    PtrTop = &f;
    f.ptr = AllocObject();
    Bar(f.ptr);
    ...
    // pop the stack
    PtrTop = f.next;
}
```

(c) Henderson's linked lists

Fig. 1. Example of previous techniques for accurate stack traversal in C++ code. In (a), we see the original code. In (b) and (c) we see the same code converted to use explicit pointer stacks and Henderson's linked frames.

(one in this case), and the epilogue decrements it by an equal quantity. References are then stored in the reserved stack slots.

Henderson's Linked Frames. Henderson proposed a different approach, taking advantage of the fact that in C a local variable's address may either be passed to another function or stored in the heap. A C or C++ compiler handles these variables specially, to ensure that changes made through these external references are visible locally. Fig. 1(c) illustrates Henderson's technique. The PtrFrame data structure is used to build a linked list of frames which hold live pointers. The translator emits a function prologue that declares a frame with sufficient space to hold all the pointers (just one in our example). places The frame is placed into a linked list which can be subsequently traversed by the garbage collector.

Both techniques pin local variables into specific memory location that cannot easily be optimized by the C/C++ compiler. In the absence of good alias analysis, any write to a pointer variable will invalidate previous reads of all other pointer variables. Hence, the effectiveness of optimizations such as register allocator is limited, as pointers can not be moved around or stored in register.

4   Accuracy with Lazy Pointer Stacks

The key to accurately obtaining references in the call stack is to force the compiler to place references in specific locations, which the approaches above do by segregating references to an explicit pointer stack or, in Henderson's case, to a linked frame structure. Both approaches are *eager* in the sense that the data structures describing live pointers are always up-to-date. We investigate here techniques that constructs the equivalent of a pointer stack on demand. We refer to this approach as *lazy pointer stacks*.

The goal of a lazy pointer stack algorithm is to produce at any GC safe point a list of all references on the call stack of each thread. We shall assume that safe points are associated to call sites, *de facto* the case in Ovm as GCs are triggered by calls to the memory allocator. Other granularities are however possible.

For every safe point, the language translator has a set of reference variables. that may be live. Each safe point is followed by a guarded sequence that saves all the live references and simply returns, as in Fig. 2. When a stack needs to be scanned, we arrange for the guard to evaluate to true and return from the topmost frame. The call stack then unwinds saving all references in the process. Once all pointers are saved to the lazy stack, the GC can use this data to work accurately.

```
void Foo(void) {
    void *ptr = AllocObject();
    Bar(ptr);
    if (save()) {
        lazyPointerStack->pushFrame(1);
        lazyPointerStack->pushPtr(ptr);
        return;
    }
    ...
}
```

Fig. 2. Lazy pointer stack construction: generated C++ code

After unwinding the stack, we restore the thread to its initial state; specifically we restore the C++ call stack and the register file. If we are unwinding a thread we just context-switched to, we already have a copy of the register file, otherwise, we save it using `setjmp`. To be able to restore the stack, we simply save the original C++ call stack before unwinding and replace the unwound stack with its copy afterwards.

This simple strategy is all that is needed if the garbage collector does not move objects. Supporting a moving collector, however, requires the ability to update the pointers contained in local variables. We developed two original solutions for this purpose: *pointer frame counting*, and the *safe point catch and thunk*.

```
void Foo(void) {
    void *ptr = AllocObject();
    Bar(ptr);
    if (save()) {
        lazyPointerStack->pushFrame(1);
        lazyPointerStack->pushPtr(ptr);
        return;
    } else if (restore()) {
        ptr = lazyPointerStack->popPtr();
        lazyPointerStack->popFrame();
    }
    ...
}
```

Fig. 3. Prototype of lazy pointer stack with frame counting guard: generated C code

4.1   Pointer Frame Counting

Updating pointers held in local variables can also be done lazily, as in Fig. 3. After collection, when each thread resumes execution, we cause each frame to perform pointer restoration as control returns to it, thanks to an additional post-safe-point guard which retrieves the possibly updated pointers. So, when the garbage collector runs, the pointers stored in the lazy pointer

```
// pointers in locals
void *ptr1, *ptr2, *ptr3, ...

height++;
functionCall();
height--;
if (save()) {
    if (height < auxHeight) {
        stop unwinding, restore the stack;
    } else {
        lazyPointerStack->pushFrame(nptrs);
        lazyPointerStack->pushPtr(ptr1);
        lazyPointerStack->pushPtr(ptr2);
        lazyPointerStack->pushPtr(ptr3);
        ...
        return;
    }
} else if (height < auxHeight) {
    ptr3 = lazyPointerStack->popPtr();
    ptr2 = lazyPointerStack->popPtr();
    ptr1 = lazyPointerStack->popPtr();
    ...
    lazyPointerStack->popFrame();
    auxHeight--;
}
```

```
// pointers in locals
void *ptr1, *ptr2, *ptr3, ...;

try {
    functionCall();
} catch (const StackScanException&) {
    if (save()) {
        lazyPointerStack->pushFrame(nptrs);
        lazyPointerStack->pushPtr(ptr1);
        lazyPointerStack->pushPtr(ptr2);
        lazyPointerStack->pushPtr(ptr3);
        ...
        throw;
    } else {
        ptr3 = lazyPointerStack->popPtr();
        ptr2 = lazyPointerStack->popPtr();
        ptr1 = lazyPointerStack->popPtr();
        ...
        lazyPointerStack->popFrame();
        if (had application exception) {
            throw application exception
        } else {
            retrieve return values
        }
    }
}
```

(a) Function call with pointer frame counting   (b) Function call, safe point catch and thunk

Fig. 4. Lazy pointer stack techniques

stack structure are used and modified. When the collector yields back to the application threads, the pointers are automatically restored from the pointer stack, frame by frame.

The restoration logic has two key aspects. First, restore() must only evaluate to true the first time we return to a frame after a collection, which may happen immediately after the collection, or later. Second, a thread may return to a frame only after several collections have occurred. This complicates the stack unwinding procedure. If at the time of a stack scanning request it is found that a frame has not been active since before a previous garbage collection, then the pointers in that frame are no longer valid, and the collector should not use that frame's pointers as roots but rather reuse the pointers in its lazy pointer stack.

We illustrate these issues in the following example. The program is composed of four method M, A, B, C, and G, which is the invocation of the memory allocator which triggers garbage collection. A frame is said to be *dirty* if it contains references to objects that were not updated after a collection (these reference are stale if the objects were moved). We denote a dirty frame using bold face.

(a) $[M]$ The main function.
(b) $[M \rightarrow A \rightarrow B]$ M calls A, which then calls B.
(c) $[M \rightarrow A \rightarrow B \rightarrow G]$ B requests memory and triggers a collection.
(d) $[M \rightarrow A \rightarrow B \rightarrow G]$ The stack is scanned and restored.

(e) [M → A → B → G] The garbage collector runs, potentially moving objects referenced from the stack. All frames below that of the garbage collector are now dirty as they contain pointers to the old locations of objects.

(f) [M → A → B] We return to a dirty frame, **B**, and must restore pointers.

(g) [M → A → B] Execution proceeds in a clean frame.

(h) [M → A → B → C] Call into C.

(i) [M → A → B] Return to B. Because it is clean, we do not restore pointers.

(j) [M → A → B → G] Consider what happens if B triggers another collection.

(k) [M → A → B → G] The stack is scanned only as far as B, since frames below it contain contain old, now invalid, pointers.

We see that there is a frontier between dirty and clean frames. For dirty frames, the lazy pointer stack has correct pointers. For clean frames, the lazy pointer stack has no information. The *pointer frame counting* technique for accurate stack scanning is shown in Fig. 4(a). We keep track of the frontier between dirty frames and clean frames by using two counters: `height` is the height of the stack below the current frame; `auxHeight` is the height of the lazy pointer stack managed by the garbage collector, and it keeps track of the frontier between dirty and clean frames. We only restore pointers in a frame when the `height` becomes smaller than `auxHeight`. After stack scanning, the collector resets the `height` to its previous value, and `auxHeight` to the same value as `height`.

Non-local returns can interfere with this scheme. In our case the language translator uses C++ exceptions, so we have to handle them appropriately, providing a way to maintain the correct value of `height`. The solution is to compile `try` blocks as shown in Fig. 5. Before entry into the `try` block we save the value of `height`, and we restore it when an exception is caught. Because the exception may have traversed multiple dirty frames, we need to pop those from the lazy pointer stack. This is the purpose of the `while` loop. Finally, we check if the current frame is dirty; if so, we restore the pointers.

This gives us a complete system, with all the features necessary to accurately scan the stack and find pointers. However, this solution still has some

```
unsigned savedHeight = height;
...
try {
    ...
} catch (const ApplicationException&) {
    // restore counts
    height = savedHeight;
    while (height < auxHeight-1) {
        // ignore pointers in frame
        lazyPointerStack->popFrame();
        auxHeight--;
    }
    if (height < auxHeight) {
        ptr = lazyPointerStack->popPtr();
        lazyPointerStack->popFrame();
        auxHeight--;
    }
    // handle application exception
    ...
}
```

Fig. 5. Compiling try blocks to restore the pointer frame counts

overheads. In particular, it is necessary to execute code that counts the stack height before and after each function call.

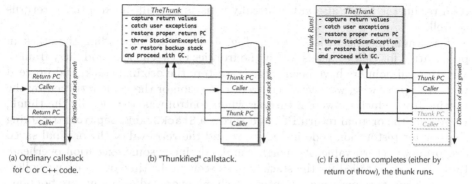

Fig. 6. Installing thunks in a C++ call stack

4.2 Safe Point Catch and Thunk

On most systems, enclosing a group of instructions in a `try/catch` block does not require any additional code to be executed when no exceptions are thrown. The fast path has virtually no overhead. Instead of using a costly conditional to protect entry to the save and restore sequences, therefore, we can obtain better performance by implementing the accurate pointer guard using C++ exceptions.

To scan the stack, we simply throw a distinguished `StackScanException`. That exception is caught by the `catch` block in Fig. 4(b) and, if the `save()` predicate is set, the pointers in the receiver frame are saved. The exception propagates until all pointers are saved. During the traversal, for every dirty frame we install a helper routine, a *thunk*, by modifying the return address in the C++ call stack. After GC, whenever control would return to a function with a dirty frame, the thunk runs instead, throwing again a `StackScanException`. That causes the pointers in the corresponding frame to be restored before normal execution resumes. At all times, thunks delimit the frontier between clean and dirty frames. This approach is illustrated in Fig. 4(b).

```
void thunk() {
  if (unwinding stack) {
    stop unwinding, restore the stack
  } else {
    if (target frame threw exception) {
      save exception
    } else {
      save return values
    }
    restore proper return PC
    throw StackScanException;
  }
}
```

Fig. 7. Thunk algorithm

Thunks are invoked on both normal and exceptional returns. During the normal return sequence, the ordinary return sequence of the target frame results in the thunk being called. Fig. 6 shows this process. During exceptional returns, the C++ runtime unwinds the stack using the return PCs to determine if a frame is able to handle exceptions of a given type. We replace the return PC with the address of our thunk; therefore, we simply have to enclose the entry point of our thunk within a suitable exception handler.

As a result, the thunk also automatically runs as a result of exceptional returns as well.

The thunk algorithm is shown in Fig. 7. If we are unwinding the stack in preparation for GC, it means we hit the frontier between clean and dirty frames. We stop (all pointers have been copied), restore the original stack, and proceed with GC. Otherwise, we save the current exception or the value returned by the routine from which we were returning when control was assumed by the thunk, we restore the original return PC, and throw a StackScanException, triggering the pointer restoration code in Fig. 4(b) and the retrieval of the original saved exception or return value. Although thunks do incur some execution overhead, they are only installed for the stack frames seen at the time of a garbage collection, and run once per frame. Hence, the thunk overhead is in any case bounded by the stack height at the time of the collection.

4.3 Practical Considerations

Henderson [8] argues that his approach is fully portable as it uses only standard C. The same holds for explicit pointer stacks. Our approach uses some platform-specific knowledge in order to save and restore the stack. We also rely on using only one stack frame at a time, not the case for lexically nested functions or if objects are on the stack. The safe point catch and thunk technique also requires some knowledge of the C++ calling convention. While the implementation of thunks does require some platform specific code, we argue that the such dependencies are small. The platform specific code in our thunking implementation amounts to just 30 lines of code, supporting both IA32 and PPC architectures.

5   Compiler Optimizations

We have described four methods for accurate stack scanning: explicit pointer stacks and Henderson's frame lists, and two new techniques, frame counting and catch & thunk. All four have been implemented in the Ovm virtual machine. We found that the overheads imposed by those techniques can be reduced by carefully applying a number of optimization strategies.

General Optimizations. The adoption of certain optimization techniques proved to have a positive effect on the performance of both eager and lazy stack scanning techniques. Inlining at the bytecode level, within our compiler, produced smaller code than relying exclusively on the GCC inliner, as we can rely on a higher-level knowledge of the program structure. Method devirtualization is more effective after bytecode inlining, as our analysis can rely on additional context. Refining our liveness analysis also proved beneficial. By reducing as much as possible the set of variables known to be live at each call site, we can both reduce the size of the added code, and improve the efficiency of the garbage collector at runtime.

Fine Tuning Further optimizations, specifically concerning our new techniques, also proved very valuable. When lazy pointer stacks are used, we treat safe points where no pointers are live as a special case. With catch & thunk, a function call with no live pointers does not require a *try/catch* block at all. In the pointer frame counting approach, empty safe points just require a simple guard, as show below. In SPECjvm, 26% of all safe points are empty.

If no variables are live across any safe point in a method, that method can avoid using the pointer stack entirely. Because we only emit poll checks on backward branches, many methods fall into this category (roughly 34% of all methods after bytecode inlining). Certain function calls do not need a guard even if pointers are live at the call. This includes function calls that are known not to return normally, for which the set of exceptions thrown is known, and whose exceptions are not caught locally. We currently use this optimization at array bounds checks, explicit type checks, and implicit type checks when writing to an array of object references. Only 5% of our runtime checks include non-empty safe points. In certain cases, we can also coalesce multiple exception handlers within each method. That allows us to further contain the code size overhead.

6   Experimental Evaluation

Our experimental evaluation was performed on a Pentium 4 machine at 1600 MHz, 512 MB of RAM, running Linux 2.6 in single-user mode. All results are based on the SPECjvm98 benchmark suite. The results reported here are the arithmetic mean of fifty individual runs of each test, using a range of heap sizes from 2MB to 256MB. We show the results from the smallest heap size in which each test ran succesfully. The heap sizes do not include static data, which is instead pre-allocated by the j2c ahead-of-time compiler at compile time. We use Ovm's most reliable production garbage collector, called *mostlyCopying*, which has two operational modes. When accurate information is available it behaves as a traditional semi-space collector. Otherwise it runs in 'conservative' mode and pins pages referenced from the stack.

Overhead of Accurate Techniques. Figure 8 shows the percent overhead of using the four accurate stack scanning techniques. catch & thunk is significantly better than other techniques. It has a geometric mean overhead of less than 3.5% over a conservative collector, while the others are no better than about 6%. In large heap configurations, many of the SPECjvm98 benchmarks only collect when the benchmark asks for it directly using *System.gc()*. Hence, results using the large heap configurations place more emphasis on the mutator overheads of the stack scanning techniques. Smaller heap configurations place more emphasis on the cost of stack scanning and collection time. Detailed overhead numbers for 32MB and 256MB heaps are shown in Figure 9.

Time Spent in GC. Sometimes thunking can lead to a speed up, as our garbage collector can work more efficiently if accurate pointer information is available. We profiled the time spent in the garbage collector, and verified that the time used for GC in mtrt is shorter in the accurate configuration, consistently with the speed-ups shown in Fig. 9.

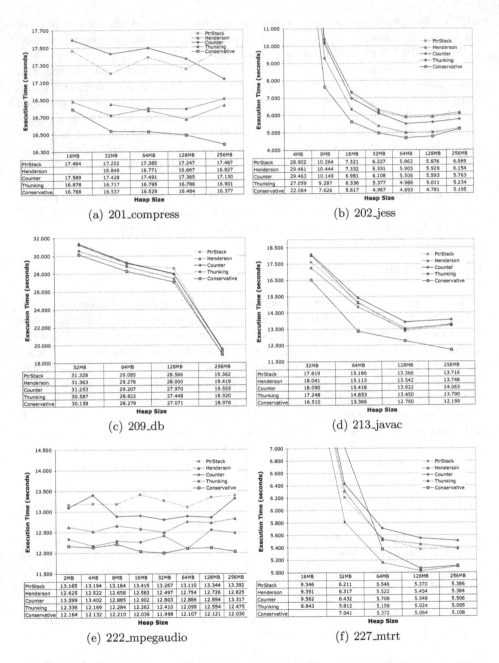

Fig. 8. Overhead of accurate collection. Execution times of SPECjvm98 benchmarks, in seconds, using the different techniques, with Ovm and bytecode inlining. The times are arithmetic means of 50 runs. (Continues on the next page.)

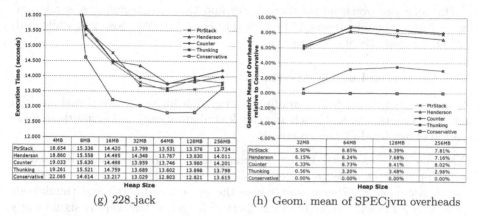

	4MB	8MB	16MB	32MB	64MB	128MB	256MB
PtrStack	18.654	15.336	14.420	13.799	13.531	13.576	13.724
Henderson	18.860	15.558	14.495	14.348	13.767	13.830	14.011
Counter	19.033	15.630	14.498	13.959	13.746	13.980	14.201
Thunking	19.261	15.521	14.759	13.689	13.602	13.898	13.798
Conservative	22.065	14.614	13.217	13.029	12.803	12.821	13.615

Heap Size

	32MB	64MB	128MB	256MB
PtrStack	5.90%	8.85%	8.39%	7.81%
Henderson	6.15%	8.24%	7.68%	7.16%
Counter	6.33%	8.73%	8.41%	8.02%
Thunking	0.56%	3.20%	3.48%	2.98%
Conservative	0.00%	0.00%	0.00%	0.00%

Heap Size

(g) 228_jack   (h) Geom. mean of SPECjvm overheads

Fig. 8. Overhead of accurate collection, SPECjvm98 execution times (*continued*)

Average of Execution time in seconds - (Overhead relative to Conservative)	Thunking	Counter	PtrStack	Henderson
201_compress	3.20%	4.60%	6.78%	2.75%
202_jess	0.75%	10.94%	16.84%	18.46%
209_db	-0.30%	3.05%	2.03%	2.33%
213_javac	13.04%	15.28%	12.43%	12.69%
222_mpegaudio	3.70%	10.69%	11.32%	6.61%
227_mtrt	-0.25%	7.80%	5.45%	5.41%
228_jack	1.34%	4.31%	0.80%	2.91%
Geometric Mean	2.98%	8.02%	7.81%	7.16%
Average of Execution time in seconds - Spec JVM 98 Benchmark vs. Ovm Configuration Ovm inlining, 65000 vars, copy propagation, Heap Size: 256m, Compiler: gcc-4.0.2, 50 runs - (Overhead relative to Conservative)				

Average of Execution time in seconds - (Overhead relative to Conservative)	Thunking	Counter	PtrStack	Henderson
201_compress	1.09%	5.39%	4.02%	1.88%
202_jess	8.26%	22.98%	25.36%	27.47%
209_db	1.42%	3.63%	3.88%	4.00%
213_javac	4.47%	9.57%	6.72%	9.27%
222_mpegaudio	3.43%	6.71%	10.58%	4.16%
227_mtrt	-17.47%	-8.65%	-11.80%	-10.29%
228_jack	5.07%	7.14%	5.91%	10.12%
Geometric Mean	0.56%	6.33%	5.90%	6.15%
Average of Execution time in seconds - Spec JVM 98 Benchmark vs. Ovm Configuration - Ovm inlining, 65000 vars, copy propagation, Heap Size: 32m, Compiler: gcc-4.0.2, 50 runs - (Overhead relative to Conservative)				

(a) 256MB heap   (b) 32 MB heap

Fig. 9. Percent overhead of accurate garbage collection in Ovm. The overhead of accurate stack walking when using the safe point catch and thunk is significantly smaller than that of the other techniques.

Comparing VMs. Our goal in implementing Ovm was to deliver a competitive Java implementation. We compare Ovm and stack walking configurations (conservative and thunking) against HotSpot Client and Server version 1.5, and GCJ version 4.0.2, with a 256 MB heap. Fig. 11 shows the results. We were unable to obtain 228_jack results for GCJ in our setup. Ovm's performance is highly competitive with that of the other systems, therefore our overhead results are likely not due to implementation inefficiencies.

Conservative	3,376
Explicit Pointer Stack	3,857
Henderson	4,031
Counter	9,320
Thunking	11,081

Fig. 10. Code Size in KB

Code Size. All accurate techniques increase code size. In the case of Ovm with j2c we can measure the code component of the Ovm executable image. Fig. 10 shows the image sizes in KBytes for the SPEC benchmark executable image (includes the application as well as the VM code, and approximately 30MB of data.)

The code size overhead for the counter and thunking techniques is relevant, but not unreasonable. It should be kept into consideration, however, while evaluating the tradeoffs of each approach.

6.1   Understanding the Overheads

We used gprof[9] to obtain profiling information for the javac benchmark in both the conservative and catch and thunk configurations, and found three main sources of overhead in these methods.

Exception Dispatch Code. Up to two call-preserving registers may be used by exception dispatch code generated by GCC. This appears to be the dominant cost in *ScannerInputStream.read*, where the presence of catch and thunk code spills a loop induction variable from %edi. The generated code is significantly more complicated where two or more exception handlers are nested.

Extra Assignments of Return Values. We replace method calls with wrapper macros that add our lazy stack walking code. Those macros may lead to extra assignments of return values. When a method produces a value, the safe point code serves as the right-hand side of an assignment expression. The return value is saved in a macro-generated variable and returned to the macro's caller using GCC's statement-in-expression syntax. These extra assignments invariably remain after GCC's optimization, but are usually simple register-to-register moves. However, in *Scanner.xscan*, these extra variables and assignments do result in

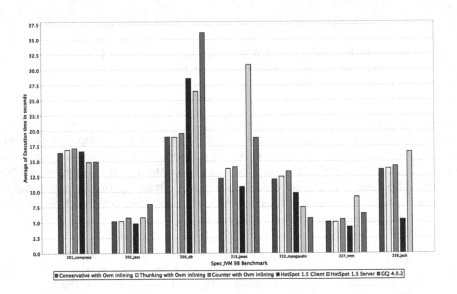

Fig. 11. Comparing Virtual Machines. 256MB heap, arithmetic mean of 50 runs. Comparing two Ovm configurations (conservative and thunking) with HotSpot Client 1.5, HotSpot Server 1.5 and GCJ 4.0.2.

additional variables being spilled to the stack, leading to a marked slowdown (about 40%). It should be possible to eliminate this overhead by treating an assignment expression whose right-hand-side is a method call as a safe point, thus moving the real assignment inside the safe point try block.

Code Motion Across Exception Handlers. Code motion across exception handlers is sometimes less profitable than it would be in the absence of exception handlers. GCC occasionaly performs extra work to ensure that variables that are not used by safe point code are available inside the safe point catch clause.

7   Validation: Real-Time Garbage Collection

One of our goals in starting this project was to support real-time garbage collection (RTGC) in the real-time configuration of Ovm. While it is reasonable to think that lazy pointer stacks are able to deliver both the level performance and predictability needed in a real-time GC, it is difficult to have confidence in such a claim without an actual implementation. We therefore implemented a real-time garbage collector within Ovm using the lazy pointer stack technique [10]. The success in this endeavor increased our confidence in the general applicability of the techniques introduced here.

The Ovm real-time collector is a mark-sweep snapshot-at-the-beginning non-copying incremental garbage collector. The collector, just as the rest of the VM, is written in Java. We thus used features of the Real-time Specification for Java in the implementation. The collector thread is a real-time Java thread with a priority high enough that, unless it yields, it will not be interrupted by application threads. When memory usage increases beyond a user-specified threshold, the collector thread is scheduled. Because of its priority, it immediately preempts any application threads. It then accurately scans the stack, the Ovm boot image, which contains immortal objects used by the VM, and then incrementally traverses the heap reclaiming unused objects. Accurate stack scanning takes less than $250\mu s$ for the `mtrt` benchmark, and the maximum collector pause time for this benchmark is $1.022ms$. Further details on our real-time collector are in [10].

8   Related Work

Language implementations that use a C or C++ compiler as a back-end have a choice between conservative collection and the accurate techniques presented here. Techniques for accurate stack scanning in uncooperative environments have been previously described in detail in [13,8]. Popular techniques for conservative garbage collection include the Boehm-Weiser collector[2] and various incarnations of mostly-copying collectors[14,15,16].

JamaicaVM uses explicit pointer stacks [13], but they differ from our implementation. First, objects referenced from the stack cannot move (in Ovm they can). Second, JamaicaVM uses write barriers on the pointer stack to enable incremental stack scanning. Ovm uses stop-the-world stack scanning. JamaicaVM may choose to place pointers on the pointer stack at safe points rather than upon each write. However, our lazy pointer stacks go further, only saving pointers when a stack scanning is actually requested, and additionally allowing for objects referenced by pointers on the stack to be moved.

The motivation behind generating C or C++ code is to create a competitive, portable language implementation with minimal effort. Jones, Ramsey, and Reig[17,18] point out that what is really needed is a portable assembly language. They propose C--, which has a structured C-like syntax and comes complete with a runtime system that supports accurate garbage collection. C-- is attractive, but its stage of development cannot compete with GCC, especially for implementations of languages that map nicely onto C++, and where either conservative collection is acceptable, or the accurate stack walking techniques within this work are applicable. The Quick C-- compiler currently only supports IA32, while Ovm is available on IA32, PPC, and ARM. Using GCC allows us to generate fast code on each of these architectures.

It possible to modify, with some effort, the GCC compiler to support accurate garbage collection. Diwan, Moss, and Hudson [19] describe changes to GCC version 2.0 to support accurate garbage collection in Modula-3. A further effort in this area is described in [20]. Our work has the advantage of not being strictly specific to GCC; the techniques described in this paper can be used with any compiler that has a reasonable binary interface for exceptions.

9   Conclusions

We have extended the state of the art for accurate garbage collection in uncooperative environments. The lazy pointer stacks technique shows significantly improved performance over previous techniques. Further, we show the need for optimizations such as inlining to be implemented in the high-level compiler for accurate garbage collection to pay off. To our knowledge, our experimental evaluation is the first to compare multiple approaches to accurate stack scanning within the same system. Of the previously known techniques, Henderson's approach fared the best in our tests; however, it showed more than twice the overhead of our new strategy. We claim therefore that our new approach improves the viability of accurate garbage collection in uncooperative environments and makes it easier for language implementors to use C++ as portable low-level representation.

References

1. Free Software Foundation: Gnu compiler collection. (http://gcc.gnu.org/)
2. Boehm, H.J., Weiser, M.: Garbage collection in an uncooperative environment. Software—Practice and Experience 18(9) (1988) 807–820
3. Boehm, H.J.: Space efficient conservative garbage collection. In: Proceedings of the ACM Conference on Programming Language Design and Implementation. Volume 26. (1991) 197–206

4. Baker, J., Cunei, A., Flack, C., Pizlo, F., Prochazka, M., Vitek, J., Armbuster, A., Pla, E., Holmes, D.: A real-time Java virtual machine for avionics. In: Proceedings of the 12th IEEE Real-Time and Embedded Technology and Applications Symposium (RTAS 2006), IEEE Computer Society (2006)
5. Vitek, J., Baker, J., Flack, C., Fox, J., Grothoff, C., Holmes, D., Palacz, C., Pizlo, F., Yamauchi, H.: The Ovm Project. (http://www.ovmj.org)
6. Palacz, K., Baker, J., Flack, C., Grothoff, C., Yamauchi, H., Vitek, J.: Engineering a common intermediate representation for the Ovm framework. The Science of Computer Programming **57**(3) (2005) 357–378
7. Flack, C., Hosking, T., Vitek, J.: Idioms in Ovm. Technical Report CSD-TR-03-017, Purdue University Department of Computer Sciences (2003)
8. Henderson, F.: Accurate garbage collection in an uncooperative environment. In: Proceedings of the ACM International Symposium on Memory Management. Volume 38., ACM (2002) 256–263
9. Free Software Foundation: Gnu binutils. (http://www.gnu.org/software/binutils/)
10. Pizlo, F., Vitek, J.: An empirical evaluation of memory management alternatives for Real-Time Java. In: Proceedings of the 27th IEEE Real-Time Systems Symposium (RTSS 2006), 5-8 December 2006, Rio de Janeiro, Brazil. (2006)
11. Baker, H.G.: List processing in real time on a serial computer. Communications of the ACM **21**(4) (1978) 280–294
12. Bacon, D.F., Cheng, P., Rajan, V.T.: A real-time garbage collector with low overhead and consistent utilization. In: Conference Record of the ACM Symposium on Principles of Programming Languages. Volume 38. (2003) 285–298
13. Siebert, F.: Constant-time root scanning for deterministic garbage collection. In: International Conference on Compiler Construction (CC). (2001) 304–318
14. Bartlett, J.F.: Compacting garbage collection with ambiguous roots. Research Report 88/2, Western Research Laboratory, Digital Equipment Corporation (1988)
15. Smith, F., Morrisett, J.G.: Comparing mostly-copying and mark-sweep conservative collection. In: Proceedings of the ACM International Symposium on Memory Management. Volume 34., ACM (1998) 68–78
16. Bartlett, J.F.: Mostly-copying garbage collection picks up generations and C++. Technical Note TN-12, Western Research Laboratory, Digital Equipment Corporation (1989)
17. Jones, S.P., Ramsey, N., Reig, F.: C--: a portable assembly language that supports garbage collection. In: International Conference on Principles and Practice of Declarative Programming. (1999)
18. C--: (http://www.cminusminus.org)
19. Diwan, A., Moss, J.E.B., Hudson, R.L.: Compiler support for garbage collection in a statically typed language. In: Proceedings of the ACM Conference on Programming Language Design and Implementation. Volume 27. (1992) 273–282
20. Cunei, A.: Use of Preemptive Program Services with Optimised Native Code. PhD thesis, University of Glasgow (2004)

Correcting the Dynamic Call Graph
Using Control-Flow Constraints*

Byeongcheol Lee, Kevin Resnick, Michael D. Bond, and Kathryn S. McKinley

The University of Texas at Austin

Abstract. To reason about programs, dynamic optimizers and analysis tools use sampling to collect a *dynamic call graph* (DCG). However, sampling has not achieved high accuracy with low runtime overhead. As object-oriented programmers compose increasingly complex programs, inaccurate call graphs will inhibit analysis and optimizations. This paper demonstrates how to use static and dynamic *control flow graph* (CFG) constraints to improve the accuracy of the DCG. We introduce the *frequency dominator* (FDOM), a novel CFG relation that extends the dominator relation to expose static relative execution frequencies of basic blocks. We combine conservation of flow and dynamic CFG basic block profiles to further improve the accuracy of the DCG. Together these approaches add minimal overhead (1%) and achieve 85% accuracy compared to a perfect call graph for SPEC JVM98 and DaCapo benchmarks. Compared to sampling alone, accuracy improves by 12 to 36%. These results demonstrate that static and dynamic control-flow information offer accurate information for efficiently improving the DCG.

1   Introduction

Well-designed object-oriented programs use language features such as encapsulation, inheritance, and polymorphism to achieve reusability, reliability, and maintainability. Programs often decompose functionality into small methods, and virtual dispatch often obscures call targets at compile time. The dynamic call graph (DCG) records execution frequencies of call site-callee pairs, and dynamic optimizers use it to analyze and optimize whole-program behavior [2,3,4,5,11,21]. Prior approaches sample to collect the DCG, trading accuracy for low overhead. Software sampling periodically examines the call stack to construct the DCG [4,12,17,20,24]. Hardware sampling lowers overhead by examining hardware performance counters instead of the call stack, but gives up portability. All DCG sampling approaches suffer from sampling error, and timer-based sampling suffers from timing bias. Arnold and Grove first measured and noted these inaccuracies [4].

* This work is supported by NSF CCF-0429859, NSF CCR-0311829, NSF EIA-0303609, DARPA F33615-03-C-4106, Samsung, Intel, IBM, and Microsoft. Any opinions, findings and conclusions expressed herein are the authors' and do not necessarily reflect those of the sponsors.

S. Krishnamurthi and M. Odersky (Eds.): CC 2007, LNCS 4420, pp. 80–95, 2007.

Figure 5(a) (appears in Section 6) shows DCG accuracy for the SPEC JVM98 benchmark *raytrace* using Jikes RVM default sampling. Each bar represents the *true* relative frequency of a DCG edge (call site and callee) from a fully instrumented execution. Each dot is the frequency according to sampling. Vertical dashed lines separate the calling method. Notice that many methods make calls with the same frequency (i.e., bars have the same magnitude between dashed lines), but sampling tells a different story (i.e., dots are not horizontally aligned). These errors are due to timing bias.

This paper presents new *DCG correction* algorithms to improve DCG accuracy with low overhead (1% on average). Our insight is that a program's static and dynamic *control flow graph* (CFG) constrains possible DCG frequency values. We introduce the static *frequency dominator* (FDOM): given statements x and y, x FDOM y if and only if x executes at least as many times as y. FDOM extends the dominator and strong region relations on CFGs. For example, FDOM tells us when two calls must execute the same number of times because the static control flow dictates that their basic blocks execute the same number of times.

We also exploit dynamic *basic block profiles* to improve DCG accuracy. Most dynamic optimizers collect accurate control-flow profiles such as basic block and edge profiles to make better optimization decisions [1,3,12,16,17]. We show how to combine these constraints to further improve the accuracy of the DCG. Our intraprocedural and interprocedural correction algorithms require a single pass over the basic block profile, which we perform periodically.

We evaluate DCG correction in Jikes RVM [3] on the SPEC JVM98 and DaCapo [8] benchmarks. Our approach improves DCG accuracy over the default sampling configuration in Jikes RVM, as well as over the *counter-based sampling* (CBS) configuration recommended by Arnold and Grove [4]. Compared to a perfect call graph, default sampling attains 52% accuracy and DCG correction algorithms boost accuracy to 71%; CBS by itself attains 76% accuracy and DCG correction boosts its accuracy to 85%, while adding 1% overhead.

Clients of the DCG include alias analysis, escape analysis, recompilation analysis, and inlining. We use inlining to evaluate accurate DCGs. The adaptive compiler in Jikes RVM periodically recompiles and inlines hot methods. We modify Jikes RVM to apply DCG correction immediately before recompilation. We measure the potential of inlining with a perfect call graph, which provides a modest 2% average improvement in application time, but significantly improves *raytrace* by 13% and *ipsixql* by 12%. DCG correction achieves a similarly high speedup on *raytrace* and improves average program performance by 1%. We speculate that these modest improvements are the result of tuning the inlining heuristics with inaccurate call graphs and that further improvements are possible.

2 Background and Related Work

This section first discusses how dynamic optimizers sample to collect a DCG with low overhead. It then compare the new frequency dominator relation to

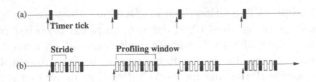

Fig. 1. Sampling. Filled boxes are taken samples and unfilled boxes are skipped. Arrows are timer ticks. (a) Timer-based sampling: one sample per timer tick. (b) CBS: multiple samples per tick, randomly skips initial samples, and strides between samples.

dominators and strong regions. Finally, it compares DCG correction to previous static call graph construction approaches for ahead-of-time compilers.

2.1   Collecting Dynamic Call Graphs

Dynamic optimizers could collect a *perfect* DCG by profiling every call, but the overhead is too high [4]. Some optimizers profile calls fully for some period of time and then turn off profiling to reduce overhead [17,20]. For example, HotSpot adds call graph instrumentation only in unoptimized code [17]. Suganama et al. insert call instrumentation, collect call samples, and then remove the instrumentation [20]. This *one-time profiling* keeps overhead down but loses accuracy when behavior changes.

Many dynamic optimizers use software sampling to profile calls and identify hot methods [4,6,12]. Software-based approaches examine the call stack periodically and update the DCG with the call(s) on the top of the stack. For example, Jikes RVM and J9 use a periodic timer that sets a flag that triggers the system to examine the call stack at the next *yield point* and update the DCG [6,12]. These systems insert yield points on method entry and exit, and on back edges.

Figure 1(a) illustrates timer-based sampling. Arnold and Grove show that this approach suffers from insufficient samples and *timing bias*: some yield points are more likely to be sampled than others, which skews DCG accuracy [4]. To eliminate bias, they present *counter-based sampling* (CBS), which takes multiple samples per timer tick by first randomly skipping zero to *stride-1* samples and then striding between samples. Figure 1(b) shows CBS configured to take three samples for each timer tick and to stride by three. By widening the profiling windows, CBS improves DCG accuracy but increases profiling overhead. They report a few percent overhead to attain an average accuracy of 69%, but to attain 85% accuracy, they hit some pathological case with 1000% overhead. With our benchmarks, their recommended configuration attains 76% accuracy compared to a perfect call graph, whereas our approach combined with the recommended configuration reaches 86% accuracy by adding 1% overhead.

Other dynamic optimizers periodically examine hardware performance counters such as those in Itanium. All sampling approaches suffer from sampling error, and timer-based sampling approaches suffer from timing bias as well. DCG correction can improve the accuracy of any DCG collected by sampling and Section 6 demonstrates improvements over two sampling configurations.

Zhuang et al. [24] present a method for efficiently collecting the calling context tree (CCT), which represents the calling context of nodes in the DCG. Their work is orthogonal to ours since they add another dimension to the DCG (context sensitivity), while we improve DCG accuracy. We believe that our correction approach could improve CCT accuracy as well.

2.2   Constructing the DCG Using Control-Flow Information

Static compilers have traditionally used control-flow information to construct a call graph [13,23]. Hashemi et al. use static heuristics to construct an estimated call frequency profile [13], and Wu and Larus construct an estimated edge profile for estimating call frequency profile [23] for C programs. These approaches use static *heuristics* to estimate frequencies, while DCG correction uses static *constraints* and combines them with dynamic profile information.

2.3   The Dominator Relation and Strong Regions

This paper introduces the *frequency dominator* (FDOM) relation, which extends *dominators* and *strong regions* [7,10,22]. The set of dominators and post-dominators of x is the set of y that will execute at least once if x does. The set that frequency dominates x, is the subset that executes at least as many times as x. While strong regions find vertices x and y that must execute the same number of times, FDOM also identifies vertices x and y where y must execute at least as many times as x.

3   Dynamic Call Graph Correction Algorithms

This section describes DCG correction algorithms. We first present formal definitions for a control flow graph (CFG) and the dynamic call graph (DCG). We introduce the *frequency dominator* (FDOM) and show how to apply its static constraints to improve the accuracy of the DCG, and how to combine them with dynamic CFG frequencies to further improve the DCG.

3.1   Terminology

A *control flow graph* represents *static* intraprocedural control flow in a method, and consists of basic blocks (V) and edges (E). Figure 2 shows an example control flow graph CFG_p that consists of basic blocks $ENTRY$, a, b, c, d, e, and $EXIT$. The dashed lines show edges between basic blocks. The dark edges show calls between methods (other CFGs). A *call edge* represents a method call, and consists of a *call site* and a *callee*. An example call edge in Figure 2 is e_5, the call from cs_c to CFG_t. The DCG of a program includes the *dynamic* frequency of each call edge, from some execution. For a call site cs, $OutEdges(cs)$ is the set of call edges that start at call site cs. $OutEdges(cs_a) = \{e_3, e_4\}$ in Figure 2. For a method m, $InEdges(m)$ is the set of call edges that end at m. $InEdges(CFG_t) = \{e_4, e_5\}$ in Figure 2.

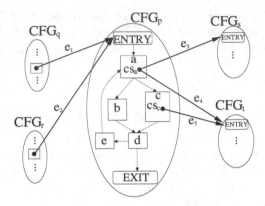

Fig. 2. Example dynamic call graph (DCG) and its control flow graphs (CFGs)

Definition 1. *The* INFLOW *of a method m is the total flow into m:*

$$\text{INFLOW}(m) \equiv \sum_{e \in \text{InEdges}(m)} f(e)$$

where $f(e)$ is the execution frequency of call edge e. INFLOW(m) *in an accurate DCG is the number of times m executes.*

Definition 2. *The* OUTFLOW *of a call site* cs *is:*

$$\text{OUTFLOW}(\text{cs}) \equiv \sum_{e \in \text{OutEdges}(\text{cs})} f(e)$$

OUTFLOW(cs) *in an accurate DCG is the number of times* cs *executes.*

Because a sampled DCG has timing bias and sampling errors, the DCG yields inaccurate *OUTFLOW* and *INFLOW* values. DCG correction corrects *OUT-FLOW* using constraints provided by static and dynamic control-flow information (doing so indirectly corrects method *INFLOW* as well).

DCG correction maintains the relative frequencies between edges coming out of the same call site (which occur because of virtual dispatch), and does not correct their relative execution frequencies. For example, DCG correction maintains the sampled ratio between $f(e_3)$ and $f(e_4)$ in Figure 2.

3.2   The Frequency Dominator (FDOM) Relation

This section introduces the *frequency dominator* relation, a static property of CFGs that represents constraints (theorems) on program statements' relative execution frequencies. Due to space constraints, we omit the algorithms for computing FDOM and only sketch the constraint propagation algorithms based on FDOM. The detailed algorithms may be found in an extended technical report [15]. The FDOM algorithm is closely related to dominator algorithms [10]. Like the dominator relation, FDOM is reflexive and transitive.

Definition 3. *Frequency Dominator (FDOM). Given statements x and y in the same method, x FDOM y if and only if for every possible path through the method, x must execute at least as many times as y. We also define FDOM(y) $\equiv \{x \mid x$ FDOM $y\}$.*

3.3   Static FDOM Constraints

We first show how to propagate the FDOM constraint to DCG frequencies.

Theorem 1. *FDOM OUTFLOW* Constraint: *Given method m and two call sites cs_1 and cs_2 in m, if cs_1 FDOM cs_2, OUTFLOW(cs_1) $\geq$ OUTFLOW(cs_2)*

Intuitively, the *OUTFLOW* constraint tells us that flow on two call edges is related if they are related by FDOM. For example, in Figure 2, cs_a FDOM cs_c and thus $OUTFLOW(cs_a) \geq OUTFLOW(cs_c)$.

Theorem 2. *FDOM INFLOW* Constraint: *Given method m, if cs FDOM ENTRY (m's entry basic block), INFLOW(m) $\leq$ OUTFLOW(cs)*

Intuitively, the *INFLOW* constraint specifies that a call site must execute at least as many times as a method that always executes the call site.

3.4   Static FDOM Correction

We use an algorithm called *FDOMOutflowCorrection* to apply the *FDOM OUT-FLOW* constraint to a sampled DCG. We give pseudocode in the technical report [15]. The algorithm compares the sampled *OUTFLOW* of pairs of call sites that satisfy the FDOM relation. If their *OUTFLOW*s violate the *FDOM OUTFLOW* constraint, *FDOMOutflowConstraint* sets both *OUTFLOW*s to the maximum of their two *OUTFLOW*s. After processing a method, *FDOMOutflow-Constraint* scales the *OUTFLOW*s of all the method's call sites to preserve the sum of the frequencies out of the method. For instance, consider a call site cs_1 and a call site cs_2 in the same method, and suppose that cs_1 executes at least as many times as cs_2 due to the *FDOMOutflowConstraint*. However, suppose also that the call graph profiler samples cs_1 10 times and cs_2 30 times since the program spends a lot of time executing the callee of cs_2. The *FDOMOutflow-Correction* algorithm corrects this anomaly and assigns 30 to $OUTFLOW(cs_1)$, and scales the two *OUTFLOW*s by $(10+30)/(30+30) = 2/3$ so the *OUTFLOW* sum is preserved. Then both call sites have 20 as their corrected execution frequency.

   We also implemented correction algorithms using the *INFLOW* constraint, but they degraded DCG accuracy in some cases. This class of correction algorithms requires high accuracy in the initial *INFLOW* for a method to subsequently correct its *OUTFLOW*. In practice, we found that errors in *INFLOW* information propagated to the *OUTFLOW*s, degrading accuracy.

3.5   Dynamic Basic Block Profile Constraints

This section describes how to incorporate constraints on DCG frequencies provided by basic block profiles, and the following section shows how to correct the DCG with them. The *Dynamic OUTFLOW* constraint computes execution ratios from the basic block execution frequency profiles, and then applies these ratios to the *OUTFLOW* of call sites in the basic blocks.

Theorem 3. *Dynamic OUTFLOW Constraint: Given two call sites cs_1 and cs_2, and execution frequencies $f_{bprof}(cs_1)$ and $f_{bprof}(cs_2)$ provided by a basic block profile,*

$$\frac{\text{OUTFLOW}(cs_1)}{\text{OUTFLOW}(cs_2)} = \frac{f_{bprof}(cs_1)}{f_{bprof}(cs_2)}$$

We apply the *Dynamic OUTFLOW* constraint within the same method, i.e., *intraprocedurally*. Edge profiles alone do not compute accurate relative basic block profiles between methods, i.e., basic block profiles with *interprocedural accuracy*. To attain interprocedural accuracy, we experiment with using low-overhead method invocation counters to provide basic block profiles interprocedural accuracy. In this case, *Dynamic OUTFLOW* can correct call sites in different methods (see Section 4).

Theorem 4. *Dynamic INFLOW Constraint: Given a method m with a single basic block and a call site cs in m,* INFLOW(m) = OUTFLOW(cs)

The *Dynamic INFLOW* constraint uses the total flow (frequency) coming into the method to constrain the flow leaving any call sites in the method (*OUTFLOW*). When basic block profiles do not have interprocedural accuracy, the *Dynamic INFLOW* constraint is useful for methods with a single basic block because the *Dynamic OUTFLOW* constraint cannot constrain the *OUTFLOW* of call sites in a single basic block.

3.6   Dynamic Basic Block Profile Correction

We use an algorithm called *DynamicOutflowCorrection* to apply the *Dynamic OUTFLOW* constraint [15]. This algorithm sets the *OUTFLOW* of each call site cs to $f_{bprof}(cs)$, its frequency from the basic block profile. The algorithm then scales all the *OUTFLOW* values so that the method's total *OUTFLOW* is the same as before (as illustrated in Section 3.4). This scaling helps to maintain the frequencies due to sampling across disparate parts of the DCG.

Since *DynamicOutFlowCorrection* determines corrected DCG frequencies using a basic block profile, accuracy may suffer if the basic block profile is inaccurate. Jikes RVM collects an edge profile (which determines the basic block profile) in baseline-compiled code only, so phased behavior may affect accuracy, although we find that the edge profile is accurate enough to improve DCG accuracy in our experiments. To avoid the effects of phased behavior, DCG correction could use edge profiles collected continuously [1,9].

We also use an algorithm called *DynamicInflowCorrection* that applies the *Dynamic INFLOW* constraints to the DCG [15]. For each method with a single basic block, *DynamicInflowCorrection* sets the *OUTFLOW* of each call site in the method to the *INFLOW* of the method. As in the case of the FDOM *INFLOW* constraint, we do not use the *Dynamic INFLOW* constraint together with an intraprocedural edge profile. However, with an interprocedural edge profile, *INFLOW* is accurate enough to improve overall DCG accuracy.

4   Implementing DCG Correction

Dynamic compilation systems perform profiling while they execute and optimize the application, and therefore DCG correction needs to occur at the same time with minimal overhead.

We minimize DCG correction overhead by limiting its frequency and scope. We limit correction's frequency by delaying it until the optimizing compiler requests DCG information. The correction overhead is thus proportional to the number of times the compiler selects optimization candidates during an execution. Correction overhead is thus naturally minimized when the dynamic optimizer is selective about how often and which methods to recompile.

We limit the scope of DCG correction by localizing the range of correction. When the compiler optimizes a method m, it does not require the entire DCG, but instead considers a localized portion of the DCG relative to m. Because we preserve the call edge frequency sum in the *OUTFLOW* correction algorithm, we can correct m and all the methods it invokes without compromising the correctness of the other portions of the DCG. Because we preserve the DCG frequency sum, the normalized frequency of a call site in a method remains the same, independent of whether call edge frequencies in other methods are corrected or not.

For better interaction with method inlining, one of the DCG clients, we limit correction to *nontrivial* call edges in the DCG. Trivial call edges by definition are inlined regardless of their measured frequencies because their target methods are so small that inlining them always reduces the code size.

Table 1 summarizes the correction algorithms and their scope. The algorithms take as input the set of call sites to be corrected. Clearly, for FDOM correction, the basic unit of correction is the call sites within a procedure boundary. For dynamic basic block profile correction, there are two options. The first limits the call site set to be within a procedural boundary, and the second corrects all the reachable methods. Since many dynamic compilation systems support only high precision intraprocedural basic profiles, the first configuration represents how much DCG correction would benefit these systems.

Because our system does not collect interprocedural basic block profiles, we implement interprocedural correction by adding method counters. DCG correction multiplies the counter value by the normalized intraprocedural basic block frequency. We find this mechanism is a good approximation to interprocedural basic block profiles.

Table 1. Call Graph Correction Implementations

Correction algorithm	Input	Correction unit	Algorithms
Static FDOM CF Correction	Sampled DCG	Call sites in method to be optimized	$FDOMOutflowCorrection$
Dynamic Intraprocedural CF Correction	Sampled DCG block profile	Call sites in method to be optimized	$DynamicOutflowCorrection$
Dynamic Interprocedural CF Correction	Sampled DCG block profile	Call sites in DCG	$DynamicOutflowCorrection$ & $DynamicInflowCorrection$

5   Methodology

This section describes our benchmarks, platform, implementation, and VM compiler configurations. We describe our methodologies for accuracy measurements against the perfect dynamic call graph (DCG), overhead measurements, and performance measurements.

We implement and evaluate DCG correction algorithms in Jikes RVM 2.4.5, a Java-in-Java VM, in its production configuration [3]. This configuration precompiles the VM methods (e.g., compiler and garbage collector) and the libraries the VM uses into a boot image. Jikes RVM contains two compilers: the *baseline compiler* and *optimizing compiler* with three optimization levels. (There is no interpreter.) When a method first executes, the baseline compiler generates assembly code (x86 in our experiments). A call-stack sampling mechanism identifies frequently executed (*hot*) methods. Based on these method sample counts, the *adaptive compilation system* then recompiles methods at progressively higher levels of optimization. Because it is sample-based, the adaptive compiler is non-deterministic.

Jikes RVM runs by default using *adaptive* methodology, which dynamically identifies frequently executed methods and recompiles them at higher optimization levels. Because it uses timer-based sampling to detect hot methods, the adaptive compiler is non-deterministic. For our performance measurements, we use *replay compilation* methodology, which forces the compiler to behave in deterministically. We use *advice files* to specify which methods to compile and at what level. For each method in the file, Jikes RVM compiles it to the specified level when it is first invoked. We use advice files that include all methods and represent the best performance of 25 adaptive runs. The advice files specify (1) the optimization level for compiling every method, (2) the dynamic call graph profile, and (3) the edge profile. Fixing these inputs, we execute two consecutive iterations of the application. During the first iteration, Jikes RVM optimizes code using the advice files. The second iteration executes only the application at a realistic mix of optimization levels. Both iterations eliminate non-determinism due to the adaptive compiler.

We use the SPEC JVM98 benchmarks [18], the DaCapo benchmarks (beta-2006-08) [8], and *ipsixql* [14]. We omit the DaCapo benchmarks *lusearch, pmd* and *xalan* because we could not get them to run correctly. We also include *pseudojbb* (labeled as *jbb*), a fixed-workload version of SPEC JBB2000 [19].

We perform our experiments on a 3.2 GHz Pentium 4 with hyper-threading enabled. It has a 64-byte L1 and L2 cache line size, an 8KB 4-way set associative L1 data cache, a 12Kμops L1 instruction trace cache, a 512KB unified 8-way set associative L2 on-chip cache, and 2GB main memory, and runs Linux 2.6.0.

Accuracy Methodology. To measure the accuracy of our technique against the perfect DCG for each application, we first generate a perfect DCG by modifying Jikes RVM call graph sampling to sample every method call (instead of skipping). We also turn off the adaptive optimizing system to eliminate non-determinism due to sampling and since call graph accuracy is not influenced by code quality. We modify the system to optimize (at level 1) every method and to inline only trivial calls. Trivial inlining in Jikes RVM inlines a callee if its size is smaller than the calling sequence. The inliner therefore never needs the frequency information for these call sites. We restrict the call graph to the application methods by excluding all call edges with both the source and target in the boot image, and calls from the boot image to the application. We include call edges into the boot image, since these represent calls to libraries that the compiler may want to inline into the application.

To measure and compare call graph accuracy, we compare the perfect DCG to the final corrected DCG generated by our approach. Because DCG clients use incomplete graphs to make optimization decisions, it would be interesting, although challenging, to compare the accuracy of the instantaneous perfect and corrected DCGs as a function of time. We follow prior work in comparing the final graphs [4] rather than a time series, and believe these results are representative of the instantaneous DCGs.

Overhead Methodology. To measure the overhead of DCG correction without including its influence on optimization decisions, we configure the call graph correction algorithms to perform correction without actually modifying DCG frequencies. We report the first iteration time because the call graph correction is triggered only at compilation time. We report the execution time as the median of 25 trials to obtain a representative result not swayed by outliers.

Performance Methodology. We use the following configuration to measure the performance of using corrected DCGs to drive inlining. We correct the DCG as the VM optimizes the application, providing a realistic measure of DCG correction's ability to affect inlining decisions. We measure application-only performance by using the second iteration time. We report the median of 25 trials.

6   Results

This section evaluates the accuracy, overhead and performance effects of the DCG correction algorithms.

We use the notation *CBS(SAMPLES, STRIDE)* to refer to an Arnold-Grove sampling configuration [4]. To compare the effect of the sampling configuration on call graph correction, we use two sampling configurations: $CBS(1,1)$ and $CBS(16,3)$, 16 samples with a stride of 3. The default sampling configuration in Jikes RVM is $CBS(1,1)$, which is equivalent to the default timer-based sampling in Figure 1(a). Arnold and Grove recommend $CBS(16,3)$, which takes more samples to increase accuracy while keeping average overhead down to 1-2%.

6.1   Accuracy

We use the overlap accuracy metric from prior work to compare the accuracy of DCGs [4].

$$overlap(DCG_1, DCG_2) =$$
$$\sum_{e \in CallEdges} min(weight(e, DCG_1), weight(e, DCG_2))$$

where *CallEdges* is the intersection of the two call edge sets in DCG_1 and DCG_2 respectively, and $weight(e, DCG_i)$ is the normalized frequency for a call edge e in DCG_i. We use this function to compare the perfect DCG to other DCGs.

Figures 3 and 4 show how DCG correction boosts accuracy over the $CBS(1,1)$ and $CBS(16,3)$ sampling configurations. The perfect DCG is 100% (not shown). The graphs compare the perfect DCG to the base system (*No Correction*), *Static FDOM CF Correction, Dynamic Intraprocedural CF Correction* and *Dynamic Interprocedural CF Correction*. Arnold and Grove report an average accuracy of 50% on their benchmarks for $CBS(1,1)$, and 69% for $CBS(16,3)$ for 1 to 2% overhead [4]. We show better base results here with an average accuracy of 52% for $CBS(1,1)$ and 76% for $CBS(16,3)$.

These results show that our correction algorithms improve over both of the sampled configurations, and that each of the algorithm components contributes to the increase in accuracy (for example, *raytrace* in Figure 3 and *jack* in Figure 4), but their importance varies with the program. FDOM and intraprocedural correction are most effective when the base graph is less accurate as in $CBS(1,1)$ because they improve relative frequencies within a method. Interprocedural correction is relatively more effective using a more accurate base graph such as $CBS(16,3)$. This result is intuitive; a global scheme for improving accuracy works best when its constituent components are accurate.

Figure 5 shows how the correction algorithms change the shape of the DCG for *raytrace* for $CBS(1,1)$, our best result. The vertical bar presents normalized frequencies of the 150 most frequently executed call edges from the perfect DCG. The call edges on the x-axis are grouped by their callers, and the vertical dashed lines show the group boundaries. The dots show the frequency from the sampled or corrected DCG. In the base case, call edges have different frequencies due to timing bias and sampling error. *Static FDOM CF Correction* eliminates many of these errors and improves the shape of the DCG; Figure 5(b) shows that FDOM eliminates frequency variations in call edges in the same routine. Since FDOM takes the maximum of edge weights, it raises some frequencies above their true values. *Dynamic Intraprocedural CF Correction* further improves the

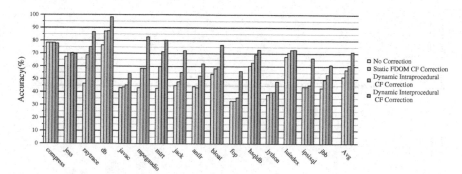

Fig. 3. Accuracy of DCG correction over the *CBS(1,1)* configuration

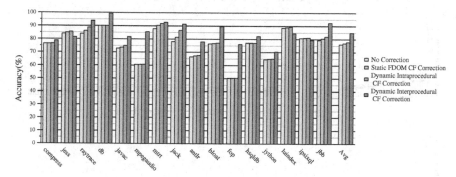

Fig. 4. Accuracy of DCG correction over the *CBS(16,3)* configuration

DCG because it uses fractional frequency between two call sites, while FDOM gives only relative frequency. We can see in Figure 5(c) several frequencies are now closer to their perfect values. Finally, *Interprocedural CF Correction* further improves the accuracy by eliminating interprocedural sampling bias. The most frequently executed method calls, on the left of Figure 5(d), show particular improvement.

6.2 Overhead

Figure 6 presents the execution overhead of DCG correction, which occurs each time the optimizing compiler recompiles a method. Correction could occur on every sample, but our approach aggregates the work and eliminates repeatedly correcting the same edges. We take the median out of 10 trials (shown as dots). *Static FDOM Correction* and *Dynamic Intraprocedural CF Correction* add no detectable overhead. The overhead of the interprocedural correction is on average 1% and at most 3% (on jython). This overhead stems from method counter instrumentation (Section 4).

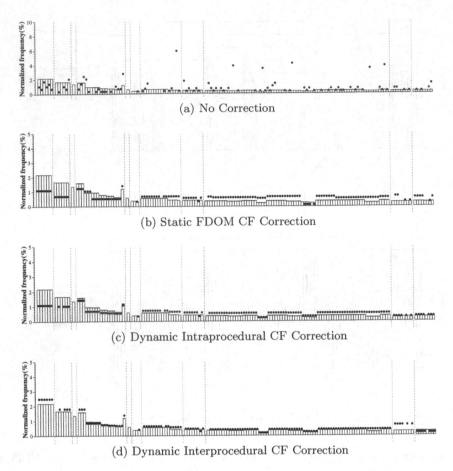

(a) No Correction

(b) Static FDOM CF Correction

(c) Dynamic Intraprocedural CF Correction

(d) Dynamic Interprocedural CF Correction

Fig. 5. Call graph frequencies for *raytrace* in *CBS(1,1)* configuration

6.3   Performance

We evaluate the costs and benefits of using DCG correction to drive one client, inlining. We use the default inlining policy with *CBS(1,1)*. Figure 7 shows application-only (second iteration) performance (median of 10 trials) with several DCG correction configurations. The graphs are normalized to the execution time without correction. We first evaluate feeding a perfect DCG to the inliner at the beginning of execution (*Perfect DCG*). The perfect DCG improves performance by a modest 2.3% on average, showing that Jikes RVM's inliner does not currently benefit significantly from high-accuracy DCGs. This result is not surprising, since the heuristics were developed together with poor-accuracy DCGs.

Static FDOM CF Correction shows the improvement from static FDOM correction, which is 1.1% on average. *Dynamic Intraprocedural CF Correction* improves performance by 1.7% on average. *Dynamic Interprocedural CF Correction*

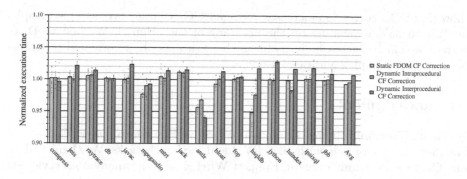

Fig. 6. The runtime overhead of call graph correction in *CBS(1,1)* configuration

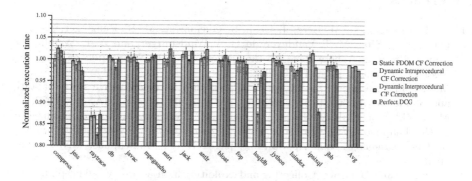

Fig. 7. The performance of correcting inlining decisions in *CBS(1,1)* configuration

shows 1.3% average improvement. However, a perfect call graph does improve two programs significantly: *raytrace* and *ipsixql* by 13% and 12% respectively, and DCG correction gains some of these improvements: 18% and 2% respectively. For *raytrace*, corrected (but imperfect) information yields better performance than perfect information. This perfect information has strictly more call edges and tends to report smaller normalized call edge frequencies as shown in Figure 5(d), leading the optimizer not to inline one important call edge. This effect occurs in *hsqldb* as well.

7   Conclusion

This paper introduces *dynamic call graph (DCG) correction*, a novel approach for increasing DCG accuracy using static and dynamic control-flow information. We introduce the *frequency dominator* (FDOM) relation to constrain and correct DCG frequencies based on control-flow relationships in the CFG. We also show how to combine these constraints with intraprocedural and interprocedural basic block profiles to correct the DCG. By adding just 1% overhead on average, we show that DCG correction increases average DCG accuracy over sampled graphs by 12% to 36% depending on the accuracy of the original. We believe DCG correction will be increasingly useful in the future as object-oriented programs become more complex and more modular.

Acknowledgments

We thank Xianglong Huang, Robin Garner, Steve Blackburn, David Grove, and Matthew Arnold for help with Jikes RVM and the benchmarks. We thank Calvin Lin, Curt Reese, Jennifer Sartor, Emmett Witchel, and the anonymous reviewers for their helpful suggestions for improving the paper.

References

1. J. M. Anderson, L. M. Berc, J. Dean, S. Ghemawat, M. R. Henzinger, S.-T. A. Leung, R. L. Sites, M. T. Vandevoorde, C. A. Waldspurger, and W. E. Weihl. Continuous Profiling: Where Have All the Cycles Gone? In *Symposium on Operating Systems Principles*, pages 1–14, 1997.
2. M. Arnold, S. Fink, V. Sarkar, and P. F. Sweeney. A comparative study of static and profile-based heuristics for inlining. pages 52–64, Boston, MA, July 2000.
3. M. Arnold, S. J. Fink, D. Grove, M. Hind, and P. Sweeney. Adaptive optimization in the Jalapeño JVM. In *ACM Conference on Object Oriented Programming, Systems, Languages, and Applications*, pages 47–65, Minneapolis, MN, October 2000.
4. M. Arnold and D. Grove. Collecting and exploiting high-accuracy call graph profiles in virtural machines. In *Symposium on Code Generation and Optimization*, pages 51–62, Mar. 2005.
5. M. Arnold and B. G. Ryder. A framework for reducing the cost of instrumented code. In *PLDI '01: Proceedings of the ACM SIGPLAN 2001 conference on Programming language design and implementation*, pages 168–179, New York, NY, USA, 2001. ACM Press.
6. M. Arnold and P. F. Sweeney. Approximating the calling context tree via sampling. Technical Report RC 21789, IBM T.J. Watson Research Center, July 2000.
7. T. Ball. What's in a region?: or computing control dependence regions in near-linear time for reducible control flow. *ACM Letters on Programming Languages and Systems*, 2(1-4):1–16, 1993.
8. S. M. Blackburn, R. Garner, C. Hoffman, A. M. Khan, K. S. McKinley, R. Bentzur, A. Diwan, D. Feinberg, D. Frampton, S. Z. Guyer, M. Hirzel, A. Hosking, M. Jump, H. Lee, J. E. B. Moss, A. Phansalkar, D. Stefanović, T. VanDrunen, D. von Dincklage, and B. Wiedermann. The DaCapo Benchmarks: Java benchmarking development and analysis. In *ACM Conference on Object-oriented programing, systems, languages, and applications*, Portland, OR, USA, Oct. 2006. http://www.dacapobench.org.
9. M. D. Bond and K. S. McKinley. Continuous path and edge profiling. In *IEEE/ACM International Symposium on Microarchitecture*, pages 130–140, Barcelona, Spain, 2005.
10. K. D. Cooper, T. J. Harvey, and K. Kennedy. A simple, fast dominance algorithm. *Software Practice & Experience*, 4:1–10, 2001.

11. J. Dean, C. Chambers, and D. Grove. Selective specialization for object-oriented languages. In *PLDI '95: Proceedings of the ACM SIGPLAN 1995 conference on Programming language design and implementation*, pages 93–102, New York, NY, USA, 1995. ACM Press.
12. N. Grcevski, A. Kielstra, K. Stoodley, M. G. Stoodley, and V. Sundaresan. Java just-in-time compiler and virtual machine improvements for server and middleware applications. In *Virtual Machine Research and Technology Symposium*, pages 151–162, 2004.
13. A. Hashemi, D. Kaeli, and B. Calder. Procedure mapping using static call graph estimation. In *Workshop on Interaction between Compiler and Computer Architecture*, San Antonio, TX, 1997.
14. J. Henkel. Colorado Bench. http://www-plan.cs.colorado.edu/henkel/projects/colorado_bench.
15. B. Lee, K. Resnick, M. D. Bond, and K. S. McKinley. Correcting the Dynamic Call Graph Using Control-Flow Constraints. Technical report, University of Texas at Austin, 2006.
16. M. C. Merten, A. R. Trick, E. M. Nystrom, R. D. Barnes, and W. mei W. Hmu. A Hardware Mechanism for Dynamic Extraction and Relayout of Program Hot Spots. In *International Symposium on Computer Architecture*, pages 59–70, 2000.
17. M. Paleczny, C. Vick, and C. Click. The java hotspot server compiler. In *Usenix Java Virtual Machine Research and Technology Symposium (JVM'01)*, pages 1–12, April 2001.
18. Standard Performance Evaluation Corporation. *SPECjvm98 Documentation*, release 1.03 edition, March 1999.
19. Standard Performance Evaluation Corporation. *SPECjbb2000 (Java Business Benchmark) Documentation*, release 1.01 edition, 2001.
20. T. Suganuma, T. Yasue, M. Kawahito, H. Komatsu, and T. Nakatani. A Dynamic Optimization Framework for a Java Just-in-Time Compiler. In *ACM Conference on Object Oriented Programming, Systems, Languages, and Applications*, pages 180–195, 2001.
21. T. Suganuma, T. Yasue, and T. Nakatani. An empirical study of method inlining for a java just-in-time compiler. July 2002.
22. R. E. Tarjan. Finding dominators in directed graphs. *SIAM Journal of Computing*, 3(1):62–89, 1974.
23. Y. Wu and J. R. Larus. Static branch frequency and program profile analysis. In *ACM/IEEE International Symposium on Microarchitecture*, pages 1–11, 1994.
24. X. Zhuang, M. J. Serrano, H. W. Cain, and J.-D. Choi. Accurate, efficient, and adaptive calling context profiling. In *ACM Conference on Programming Language Design and Implementation*, pages 263–271, 2006.

Obfuscating Java: The Most Pain for the Least Gain*

Michael Batchelder and Laurie Hendren

School of Computer Science, McGill University, Montreal, QC, Canada
mbatch@cs.mcgill.ca, hendren@cs.mcgill.ca

Abstract. Bytecode, Java's binary form, is relatively high-level and therefore susceptible to decompilation attacks. An obfuscator transforms code such that it becomes more complex and therefore harder to reverse engineer. We develop bytecode obfuscations that are complex to reverse engineer but also do not significantly degrade performance. We present three kinds of techniques that: (1) obscure intent at the operational level; (2) complicate control flow and object-oriented design (i.e. program structure); and (3) exploit the semantic gap between what is legal in source code and what is legal in bytecode. Obfuscations are applied to a benchmark suite to examine their affect on runtime performance, control flow graph complexity and decompilation. These results show that most of the obfuscations have only minor negative performance impacts and many increase complexity. In almost all cases, tested decompilers fail to produce legal source code or crash completely. Those obfuscations that are decompilable greatly reduce the readability of output source.

1 Introduction

Reverse engineering is the act of uncovering the underlying design of a product through analysis of its structure, features, functions and operation. It has a long history, including applications in military and pharmacology industries, but it could be argued that software has proven to be among the most susceptible to its attacks. Since software is an easily and cheaply reproduced product it must rely on either passive protection such as a patent or some form of active protection such as hiding software on servers, encryption, or obfuscation.

Obfuscation is the obscuring of intent in design. It is one way of foiling decompilers. With software this means transforming code such that it remains semantically equivalent to the original, but is more esoteric and confusing. A simple example is the renaming of variable and method identifiers. By changing a method from getName to a random sequence of characters such as sdfhjioew, information about the method is hidden that a reverse engineer could otherwise have found useful. A more complex example is introducing unnecessary control flow that is hidden using opaque predicates, expressions that will always evaluate to the same answer (true or false) but whose value is not possible to estimate statically. Obfuscation is one of the more promising forms of code protection because, while it may be obvious to a malicious attacker that a program has been obfuscated, this fact will not necessarily improve their chances at decompilation. Also, obfuscation can severely complicate a program such that even if it is

---

* This work was supported, in part, by NSERC and FQRNT.

S. Krishnamurthi and M. Odersky (Eds.): CC 2007, LNCS 4420, pp. 96–110, 2007.
© Springer-Verlag Berlin Heidelberg 2007

decompilable it is very difficult to understand, making extraction of tangible intellectual property close to impossible, without serious time investment.

Java is particularly vulnerable to reverse engineering because its binary form, byte-code, is relatively high-level and contains considerable information about types, and field and method names. There are also many references in the code to known fields and methods in publicly-available class libraries, including the standard ones provided with a Java implementation. Java decompilers exploit these weaknesses and there are quite a few products that convert bytecode into Java source code that very similar to the original and is quite readable, particularly when the bytecode is in exactly the format produced by known javac compilers [20, 15, 12, 17, 14, 13].

This paper presents and studies a wide range of techniques for obfuscating Java bytecode. However, a very important factor is that one wants the obfuscations to make reverse engineering difficult (the most pain), but at the same time not hurt performance of the obfuscated application (the least gain). This tradeoff is not obvious, since the same obfuscations that make it hard for a decompiler may also severely impact the analysis and optimizations in JIT compilers found in modern Java Virtual Machines (JVMs).

This tradeoff is the main goal of our work. We developed and implemented a collection of obfuscations that hinder reverse engineering attempts, while at the same time do not affect performance too much. We examine some variations of previously suggested obfuscations and we also develop some new techniques, most notably those which exploit the semantic gap between what can be expressed in Java bytecode and what is allowed in valid Java source.

The remainder of the the paper is organized as follows. In Section 2 we give a short summary of previous work. Section 3 gives a high-level overview of our software obfuscator, the Java Bytecode Obfuscator (JBCO). Sections 4 through 6 present our obfuscations grouped by type: operator-level obfuscation, program structure modification, and semantic gap exploitation. Each section ends with a summary of the impact of the obfuscations on three decompilers. Due to space limitations we briefly describe each obfuscation. However, detailed code examples and challenge cases for decompilers can be found at http://www.sable.mcgill.ca/JBCO. In Section 7 we introduce a benchmark set and provide a summary of the impact of each obfuscation on runtime performance and control flow complexity. Finally, Section 8 gives conclusions and future work.

2   Related Work

Obfuscation is a form of *security through obscurity*. While Barak argues that there are seemingly few truly irreversible obfuscations [2] and, in theory, "deobfuscation" under certain general assumptions has been shown by Appel to be NP-Easy [1], obfuscation is nevertheless a valid and viable solution for general programs.

Early attempts involved machine-level instruction rewriting. Cohen used a technique he called "program evolution" to protect operating systems that included the replacement of instructions, or small sequences of instructions, with ones that perform semantically equal functions. Transformations included instruction reordering, adding or removing arbitrary jumps, and even de-inlining methods [5].

Much later, a theoretical approach was presented by Collberg *et al.* [6]. They outline obfuscations as program transformations and develop terminology to describe them in terms of performance effect and quality. They rely on a number of well-known software metrics [4, 11, 16] to measure quality. Later, in [7], they reconsider lexical obfuscations (name changing) and data transformations (*e.g.*, splitting boolean values into two discrete numerics that are combined only at evaluation time). However, their chief contributions are in control-flow modifications. They make use of opaque predicates to introduce dead code, specifically engineering the dead branches to have buggy versions of the live branches.

Sakabe *et al.* concentrate their efforts on the object-oriented nature of Java — the high-level information in a program. Using polymorphism, they invent a unique return type class which encapsulates all return types and then modify every method to return an object of this type [18]. Method parameters are encapsulated in a similar way and method names are cloned across different classes. In this way the true return types of methods and the number and types of a method's parameters are hidden. They further obfuscate typing by introducing opaque predicates that branch around new object instantiations which confuses the true type of the object and they use exceptions as explicit control flow. Unfortunately, their empirical results show significantly slower execution speeds — an average slowdown of 30% — and a 300% blowup in class file size.

Sonsonkin *et al.* present more high-level obfuscations which attempt to confuse program structure [19]. They suggest the coalescing of multiple class files into one — combining the logic of two or more functionally-separate sections of the program — and its reverse, splitting a single class file into multiples.

The obfuscations presented in this paper build upon both the simple operation-level obfuscations as well as control flow and program structure obfuscations. We have also developed a new set of obfuscations, which exploit the semantic gap between Java bytecode and Java source. Many of these were inspired by our experiences in building Java bytecode optimizers and and decompilers. The cases that are difficult for those tools are exactly the cases that should be created by obfuscators.

3   JBCO Structure

JBCO – our Java ByteCode Obfuscator – is built on top of Soot [21]. Soot is a Java bytecode transformation and annotation framework providing multiple intermediate representations and infrastructure for dataflow analysis and transformations. JBCO uses two intermediate representations: Jimple, a typed 3-address intermediate form; and Baf, a typed abstraction of bytecode.

JBCO is a collection of Jimple and Baf transformations and analyses. Whenever possible, we analyze and transform Jimple, since it is at a higher abstraction and easier to work with. However, some low-level obfuscations are implemented in Baf since they require modifying actual bytecode instructions. There are three categories of analyses and transformations:

Information Aggregators: collect data about the program for the transformationsi, such as constant usage and local variable-to-type pairings.

Code Analyses: collect information about the code such as control flow graphs, type data, and use-def chains, which help identify where in the program transformations can be applied (e.g. in order to produce verifiable bytecode we must ensure proper matchings between allocations of objects and their initializations).

Instrumenters: are the actual obfuscations, ransforming the code to obscure meaning.

JBCO can be used as a command-line tool or via a graphical user interface.[1] Each obfuscation can be activated independently and, depending on the severity of the obfuscation desired, a weight of 0-9 can be given where 0 turns it off completely and 9 corresponds to applying it everywhere possible. We also provide a mechanism to limit the obfuscations to specific regions of a program by using regular expressions to specify certain classes, fields or methods. This is useful if a user wants certain parts to be heavily obfuscated or when a specific hot method should not be obfuscated because of performance considerations.

4   Operator-Level Obfuscation

Our first group of obfuscations works at the operator level. That is, we convert a local operation into a semantically equivalent computation that is harder for a reverse engineer to understand. These obfuscations should be decompilable, but the decompiled code is expected to be harder to understand.[2,3]

4.1   Embedding Constant Values as Fields (ECVF)

Programmers often use constants, particularly string constants, to convey important information. For example, a statement of the form `System.err.println("Illegal argument, value must be positive.");` provides some context to the reverse engineer. The point of the ECVF obfuscation is to move the constant into a static field and then change references to the constant into references to the field. This could lead to something like `System.err.println(ObjectA.field1);`, which conveys significantly less meaning. An interprocedural constant propagation could potentially undo this obfuscation. However, if the initialization of the field is further obfuscated through the use of an opaque predicate, this is no longer possible.

4.2   Packing Local Variables into Bitfields (PLVB)

In order to introduce a level of obfuscation on local variables with primitive types (boolean, char, byte integer), it is possible to combine some variables and pack them

---

[1] JBCO will soon be released as a new component of Soot.

[2] Our identifier renamer obfuscation was left out of the paper due to space limits. We developed a unique approach to garbleing names, but the overall technique is quite common.

[3] For each obfuscation, we give the acronym we use for it. This acronym is used both in the experimental results and also as the flag used to enable the obfuscation in JBCO.

into one variable which has more bits. To provide maximum confusion we randomly choose a range of bits to use for each local variable. For example, an integer variable may get packed into bits 9 through 43 of a 64-bit long. Each read or write of the original variable must be replaced by packing and unpacking operations in the obfuscated code and this might slow down the application. Thus, it is used sparingly and applied randomly to only some locals. Without further obfuscation of the bitshifting and bit-masking constants used for packing and unpacking, however, a clever decompiler could overcome this technique.

4.3   Converting Arithmetic Expressions to Bit-Shifting Operations (CAE2BO)

Optimizing compilers sometimes convert a complex operation such as multiplication or division into a sequence of cheaper ones. This same trick can be used to obfuscate the code. In particular, we look for instances of expressions in the form of $v * C$ (a similar technique is used for v/C), where v is a variable and C is a constant. We extract from C the largest integer i where $i < C$ and is also a power of 2, $i = 2^s$, where $s = floor(log_2(v))$. We then compute the remainder, $r = v - i$. If s is in the range of $-128 \ldots 127$, we can convert the original to $(v << s) + (v * r)$ and the expression $v * r$ can be further decomposed. In order to further obfuscate we don't use the shift value s directly, but rather find an equivalent value s'. To do this we take advantage of the fact that shifting a 32-bit word by 32 (or a multiple of 32) always returns the original value. We choose a random multiple m, and compute a new but equivalent shift value, $s' = (byte)(s + (m * 32))$.

As an example, an expression of the form $v * 195$ would be converted first to $(v << 7) + (v << 6) + (v << 1) + v$ and then the three shift values would be further obfuscated to something like $(v << 39) + (v << 38) + (v << -95) + v$.

A decompiler that is aware of this calculation could potentially reverse it, but if one or more of the constants were hidden with an opaque predicate, it could stymie the attempt.

4.4   Impact of Operator-Level Obfuscations on Decompilers

Although we fully expected all of these simple, operator-level, obfuscations to be decompilable (i.e. correct and compilable source code would be produced, even if less readable than the original), we were surprised to find the results in Table 1. For these and subsequent decompiler tests in this paper, we created some small micro-tests for each obfuscation.[4] A score of *Pass* indicates that the decompiler produced correct Java source that could be recompiled by javac, *Fail* indicates that the produced code would not recompile, and *Crash* is the result of a decompiler not terminating normally.

Why do decompilers fail on these simple obfuscations? The three obfuscations unwittingly exploit a semantic gap between bytecode and Java source. Booleans, bytes and

---

[4] We used micro-tests because some decompilers, most notably pattern-based Jad, are very sensitive to whether the bytecode looks exactly like it came from a javac compiler or not. Since all of our tests have been run through Soot, which even without obfuscations is sometimes enough to confuse decompilers, we wanted to ensure that our tests were small enough to measure the impact of the obfuscation itself and not indirect effects due to processing with Soot.

Table 1. Measuring Decompiler Success against Operator-level Obfuscations

Obfuscation	Jad	SourceAgain	Dava
Embedding Constant Values as Fields	Fail	Fail	Fail
Packing Local Variables into Bitfields	Fail	Fail	Fail
Converting Arithmetic Expressions to Bit-Shifting Ops	Fail	Fail	Pass

chars are expressed as integers in bytecode, whereas in source these are given unique types which must be used consistently and in a manner so as not to lose precision. The decompilers failed to properly type and cast for these computations and produced output that was not recompilable.[5]

5   Obfuscating Program Structure

Program structure can be thought of as the framework. In a building this would be the supporting beams, the floors, and the ceiling. It would not be the walls or the carpeting. We define structure to include two facets: low-level method control flow and high-level object-oriented design. Modern decompilers such as SourceAgain and Dava should be able to handle these techniques, in principle.

5.1   Adding Dead-Code Switch Statements (ADSS)

The switch construct in bytecode offers a useful control flow obfuscation tool. It is the only organic way (other than the try-catch structure) to manufacture a control flow graph that has a node whose successor count is greater than two. This can severely increase the complexity of a method.

This obfuscation adds edges to the control flow graph by inserting a dead switch. To ensure that the switch itself is never executed it is wrapped in an opaque predicate. All bytecode instructions with a stack height of zero are potentially safe jump targets for cases in the switch. We implemented an analysis to find these zero-height locations and we randomly select some as targets for the cases switch. This increases the connectedness and overall complexity of a method. A decompiler cannot remove the dead switch because it cannot statically determine the value of the opaque predicate.

5.2   Finding and Reusing Duplicate Sequences (RDS)

Because of the nature of bytecode, there is often a fair amount of duplication even within a single method. By finding these clones and replacing them with a single switched instance we can potentially reduce the size of the method while also confusing the control flow, creating patterns not naturally expressed in Java.

We determine when a duplicate sequence D is a clone of the original sequence O using the following rules:

---

[5] Clearly our research group would like to fix Soot/Dava to properly handle this variation of the typing problem - it is quite interesting to have one subgroup building a decompiler, while at the same time another subgroup is trying to break it!

- D must be of the same length as O and for each index i, instruction D_i must equal O_i.
- Each D_i must be protected by the same (or no) try blocks as the original O_i.
- Every instruction in a sequence other than the first must have no predecessors that fall *outside* the sequence (*i.e.* no branching into the middle of a sequence).
- Each D_i must share the same stack height and types as the original O_i.
- Each D_i must not have the same offset within the method as *any* instruction O_j.

The algorithm searches for duplicates of length 3 to 20. When a duplicate sequence is found, a new integer is created to act as a control flag. Each duplicate is removed and replaced with an assignment of the flag to a unique id followed by a goto directed at the first instruction in the original sequence. The original sequence is prepended with instructions which store 0 to the flag (the "first" unique id) and appended with a switch. The default switch jump falls through to the next instruction (the successor of the original sequence). A jump to the successor of each duplicate sequence is added to the switch based on its flag id.

5.3 Building API Buffer Methods (BAPIBM)

A lot of information is inherent in Java programs because of the widespread use of the Java libraries. These libraries have clear and well-defined documentation. The very existence of library objects and method calls can give shape and meaning to a method based entirely on how they are being used. The method calls that direct execution into the native Java libraries cannot be renamed because the obfuscator should not change library code[6]. Therefore, the next best option is to hide library method calls. We do this by indirecting library calls through intermediate methods that have nonsensical identifiers.

Each program method is checked for library calls. A new method M is then created for each library method L referenced in the program. M is modified to invoke L. M is placed in a randomly chosen class in order to cause "class-coagulation" — an increase in class interdependence. Therefore, this obfuscation is two-fold. It confuses the object-oriented design of the program and hides the library method calls by indirecting them through a different "physical" part of the program.

5.4 Building Library Buffer Classes (BLBC)

Having a class that extends a library class directly can also lend a certain amount of clarity to a program. Parent class methods that are over-ridden in the child are more obvious as well. Experienced Java programmers are able to quickly grasp design intent from this information.

This obfuscation attempts to cloud this particular design structure of Java. For each class C, which directly extends a library class L, we create a new buffer class B. It is inserted as a child of L and a parent of C. Since no part of the program itself ever uses

---

[6] While it is not impossible, it is not reasonable. Obfuscating library code would mean that those modified libraries would have to be distributed with the program, causing both licensing issues and an unreasonable increase in the program's distribution size.

B directly, methods over-ridden in C can be defined as nonsense methods in B, further adding confusion. This complicates and confuses the design of the program by adding extra layers. Ultimately, it spreads the single-intent class structure over multiple files making it difficult for a reverse engineer to understand.

5.5 The Impact of Program Structure Obfuscations on Decompilers

The results are shown in Table 2. Jad fairs badly when decompiling our structure obfuscations, most likely due to its lack of control flow analysis. It resorts to leaving pure bytecode in its output where it is unable to produce correct source. More surprisingly, SourceAgain also has difficulty with the heavier control flow obfuscations. RDS causes it to crash completely.

Table 2. Measuring Decompiler Success against Structure Obfuscations

Obfuscation	Jad	SourceAgain	Dava
Adding Dead-Code Switch Statements	Fail	Fail	Pass
Finding and Reusing Duplicate Sequences	Fail	Crash	Pass
Building API Buffer Methods	Fail	Fail	Fail
Building Library Buffer Classes	Fail	Pass	Pass

None of the decompilers were able to properly mark which methods might throw exceptions, which is a requirement of Java source. Because some methods indirected by BAPIBM might throw exceptions the new methods that call them are required to as well.

6 Exploiting the Design Gap

Certain gaps between what is representable in Java source code and what is representable in bytecode exist. The classic example is the goto instructioni that has no direct counterpart in source[7].

The obfuscations detailed in this section were designed to exploit these bytecode-to-source gaps. Smart decompilers can sometimes transform the obfuscated bytecode into a semantically equivalent form of source code yet it is usually unreadable. Often, however, the result is incorrect decompiled code or no decompiler output whatsoever. Sometimes a decompiler crashes altogether.

6.1 Converting Branches to jsr Instructions (CB2JI)

The jsr bytecode[8], short for Java subroutine, is analogous to the goto other than the fact that it pushes a return address on the stack. Normally, the return address is stored

---

[7] Abrupt jumps in source must be performed through the break or continue statements which force a certain level of structure since they must always be directly associated with well-defined statement blocks.

[8] The jsr was originally introduced to handle finally blocks — sections of code that are ensured to run after a try block whether an exception is thrown or not. It is a historical anomaly that is no longer used by modern javac compilers.

to a register after a `jsr` jump and when the subroutine is complete the `ret` bytecode is used to return.

The `jsr - ret` construct is very difficult to handle when dealing with typing issues because each subroutine can be called from multiple places, requiring that type information be merged which gives a more conservative estimate. Also, decompilers will usually expect to find a specific `ret` for every `jsr`.

This obfuscation replaces `if` and `goto` targets with `jsr` instructions. The old jump targets are each prepended by a `pop` in order to throw away the return address which is pushed onto the stack. If the jump target's predecessor in the instruction sequence falls through then a `goto` is inserted after it which jumps directly to the old target (stepping over the `pop`).

6.2 Reordering `load` Instructions Above `if` Instructions (RLAII)

Patterns in bytecode produced by `javac` can be examined for areas of possible obfuscation. This simple obfuscation looks for situations where a local variable is used directly following both paths of an `if`. That is, along both branches the first instruction loads the variable on to the stack. This is a somewhat common occurance.

The obfuscation then moves the `load` instruction above the `if`, removing its clones along both branches. While a modern decompiler like Dava, which is based on a 3-address intermediate representation, will be able to overcome this change, any decompiler relying on pattern matching (such as Jad) will become very confused.

6.3 Disobeying Constructor Conventions (DCC)

The Java language specification [8] stipulates that class constructors – those methods used to instantiate a new object of that class type – must always call either an alternate constructor of the same class or their parent class' constructor as the *first directive*. In the event that neither is specified in source `javac` explicitly adds a call to the parent at the beginning of the method.

While this super call, as a rule, must be the first statement in the Java *source* it is, in fact, not required to be the first within the bytecode. By exploiting this fact it is possible to create constructors with no valid source code representation. This obfuscation randomly chooses among four different approaches in order to confuse decompilers:

Wrapping the super call within a try block: This ensures that any decompiled source will be *required* to wrap the call in a try as well to conform to the rules of Java. To properly allow the exception to propagate, the handler unit — a `throw` instruction — is appended to the end of the method.

Taking advantage of classes which are children of java.lang.Throwable: This approach inserts a `throw` before the super call and creates a new try block that traps just the new `throw`. The handler unit is designated to be the super call itself. This takes advantage of the fact that the class is throwable and can be pushed onto the stack through the throw mechanism instead of the standard load.

Inserting a `jsr` jump and a `pop` directly before the super constructor call: The `jsr`'s target is the `pop`, which removes the subsequent return address that is pushed on the stack by the `jsr`. This confuses the majority of decompilers which have problems dealing with `jsr` instructions.

Adding new instructions before the super call: This approach inserts a `dup` followed by an `ifnull` before the super call. The `ifnull` target is the super call. The `if` branch instruction will always be `false` since the object it is comparing is the object being instantiated in the current constructor. A `push null` is inserted, followed by a `throw`, along the false branch of the `if`. A try block is created spanning from the `ifnull` up to the super call. The catch block is appended to the end of the method as a sequence of `pop`, `load o`, `goto sc` (o is the object being instantiated and `sc` is the super call). This confuses decompilers because it is more difficult to deduce which local will be on the stack when the super call site is reached.

6.4   Partially Trapping Switch Statements (PTSS)

There is a big gap between high-level structured use of try-catch blocks in Java source and their low-level byte implementation. The Java construct allows only well-nested and structured uses, but the bytecode implementation is at a lower abstraction. A bytecode trap specifies a bytecode range $a \ldots b$, a handler unit h, and an exception type E. If an exception T is raised within the method at bytecode c then the JVM searches for a trap in the list matching either the type of T or a parent type of T whose bytecode range $a \ldots b$ contains c. If a trap is found then the stack is emptied, T is pushed on top, and the program counter is set to the handler h. There are no rules that enforce nesting of these ranges. They may overlap or even share code with handler code.

Thus, one way of confusing decompilers is to trap sequential sections of bytecode that are not necessarily sequential in Java source code. An example of this is the switch construct. In source, the switch encapsulates different blocks of code as *targets* of the switch. However, in bytecode there is nothing explicitly tying the `switch` instruction to the different code blocks (*i.e.* there is no explicit encapsulation).

If the `switch` is placed within a trap range along with only *part* of the code blocks which are associated as its targets then there will be no way for an automatic decompiler to output semantically equivalent code that looks anything like the original source. It *must* reproduce the trap in the output, potentially by duplicating code.

This transformation is conservatively limited to those switch constructs which are *not* already trapped, which alleviates some analysis work. This implies that the `switch` instruction itself and any additional instructions that are selected for trapping were not previously trapped in any way.

6.5   Combining Try Blocks with Their Catch Blocks (CTBCB)

Java source code can only represent try-catch blocks in one way: with a try block directly followed by one or more catch blocks associated with it. In bytecode, however, try blocks can protect the same code that is used to handle the exceptions it throws or one of its catch blocks can appear "above" it in the instruction sequence.

This obfuscation combines a try-catch block such that both the beginning of the try block and the beginning of the catch block are the same instruction. This is accomplished by prepending the first unit of the try block with an `if` that branches to either the try code or the catch code based on an integer control flow flag. Once the try section has been officially entered, the flag is set to indicate that any execution of the `if` in the future should direct control to the catch section. The integer flag is reset to its original value when the try section is completed.

6.6   Indirecting `if` Instructions (III)

While `javac` always produces predictable try blocks it is possible to abuse them in other ways. This obfuscation takes advantage of this by indirecting `if` branching through `goto` instructions which are within a special try block. Normally, modern compilers would remove the `goto` and modify the `if` to jump directly to its final target. However, since a try block protects all these gotos it is not valid to remove them unless the code can be statically shown to never raise an exception. Since there is no explicit `goto` allowed in Java source, it is difficult for decompilers to synthesize equivalent source code.

6.7   `Goto` Instruction Augmentation (GIA)

Explicit `goto` statements are not allowed in Java source.[9] One must use abrupt statements instead. However, the `goto` exists in bytecode. It is possible to insert an explicit `goto` in bytecode. While reversible using control flow graph analysis, some simple decompilers will still struggle with this.

Our obfuscation randomly splits a method into two sequential parts: The first, containing the start of the method, P_1 and a second, containing the end of the method, P_2. It then reorders these two parts and inserts two `goto` instructions. One is made the first instruction in the method and points to the start of P_1. The other is appended to P_1 and targets P_2. The new layout is now: { `goto` P_1, P_2, P_1, `goto` P_2}. A try block is then created, spaning from the end of P_2 to the beginning of P_1, thereby "gluing" the two together. This makes it difficult to shuffle them back to their original order.

6.8   The Impact of Exploiting the Semantic Gap on Decompilers

All of the decompilers have difficulty with the obfuscations from this section. Table 3 shows that both Jad and SourceAgain fail all tests and Dava is only successful once. Jad generates source with much bytecode left in it, making it difficult to identify anything specific as the cause. SourceAgain was unable to analyze the scope of local variables. It would declare a local within a nested block even when the parent block used that local. Both SourceAgain and Dava had difficulties marking methods which might throw exceptions. They also could not recognize the super constructor method calls in DCC

---

[9] Studies have shown this to be a good design decision [3].

Table 3. Measuring Decompiler Success against Semantic Gap Obfuscations

Obfuscation	Jad	SourceAgain	Dava
Converting Branches to jsr Instructions	Fail	Fail	Crash
Reordering loads Above if Instructions	Fail	Fail	Pass
Disobeying Constructor Conventions	Fail	Fail	Crash
Partially Trapping Switch Statements	Fail	Fail	Fail
Combining Try Blocks with their Catch Blocks	Fail	Fail	Fail
Indirecting if Instructions	Fail	Fail	Fail
Goto Instruction Augmentation	Fail	Fail	Fail

either, leaving the bytecode name `<init>` which is not legal. Dava crashed on DCC due to its inability to handle explicitly null exceptions.[10]

7 Empirical Evaluation

An important aspect of our work is the evaluation of the impact of obfuscations on performance. To test this we have gathered a set of computation-extensive benchmarks. They represent a wide array of programs each with their own unique coding style, resource usage, and ultimate task. Below is a list of brief descriptions of the programs.

Asac: compares the performance of the Bubble Sort, Selection Sort, and Quick Sort algorithms. It creates a thread for each algorithm.

Chromo: runs a genetic algorithm; a technique using randomization instead of a deterministic search strategy. It instantiates many chromosome objects and performs many 64-bit array comparisions for each generation it simulates.

Decode: implements Shamir's Secret Sharing algorithm for decoding encrypted messages.

FFT: performs fast fourier transformations on double precision data.

Fractal: generates a fractal image. It performs many trigonometric functions and is deeply recursive.

LU: implements Lower/Upper Triangular Decomposition for matrix factorization.

Matrix: performs the inversion function on matrices.

Probe: uses the Poisson distribution to compute a theoretical approximation of pi.

Triphase: contains three programs: (1) a Linpack linear system solver performing heavy floating-point math; (2) a multithreaded matrix multiplier; and (3) a multithreaded Sieve prime-finder algorithm.

7.1 Impact of Obfuscations on Performance

Figure 1(a) summarizes the ratio of the execution times of the obfuscated benchmark to the original benchmark.[11] A ratio of 1 indicates no effect on performance, a ratio of

---

[10] Soot is unable to read in classfiles that include `jsr` instructions with no matching `ret`. This is not a limitation of Dava itself but we marked it as having crashed on the CB2JI obfuscation because of this.

[11] To time the original benchmark, we first processed it via Soot with no obfuscations turned on. This is to factor out any differences due to Soot processing.

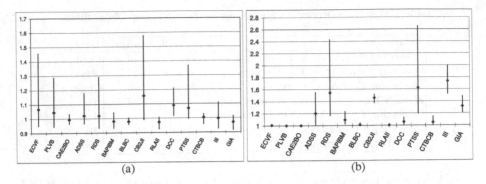

Fig. 1. Comparing obfuscated programs to their original forms: (a) Performance Ratio — (average execution time of obfuscated program)/(average execution time of original program); (b) Complexity Ratio — (sum of edges and nodes in obfuscated CFG)/(sum of edges and nodes in original CFG)

less than 1 indicates that the obfuscated benchmark was faster, and a ratio greater than 1 indicates that it was slower.[12] Each bar corresponds to one obfuscation, the diamond on the bar indicates the average over all the benchmarks. The bars show the range of ratios with the bottom of the bar indicating the benchmark with the lowest ratio and the top of the bar corresponds to the benchmarks with the highest ratio.

All experiments were run on an AMD Athlon™64 X2 3800+ machine with 4GB of RAM running Ubuntu 6.06 Linux. Sun Microsystem's Java HotSpot™64-Bit Server VM (build 1.5.0 06 b05) was used with the initial and maximum Java heap sizes set to 128MB and 1024MB, respectively.

As shown by recent empirical studies by Gu *et al.* [9, 10], small variations in code layout can lead to relatively large performance differences in Java (on the order of 5-10%). Thus, we can expect some performance differences between the original and obfuscated code just because the obfuscated code leads to different code layouts. Notable performance differences are those less than .95 or greater than 1.05.

Average performance of the obfuscated code is very reasonable and quite a few are, in fact, faster. The most expensive is CB2JI, which converts branches to jsr instructions, with an average slowdown of 1.16 and a maximum slowdown of almost 1.6.[13] Only 6 obfuscations lead to a maximum slowdown > 1.2. These should be used carefully, avoiding hot methods if possible.

In some cases the obfuscations actually seem to slightly improve peformance. The RLAII obfuscation that moves loads above ifs is one such case.[14]

---

[12] The execution time is computed by timing 10 runs, dropping the slowest and fastest and averaging the remaining 8. The largest standard error we saw was 2.6% and most measurements were well below that.

[13] The maximum slowdown was in the LU benchmark and we found th entire slowdown was caused by one deeply nested loop which had very complex control flow after obfuscation. The JIT compiler struggled to analyze this, causing a 5-fold slowdown in compilation time.

[14] This makes sense since it is moving a load that is known to be needed on both branches earlier in the computation.

7.2 Impact of Obfuscations on Control-Flow Complexity

Figure 1(b) shows the increase in code complexity due to obfuscations (the pain). We have opted for a simple measure of complexity based on the total number of nodes and edges in the control flow graphs of the program. Each node is a basic block and each edge is a control flow edge. Obfuscations which change the structure of the code may introduce new edges and/or redirect existing edges to split basic blocks. Figure 1(b) displays the ratio of the sum of nodes and edges of the obfuscated code over the sum of the original. This count captures the impact of control flow obfuscations well.[15]

Some structure obfuscations show a signficant increase in complexity.[16]

As we have shown in Table 3, the third group of obfuscations are those that are most effective in breaking decompilers. Some of these also show significant increases in complexity. Based on our experiences with Dava, which can partially handle many of these cases, we expect that a complete decompilation will lead to source code with a lot of code duplication and heavy use of labeled blocks.

8   Conclusions and Future Work

Fourteen obfuscations have been presented. The intent was to hinder reverse engineering while maintaining performance. The operator-level techniques are intended to make the code less readable. We didn't expect these to break decompilers, yet several decompilers failed to properly type the obfuscated code. The structure obfuscations were meant to confuse control flow and object-oriented design. The decompilers also had trouble with some of these techniques, although they should in principle be decompilable. These failures were mostly due to obfuscations creating unstructured control flow which is more difficult to handle than structured control flow. The gap obfuscations were new techniques and were aimed at exploiting the differences between bytecode and Java source. These were very successful in increasing the complexity of the code and breaking the decompilers.

The effect on performance varied. The average performance ratio of obfuscated/original ranged from .96 to 1.16. The maximum ratio reached almost 1.6 but only 6 of 14 obfuscations were over 1.2. These 6 should not be used heavily in hot methods of a program. More detailed analysis of specific instances showed that performance slowdowns were often due to the increased time needed by the JIT compilers to analyze the complex control flow created by our modifications. Hence the obfuscations are not just more difficult for reverse engineers to understand, they also cause problems for tools like compilers and decompilers.

We presented obfuscations we developed and this paper has shown how they work individually. The next step is to develop techniques to automatically determine optimized obfuscation sites and how to best select a combination of obfuscations so that the best

---

[15] As expected, the operation-level obfuscations have no impact on control flow complexity. Complexity for these obfuscations is better demonstrated by an increase in the number of operations. We have collected these kinds of metrics, which do demonstrate an increase.

[16] The two obfuscations that confuse the object-oriented design, BAPIBM and BLBC, do not increase complexity, but would affect other metrics which measure coupling.

overall protection is acheived. We have also started to develop metrics to quantify the effect of obfuscators and decompilers.

References

1. A. W. Appel. Deobfuscation is in NP, Aug. 21 2002.
2. B. Barak, O. Goldreich, R. Impagliazzo, S. Rudich, A. Sahai, S. Vadhan, and K. Yang. On the (im)possibility of obfuscating programs. *Lecture Notes in Computer Science*, 2139:1–??, 2001.
3. B. A. Benander, N. Gorla, and A. C. Benander. An empirical study of the use of the goto statement. *J. Syst. Softw.*, 11(3):217–223, 1990.
4. S. R. Chidamber and C. F. Kemerer. A metrics suite for object oriented design. *IEEE Trans. Softw. Eng.*, 20(6):476–493, 1994.
5. F. B. Cohen. Operating system protection through program evolution. *Comput. Secur.*, 12(6):565–584, 1993.
6. C. Collberg, C. Thomborson, and D. Low. Breaking abstractions and unstructuring data structures. In *ICCL '98: Proceedings of the 1998 International Conference on Computer Languages*, page 28, Washington, DC, USA, 1998. IEEE Computer Society.
7. C. S. Collberg and C. Thomborson. Watermarking, tamper-proofing, and obfuscation - tools for software protection. In *IEEE Transactions on Software Engineering*, volume 28, pages 735–746, Aug. 2002.
8. J. Gosling, B. Joy, G. Steele, and G. Bracha. *The Java Language Specification, Second Edition*. Addison Wesley, 2000.
9. D. Gu, C. Verbrugge, and E. Gagnon. Code layout as a source of noise in JVM performance. In *Component And Middleware Performance workshop, OOPSLA 2004*, 2004.
10. D. Gu, C. Verbrugge, and E. M. Gagnon. Relative factors in performance analysis of Java virtual machines. In *VEE '06: Proceedings of the 2nd international conference on Virtual execution environments*, pages 111–121. ACM Press, 2006.
11. S. Henry and K. Kafura. Software structure metrics based on information flow. *IEEE Transactions on Software Engineering*, 7(5):510–518, 1981.
12. Jad - the fast Java Decompiler. Available on: http://www.kpdus.com/jad.html.
13. J. Miecnikowski and L. J. Hendren. Decompiling Java bytecode: problems, traps and pitfalls. In R. N. Horspool, editor, *Compiler Construction*, volume 2304 of *Lecture Notes in Computer Science*, pages 111–127. Springer Verlag, 2002.
14. J. Miecznikowski and L. Hendren. Decompiling Java using staged encapsulation. In *Proceedings of the Working Conference on Reverse Engineering*, pages 368–374, October 2001.
15. Mocha, the Java Decompiler. Available on: http://www.brouhaha.com/~eric/computers/mocha.html.
16. J. C. Munson and T. M. Khoshgoftaar. Measurement of data structure complexity. *J. Syst. Softw.*, 20(3):217–225, 1993.
17. N. A. Naeem and L. Hendren. Programmer-friendly decompiled Java. In *Proceedings of the 14th IEEE International Conference on Program Comprhension*, 2006.
18. Y. Sakabe, M. Soshi, and A. Miyaji. Java obfuscation with a theoretical basis for building secure mobile agents. In *Communications and Multimedia Security*, pages 89–103, 2003.
19. M. Sosonkin, G. Naumovich, and N. Memon. Obfuscation of design intent in object-oriented applications. In *DRM '03: Proceedings of the 3rd ACM workshop on Digital rights management*, pages 142–153, New York, NY, USA, 2003. ACM Press.
20. Source Again - A Java Decompiler. Available on: http://www.ahpah.com/.
21. R. Vallée-Rai, L. Hendren, V. Sundaresan, P. Lam, E. Gagnon, and P. Co. Soot - a Java optimization framework. In *Proceedings of CASCON 1999*, pages 125–135, 1999.

A Fast Cutting-Plane Algorithm
for Optimal Coalescing

Daniel Grund[1],* and Sebastian Hack[2]

[1] Department of Computer Science, Saarland University
grund@cs.uni-sb.de
[2] Department of Computer Science, University of Karlsruhe
hack@ipd.info.uni-karlsruhe.de

Abstract. Recent work has shown that the subtasks of register allocation (spilling, register assignment, and coalescing) can be completely separated. This work presents an algorithm for the coalescing subproblem that relies on this separation. The algorithm uses 0/1 Linear Programming (ILP), a general-purpose optimization technique, to derive optimal solutions.

We provide the first optimal solutions for a benchmark called "Optimal Coalescing Challenge", i.e., our ILP model outperforms previous approaches. Additionally, we use these optimal solutions to assess the quality of well-known heuristics. A second benchmark on SPEC CPU2000 programs emphasizes the practicality of our algorithm.

1 Introduction

Coalescing is an important compiler optimization that removes useless copy instructions from a program to improve its performance. Because it needs information about assigned registers it is commonly performed as a subtask of register allocation besides spilling and register assignment.

The first published coalescing heuristic [1] did not know about the negative influence of aggressive coalescing on spilling. Later approaches discovered these effects and restricted coalescing [2,3] or avoided harmful cases by partial undoing [4].

Latest work [5] suggests to perform register allocation while the program is in SSA form (static single assignment). The chordality of the SSA programs' interference graphs allows for an allocation scheme in which each subtask needs to be processed only once, see Figure 1. For the same reason the effects of coalescing on the colorability of an already colored interference graph can be predicted precisely.

Our main contribution is an algorithm for optimal coalescing using 0/1 linear programming (ILP) that outperforms previous approaches, e.g., most recently [6]. Basically, the algorithm only relies on the strict separation of spilling

---

* Partially supported by the German Research Foundation (DFG) GK 623.

S. Krishnamurthi and M. Odersky (Eds.): CC 2007, LNCS 4420, pp. 111–125, 2007.
© Springer-Verlag Berlin Heidelberg 2007

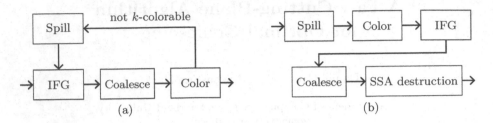

Fig. 1. Rough register allocation schemes: (a) Traditional, "iterative" Chaitin style allocator. (b) "Sequential" SSA form allocator. For spilling and coloring an interference graph is *not* strictly necessary.

and coalescing, although there is one step that can be handled more efficiently for chordal graphs.

Optimization of the ILP solution process is key to obtain suitable solution times. We present optimizations including a preprocessing that reduces the problem size, cutting planes pruning the search space as well as alternative ILP constraints that are most easily generated for chordal graphs.

We use a set of interference graphs published by Appel [7] to assess the speed of our algorithm. Our algorithm is the first to actually compute optimal solutions thereby outperforming Appel's approach [6]. Furthermore, we use the obtained solutions to absolutely qualify coalescing heuristics presented in [8] and [7] and the well-known ones presented in [3] and [4]. I.e., we judge them by how close they are to the optimum; we do not ask how much they improved some objective function but how much potential is left over.

The next section gives the necessary concepts from graph theory and integer linear programming. Section 3 describes in detail all sources of copy instructions (especially the handling of ϕ-functions) and defines the coalescing problem in terms of an augmented interference graph. The main contribution is presented in Section 4: The first part deals with the basic ILP model while the second part presents the optimizations. The benchmark results are contained in Section 5. Finally, Section 6 contrasts this paper to related work and Section 7 concludes.

2   Foundations

Concepts from **graph theory:** A *chord* is an edge connecting two non-adjacent nodes on a cycle. A cycle with k nodes and without chords is called a *k-hole*. A graph is called *chordal* if it does not contain any k-holes for $k \geq 4$. A *clique* is a completely connected subgraph. An alternative characterization of chordal graphs can be given iteratively: A clique is a chordal graph. Gluing together two chordal graphs such that the shared nodes are a clique is again a chordal graph. More precisely, $G = G_1 \cup G_2$ is chordal if the subgraphs G_i are chordal and $G_1 \cap G_2$ is a clique.

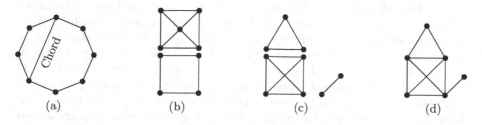

Fig. 2. Concepts from graph theory related to chordality: (a) A chord in a cycle building a 4-hole and a 6-hole. (b) Two non-chordal graphs. (c) Some cliques. (d) A chordal graph constructed with the cliques of (c).

Integer linear programming (ILP) is the problem of maximizing or minimizing an objective function subject to (in)equality constraints and integrality restrictions on a (sub)set of variables. In general, solving an ILP is $\mathcal{NP}$ hard, but in practice even large instances can be solved. Let $P = \{x \mid Ax \geq b, x \in \mathbb{R}^n_+\}, c \in \mathbb{R}^n, b \in \mathbb{R}^m, A \in \mathbb{R}^{m \times n}$. Then ILP is the problem:

$$\min f = c^T x, \quad x \in P \cap \mathbb{Z}^n$$

The set P is called the *feasible region*. P is called *integral* if it is equal to the convex hull $P_I = conv(P \cap \mathbb{Z}^n)$ of the integer points I. In case of an integral feasible region, an optimal solution of the ILP can be efficiently computed by solving the LP relaxation of the problem by dropping all the integrality constraints. The figure to the right illustrates the coherence of these sets. Closing the gap be-

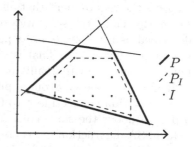

tween the feasible region and the convex hull by an efficient problem formulation or by adding additional constraints/cuts helps ILP solvers to find good or optimal solutions more quickly. In contrast to constraints cuts do not rule out any feasible integer points. For more details on (I)LP refer to [9,10].

3   The Problem

Let us first briefly summarize register allocation for SSA-form programs as described in [5] and illustrated in Figure 1. First, the register pressure is reduced to the number of available registers k by selecting certain abstract values and generating spill code for them. Then the actual assignment of registers takes place by performing a walk over the dominance tree of the program. Coalescing is an optional optimization that may be disregarded. If applied, it may either improve a given coloring or it can subsume coloring by combining the two phases.

At last, the SSA form is destructed by replacing the ϕ functions with register permutations. For the details we have to refer to [11] or most recently to [8].

In such a setting, the starting point for coalescing is a k-colored chordal interference graph $G = (V, E)$. To express the subjects of coalescing we add a second type of undirected, so called *affinity edges* to the graph yielding $G = (V, E, A)$. An affinity edge is assigned an additional positive weight that represents the penalty incurred whenever the two incident nodes have *different* colors. Thus, coalescing is the optimization problem to color as many affinity pairs as possible with only one color each, while retaining a correct coloring. In the following, we list the origin of these edges (how they emerge) and describe their construction.

ϕ **functions** represent control-flow-dependent data flow. Because there is no immediate hardware support for this abstraction, one has to realize them with suitable instruction sequences. This is called SSA destruction. All prior SSA destruction algorithms insert sequences of copy instructions in the predecessor blocks to implement the behavior of the ϕ functions and (try to) merge nodes in the resulting interference graph to reduce the number of copy instructions.

But as described in [5], inserting *sequences* of copy instructions is in general neither desirable (may destroy chordality) nor possible (may raise register demand). Instead, the intermediate step of implementing ϕs with permutations respects the requirement that all ϕs in a basic block must be carried out *simultaneously*. Thus, the semantics of ϕ functions in the same basic block may be described as the *simultaneous* permutation of registers contents on the incoming control flow edges. That is why ϕ functions should or must be replaced by permutations that are finally implemented by copy or swap instructions.

Regarding coalescing, our approach is to add an affinity edge for each operand of a ϕ function connecting it to the result of the ϕ. Coalescing may assign such a pair of nodes the same color, in which case no value movement is necessary. When SSA destruction inserts permutations, the prior optimization has already maximized the number of fixed points of these permutations. Figure 3 shows an exhaustive example.

Register constraints, the requirement that the assignable registers of certain arguments or results of an instruction are limited to a subset of all registers, are another source of permutations.[1] But as they are beyond the scope of this paper, we will not elaborate this topic deeply. In general, completing the coloring of a graph with pre-colored nodes is $\mathcal{NP}$ complete, even for chordal graphs [12]. But if each color is used only once by the pre-coloring the problem becomes easy for chordal graphs.

As shown in Figure 4, we insert a permutation in front of each instruction having a register constraint on one of its arguments or results (e.g., `mul` or `div` on IA32 architecture). Therefore, every live range ends before such an instruction and the interference graph is split into several unconnected components, each containing every constraint color only once. To maximize the number of fixed

---

[1] Permutations for register constraints are inserted before coloring, permutations for ϕ functions during SSA destruction, after coalescing.

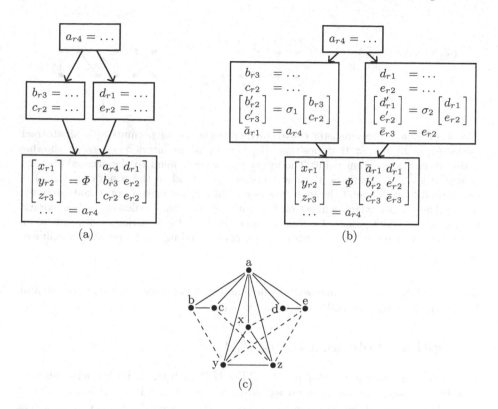

Fig. 3. Connection between Φs, permutations, and SSA destruction. **(a)** Example SSA program. The subscripts of the variables denote the assigned registers. **(c)** Interference graph of the program in (a) with dashed affinity edges ($[a, x]$ was left out due to infeasibility). **(b)** The program after SSA destruction *without* prior coalescing. The abstract values v' hold the results of the permutations. σ_1 is inserted to swap the registers of b and c. σ_2 is the identity function. Its insertion is not strictly necessary. Now the Φ function can be omitted because the registers of arguments and corresponding results match. In addition this example contains *all* details and special cases one has to consider: The abstract values $\bar{v}$ are introduced to duplicate values. The value of a must be duplicated because it is used at the end of the last basic block and thus interferes with x. The value e must be duplicated because upon entering the last block the value must be present in two registers (y and z). The duplicated value $\bar{e}$ could be assigned to y or z. Since the registers of e and y match, $\bar{e}$ is assigned to z.

points of a permutation of size k we add k affinity edges to the interference graph connecting the corresponding nodes of a permutation.

Register identity in two-address code, the requirement that the same register must be assigned to the first operand and the result of an instruction, can be seen as a register constraint. But it is handled differently to keep the number of affinity edges small. We simply express the wish to have the result and the first operand in the same register by adding an affinity edge between the two

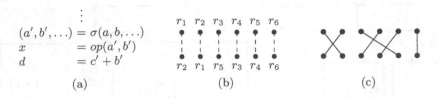

$$
\begin{aligned}
(a', b', \ldots) &= \sigma(a, b, \ldots) \\
x &= op(a', b') \\
d &= c' + b'
\end{aligned}
$$

(a)   (b)   (c)

Fig. 4. (a) Before every register-constrained operation op we permute by σ all abstract values $(a, b, \ldots)$ live at that position. (b) Cutout of an interference graph showing nodes at such a program point: The upper nodes correspond to the original abstract values $(a, b, \ldots)$ to permute, the lower nodes correspond to the results $(a', b', \ldots)$ of the permutation. Some of the lower nodes are subject to register constraints imposed by op. The affinity edges connect each v with its v'. Thus, coalescing will maximize the number of fixed points of σ, and a lower number of instructions will result when generating code for σ. (c) The permutation corresponding to the register assignment in (b).

corresponding nodes. If this wish is declined one can still fulfill this constraint by generating suitable code not considered here.

4   Optimal Solutions Using ILP

In this section, we will develop a 0/1-LP (an ILP with all variables being binary) to solve coalescing problems represented by a graph $G = (V, E, A)$ as introduced in Section 3. The idea is to use a standard ILP to model the graph-coloring problem and to introduce separate variables to express the target function to optimize. Finally, one has to interrelate these two components with additional, well chosen constraints.

4.1   Formalization

Let us first model the correct coloring of the interference graph $G = (V, E, A)$ with k available colors. For each node $v_i \in V$, we add k binary variables $x_{i1} \ldots x_{ik}$ to the model (we know that the graph is k-colorable), where $x_{ic} = 1$ if and only if node v_i has color c. To express that each node gets assigned exactly one color, we add the constraints $\sum_{c=1}^{k} x_{ic} = 1$.

For each interference edge $e_{ij} \in E$ connecting two nodes v_i and v_j we must assure the nodes get assigned different colors. This is simply achieved by adding $x_{ic} + x_{jc} \leq 1$ for each color c. So far this corresponds to Appel's formulation [6].

Now let us focus on the affinity edges. First we model the objective function: For each affinity edge $a_{ij} \in A$ with the positive weight w_{ij}, we add the summand $w_{ij}y_{ij}$ to the objective function being minimized. The binary variables y_{ij} shall be 1 if and only if the adjacent nodes v_i and v_j have *different* colors. Therefore the costs w_{ij} are incurred iff $y_{ij} = 1$ iff the two nodes have different colors.

So far, the last property is not modelled, yet, because the optimality variables y_{ij} are completely unconstrained. We have to interrelate these variables with the coloring variables. All the variables y_{ij} are optimized to 0 automatically, if possible. Thus, we only have to take care of the case where two affinity nodes have different colors. In this case we force y_{ij} to be 1 with the following constraints: $y_{ij} \geq x_{ic} - x_{jc}$ for each color c. If the two involved nodes have different colors, there exists an inequality constraint with the right hand side evaluating to 1, and therefore enforcing $y_{ij} = 1$. If the two nodes have the same color, all right hand sides evaluate to 0 and the variable y_{ij} is effectively not constrained by these constraints and will be minimized to 0.

To sum things up, here is the complete model:

$$\min f = \sum_{a_{ij} \in A} w_{ij} y_{ij}$$
$$\text{where} \quad \sum_{c=1}^{k} x_{ic} = 1 \quad v_i \in V$$
$$x_{ic} + x_{jc} \leq 1 \quad (v_i, v_j) \in E, c = 1 \ldots k$$
$$y_{ij} \geq x_{ic} - x_{jc} \quad (v_i, v_j) \in A, c = 1 \ldots k$$
$$y_{ij}, x_{ic} \in \{0, 1\}$$

4.2 Optimizations

Although the above model yields correct results, even the runtimes of industry strength ILP solvers are unsatisfactory as we will show later in the measurements section. Therefore we increase the performance of the solution process by taking the following measures.

Data Size Reduction. The first optimization is a preprocessing that takes place before the graph is transformed to an ILP. We unburden the ILP solver by reducing the problem to its core, thereby reducing the number of variables and constraints it has to deal with. More precisely, we want the solver to only think about the parts of the graph related to affinity edges, and complete the optimal partial coloring by a standard algorithm.

Remember that a node with degree strictly less than k (insignificant degree) can be colored regardless of the colors assigned to its neighbors and can be removed from the graph. This elimination was already used in Chaitin's allocator [1]. With this in mind, we remove a maximum number of nodes from the graph that satisfy the following conditions:

- The node removed is not incident with an affinity edge.
- The node is not subject to any register constraints.
- The node has insignificant degree in the current graph.

Thus, we end up with a maximal prefix of an elimination order. The remaining nodes are the core of the problem that is solved by the ILP solver. Afterwards, the removed nodes are colored in reverse order resulting in a global optimal solution.

Note, that this reduction can split the graph into unconnected components. Solving each connected component separately reduces the total solution time significantly.

Clique Inequalities. The second optimization modifies the ILP model. It uses the well known *clique inequalities* [10] to model the interference edges. Given an interference clique $v_1 \ldots v_n$, it is clear that each color can appear at most once in this clique. Thus, instead of modeling each of the interference edges one by one, we replace the $O(n^2)$ constraints $x_{ic} + x_{jc} \leq 1$ with just one $\sum_{i=1}^{n} x_{ic} \leq 1$ per color. If the clique is of size k such constraints are always satisfied at equality. Thus, one can demand equality to add more explicit knowledge to the model.

In general, computing a minimum clique cover is $\mathcal{NP}$ complete [13]. However, there is an efficient $O(|V| + |E|)$ algorithm for chordal graphs [14]. For arbitrary graphs one must fall back to a heuristic computing some clique cover.

Reverse Affinity Cuts. As we have seen, only one of the two possible sets of inequations $y_{ij} \geq x_{ic} - x_{jc}$ and $y_{ij} \geq x_{jc} - x_{ic}$ is necessary to model an affinity edge $[i, j] \in A$. But the other one can be used to tighten the LP relaxation. Consider the following example with three colors. The fractional values of the x variables might occur as a solution of the LP relaxation:

$$\left\{ \begin{array}{l} y \geq 0.4 - 1.0 \\ y \geq 0.3 - 0.0 \\ y \geq 0.3 - 0.0 \end{array} \right\}$$

Effectively this only yields $y \geq 0.3$. Adding all inequations with switched minuend and subtrahend results in $y \geq 0.6$.

Path Cuts. In some sense, an ILP solver is a *generic* piece of software. As described in Section 2 supporting it with cuts that describe *problem specific* knowledge can lead to better performance. The last two optimizations provide such cuts: They encode a lower bound for certain subsets of affinity edges.

The first class of cuts uses the contradictoriness of affinity and interference edges. Affinity edges represent the wish to assign the *same* colors, but interference edges are hard constraints for *different* colors. Consider a path of affinity edges where only its ends are connected by an interference edge, e.g., Figure 5: Clearly, one of the affinity edges must break, because along the path the coloring must change at least once. To be precise:

Definition 1 (Affinity-connected). *Let the graph $G = (V, E, A)$. Two nodes $a, b \in V$ are affinity-connected, if a and b are connected by a path of affinity edges and no inner nodes of this path are connected with an interference edge:*
$\exists v_1, \ldots, v_n \in V :$

- $a = v_1, b = v_n$
- $v_i = v_j \Rightarrow i = j$
- $\forall 1 \leq i < n : (v_i, v_{i+1}) \in A$
- $\forall 1 \leq i < j \leq n : (v_i, v_j) \in E \Rightarrow \{v_i, v_j\} = \{a, b\}$

Lemma 1 (Path Cut). *If two nodes interfere and are affinity-connected with the path $v_1, \ldots, v_n$ the following inequation holds: $\sum_{i=1}^{n-1} y_{i,i+1} \geq 1$*

Clique-Ray Cuts

Definition 2 (Clique Ray). *A subgraph consisting of an interference clique* $C = \{v_1, \ldots, v_n\}$ *and a node* $a \notin C$ *with affinity edges to all* $v \in C$ *is called a clique ray.*

At first, this compound of cliques and affinity edges illustrated in Figure 5 may seem very special. But this pattern occurs in real problems, e.g., if one and the same variable is used multiple times in different ϕ functions in the same basic block at the same argument position. Due to the simultaneous execution of all ϕ functions in a basic block, all results interfere pairwise and form an interference clique. The affinity edges to the multiply used node/variable build the rest of the clique ray.

Lemma 2 (Clique-Ray Cut). *For a given clique ray* (C, a) *the following inequation holds:* $\sum_{v \in C} y_{v,a} \geq |C| - 1$

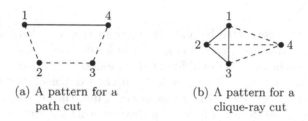

(a) A pattern for a   (b) A pattern for a
    path cut   clique-ray cut

Fig. 5. (a) At least one affinity edge must break due to the interference edge: $y_{12} + y_{23} + y_{34} \geq 1$ (b) At most one affinity edge can hold: $y_{14} + y_{24} + y_{34} \geq 2$

5   Measurements

5.1   The Optimal Coalescing Challenge

The first benchmark is a collection of interference graphs provided by Appel [7] known as the optimal coalescing challenge (OCC). These graphs were produced using a variant of SML/NJ that implements optimal register spilling as described in [6] and live-range splitting after each instruction. This kind of splitting adds an extreme amount of affinity edges, which makes the problems harder to solve. Strictly speaking, the problem to solve is optimal live-range splitting, which subsumes optimal coalescing that is not allowed to split live ranges to coalesce others.

We compared Appel's approach [6] to some variations of our proposal by building and solving all ILPs on an ATHLON 64 3200+ using CPLEX 9.0. The cuts described in Section 4.2 were all generated before invoking the ILP solver, which only used the necessary ones out of a so called cut pool. We generated the clique-ray cuts for each applicable node by taking the subgraph induced by its affinity neighborhood and computing a minimum clique cover of this subgraph.

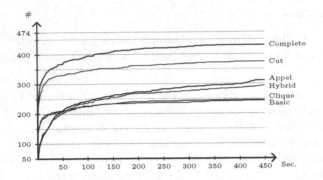

Fig. 6. Distribution of the solution times of the 474 OCC problems. The #-axis gives the number of problems solved within a certain time. The *basic* model is described in Section 4.1, *clique* uses clique inequalities to model interferences, *cut* extends the clique model by path cuts and clique-ray cuts, *complete* additionally includes reverse affinity cuts. Finally, *hybrid* combines Appel's model with our cuts.

The path cuts were generated by a simple recursive search[2], looking for a cycle containing exactly one interference edge and at least three affinity edges.

Figure 6 shows the runtimes of different ILP models. The use of clique inequalities improves the performance very little (compared to basic), because CPLEX analyses dependencies between binary variables. Thus, the lack of clique inequalities in Appel's model does not greatly matter, at least for mature solvers.

Adding the cuts to the model (cut, complete) increases the performance significantly: The number of optimally solved problems rises from 243 to 430. Lowering the time limit to 6 seconds would still yield 300 solved problems, i.e., most problems can easily be solved using the cuts.

Interestingly, for the easy problems our basic model performs better than Appel's, but solves less problems in the end. Intuitively, one would expect better results when combining his model with our cuts, but the combination (hybrid) increases the overhead and degrades performance. Therefore, the performance of our best model must come from our tighter affinity encoding *combined* with the application of cuts.

Table 1. Solution times (in seconds) of the 309 OCC instances optimally solved by both ILPs within 450 seconds

ILP	Appel	Complete
Sum	20852.7	1332.3
Average	67.5	4.3
Max	432.4	195.1

---

[2] This may be intractable for arbitrary graphs, i.e., with high affinity degree.

To complement the big picture with some numbers, Table 1 shows the solution times for the 309 problems optimally solved by both, Appel's model and our complete model. Our method is approximately 15 times faster in these cases and could optimally solve 430 problems within time in contrast to the 311 solved by Appel's.

Another indicator for the strength of our ILP is the solution quality produced within a given time limit. Table 2 lists properties of the best known solutions after 450 seconds of computing, including and excluding the optimally solved problems. The objective is minimized, so lower is better here. The gap absolute and gap relative rows show the distance between the best known solution and the optimal solution theoretically still possible.

Table 2. Solution quality (in millions of objective units) of feasible solutions after the time limit, excluding (EO) and including (IO) optimally solved problems

ILP	Appel EO	Complete EO	Appel IO	Complete IO
Sum	126.7	2.7	128.1	3.0
Gap abs	126.1	1.3	127.4	1.3
Gap rel	99.5%	49.4%	99.4%	44.5%

First of all, our method produced solutions being 50 times better. Second, the lower gap values indicate that our ILP produces tighter relaxations, which is useful to argue about solution quality. These advantages can be used if one is only interested in a solution provably lying in a certain distance to the optimum. However the tightness has one negligible drawback: There were 7 problems for which our ILP did not even yield a feasible solution in time. Although Appel's approach did yield feasible solutions, this is negligible because these solutions were far from optimal. Informally speaking, our first integer solution might take some time longer to pop up but then is better than those produced by Appel's ILP in the same time.

Last but not least we dropped the time limit to compute all optimal solutions. These were used to determine the absolute quality of the following coalescing heuristics: Iterated Coalescing [3], Optimistic Coalescing [4], a heuristic by Hack [8] directly designed for the SSA case, and another result set by Fang, which was produced with a local search SAT solver and is published on [7].

Figure 7 illustrates the big picture and Table 3 gives the corresponding numbers. The best heuristics solve about 175 problems optimally. Most of the problems can be solved with an objective function below $2 \cdot OPT$ (100%). The graph shows, again, previous experience [4,15] that optimistic coalescing performs better than iterated coalescing. From the table, one can derive that optimistic coalescing has a good average-case behavior (34%), but some difficult problems raised the overall deviation to 53%. A tuned version (Optimistic II) behaves vice versa: 60% on average but only 44% in total. Our SSA heuristic is competitive and comparable to optimistic coalescing, but more balanced (46%, 51%).

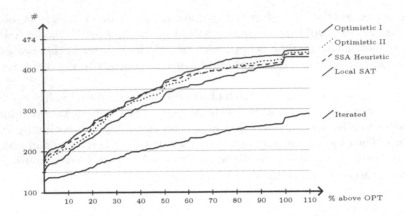

Fig. 7. Distribution of the solution qualities for coalescing heuristics. The %-axis gives the quality in terms of the allowed deviation from an optimal solution. The #-axis gives the number of solutions within a certain quality. E.g., iterated coalescing produces 200 solutions such that each is not more than 40% above the respective optimal solution.

Table 3. Comparison of different coalescing algorithms. The first two rows are given in millions of objective function units, the last was obtained by first calculating the percentage differences for all problems and then taking their arithmetic mean. (3 ILP solutions might not be optimal, but tight bounds can be given).

Algorithm	ILP	Iterated	Optimistic I	Optimistic II	SSA Heur	Local SAT
Objective sum	26.3	66.4	40.4	37.8	38.4	38.9
Difference to Opt	0.1	40.0	14.0	11.5	12.1	12.6
% above Opt	0.4	152	53	44	46	48
Average % above Opt	0	219	34	60	51	60

No heuristic yields solutions better than 44% (over all cases) above the optimal solution. This picture changes only little if one removes the outliers.

Some last remarks on the OCC: Due to the live-range splitting after each instruction we could only generate 22 clique-ray cuts, all equivalent to a path cut of length two, compared to 135942 path cuts. For the same reason the data size reduction was not applicable at all to this test set.

5.2   SPEC CPU2000 Benchmarks

To compensate the disadvantages of the OCC we performed a second benchmark, this time on a PENTIUM 4 2400. We compiled a subset of the SPEC CPU2000-benchmarks [16] consisting of C programs using FIRM [17] with its SSA-based x86 backend. In this setting, live-range splitting is limited to SSA construction, spilling[3] and the handling of register constraints.

---

[3] All subranges between two references (def/use) can be spilled separately.

Here, the data size reduction is applicable and worthwhile: The average number of removed nodes was 10%. Since live-range splitting is frequent for x86 (high number of constrained instructions), we assume that this percentage is even higher for standard RISC architectures. The number of generated clique-ray cuts was 227 and the number of path cuts was 112486.

Prior to the ILP, we ran the SSA heuristic on the graph and provided its solution as a start value to the ILP solver. Hence, there always was at least a feasible solution. Out of 4459 problems, only 211 (4.7%) were not solved *optimally* within 5 minutes. In those cases we also recorded the best lower bound (BLB in the following) known to the solver after the time limit was reached. The optimal solution of a problem lies between the BLB and the objective value returned. However, a common observation in practice is that the solver lowers the objective value and then remains a long time at the same best solution, only raising the lower bound, i.e., proving optimality of that solution. Therefore, some of the 211 feasible solutions might be optimal but the solver failed to prove it within time.

Table 4. Results of the SPEC2000 benchmark

	Max Costs	5min	BLB 5min	%5min	%BLB 5min
164.gzip	3456885	97356	30935	2.82	0.89
175.vpr	17105748	218105	215758	1.28	1.26
176.gcc	221483452	3429671	2641368	1.55	1.19
181.mcf	136390	6925	4567	5.08	3.35
186.crafty	27781660	852833	390419	3.07	1.41
197.parser	22227033	678415	609249	3.05	2.74
253.perlbmk	49321969	1596567	1424011	3.24	2.89
254.gap	131547137	2908392	1930799	2.21	1.47
255.vortex	28572683	1292513	1248252	4.52	4.37
256.bzip2	7007580	239528	196840	3.42	2.81
300.twolf	162497955	2915713	1253567	1.79	0.77

Table 4 shows the results of the benchmark. The column "Max Costs" lists the maximal costs of the benchmark, "5min" shows the remaining costs after at most five minutes of optimization. "BLB 5min" shows the costs if the best lower bound is assumed as the optimal objective value for problems that could not be solved within five minutes. "%5min" and "%BLB 5min" show the respective percentages regarding "Max Costs". The ILP formulation was able to compute optimal solutions in 95% of all cases and the other solutions were near-optimal.

6   Related Work

Goodwin and Wilken [18] were the first applying ILP to register allocation. They addressed the full problem of register allocation including spilling, rematerialization, callee/caller save register handling, register assignment and coalescing.

Thus, they solved a much harder problem on older hardware with older ILP solver technology. The only optimization they performed, was to reduce the size of the ILP by restricting the spill and reload decisions to sensible program points.

Fu and Wilken [19] improved this work by speeding up solution times. They identified several kinds of redundant or symmetric decisions and removed them from the ILP formulation. These optimizations together with faster hardware and better ILP solvers (7 years in between), resulted in significantly more functions being optimally allocated in less time.

Between these two publications, Appel and George [15] proposed decomposing this problem into two subproblems: Spill code placement and register coalescing, of which the latter also includes the actual assignment. They solved both problems by ILP and empirically showed that decomposing the problem does not significantly worsen the overall allocation quality. One point is unique to their approach: They potentially allow splitting live ranges after each instruction. However, this may be one of the reasons why the authors called their coalescing ILP far too slow and left an efficient algorithm for optimal coalescing as an open problem [7].

Our setting compares best to Appel's: We also separate spilling and coalescing, but for a better reason (chordality), and have basically the same starting point for coalescing, with the following differences: We do not allow live-range splitting after each instruction, although we are capable of solving such problems. Instead, our split points are limited to those introduced by SSA construction, spilling, and the handling of register constraints.

Concerning the ILP, our formulation differs from Appel's in the following points: We use a smaller and more efficient encoding of the affinity edges and efficiently generate clique inequalities to express the interference constraints. Admittedly, the clique inequalities contribute little to the performance because modern solvers have this optimization as a built-in function. Furthermore, all prior approaches focused on reducing the size of the ILP formulation. Additionally, we add supplementary cuts to cut down the search space, which is more sensible than a smaller formulation with a larger feasible region.

7   Conclusions and Further Work

Although this work began in a SSA context, the algorithm and all optimizations are applicable to the non-SSA case, as long as coalescing is separated from spilling. Our ILP model performs better than previous approaches: It needs significantly less time to compute optimal solutions or it can produce better solutions within a given time limit. If one should point out one crucial point it is the cutting planes. But to achieve top performance all the optimizations must go hand in hand.

For very large problems and extreme live-range splitting scalability comes to an end: The ILPs are so large (200000×200000 matrix) that solving the continuous relaxations consumes too much time. Future work could push this limit and investigate whether a benders decomposition or the new feature of CPLEX 10 to model implications are worthwhile. Other constraint solving techniques could be considered but 0/1-LP already is a very special problem class and ILP has the advantage to provide lower bounds. Another point that could be interesting for practical and theoretical reasons is the question which live-range splitting points are really necessary to achieve an optimally coalesced program.

References

1. Chaitin, G.J.: Register allocation & spilling via graph coloring. In: SIGPLAN symposium on Compiler construction, New York, NY, USA, ACM Press (1982)
2. Briggs, P., Cooper, K.D., Torczon, L.: Improvements to graph coloring register allocation. ACM Trans. Program. Lang. Syst. **16** (1994)
3. George, L., Appel, A.: Iterated Register Coalescing. ACM TOPLAS **18** (1996)
4. Park, J., Moon, S.M.: Optimistic Register Coalescing. ACM TOPLAS **26** (2004)
5. Hack, S., Grund, D., Goos, G.: Register Allocation for Programs in SSA-Form. In: Compiler Construction 2006. Volume 3923., Springer (2006)
6. Appel, A., George, L.: Optimal Spilling for CISC Machines with Few Registers. Technical report, Princeton University (2000)
7. Appel, A.: Optimal Coalescing Challenge. `http://www.cs.princeton.edu/~appel/coalesce` (2000)
8. Hack, S.: Register Allocation for Programs in SSA-Form (to appear). PhD thesis, University of Karlsruhe (2006)
9. Schrijver, A.: Theory of Linear and Integer Programming. J. Wiley & Sons (1986)
10. Nemhauser, G., Wolsey, L.: Integer and Combinatorial Optimization. Wiley-Interscience New York (1988)
11. Hack, S., Grund, D., Goos, G.: Towards Register Allocation for Programs in SSA-form. Technical report, University of Karlsruhe (2005)
12. Biró, M., Hujter, M., Tuza, Z.: Precoloring extension. I. Interval graphs. Discrete Mathematics **100** (1992)
13. Garey, M.R., Johnson, D.S.: Computers and Intractability: A Guide to the Theory of NP-Completeness. W. H. Freeman (1979) ISBN: 0716710455.
14. Gavril, F.: Algorithms for Minimum Coloring, Maximum Clique, Minimum Covering by Cliques, and Independent Set of a Chordal Graph. SIAM Journal on Computing **1** (1972)
15. Appel, A., George, L.: Optimal Spilling for CISC Machines with Few Registers. In: ACM SIGPLAN Conference PLDI. (2001)
16. Standard Performance Evaluation Corp.: `http://www.spec.org/cpu2000/` (2000)
17. Lindenmaier, G., Beck, M., Boesler, B., Geiß, R.: Firm, an Intermediate Language for Compiler Research. Technical Report 2005-8, University of Karlsruhe (2005)
18. Goodwin, D.W., Wilken, K.D.: Optimal and Near-optimal Global Register Allocations Using 0-1 Integer Programming. Softw. Pract. Exper. **26** (1996)
19. Fu, C., Wilken, K.: A Faster Optimal Register Allocator. In: Proceedings of the ACM/IEEE international symposium on Microarchitecture, Los Alamitos, CA, USA, IEEE Computer Society Press (2002)

Register Allocation and Optimal Spill Code Scheduling in Software Pipelined Loops Using 0-1 Integer Linear Programming Formulation

Santosh G. Nagarakatte[1] and R. Govindarajan[1,2]

[1] Department of Computer Science and Automation,
[2] Supercomputer Education and Research Center,
Indian Institute of Science, Bangalore 560012, India
{santosh,govind}@csa.iisc.ernet.in

Abstract. In achieving higher instruction level parallelism, software pipelining increases the register pressure in the loop. The usefulness of the generated schedule may be restricted to cases where the register pressure is less than the available number of registers. Spill instructions need to be introduced otherwise. But scheduling these spill instructions in the compact schedule is a difficult task. Several heuristics have been proposed to schedule spill code. These heuristics may generate more spill code than necessary, and scheduling them may necessitate increasing the initiation interval.

We model the problem of register allocation with spill code generation and scheduling in software pipelined loops as a 0-1 integer linear program. The formulation minimizes the increase in initiation interval (II) by optimally placing spill code and simultaneously minimizes the amount of spill code produced. To the best of our knowledge, this is the first integrated formulation for register allocation, optimal spill code generation and scheduling for software pipelined loops. The proposed formulation performs better than the existing heuristics by preventing an increase in II in 11.11% of the loops and generating 18.48% less spill code on average among the loops extracted from Perfect Club and SPEC benchmarks with a moderate increase in compilation time.

1   Introduction

Software pipelining [14] is the most commonly used loop scheduling technique for exploiting higher instruction level parallelism. In a software pipelined loop, instructions from multiple iterations are executed in an overlapped manner. Several heuristic methods [2,19] have been proposed to construct a software pipelined schedule. In addition a number of methods [10] have also been proposed to find an optimal schedule considering resource constraints. A schedule is said to be optimal if the initiation interval (II) of the schedule is not greater than that of any other schedule for the loop with the given resource constraints.

Software pipelining, like other instruction scheduling techniques, increases the register pressure. A number of heuristic approaches to reduce the register pressure

S. Krishnamurthi and M. Odersky (Eds.): CC 2007, LNCS 4420, pp. 126–140, 2007.

of the software pipelined schedule have been proposed [11]. Also, approaches to minimize the register pressure of the software pipelined schedule using linear [16] and integer linear program formulation have been reported in literature. However, these methods do not guarantee that the register requirements of the constructed schedule is less than the available registers. If the register need of the constructed schedule is greater than the available number of registers, either spill code needs to be introduced or the initiation interval needs to be increased [21]. In order to determine whether the constructed schedule is feasible for the given number of registers, register allocation must be performed with necessary spill code generation. Further the spill code must be scheduled in the compact schedule, without violating any resource or dependence constraints. Currently heuristic approaches [21] have been proposed for the introduction of spill code. Unfortunately, introduction of spill code can saturate the memory units and thereby force an increase in the initiation interval.

In this paper, we are interested in addressing the following problem: Given a modulo scheduled loop L, a machine architecture M and an initiation interval II, is it possible to perform register allocation with the given registers and optimally generate and schedule necessary spill code such that the register requirement of the schedule is lesser than or equal to the available number of registers? We propose a 0-1 integer linear programming formulation for register allocation, optimal spill code generation and spill code placement in software pipelined loops. The proposed approach is guaranteed to identify a schedule with necessary spill code, whenever such a schedule exists, without increasing the initiation interval. Further the proposed approach generates minimal spill code, thereby improving the code quality. The proposed formulation takes into account both the compactness of the schedule and memory unit usage. Further the formulation incorporates live range splitting [4] which allows a live range to be assigned to a register at specific time instances and be resident in memory in rest of the time instances. To the best of our knowledge, this is the first integrated formulation for register allocation, optimal spill code generation and scheduling for software pipelined loops. The formulation is useful in evaluating various heuristics and one can generate a better quality code with a moderate increase in compilation time. We have implemented the solution method on loops from Perfect Club and SPEC2000 benchmarks. On an average, we prevent an increase in the initiation interval in 11.11% of the 90 loops on an architecture with 32 registers and in 12% of the 157 loops on an architecture with 16 registers when compared to the heuristic approach [21]. We also generate roughly 18.48% less spill code compared to the heuristic solution.

The paper is organized as follows: Section 2 provides a brief motivation for optimal spill code generation and scheduling. In Section 3, we explain our integer linear programming formulation. Section 4 presents the simplified formulation. Section 5 presents the experimental methodology and results. In Section 6, we discuss the related work and concluding remarks are provided in Section 7.

2 Motivation

Traditionally, the process of adding spill code is done iteratively [21] for architectures with no rotating registers. First, the loop is modulo scheduled, then register allocation is performed. If the register pressure of the schedule is greater than the available number of registers, then spill candidates are chosen. Subsequently spill code is added and the loop is rescheduled. In the process above, since the selection of spill candidates is based on a certain heuristic, it may result either in the addition of extra spill code or the introduction of spill code at a time step where no memory unit is available. These, in turn, may increase the memory unit usage necessitating an increase in the initiation interval. Various heuristics have been proposed for generating spill code and scheduling spill code [1].

Critical cycle is one of the key characteristics used by heuristics to decide on the spill candidates. A time step t is said to be a *Critical cycle* in the kernel if the number of live ranges at that instant is greater than the number of available registers. In Figure 1(a), we show the live ranges of a software pipelined schedule with $II = 6$ and assume there are four registers available. For this schedule, cycle 2 is the critical cycle. To perform register allocation with the available four registers for the given schedule, one of the live ranges must be spilled. A commonly used heuristic gives priority to the spill candidate with longest live range [21]. Unfortunately, it is possible that the longest live range does not span through critical cycle. Hence, spilling the longest live range may not necessarily reduce the register pressure. A refined heuristic considering the above prioritizes the spill candidate which is live at the critical cycle and has the longest lifetime among the the the spill candidates [21]. The heuristics may not be able to capture all the scenarios.

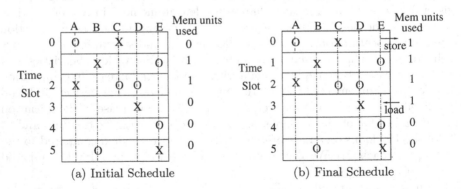

Fig. 1. Initial kernel with II = 6. X is the definition and O is the use of the live range.

Consider the kernel shown in Figure 1(a). In this example, we have assumed a load and a store latency of 1 cycle and the presence of a single memory unit and 4 registers. The memory unit usage in the kernel is indicated in the figure. The kernel is obtained for an initiation interval of 6. The register need of the schedule is 5. So we need to insert spills in order to reduce register need. Figure 1(b) shows the kernel after the spill code has been scheduled. Among the spill candidates, variables D and E have the longest live range and pass through the critical cycle 2. In the kernel in Figure 1(b), though the spill store for E is scheduled at cycle 0, the value in the register continues and ends only at cycle 1. If we had chosen D as the spill candidate, we would not have been able to spill and hence reduce the register pressure at cycle 2. This is because of the use of D in cycle 2. As a result, it is not only necessary to select the right spill candidate but also to schedule the spill loads and stores so that the register need of the loop is reduced without unnecessarily requiring an increase in the initiation interval.

The recent work in spill code generation [21] addresses the iterative process of adding spill code by selecting a finite number of candidates for spilling based on a *quantity factor* which is determined experimentally. By adopting the notion of quantity factor, we are making the decision of selecting the spill candidate and scheduling them incrementally, considering a few candidates. It is possible that the greedy approach can fail. In our experimentation, the quantity factor of 0.5 resulted in an increase in the initiation interval in 12% of the loops that had sufficent register pressure and needed the addition of spill code.

Moreover, there are a plethora of factors that need to be considered while choosing the right spill candidate which can be suitably scheduled with a minimal amount of spill code. An injudicious selection and subsequent scheduling can result in an unnecessary increase in the initiation interval, which can be attributed to addition of otherwise superfluous spill code saturating the memory usage.

3   ILP Formulation for Spill Code Minimization and Scheduling

In this section, we explain our 0-1 integer linear programming formulation for register allocation and spill code scheduling in software pipelined loops assuming a load-store architecture with no rotating registers. A solution to the ILP formulation would represent a valid schedule with spill code suitably scheduled satisfying the register and functional resource constraints. Given a software pipelined loop with modulo variable expansion [14] carried out, our efficient register allocation and spill code scheduling formulation involves the association of decision variables to the live range, formulation of relationship between the decision variables that need to be satisfied, solving the integer linear program and rewriting the original code.

3.1   Generation of Decision Variables

Given a data dependence graph and a periodic schedule, we model a live range with a set of decision variables. The live range produced by instruction i is denoted by the temporary name TN_i. Without the loss of generality, we use the term temporary variable and live range interchangeably as each temporary variable has exactly one definition point. The live range TN_i is represented with a series of liveness decision variables from its definition time (T_i^{def}) to its last use time (T_i^{end}). A live range can be allocated to any of the R registers. Hence corresponding to each time instant $t \in [T_i^{def}, T_i^{end}]$ and register r, we create liveness decision variables of the form $TN_{i,r,t}$. The decision variable $TN_{i,r,t} = 1$ represents the fact that the TN_i is allocated to register r at time instant t.

To determine where to introduce spill stores and loads in the schedule, we introduce two kinds of spill decision variables namely store decision and load decision variables.

1. Store decision variable: We introduce store decision variables $STN_{i,r,t}$ for every live range TN_i, for register r and time t. The store decision variable $STN_{i,r,t} = 1$ implies that there is a spill store of the live range TN_i in register r at time instant t. The store decision variable is defined only for a subset of the time steps in the kernel. More specifically, it is defined only for time step $t \in [T_i^{def} \oplus lat_i, T_i^{end} \ominus lat_{store} \ominus lat_{load}]$ where lat_i, lat_{store} and lat_{load} are latencies of instruction i, store and load respectively. This is because the spill store can be scheduled only after $T_i^{def} \oplus lat_i$. Further the spill store must be scheduled $lat_{store} + lat_{load}$ cycles before the last use. Since all time steps should be within $[0, II - 1]$, the add and subtract operations are performed modulo II and represented as $\oplus$ and $\ominus$ respectively. The store decision variable $STN_{i,r,t}$ is defined for time steps $t \in storeset(i)$ where $storeset(i) = [T_i^{def} \oplus lat_i, T_i^{end} \ominus lat_{load} \ominus lat_{store}]$.

2. Load decision variable: We introduce load decision variable $LTN_{i,r,t}$ for every live range TN_i, register r, and time step t. The load decision variable $LTN_{i,r,t} = 1$ implies that there is a spill load of the live range TN_i scheduled at time instant t. The load decision variable $LTN_{i,r,t}$ is defined for time steps $t \in loadset(i)$ where $loadset(i) = [T_i^{def} \oplus lat_i \oplus lat_{store}, T_i^{end} \ominus lat_{load}]$.

We illustrate the introduction of live range and spill decision variables with a specific example in Figure 2. An instruction which defines the value of a temporary variable TN_1 is scheduled at time 0. The last use of TN_1 is scheduled at time 9. The liveness, spill load and store decision variables introduced corresponding to register R0 are shown in Figure 2. In this example, the latency of the instruction producing the live range TN_1 is 1, and that of store or load is 2. To represent whether the live range TN_1 is live in register R0 at various time steps during its live range, we use decision variables $TN_{1,0,0}, \ldots TN_{1,0,9}$. The store decision variables are defined for time steps $[1, 5]$. We do not define the store decision variable at time instant 0 since it is the definition time. Similarly the store decision variable is not defined for time steps $[6, 9]$ as splitting the live range beyond time step 5 does not result in a meaningful spill load to be scheduled before the last use of TN_1. Similarly we do not create spill load decision variables at time steps $[0, 2]$, since spill store would not have completed by that time, and at time steps $[8, 9]$, as the spill load would not complete before the last use at 9.

Time		Decision variables for register R0		
0	$TN_1 =$	$TN_{1,0,0}$		
1		$TN_{1,0,1}$	$STN_{1,0,1}$	
2		$TN_{1,0,2}$	$STN_{1,0,2}$	
3		$TN_{1,0,3}$	$STN_{1,0,3}$	$LTN_{1,0,3}$
4		$TN_{1,0,4}$	$STN_{1,0,4}$	$LTN_{1,0,4}$
5	$= .. \text{ op } TN_1$	$TN_{1,0,5}$	$STN_{1,0,5}$	$LTN_{1,0,5}$
6		$TN_{1,0,6}$		$LTN_{1,0,6}$
7		$TN_{1,0,7}$		$LTN_{1,0,7}$
8		$TN_{1,0,8}$		
9	$= .. \text{ op } TN_1$	$TN_{1,0,9}$		

Fig. 2. Decision variables associated with live range TN_1 and register 0 with an II=10

3.2 Constraints

Having discussed the liveness, spill store and spill load decision variables corresponding to each time instant and register, we now explain how register allocation and spill code scheduling can be formulated using a set of constraints. Satisfaction of these constraints results in a schedule with valid register allocation and appropriate spill code placement.

Must-Allocate Definition Constraint: The Must-Allocate Definition Constraints ensure that a register is allocated to a live range when the live range is defined. That is, for each instruction that produces a value, a register must be allocated to the live range. If I is the set of instructions that produce a result value and TN_i be the temporary variable corresponding to instruction $i \in I$, the following must-allocate definition constraint must be satisfied.

$$\sum_{r \in R} TN_{i,r,t} = 1 \quad \forall i \in I \text{ and } t = T_i^{def} \tag{1}$$

There are exactly $|I|$ constraints produced by the above equation. For the example shown in Figure 2, corresponding to TN_1, the following must-allocate definition constraint must be satisfied.

$$\sum_{r \in R} TN_{1,r,0} = 1$$

Must-Allocate Use Constraint: Must-Allocate Use Constraints ensure that a live range is in a register at the time instant where there is an use. Let use(TN_i) represent the set of instructions that use the temporary variable TN_i produced by instruction i. The live range TN_i must be available in a register at time instant t corresponding to its use since we assume a load-store architecture.

For each instruction $j \in use(TN_i)$, scheduled at time instant t,

$$\sum_{r \in R} TN_{i,r,t} - \sum_{r,t'} LTN_{i,r,t'} \geq 1 \quad for \ all \ t = T_j^{def} \ and \ j \in use(TN_i) \qquad (2)$$

where $t' \in (t \ominus lat_{load}, \ t]$. There are exactly $\sum_{i \in I} |use(TN_i)|$ constraints corresponding to the above equation. We refer to these as must-allocate use constraints.

For the example shown in Figure 2, corresponding to TN_1, the following must-allocate use constraints must be satisfied.

$$\sum_{r \in R} TN_{1,r,5} - \sum_{r \in R} (LTN_{1,r,4} + LTN_{1,r,5}) \geq 1; \quad \sum_{r \in R} TN_{1,r,9} \geq 1$$

At-most Single Store Constraints: The live range TN_i need to be stored at-most once. For every instruction $i \in I$, at-most one store constraint is given by

$$\sum_{t} \sum_{r \in R} STN_{i,r,t} \leq 1 \qquad (3)$$

where t is in the range $[(T_i^{def} \oplus lat_i), (T_i^{end} \ominus lat_{load} \ominus lat_{store})]$.

As the objective minimizes the spill loads and stores, this constraint is redundant. However, this constraint reduced the solution time taken by the ILP solver.

Store Before Load Constraints: A spill load can be scheduled for a live range provided there is an earlier spill store for that temporary name. At every time instant where a spill load is possible, there must be a store which has been scheduled earlier. For every spill load corresponding to live range TN_i, the following constraints must be satisfied.

$$\sum_{r} LTN_{i,r,t} \leq \sum_{r} \sum_{t'} STN_{i,r,t'} \quad \forall t \in loadset(i) \qquad (4)$$

where t' is in the range $[(T_i^{def} \oplus lat_i), (t \ominus lat_{store})]$. There are exactly $|loadset(i)|$ such constraints for each TN_i

In Figure 2, each of the spill loads corresponding to time steps [3, 7] must satisfy the following constraints. We have assumed a store latency of 2.

$$\sum_{r \in R} LTN_{1,r,3} \leq \sum_{r \in R} STN_{1,r,1}$$

$$\sum_{r \in R} LTN_{1,r,4} \leq \sum_{r \in R} (STN_{1,r,1} + STN_{1,r,2})$$

$$\sum_{r \in R} LTN_{1,r,5} \leq \sum_{r \in R} (STN_{1,r,1} + STN_{1,r,2} + STN_{1,r,3})$$

$$\sum_{r \in R} LTN_{1,r,6} \leq \sum_{r \in R} (STN_{1,r,1} + STN_{1,r,2} + STN_{1,r,3} + STN_{1,r,4})$$

$$\sum_{r \in R} LTN_{1,r,7} \leq \sum_{r \in R} (STN_{1,r,1} + STN_{1,r,2} + STN_{1,r,3} + STN_{1,r,4} + STN_{1,r,5})$$

Spill Load Store Constraints: In order to schedule spill code in the compact schedule, we have introduced store and load decision variables at multiple time instants. The following set of constraints ensure that there are no unnecessary spill code instructions and formulation generated schedule is valid.

At each time instant t for any live range, if $t \in loadset(i)$ and $t \in storeset(i)$, then the store before load and at-most only one store constraints ensure that both load and store cannot be scheduled at t. For each store decision variable at time t corresponding to live range TN_i, a store can actually take place at that instant only if the variable is in the register.

$$STN_{i,r,t} \leq TN_{i,r,t} \quad \forall r \in R \ and \ \forall t \in \ storeset(i) \tag{5}$$

In Figure 2, the following constraints corresponding to store of live range TN_1 in register 0, at time steps $[1, 5]$ must be satisfied.

$$STN_{1,0,1} \leq TN_{1,0,1}; \quad STN_{1,0,2} \leq TN_{1,0,2}; \quad STN_{1,0,3} \leq TN_{1,0,3};$$

$$STN_{1,0,4} \leq TN_{1,0,4}; \quad STN_{1,0,5} \leq TN_{1,0,5};$$

After a spill store, the live range in a register may continue to exist or cease to exist. But if there is a load in the subsequent time instant, then the load constraints can bring the live range back into existence in the register. If a spill store is possible for live range TN_i at time instant t and spill load is not possible at time instant $t + 1$, then the following constraints need to be satisfied.

$$TN_{i,r,t\oplus1} \leq TN_{i,r,t} \quad \forall r \in R, for \ all \ t \in storeset(i) \ and \ t \oplus 1 \notin loadset(i) \tag{6}$$

In Figure 2, the following constraints must be satisfied corresponding to the live range TN_1 at time instant 1

$$TN_{1,0,2} \leq TN_{1,0,1}$$

The spill load brings back the live range into the register. There is no necessity of a spill load for any live range TN_i corresponding to register r if the live range is already in the register r. Further, a temporary name is live in a register r at time t either if it was live at time step $t \ominus 1$ or if a spill load is scheduled in time step t. For a spill load at time instant t, the following constraints need to be satisfied.

$$TN_{i,r,t} \leq TN_{i,r,t\ominus1} + LTN_{i,r,t} \quad \forall r \in R, \forall t \in loadset(i) \tag{7}$$

In Figure 2, the spill loads at time steps [3, 7] in register 0 must satisfy the following constraints.

$$TN_{1,0,3} \leq TN_{1,0,2} + LTN_{1,0,3}; \quad TN_{1,0,4} \leq TN_{1,0,3} + LTN_{1,0,4}$$

$$TN_{1,0,5} \leq TN_{1,0,4} + LTN_{1,0,5}; \quad TN_{1,0,6} \leq TN_{1,0,5} + LTN_{1,0,6}$$

$$TN_{1,0,7} \leq TN_{1,0,6} + LTN_{1,0,7}$$

If a spill load is not possible at time instant t, i.e $t \notin loadset(i)$ and a spill store is not possible at time instant $t \ominus 1$, i.e $t{\ominus}1 \notin storeset(i)$, then the following continuation constraints must be satisfied.

$$TN_{i,r,t} \leq TN_{i,r,t\ominus1} \quad \forall r \in R, for\ all\ t \notin loadset(i) \wedge t \ominus 1 \notin storeset(i) \quad (8)$$

In Figure 2, the continuation constraints corresponding to time instants 1, 8 and 9 for register 0 and live range TN_i are

$$TN_{1,0,1} \leq TN_{1,0,0}; \quad TN_{1,0,8} \leq TN_{1,0,7}; \quad TN_{1,0,9} \leq TN_{1,0,8}$$

Interference Constraints: It is important to ensure that the same register is not allocated to multiple live ranges. Interference constraints ensure that at any instant of time, a register holds a single live range. It is sufficient to ensure that after each live range definition, the register holds a single live range. At time instant t which is the definition time of live range TN_i, the following constraints must be satisfied for each register r

$$\sum_j TN_{j,r,t} \leq 1 \tag{9}$$

where $TN_{j,r,t} = 0$ for $t \notin [T_j^{def}, T_j^{end}]$.

Functional Unit Constraints: The spill loads and store generated require memory functional units. Thus a spill load or a store can be scheduled at a particular instant t provided there is a free memory unit available. Hence for scheduling spill loads or stores, the following memory unit constraints need to be satisfied for each time slot t' $\in$ [0, II-1].

$$\sum_{i,r} LTN_{i,r,t} + \sum_{j,r} STN_{j,r,t} \leq M \quad for\ all\ t \in [0, II - 1] \tag{10}$$

TN_i is the live range with $t \in$ loadset(i) and TN_j is the live range with $t \in$ storeset(j). M is the number of memory units available for spill loads and stores after the memory requirements of instructions that are scheduled at time instant t in the kernel are satisfied. The above constraint ensures that sum of all spill loads and stores scheduled at any time instant t in the kernel is lesser than or equal to the number of free memory units available.

3.3   Objective Function

The objective function is to minimize the number of spill loads and stores.

$$Minimize: \sum_{i,r,t}(STN_{i,r,t} + LTN_{i,r,t}) \tag{11}$$

4   Simplified Formulation

The previous formulation can be simplified by omitting the r indices from the spill load and store decision variables. In this formulation, we decide whether a spill load or a store is necessary at a given time step without considering which register the store or load should use. The constraints are suitably modified to reflect the same. The register used by the spill store and loads can be easily inferred from the $TN_{i,r,t}$ variables as a post-processing step. The simplified formulation is given below:

$$Minimize \sum_{i,t}(STN_{i,t} + LTN_{i,t})$$

$$\sum_{r\in R} TN_{i,r,t} = 1 \qquad \forall i \in I \text{ and } t = T_i^{def} \tag{12}$$

$$\sum_{r} TN_{i,r,t} - \sum_{t'} LTN_{i,t'} \geq 1 \qquad \forall t = T_j^{def} \text{ and} \tag{13}$$

$$j \in use(TN_i)$$
$$t' \in (t \ominus lat_{load}, t]$$

$$LTN_{i,t} - \sum_{t''} STN_{i,t''} \leq 0 \qquad \forall t \in loadset(i) \; \forall i \tag{14}$$

$$t'' \in [T_i^{def} + lat_i, t \ominus lat_{store}]$$

$$STN_{i,t} - \sum_{r} TN_{i,r,t} \leq 0 \qquad \forall t \in storeset(i) \; \forall i \tag{15}$$

$$TN_{i,r,t} - TN_{i,r,t\ominus 1} - LTN_{i,t} \leq 0 \qquad \forall t \in loadset(i) \; \forall i \tag{16}$$

$$\sum_{r} TN_{i,r,t} - \sum_{r} TN_{i,r,t\ominus 1} - LTN_{i,t} \leq 0 \qquad \forall t \in loadset(i) \; \forall i \tag{17}$$

$$\sum_{j} TN_{j,r,t} \leq 1 \qquad \forall t \in [0, II - 1] \; \forall r \tag{18}$$

$$\sum_{i} LTN_{i,t} + \sum_{j} STN_{j,t} \leq M \qquad \forall t \in [0, II - 1] \tag{19}$$

$$TN_{i,r,t\oplus 1} - TN_{i,r,t} \leq 0 \qquad \forall t \oplus 1 \notin loadset(i) \; \forall i \; \forall r \tag{20}$$

Equation 17 ensures that each spill load loads the live range in at-most one register.

5   Experimental Evaluation

5.1   Experimental Methodology

We have used the SUIF [12] as the compiler front end for the benchmarks. For the compiler back end, we have used Trimaran [13] compilation and simulation environment for VLIW architectures. The data dependence graphs are generated using the Trimaran's back end . The initial modulo schedule is obtained using an integer linear program formulation [10]. The machine architecture used in the formulation is a load-store architecture with 3 memory units, 3 integer units and 4 floating point units. For the constructed schedule, modulo variable expansion [14] is performed to ensure that no live range is longer than II. We then generate the formulation proposed in this paper to perform register allocation and necessary spill code generation and scheduling. We have considered architectures with 16 and 32 registers. The integer linear programming formulation is solved using the CPLEX 9.0 solver [5] running on a Pentium 4, operating at 3.06 GHz with 4 GB RAM. A CPU-time limit of 600 seconds is used for solving our integer linear program. The loops in which the integer linear program timed out are not considered for evaluation.

5.2   Results

We compare our approach with the best performing heuristic [21], viz spilling uses, with a quantity factor of 0.5 and a traffic factor of 0.3. The quantity factor is used for deciding the number of spill candidates and traffic factor is used for the selection of spill candidates. We refer to the above heuristic as SU and our formulation as ILP.

Spill Code. The amount of spill code introduced impacts the code quality of the schedule. We evaluated the amount of spill code generated by ILP and SU. In this result, we do not consider amount of spill code generated with the loops requiring an increase in II with SU as it is not fair to compare schedules with

Table 1. Spill code and prevention of II increase with 32 registers

Benchmark	#loops	#loops with reg pressure	Total spill code ILP	SU	% decrease in spill code(ILP)	#loops without II increase(ILP)	% loops without II increase(ILP)
168.wupwise	25	12	96	123	21.95	1	8.33
179.art	40	15	46	57	19.3	1	6.67
183.equake	42	9	44	53	16.98	1	11.11
188.ammp	46	14	56	63	11.11	2	14.29
200.sixtrack	46	9	70	84	16.67	1	11.11
Perfect Club	69	31	191	237	19.41	4	12.9
Total	268	90	503	617	18.48	10	11.11

Table 2. Spill code and prevention of II increase with 16 registers

Benchmark	#loops	#loops with reg pressure	Total spill code ILP	Total spill code SU	% decrease in spill code(ILP)	#loops without II increase(ILP)	% loops without II increase(ILP)
168.wupwise	25	19	128	152	15.79	0	0
179.art	40	26	85	106	19.81	1	3.85
183.equake	42	19	88	104	15.38	4	21.05
188.ammp	46	21	88	95	7.37	2	9.52
200.sixtrack	46	23	112	131	14.50	3	13.04
Perfect Club	69	49	313	346	9.54	9	18.37
Total	268	157	814	934	12.85	19	12.10

different initiation intervals. Table 1 and Table 2 report the amount of spill generated for an architecture with 32 and 16 registers respectively. Though number of loops with higher register pressure (greater than the available registers) is small, we find that there is fairly large spill code being generated. The amount of spill code reduction with *ILP* when compared to *SU* ranges from 11.11% to 21.95% for 32 registers and it ranges from 7.37% to 19.81% for 16 registers. On an average *ILP* produces 18.48% less spill code on an average for an architecture with 32 registers and 12.85% less spill code on an average for an architecture with 16 registers.

Initiation Interval. The throughput of a software pipelined loop is measured in terms of the initiation interval. Table 1 and Table 2 report the number of loops requiring an increase in the initiation interval in *SU* and do not require an increase in II while using *ILP*. *ILP* eliminates the need for an increase in II when compared to *SU* in 6.67% to 14.29% of the loops in various benchmarks. On an average, *ILP* eliminates an increase in II in 11% of the loops for an architecture with 32 registers and 12% of the loops for 16 registers.

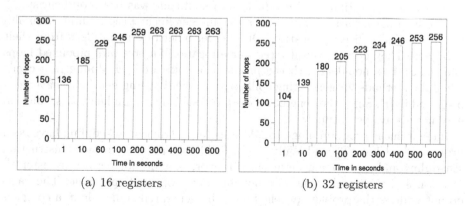

(a) 16 registers   (b) 32 registers

Fig. 3. Solution time taken by ILP

In summary, we observe that our ILP approach is able to reduce the amount of spill code by 18.48% and eliminate an increase in II by 11.11% on average among 90 loops on an architecture with 32 registers.

Solution Time. In Figure 3(a) and Figure 3(b), we report the time taken by the ILP, where the X-axis represents the time taken and Y-axis, the number of loops for which the solution can be found with the given time. For example, for the case of 16 registers, 136 out of 268 loops take less than one second each. The arithmetic mean of the time taken by ILP for each loop is 18.44 seconds in the case of 16 registers and is 77.79 seconds in the case of 32 registers.

6   Related Work

Software pipelining has been extensively studied and few of the contributions in this area are in [6,7,14,17,19]. A comprehensive survey is available in [2]. A considerable amount of work has been done to minimize the register requirements of the the software pipeline schedule. Among these, Huff [11] uses slack scheduling and tries to minimize the combined register pressure. In [8], ILP formulation for generating the schedule has been proposed and minimization of the number of buffers required in such a scenario is addressed in [10]. A number of modulo scheduling heuristics that reduce the register pressure and generate schedules with smallest number of registers have been proposed in [15]. All these do not consider the dual problem of scheduling with a given number of registers.

Register allocation for software pipelined loops was proposed by Rau et al. [18]. They consider an architecture that incorporates rotating registers. However spill code generation and scheduling was not considered. Ning et al. [16] have proposed an algorithmic framework for concurrent scheduling and register allocation. Their approach estimates the register requirement with the help of buffers. Zalamea et al. [21] have described methods for generating spill code when the register pressure is greater than the number of registers. But they did not consider register allocation and introduction of spill code was based on heuristics.

Goodwin et al. [9] have proposed a 0-1 integer linear programming formulation for global register allocation. Our model inherits certain ideas from their approach. They do not consider register allocation for software pipelined loops and hence does not deal with the problem of spill code scheduling in a cyclic schedule. Methods for generating spill code on-the-fly using heuristics have been proposed in [1]. Since the generation of spill code is based on heuristics, solution may not always be optimal.

Integer linear programming formulations for instruction scheduling have been proposed by Chang [3] and Wilken [20]. In [3], the authors consider instruction scheduling and spill code generation. However, they do not perform register allocation and their technique does not guarantee optimal spill code. They also do not address the problem of scheduling the generated spill code in a compact cyclic schedule. Our work, for the first time proposes an integrated formulation for register allocation, optimal spill code generation and scheduling in software pipelined schedules.

7 Conclusions

The paper presents an optimal method for integrated register allocation and spill code scheduling in software pipelined loops, using a 0-1 integer linear programming formulation. We formulate it as an integer linear program because the selection of a spill candidate based on a certain heuristic can generate extraneous spill code, which in turn may necessitate an increase in the initiation interval. The formulation serves as a framework with which various heuristics can be evaluated. Experiments show that our formulation outperforms the best performing heuristic proposed in [21]

- By eliminating an increase in the initiation interval in 11.11% of the 90 loops that had sufficient register pressure for an architecture with 32 registers and in 12% of the cases with 157 loops on a machine with 16 registers.
- By generating on an average, 18.48% less spill code for an architecture with 32 registers and 12.85 % less spill code for an architecture with 16 registers.

Acknowledgments

The authors are thankful to the members of the High Performance Computing Laboratory for their useful comments and discussions. The authors are also thankful to the anonymous reviewer for suggesting the simplified formulation. The first author acknowledges the partial support provided by the Philips research fellowship.

References

1. Alex Aleta, Josep M. Codina, Antonio Gonzalez, and David Kaeli. Demystifying on-the-fly spill code. *SIGPLAN Not.*, 40(6):180–189, 2005.
2. Vicki H. Allan, Reese B. Jones, Randall M. Lee, and Stephen J. Allan. Software pipelining. *ACM Comput. Surv.*, 27(3):367–432, 1995.
3. C.M Chen C.M Chang and C.T King. Using integer linear programming for instruction scheduling and register allocation in multi-issue processors. *Computers and Mathematics with Applications*, 34(9):1–14, 1997.
4. Keith D. Cooper and L. Taylor Simpson. Live range splitting in a graph coloring register allocator. In *CC '98: Proceedings of the 7th International Conference on Compiler Construction*, pages 174–187, London, UK, 1998. Springer-Verlag.
5. ILOG CPLEX:. http://www.ilog.com.
6. James C. Dehnert and Ross A. Towle. Compiling for the cydra 5. *J. Supercomput.*, 7(1-2):181–227, 1993.
7. Kemal Ebcioglu and Alexandru Nicolau. A global resource-constrained parallelization technique. In *ICS '89: Proceedings of the 3rd international conference on Supercomputing*, pages 154–163, New York, NY, USA, 1989. ACM Press.

8. Paul Feautrier. Fine-grain scheduling under resource constraints. In *LCPC '94: Proceedings of the 7th International Workshop on Languages and Compilers for Parallel Computing*, pages 1–15, London, UK, 1995. Springer-Verlag.
9. David W. Goodwin and Kent D. Wilken. Optimal and near-optimal global register allocations using 0-1 integer programming. *Softw. Pract. Exper.*, 26(8):929–965, 1996.
10. R. Govindarajan, Erik R. Altman, and Guang R. Gao. A framework for resource-constrained rate-optimal software pipelining. *IEEE Transactions on Parallel and Distributed Systems*, 07(11):1133–1149, 1996.
11. Richard A. Huff. Lifetime-sensitive modulo scheduling. In *SIGPLAN Conference on Programming Language Design and Implementation*, pages 258–267, 1993.
12. SUIF Compiler Infrastructure. http://suif.stanford.edu/suif/.
13. Trimaran: An infrastructure for research in instruction level parallelism. http://www.trimaran.org.
14. M. Lam. Software pipelining: an effective scheduling technique for vliw machines. In *PLDI '88: Proceedings of the ACM SIGPLAN 1988 conference on Programming Language design and Implementation*, pages 318–328, New York, NY, USA, 1988. ACM Press.
15. Josep Llosa, Mateo Valero, and Eduard Ayguade. Heuristics for register-constrained software pipelining. In *MICRO 29: Proceedings of the 29th annual ACM/IEEE international symposium on Microarchitecture*, pages 250–261, Washington, DC, USA, 1996. IEEE Computer Society.
16. Qi Ning and Guang R. Gao. A novel framework of register allocation for software pipelining. In *Conference Record of the Twentieth Annual ACM SIGPLAN-SIGACT Symposium on Principles of Programming Languages*, pages 29–42, Charleston, South Carolina, 1993.
17. B. R. Rau and C. D. Glaeser. Some scheduling techniques and an easily schedulable horizontal architecture for high performance scientific computing. In *MICRO 14: Proceedings of the 14th annual workshop on Microprogramming*, pages 183–198, Piscataway, NJ, USA, 1981. IEEE Press.
18. B. R. Rau, M. Lee, P. P. Tirumalai, and M. S. Schlansker. Register allocation for software pipelined loops. *SIGPLAN Not.*, 27(7):283–299, 1992.
19. B. Ramakrishna Rau. Iterative modulo scheduling: an algorithm for software pipelining loops. In *MICRO 27: Proceedings of the 27th annual international symposium on Microarchitecture*, pages 63–74, New York, NY, USA, 1994. ACM Press.
20. Kent Wilken, Jack Liu, and Mark Heffernan. Optimal instruction scheduling using integer programming. In *PLDI '00: Proceedings of the ACM SIGPLAN 2000 conference on Programming language design and implementation*, pages 121–133, New York, NY, USA, 2000. ACM Press.
21. Javier Zalamea, Josep Llosa, Eduard Ayguade, and Mateo Valero. Improved spill code generation for software pipelined loops. In *PLDI '00: Proceedings of the ACM SIGPLAN 2000 conference on Programming language design and implementation*, pages 134–144, New York, NY, USA, 2000. ACM Press.

Extended Linear Scan: An Alternate Foundation for Global Register Allocation

Vivek Sarkar[1] and Rajkishore Barik[2]

[1] IBM T.J. Watson Research Center
vsarkar@us.ibm.com
[2] IBM India Research Laboratory
rajbarik@in.ibm.com

Abstract. In this paper, we extend past work on Linear Scan register allocation, and propose two *Extended Linear Scan* (*ELS*) algorithms that retain the compile-time efficiency of past Linear Scan algorithms while delivering performance that can match or surpass that of Graph Coloring. Specifically, this paper makes the following contributions:

- We highlight three fundamental *theoretical limitations* in using Graph Coloring as a foundation for global register allocation, and introduce a *basic* Extended Linear Scan algorithm, ELS_0, which addresses all three limitations for the problem of Spill-Free Register Allocation.
- We introduce the ELS_1 algorithm which extends ELS_0 to obtain a greedy algorithm for the problem of Register Allocation with Total Spills.
- Finally, we present experimental results to compare the Graph Coloring and Extended Linear Scan algorithms. Our results show that the compile-time speedups for ELS_1 relative to GC were significant, and varied from 15× to 68×. In addition, the resulting execution time improved by up to 5.8%, with an average improvement of 2.3%.

Together, these results show that Extended Linear Scan is promising as an alternate foundation for global register allocation, compared to Graph Coloring, due to its compile-time scalability without loss of execution time performance.

1 Introduction

Register allocation is the process of determining which variables (symbolic registers) should be held in physical machine registers at different program points and which should be *spilled*. *Register assignment* is the sub-process of identifying which specific machine registers should be used at different program points to hold which variables. The scope of register allocation may be *local* (restricted to a small region of a procedure, such as an innermost loop or an extended basic block), *global* (performed on an entire procedure) or *interprocedural* (performed across multiple procedures). Ever since its inclusion in the first compiler for FORTRAN five decades ago, register allocation has retained its role as one of the most important optimizations performed by compilers for high-level programming languages, and the algorithms used for register allocation have matured accordingly.

Starting with the seminal paper by Chaitin [5], the dominant approaches for global register allocation have been based on the idea of building an *Interference Graph* (IG)

S. Krishnamurthi and M. Odersky (Eds.): CC 2007, LNCS 4420, pp. 141–155, 2007.
© Springer-Verlag Berlin Heidelberg 2007

for variables in a procedure, and employing *Graph Coloring* (GC) heuristics to perform the allocation. Significant advances have been achieved over these years through the introduction of new coloring, spilling, and coalescing heuristics based on the IG *e.g.,* [2, 3, 4, 6, 7, 12]. However, a key limitation that underlies all register allocation algorithms based on Graph Coloring is that the number of variables that can be processed by the register allocation phase in an optimizing compiler is limited by the size of the IG. The number of edges in the IG can be quadratic in the number of nodes in the worst case, and is usually observed to be super-linear in practice. The results in Section 4 show that the IG size is typically $O(n^{1.5})$ for n nodes. This non-linear complexity in space and time limits the code size that can be optimized and thereby has a damping effect on aggressive use of code transformations that can potentially increase opportunities for register allocation, such as *variable renaming*, *loop unrolling* and *procedure inlining*, but which also have the side effect of increasing the size of the IG. Finally, the non-linear complexity makes it prohibitive to use Graph Coloring for register allocation in just-in-time and dynamic compilers, where compile-time overhead contributes directly to run-time.

Recent work on *Linear Scan* algorithms [14, 16] has led to more efficient algorithms for global register allocation that use data structures with size that is linear in the number of variables. The results reported thus far suggest that Linear Scan should be used when compile-time space and time overhead is at a premium (as in dynamic compilation), but an algorithm based on Graph Coloring should be used when the best runtime performance is desired.

This paper extends past work on Linear Scan register allocation, and proposes two *Extended Linear Scan* (*ELS*) algorithms that retain the compile-time efficiency of past Linear Scan algorithms while delivering performance that can match or surpass that of Graph Coloring. The focus of this paper is on revisiting the premise that Graph Coloring is the most suitable foundation for global register allocation, and on evaluating *ELS* as an alternate foundation. Specifically, this paper makes the following contributions:

1. It highlights three fundamental *theoretical limitations* in using Graph Coloring as a foundation for global register allocation (Section 2.2).
2. It introduces the *basic* Extended Linear Scan algorithm, ELS_0 (Section 2.3), which addresses all three limitations for the problem of Spill-Free Register Allocation.
3. It introduces the ELS_1 algorithm (Section 3), which extends ELS_0 to obtain a greedy algorithm for the problem of Register Allocation with Total Spills (RATS).
4. It includes experimental results for eight SPECint2000 benchmarks to compare the Graph Coloring and Extended Linear Scan algorithms (Section 4). The results show that the space and time used by ELS_1 is significantly smaller than those used by GC – the compile-time speedups for ELS_1 relative to GC varied from $15\times$ to $68\times$. In addition, the runtime performance improved by up to 5.8% for ELS_1 relative to GC, with an average improvement of 2.3%. This is a significant improvement over past Linear Scan algorithms which delivered compile-time efficiency but lagged behind Graph Coloring in runtime performance.

Together, these results show that Extended Linear Scan is promising as an alternate foundation for global register allocation, compared to Graph Coloring, due to its compile-time scalability without loss of execution time performance. Our expectation is that the coloring, spilling, and coalescing heuristics that have been developed over the past decades as refinements to Graph Coloring, will be equally amenable to adaptation in an Extended Linear Scan foundation.

2   Spill-Free Register Allocation

This section introduces the Spill-Free Register Allocation (SFRA) problem as a theoretical foundation for comparing the fundamental differences between the Graph Coloring and Extended Linear Scan algorithms.

Spill-Free Register Allocation (SFRA): Given a set of symbolic registers, $\Re$, and k physical registers, determine if it is possible to assign each symbolic register $s \in \Re$ to a physical register, $reg(s, P)$ at each program point P where s is live. If so, report the register assignments, including any register-to-register copy statements that need to be inserted. If not, report that no feasible solution exists.   □

Two key assumptions in the specification of the SFRA problem are as follows. First, two "program points" are defined for each instruction, i_k. i_k^- denotes the point at which the input operands of instruction i_k are read, and i_k^+ denotes the point at which the output operands of instruction i_k are written. Second, we assume that register allocation is performed as a separate pass from instruction scheduling — instruction scheduling considerations for register allocation [1, 9, 11, 13] are beyond the scope of this paper.

2.1   Basic Graph Coloring Solution to the SFRA Problem

Figure 1 summarizes the basic Graph Coloring algorithm for Spill-Free Register Allocation as described by Chaitin [5]. The correctness of this algorithm has also been established earlier in [5]. It is easy to see that the algorithm requires $O(|\Re|^2)$ space, since the interference graph can be quadratic in the number of symbolic registers. The major overhead in execution time occurs in constructing the interference graph in step 2, which takes $O(|\Re|^2)$ time. (This assumes that the liveness information in input 3 has been precomputed in a way such that each instance of the *simultaneously live* condition in step 2 can be computed in constant time. Otherwise, the execution time for step 2 could be larger than $O(|\Re|^2)$.)

2.2   Theoretical Limitations of Graph Coloring Solution

In this section, we summarize three fundamental theoretical limitations in using Graph Coloring as a foundation for global register allocation.

First, Graph Coloring is a *more limited problem than Register Allocation*. Transforming Register Allocation to Graph Coloring ensures that finding a k-coloring of an Interference Graph will lead to a feasible solution to the SFRA problem, but the converse is not true *i.e., it is not necessary that an SFRA problem instance for which a solution exists can be transformed into a Graph Coloring problem for which a solution exists*. Consider the two examples in Figure 2, assuming that there are two physical registers available. In each case, a spill-free solution exists for the SFRA problem instance, but not for the Graph Coloring instance. In Example #2, the solution to the SFRA problem includes a register move instruction in the loop, but a solution based on Graph Coloring

Inputs:

1. *IR*, intermediate representation for program to be optimized.
2. $\Re$, set of *symbolic registers* that are candidates for allocation.
3. Liveness information that can be used to query if a symbolic register $s \in \Re$ is live at program point P
4. k, number of registers available for allocation.

Outputs:

1. *Success*, a boolean value that indicates whether or not a spill-free allocation was found for all symbolic registers in $\Re$.
2. If *Success* = *true*, then *reg*(*s*) specifies the physical register assigned to symbolic register *s*, for all $s \in \Re$. (For basic Graph Coloring, no register moves are necessary because the register assignment will be the same for *s* at all program points.)

Algorithm:

1. Initialize an empty undirected *Interference Graph* (IG) with one node for each symbolic register.
2. **for each** pair of distinct symbolic registers, s_i and s_j, such that there exists a program point P where both s_i and s_j are simultaneously live **do**
   (a) Insert an edge in IG between node s_i and s_j
   end for
3. /* "Simplify" step in graph coloring heuristic */
   Initialize $T :=$ an empty stack;
4. Initialize $IG' :=$ copy of IG;
5. **while** $\exists$ a node s_i in IG' with degree $< k$ **do**
   (a) Delete node s_i from IG'
   (b) Push s_i on T
   end while
6. **if** IG' is now an empty graph **then** *Success* := *true*;
   else *Success* := *false*; **return**;
   end if
7. /* "Assignment" step in graph coloring heuristic */
   Initialize $reg(s_i) := null$ for each node s_i in IG;
   while T is non-empty **do**
   (a) $s_i := pop(T)$;
   (b) $reg(s_i) :=$ any register in $1 \ldots k$ that is distinct from $reg(s_j)$ for all nodes s_j that are adjacent to s_i in IG;
   end while

Fig. 1. Overview of Graph Coloring algorithm for Spill-Free Register Allocation

instead inserts a spill instruction in the loop. It is of course well known (*e.g.*, [2]) that *renaming* of variables or *live-range splitting* can be performed to obtain spill-free solutions with Graph Coloring for the examples in Figure 2. The observation being made here is that these transformations are orthogonal to Graph Coloring and are equally

SFRA problem instance #1: Find a spill-free register allocation for symbolic registers s_A, s_B, s_C in the program shown below, assuming that there are $k = 2$ physical registers available.

```
switch ( ... ) {
                case 0:                    case 1:                    case 2:
        i₁:  sₐ := ...          i₄:  s_B := ...          i₇:  sₐ := ...
        i₂:  s_B := ...          i₅:  s_C := ...          i₈:  s_C := ...
        i₃:  ... := sₐ op s_B     i₆:  ... := s_B op s_C    i₉:  ... := sₐ op s_C
             break;                   break;                   break;
}
```

Graph Coloring problem instance: the Interference Graph is a complete clique for the three nodes s_A, s_B, s_C, and is therefore not 2-colorable.

SFRA solution: A simple solution exists to the above SFRA problem instance as follows, assuming that the two physical registers available are r_1 and r_2. No register moves are necessary for this solution:

$reg(s_A, [i_1^+, i_3^-]) = r_1,\ reg(s_B, [i_1^+, i_3^-]) = r_2,\ reg(s_B, [i_4^+, i_6^-]) = r_1,\ reg(s_C, [i_4^+, i_6^-]) = r_2,$
$reg(s_A, [i_7^+, i_9^-]) = r_1, reg(s_C, [i_7^+, i_9^-]) = r_2.$

SFRA problem instance #2: Find a spill-free register allocation for symbolic registers s_A, s_B, s_C in the program shown below, assuming $k = 2$ physical registers.

```
i₁:     s_C := ...
        /* Start of loop */
i₂:     sₐ := ...
i₃:     ... := s_C op ...
i₄:     s_B := ...
i₅:     ... := sₐ op ...
i₆:     s_C := ...
i₇:     ... := s_B op ...
i₈:     if s_C <= 0 goto i₁₀
i₉:     goto i₂
        /* End of loop */
i₁₀:    ...
```

Graph Coloring problem instance: the Interference Graph is again a complete clique for the three nodes s_A, s_B, s_C, and is therefore not 2-colorable.

SFRA solution: The following solution exists to the above SFRA problem instance assuming that there are two physical registers available, r_1 and r_2. It also requires the insertion of a register-move instruction $r_1 := r_2$ between instructions i_8 and i_9.

$reg(s_C, [i_1^+, i_3^-]) = r1, reg(s_A, [i_2^+, i_5^-]) = r2, reg(s_B, [i_4^+, i_7^-]) = r1, reg(s_C, [i_6^+, i_8^+]) = r2.$

Fig. 2. Examples #1 and #2 for which a solution exists to the SFRA problem instance, but no solution exists to the corresponding Graph Coloring instance

applicable to Extended Linear Scan (*ELS*). Also, these transformations come at the cost of increasing the number of nodes and edges in IG, thereby further exacerbating the time and space complexity of register allocation based on Graph Coloring.

Second, the $O(|\Re|^2)$ space requirement for constructing the interference graph is a *scalability limitation* because the overhead of any register allocation algorithm based on Graph Coloring becomes prohibitively large when compiling procedures with a large number of symbolic registers (especially after transformations such as procedure inlining and loop unrolling are performed), or in scenarios where compiler space and time overhead is at a premium (as in dynamic compilation).

Third, Graph Coloring is an *NP-hard* optimization problem (without even the guarantee of a constant performance bound), whereas an exact solution can be obtained for SFRA in time that is linear in the number of live intervals for all symbolic registers as shown below in Section 2.3.

Together these limitations suggest that the Graph Coloring formulation may have made the global register allocation algorithm harder to solve than necessary, and thereby provide the motivation for our work on Extended Linear Scan.

2.3 Basic Extended Linear Scan Algorithm, ELS_0

In this section, we introduce the basic Extended Linear Scan algorithm, ELS_0, for the SFRA problem. ELS_0 addresses the three limitations of Graph Coloring outlined in the previous section, and also serves as the foundation for the ELS_1 algorithm. A summary of the ELS_0 algorithm can be found in Figures 3 and 4. The *live range* of a symbolic register s is represented by an *Interval Set*, $\mathscr{I}(s)$. Each interval, $[P,Q]$ in $\mathscr{I}(s)$ represents a range of program points at which s is live. The interval set is a precise representation

Inputs: Same as in Figure 1 (*IR*, $\Re$, liveness information, k).
Outputs:

1. *Success*, a boolean value as in Figure 1.
2. If *Success* = *true*, then $reg(s, [P,Q])$ specifies the physical register assigned to symbolic register s, for all program points in interval $[P,Q] \in \mathscr{I}(s)$. This *reg* mapping can be used to easily compute $reg(s,x)$ for any program point x where s is live, by identifying the interval in $\mathscr{I}(s)$ that contains x.
3. Modified *IR* with insertion of register-move instructions to handle cases when different physical registers may be assigned to the same symbolic register in different intervals.

Data structure initialization:

1. Interval Set $\mathscr{I}(s)$ for each symbolic register s
2. $\mathscr{I} = \cup_{s \in \Re} \mathscr{I}(s)$, the set of all intervals in the program (each interval is labeled with its symbolic register)
3. *IEP*, the set of interval endpoints in $\mathscr{I}$
4. *numlive* := 0
5. *count*[P] := 0, for each point in *IEP*

Fig. 3. Inputs, Outputs, Initialization for Extended Linear Scan algorithm ELS_0 for Spill-Free Register Allocation (see Figure 4)

Algorithm:

1. **for each** program point P in *IEP*, in increasing order **do**
   (a) **for each** interval $[O,P] \in \mathscr{I}$ **do** *numlive--* **end for**
   (b) **for each** interval $[P,Q] \in \mathscr{I}$ **do** *numlive++* **end for**
   (c) *count*[P] := *numlive*
   end for
2. **if** ($\exists$ a program point P in *IEP* with *count*[P] > k) **then**
   (a) *Success* := *false*; **return**;
   end if
3. /* A feasible solution exists. Compute *reg* mapping and register-moves. */
   Success := *true*;
4. Initialize *avail* := set of all physical registers, $1 \ldots k$
5. **for each** program point P in *IEP*, in increasing order **do**
   (a) **for each** interval $[O,P] \in \mathscr{I}$ **do**
      i. *avail* := *avail* $\cup$ { r_j }, where r_j is the physical register that had been previously assigned to interval $[O,P]$
      end for
   (b) **for each** interval $[P,Q] \in \mathscr{I}$ **do**
      i. Let s := symbolic register corresponding to $[P,Q]$
      ii. Select a physical register r_j from *avail*, using the following heuristics:
         – If s is live at P, then prefer selecting r_j previously assigned to s, and
         – If program point P corresponds to a register-to-register copy statement of the form, $s := t$, then prefer selecting r_j reviously assigned to t.
      iii. $reg(s,[P,Q]) := r_j$ /* s is assigned r_j for all points in $[P,Q]$ */
      iv. *avail* := *avail* - { r_j } ;
   end for
6. /* Insert register move instructions as needed. */
   for each program point P **do**
   for each program point Q that is a control flow successor to P **do**
   (a) Initialize M to be an empty set of move instructions
   (b) **for each** symbolic reg. s such that s is live at P and Q **do**
      i. **if** $(reg(s,P) \neq reg(s,Q))$ **then**
         insert a move instruction "$reg(s,Q) := reg(s,P)$" into set M **end if**
      end for
   (c) Treat the move instructions in M as a directed graph G in which there is an edge from move instruction m_1 to move instruction m_2 if m_1 reads the register written by m_2
   (d) Compute the strongly connected components (SCC's) of directed graph G
   (e) For each SCC, create a sequence of move and xor instructions to implement its register moves without the use of a temporary register, and insert these instructions on the control flow edge from P to Q (as part of Output 3 in Figure 3)
   end for
   end for

Fig. 4. Overview of Extended Linear Scan algorithm ELS_0 for Spill-Free Register Allocation (see Figure 3)

of liveness — as in [16], there may be "holes" in the interval set corresponding to program points where s is not live. We also define $\mathscr{I} = \cup_{s \in \mathfrak{R}} \mathscr{I}(s)$ to be the set of all intervals in the program, and *IEP* to be the set of *interval endpoints i.e.,* program points that correspond to endpoints of intervals in $\mathscr{I}$. In the worst case theoretically, the size of $\mathscr{I}$ can be quadratic ($|\mathfrak{R}| \times |IR|$), where $\mathfrak{R}$ is the set of symbolic registers and IR is the intermediate representation of the procedure. The worst case can be achieved (for example) when each symbolic register is live at every other instruction in IR and therefore has $|IR|/2$ intervals. However, as shown in Section 4, in practice the average number of intervals per symbolic register is bounded by a small constant (≈ 2).

The outputs listed for the ELS_0 algorithm in Figure 4 are an extension of the outputs for the Graph Coloring algorithm in Figure 1. The boolean value, *Success*, indicates if a feasible SFRA solution can be found. The register map, *reg* is finer-grained for ELS_0 than for GC since it is capable of assigning different physical registers to different intervals in the Interval Set of a given symbolic register. The third output of the ELS_0 algorithm is a set of register-move instructions needed to support the register map. We assume that it is preferable to generate register-register moves than spill loads and stores on current and future systems, even for loads and stores that results in cache hits. This is because many processors incur a coherence overhead for loads and stores, compared to register accesses. Further, register-register moves can be optimized by efficient copy coalescing algorithms such as the one presented in [3].

We now outline how the ELS_0 algorithm addresses the three limitations for Graph Coloring discussed in Section 2.2:

1. The ELS_0 algorithm is guaranteed to find a feasible solution to an SFRA problem instance if and only if a feasible solution exists (Theorem 1).
2. The ELS_0 algorithm has a space requirement that is linear in the size of the input SFRA problem instance (Theorem 2).
3. The ELS_0 algorithm also has a time complexity that is linear in the size of the input SFRA problem instance (Theorem 2).

Theorem 1. *The* ELS_0 *algorithm always computes a correct solution for the SFRA problem.*

Proof: [Sketch] The ELS_0 algorithm returns *Success* = *false* only if there exists a program point P with $count[P] > k$ *i.e.,* with more than k symbolic registers that are live at P (which means that a spill-free register allocation is not possible). If the ELS_0 algorithm returns *Success* = *true* then $count[P] \leq k$ must be true at all program points $P \in IEP$. Therefore, there must be a physical register available in the *avail* set for each symbolic register at each program point. The register-move instructions inserted by step 6 ensure that a symbolic register's value is correctly carried across different physical registers that may be assigned to the same symbolic register. $\square$

Theorem 2. *The* ELS_0 *algorithm takes* $O(|IR| + |\mathscr{I}|)$ *space and* $O(|IR| + |\mathscr{I}|)$ *time.*

Proof: [Sketch] It is easy to see that steps 1–5b take $O(|IR| + |\mathscr{I}|)$ space and time, assuming that all liveness information is precomputed (as in the Graph Coloring algorithm in Figure 1). Note that the size of the *avail* set is bounded by a constant, k (= number of physical registers). For step 6, the key observation is that there can be at most k register move instructions inserted on any control flow edge. $\square$

3   Register Allocation with Total Spills

In this section, we extend the SFRA problem statement to allow for *total spills i.e.,* for identifying a subset of symbolic registers for which all accesses will be performed through memory instead of registers, with the goal of finding a solution with the smallest spill cost. Since the GCC compiler used to obtain our experimental results lacks support for pseudo-register live range splitting [8], an investigation of *live range splitting* and *partial spills* in the ELS framework is a subject for future work.

Register Allocation with Total Spills (RATS): Given a set of symbolic registers, $\mathfrak{R}$, k physical registers, and estimated execution frequency $freq[P]$ for each program point P, a register allocation with total spills consists of

1. a boolean function, $spilled(s)$, which indicates if s is to be spilled, and
2. for each symbolic register with $spilled(s) = false$, a register assignment, $reg(s, P)$ at each program point P where s is live.

There are two versions of the RATS problem, depending on whether or not insertion of register-move instructions is permitted:

- *regMoves = false.* In this version, no register-move instructions are allowed to be inserted, and the optimization problem is to find a register allocation with lowest *spill cost i.e.,* the lowest number of dynamic load and store instructions for the spilled symbolic registers, as determined by the $freq[P]$ values.
- *regMoves = true.* In this version, register-move instructions are permitted as in the SFRA problem statement, and the optimization goal is to minimize the combined overhead of *spill cost* and *register moves*. The relative weightage to be given to spill costs and register moves is architecture-specific.   □

The SFRA problem in Section 2.3 is a *decision problem* which indicates whether a feasible spill-free register allocation can be obtained or not. In contrast, the RATS problem is an *optimization problem*, with the goal of minimizing spill costs (for the *regMoves = false* version) and a combination of spill costs and register-move cost (for the *regMoves = true* version). Note that it is trivial to obtain a feasible solution to the RATS problem by marking all symbolic registers as spilled — the challenge is to find a least-cost solution. It is well known that both versions of the RATS problem outlined above (with *regMoves = false* or *true*) are NP-hard.

The original algorithm by Chaitin addressed the *regMoves = false* version of the RATS problem by extending the algorithm in Figure 1 with a *priority function* that favored spilling symbolic register s with the smallest value of $totalSpillCost(s)/iDegree(s)$, where

$$totalSpillCost(s) = \sum_{\text{point } P \text{ w/ read of } s} freq[P] + \sum_{\text{point } Q \text{ w/ write of } s} freq[Q]$$

is the frequency-weighted sum of all read and write accesses to s, and $iDegree(s)$ is the degree of s in the simplified Interference Graph. There has been a very substantial amount of past work on augmenting and refining this priority function, starting with [6]. As mentioned earlier, we expect that these advanced spill heuristics designed for GC will be equally applicable to an ELS foundation.

Inputs:

1. *IR*, $\mathfrak{R}$, *k*, as in Figure 1.
2. *freq*[*P*], estimated frequency for program point $P \in IEP$.
3. *regMoves*, version of the RATS problem to be solved.

Outputs:

1. *spill*(*s*), indicates if symbolic register *s* was spilled.
2. If *spill*(*s*) = *false*, then *reg*(*s*, *P*) specifies the physical register assigned to *s* at each program point *P* where *s* is live.
3. If *regMoves* = *true*, the *IR* is modified with insertion of register-move instructions as in Figure 4.

Data structure initialization:
Initialize $\mathscr{I}(s)$, $\mathscr{I}$, *IEP*, and *count* as in Figure 3, an empty stack *T*, and *spill*(*s*) := *false* and *totalSpillCost*(*s*) as defined in Section 3.

Fig. 5. Inputs, Outputs, and Initialization for Extended Linear Scan algorithm ELS_1 for Register Allocation with Total Spills (see Figure 6)

Figures 5 and 6 summarize our Extended Linear Scan algorithm for the RATS problem, ELS_1. This algorithm uses an input parameter, *regMoves*, to address both versions of the RATS problem. Figure 5 includes initialization steps from the ELS_0 algorithm, and also initializes *spill*(*s*) and *totalSpillCost*(*s*). Figure 6 contains the main ELS_1 algorithm. Step 1 in Figure 6 is the *Spill Identification* pass. It uses the observation from the SFRA problem that the only program points *P* for which spill decisions need to be made are those for which *count*[*P*] > *K*. The heuristic used in step 1a is to process these program points in decreasing order of *freq*[*P*]. As in Chaitin's Graph Coloring algorithm, Step 1b selects the symbolic register with the smallest value of *totalSpillCost*(*s*)/*iDegree*(*s*, *P*) for spilling. A key difference with graph coloring is that this decision is driven by the choice of program point *P*, and allows for assigning different physical registers to the same symbolic register at different program points, when *regMoves* = *true*. We define *iDegree*(*s*, *P*) = *count*[*P*] − 1 to be the number of symbolic registers that interfere with *s* at some program point *P* with *count*[*P*] > *k*, when computed in step 1b of ELS_1 algorithm. After Step 1 has completed, a feasible register allocation is obtained with *count*[*P*] ≤ *k* at each program point *P*. The set of registers selected to be spilled are identified by *spill*(*s*) = *true*, and are also pushed on to stack *T*. Step 2 is the *Spill Resurrection* pass. It examines the symbolic registers pushed on the stack to see if any of them can be "unspilled". Opportunities for resurrection arise when a later spill decision causes an earlier spill decision to become redundant.

Step 3 is the *Register Assignment* pass. If *regMoves* is *true*, the algorithm uses steps 4, 5, 6 of the ELS_0 algorithm in Figure 4. If *regMoves* is *false*, then we use a different register assignment algorithm that does not insert any register-move instructions. As indicated in step 3, the *regMoves* = *false* case can result in additional symbolic registers being spilled.

Algorithm:

1. /* Spill Identification. */
   while (∃ a program point $Q \in IEP$ with $count[Q] > k$) **do**
     (a) $P :=$ program point in IEP with $count[P] > k$ and $largest$ estimated frequency, $freq[P]$;
     (b) $s :=$ symbolic register s that is live at P, has $spill(s) = false$, and has the $smallest$ value
        of $totalSpillCost(s)/iDegree(s,P)$;
     (c) Set $spill(s) := true$ and push s on stack T ;
     (d) **for each** program point $X \in IEP$ where s is live **do**
        $count[X] := count[X] - 1$;
        end for
     end while
2. /* Spill Resurrection. */
   while (stack T is non-empty) **do**
     (a) $s := pop(T)$;
     (b) **if** ($count[Q] < k$ at each point Q where s is live) **then**
        /* Resurrect symbolic register with $largest$ spill cost. */
        i. Set $spill(s) := false$
        ii. **for each** program point X where s is live **do**
          $count[X] := count[X] + 1$; **end for**
        end if
     end while
3. /* Register Assignment. */
   if ($regMoves$) **then**
     Run steps 4, 5, 6 of the ELS_0 algorithm, restricted to symbolic registers s with $spill(s) = false$
     else /* Modified version of steps 4 and 5 in Figure 4. */
     for each program point P in IEP, in decreasing order of $freq[P]$ **do**
     (a) $avail :=$ set of physical registers that have not been assigned to a symbolic register that
        is live at P
     (b) **for each** symbolic register s that is live at P and does not have an assigned physical
        register, in decreasing order of $totalSpillCost(s)$ **do**
        i. Select a physical register r_j from $avail$ using the copy heuristic from step 5(b)ii in
          Figure 4.
        ii. **if** no register r_j was found **then** $spill(s) := true$;
          else $reg(s, *) := r_j$; $avail := avail - \{r_j\}$;
          end if
        end for
     end for
     end if

Fig. 6. Overview of Extended Linear Scan algorithm ELS_1 for Register Allocation with Total Spills (see Figure 5)

Theorem 3. *The ELS_1 algorithm always computes a correct solution to the RATS problem.*

Proof: [Sketch] The solution obtained after step 2 in the ELS_1 algorithm (Figure 6) is guaranteed to have $count[P] \leq k$ at each program point P. If $regMoves = true$, then the

RATS problem degenerates to SFRA in Step 3, and the correctness result from Theorem 1 holds. If $regMoves = false$, then steps 3(b)i and 3(b)ii ensure that each non-spilled symbolic register is assigned a physical register, or is spilled if no physical register is available, for each program point in IEP. ☐

Theorem 4. *The ELS_1 algorithm takes $O(|IR| + |\mathscr{I}|)$ space and $O(|IR| + |\mathscr{I}|(log(count_{max}) + log|IR|))$ time, where $count_{max}$ is the maximum value of $count[P]$ at any program point P.*

Proof: It is easy to see that the initialization in Figure 5 will take $O(|IR| + |\mathscr{I}|)$ space and $O(|IR| + |\mathscr{I}|)$ time. Note that the computation of $totalSpillCost(s)$ just takes $O(|IR|)$ time because each instruction in the intermediate representation can result in the increment of $totalSpillCost(s)$ for at most a constant number of symbolic registers.

For Step 1 (Spill Identification), the selection in step 1a of program point P with $count[P] > k$ and largest estimated frequency, $freq[P]$, contributes $O(|\mathscr{I}|log|IR|)$ time and step 1b contributes $O(|\mathscr{I}|log(count_{max}))$ time, assuming that a heap data structure (or equivalent) is used in both cases. Finally, step 2 (Spill Resurrection) and step 3 (Register Assignment) contribute at most $O(|\mathscr{I}|)$ time. ☐

4 Experimental Results

In this section, we report on experimental results obtained from a prototype implementation of Graph Coloring (as described in [10]) and ELS_1 in version 4.1 of the *gcc* compiler using the -O3 option. Compile-time and execution time were measured on a POWER5 processor running at 1.9GHz with 31.7GB of real memory running AIX 5.3.

Experimental results are presented for eight out of twelve programs from v2 of the SPECint2000 benchmark suite. Results were not obtained for 252.eon because it is a C++ benchmark, and for the three other benchmarks — 176.gcc, 253.perlbmk, and 255.vortex — because of known issues [15] that require benchmark modification or installation of v3 of the CPU2000 benchmarks.

Table 1 summarizes compile-time overheads of the Graph Coloring and Extended Linear Scan algorithms. The measurements were obtained for functions with the largest interference graphs in the eight SPECint2000 benchmarks, using the -O3 -finline-limit=3000 -ftime-report options in gcc. It is interesting to note that the Interference Graph size, $|IG|$, typically grows as $O(|S|^{1.5})$, where as the number of intervals, $|\mathscr{I}|$ is always $\leq 2|S|$. This is one of the important reasons behind the compile-time efficiency of the Linear Scan and Extended Linear Scan algorithms. While it is theoretically possible for the number of intervals for a symbolic register to be as high as half the total number of instructions in the program (e.g., if every alternate instruction is a "hole" – which could lead to a non-linear complexity for ELS), we see that in practice the average number of intervals per symbolic register is bounded by a small constant (≈ 2). We see that the Space Compression Factor (SCF) = $|\mathscr{I}|/|IG|$ varies from 4.5% to 22.7%, indicating the extent to which we expect the interval set, $\mathscr{I}$, to be smaller than the interference graph, IG. Finally, the last two columns contain the compile-time spent in global register allocation for these two algorithms. For improved measurement accuracy, the register allocation phase was repeated 100 times, and the timing (in ms)

Table 1. Compile-time overheads for functions with the largest interference graphs in SPECint2000 benchmarks. $|S|$ = # symbolic registers, $|IG|$ = # nodes and edges in Interference Graph , $|\mathscr{I}|$ = # intervals in interval set, Space Compression Factor (SCF) = $|\mathscr{I}|/|IG|$, GC = graph coloring compile-time, ELS_1 = ELS_1 compile-time with *regMoves = true*.

Function	$|S|$	$|IG|$	$|\mathscr{I}|$	SCF	GC	ELS_1
164.gzip.build_tree	161	2301	261	11.3%	141.4ms	9.4ms
175.vpr.try_route	254	2380	445	18.7%	208.7ms	9.5ms
181.mcf.sort_basket	138	949	226	22.7%	6.8ms	0.1ms
186.crafty.InputMove	122	1004	219	21.8%	150.2ms	7.8s
197.parser.list_links	352	9090	414	4.5%	114.4ms	7.4ms
254.gap.SyFgets	547	7661	922	12.0%	118.8ms	8.0ms
256.bzip2.sendMTFValues	256	2426	430	17.7%	133.0ms	7.4ms
300.twolf.closepins	227	5105	503	9.8%	212.8ms	9.1ms

reported in Table 1 is the average over the 100 runs. While compile-time measurements depend significantly on the engineering of the algorithm implementations, the early indications are there is a marked reduction in compile-time when moving from GC to ELS_1 for all benchmarks. The compile-time speedups for ELS_1 relative to GC varied from $15\times$ to $68\times$, with an overall speedup of $18.5\times$ when adding all the compile-times.

Figure 7 shows the *SPEC rates* obtained for the Graph Coloring and ELS_1 algorithms, using the -O3 option in gcc. Recall that a larger SPEC rate indicates better

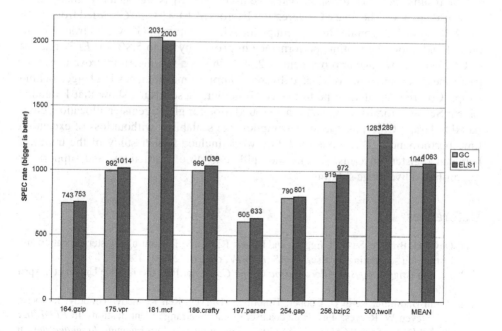

Fig. 7. SPEC rates for Graph Coloring and ELS_1 with *regMoves = true*

performance. In summary, the runtime performance improved by up to 5.8% for ELS_1 relative to GC (for 197.parser), with an average improvement of 2.3%. There was only one case in which a small performance degradation was observed for ELS_1, relative to GC – a slowdown of 1.4% for 181.mcf. These results clearly show that the compile-time benefits for Extended Linear Scan can be obtained without sacrificing runtime performance — in fact, ELS_1 delivers a net improvement in runtime performance relative to GC. Further, these measurements were obtained with *regMoves* = *true*, indicating that the extra register moves did not contribute a significant performance degradation. Runtime results were not obtained for the original Linear Scan algorithms, because it has already been established in prior work that their performance is inferior to that of Graph Coloring [14, 16].

5   Conclusions

This paper makes the case for using Extended Linear Scan as an alternate foundation to Graph Coloring for global register allocation. It highlighted three fundamental theoretical limitations with Graph Coloring as a foundation (Section 2.2). It introduced the basic Extended Linear Scan algorithm, ELS_0 (Section 2.3), which addressed all three limitations for the problem of Spill-Free Register Allocation (SFRA). It also introduced the ELS_1 algorithm (Section 3), which extended ELS_0 to obtain a greedy algorithm for the problem of Register Allocation with Total Spills (RATS). Finally, it included experimental results for eight SPECint2000 benchmarks to compare the Graph Coloring and Extended Linear Scan algorithms (Section 4).

The results show that the space and time used by ELS_1 is significantly smaller than those used by GC. The Space Compression Factor (SCF) = $|\mathscr{I}|/|IG|$ varied from 4.5% to 22.7%, and the compile-time speedups for ELS_1 relative to GC varied from $15\times$ to $68\times$. In addition, the runtime performance improved by up to 5.8% for ELS_1 relative to GC, with an average improvement of 2.3%. This is a significant improvement over past Linear Scan algorithms which delivered compile-time efficiency but lagged behind Graph Coloring in runtime performance. Together, these results show that Extended Linear Scan is promising as an alternate foundation for global register allocation, compared to Graph Coloring, due to its compile-time scalability without loss of execution time performance. Directions for future work include further study of the trade-off between register-move instructions and spill load/store instructions, and support for region-based live range splitting.

References

[1] David G. Bradlee, Susan J. Eggers, and Robert R. Henry. Integrating register allocation and instruction scheduling for riscs. In *ASPLOS-IV*, pages 122–131, 1991.
[2] Preston Briggs. *Register Allocation via Graph Coloring*. PhD thesis, Rice University, April 1992.
[3] Zoran Budimlic, Keith D. Cooper, Timothy J. Harvey, Ken Kennedy, Timothy S. Oberg, and Steven W. Reeves. Fast copy coalescing and live-range identification. In *PLDI '02: Proceedings of the ACM SIGPLAN 2002 Conference on Programming language design and implementation*, pages 25–32, 2002.

[4] David Callahan and Brian Koblenz. Register allocation via hierarchical graph coloring. In *PLDI '91: Proceedings of the ACM SIGPLAN 1991 conference on Programming language design and implementation*, pages 192–203, 1991.

[5] Gregory J. Chaitin. Register allocation and spilling via graph coloring. In *ACM SIGPLAN '82 Symposium on Compiler Construction*, pages 98–105, June 1982.

[6] Frederick Chow and John Hennessy. Register allocation by priority-based coloring. In *Proceedings of the 1984 SIGPLAN symposium on Compiler construction*, pages 222–232, 1984.

[7] Lal George and Andrew W. Appel. Iterated register coalescing. *ACM Transactions on Programming Languages and Systems*, 18(3):300–324, May 1996.

[8] Vladimir N. Makarov. Yet another gcc register allocator. In *Proceedings of the GCC Developers Summit*, pages 148–157, May 2005.

[9] Rajeev Motwani, Krishna V. Palem, Vivek Sarkar, and Salem Reyen. Combining register allocation and instruction scheduling. In *Technical Report STAN-CS-TN-95-22, Department of Computer Science, Stanford University*, 1995.

[10] Steven Muchnick. *Advanced Compiler Design and Implementation*. Morgan Kaufmann Publishers, 1997.

[11] Cindy Norris and Lori L. Pollock. An experimental study of several cooperative register allocation and instruction scheduling strategies. In *MICRO 28*, pages 169–179, 1995.

[12] Jinpyo Park and Soo-Mook Moon. Optimistic register coalescing. In *International Conference on Parallel Architectures and Compilation Techniques*, pages 196–204, October 1998.

[13] Shlomit S. Pinter. Register allocation with instruction scheduling. In *PLDI '93: Proceedings of the ACM SIGPLAN 1993 conference on Programming language design and implementation*, pages 248–257, 1993.

[14] Massimiliano Poletto and Vivek Sarkar. Linear scan register allocation. *ACM Transactions on Programming Languages and Systems*, 21(5):895–913, 1999.

[15] Standard Performance Evaluation Corporation (SPEC). http://www.spec.org/cpu2000/issues/, 2006.

[16] Omri Traub, Glenn H. Holloway, and Michael D. Smith. Quality and speed in linear-scan register allocation. In *SIGPLAN Conference on Programming Language Design and Implementation*, pages 142–151, 1998.

Program Refactoring, Program Synthesis, and Model-Driven Development

Don Batory

Department of Computer Sciences
University of Texas at Austin

Abstract. Program refactoring, feature-based and aspect-oriented software synthesis, and model-driven development are disjoint research areas. However, they are all architectural metaprogramming technologies as they treat programs as values and use functions (a.k.a. *transformations*) to map programs to other programs. In this paper, I explore their underlying connections by reviewing recent advances in each area from an architectural metaprogramming perspective. I conjecture how these areas can converge and outline a theory that may unify them.

1 Introduction

Among the greatest challenges that we face today is dealing with the alarming complexity of software, and the alarming rate at which software complexity is increasing. Brooks observed 20 years ago that programmers spent a majority of their time on accidental complexity, rather than essential complexity [12]. Unfortunately, we often can't tell the difference between the two.

Complexity is controlled by imposing structure. This paper is about the essential complexity of software structure. There are increasingly overlapping ideas in the areas of program refactoring, program synthesis, and model-driven development, all of which deal with program structure and maintenance. I conjecture how these areas can converge and outline a theory that may unify them.

I have long believed there is a common conceptual foundation for what we do in programming, software design, and maintenance. The results I expect from making these foundations explicit are increasing automation, building better tools, writing better code, and reducing program development and maintenance costs. All are worthy goals. But there may be an even bigger prize: discovering the material that will be taught to future graduates and undergraduates.

By, say, 2020 (which I hope will be a good year), programmers will be writing functions, objects, classes, and methods just as they do today. But there will be a difference in the level of abstraction at which programs are written. I expect the rise of *architectural metaprogramming*: the idea that programming and design is a computation, where programs are values and functions (a.k.a. *transformations*) map programs to programs.

In the following sections, I sketch the ideas architectural metaprogramming, and then reflect on recent advances in program refactoring [17][18], program synthesis [26], and model-driven development [7][37] from its perspective.

S. Krishnamurthi and M. Odersky (Eds.): CC 2007, LNCS 4420, pp. 156–171, 2007.

2 Basics of Architectural Metaprogramming

```
class c {
  int x;
  void inc() {x++;}
}
```
(a) value C

```
class d {
  int compute() {}
}
```
(b) value D

Fig. 1. Values C and D

Programs are values. Figure 1a shows a value C that is the Java definition of a class c. Figure 1b shows another value D; it is the Java definition of a class d. (I use Java, but any language could be used provided that one shows how concepts translate).

Values can be added. The sum C+D is a program with classes c and d. As another example: let C1 be the definition of a class c with a comp() method (Figure 2a), and let C2 be another definition of class c which has an x field and an inc() method (Figure 2b). C1+C2 yields a single definition of class c (Figure 2c), formed by the disjoint union of the members in C1 and C2.[1]

```
class c {
  int comp() {}
}
```
(a) value C1

```
class c {
  int x;
  void inc() {x++;}
}
```
(b) value C2

```
class c {
  int comp() {}
  int x;
  void inc() {x++;}
}
```
(c) value C1+C2

Fig. 2. Sum

Summation (or simply "sum") is disjoint set union with the properties:

- Sum identity 0 is the *null program* or *null value*. For any program P: P+0=P
- Sum is commutative (as disjoint set union is commutative): A+P=P+A
- Sum is associative (as disjoint set union is associative): (A+B)+C=A+(B+C)

Values can be subtracted. *Subtraction* is set difference; if a program is formed by C+D, and C is subtracted, the result is D: (D+C)-C=D. Subtraction has the properties:

- 0 is the identity: P-0=P and P-P=0
- Subtraction is left associative: P-C-D=((P-C)-D)
- Subtraction is not commutative: P-C ≠ C-P

```
class c {
  int z;
  void inc(){z++;}
}
```
Fig. 3. Value C3

A third operation is really a menagerie of operations called *distributive transformations (DTs)*. (The reason for the name will become clear shortly). One is rename(p,q,r): in program p, replace name q with name r. Recall program C2 (Figure 2b). Suppose we want to replace name "x" with name "z". The computation rename(C2,x,z) does this replacement and yields value C3, shown in Figure 3.

---

[1] Think of a primitive value as an aspect-oriented introduction that defines a member and its class (e.g., "int c.x;") . The same for other declarations such as initialization blocks, **extends** clauses, etc. When values are converted to source code, their members are collected into classes, and classes into packages, to show their hierarchical modularities.

Consider another computation: `rename(D,x,z)` which equals D. That is, `rename` leaves D unaltered as D does not reference **x**. In mathematics this is a *fixed point*, i.e., a value **x** such that `f(x)=x`. DTs usually have many fixed points.

The key property of DTs is that they distribute over + and – (hence their name). That is, a DT **f** of a sum equals the sum of the transformed values. The same for subtraction:

$$f(A+B) = f(A) + f(B)$$

$$f(A-B) = f(A) - f(B) \tag{1}$$

As an illustration, consider renaming "**x**" to "**z**" in program **C2+D**. This computation, `rename(C2+D,x,z)`, is performed by applying `rename` to programs **C2** and **D** individually, and summing their results:

```
rename(C2+D,x,z)
= rename(C2,x,z) + rename(D,x,z)   // distribution
= C3 + D                           // evaluation
```

DTs have other properties. Transforming a non-null value yields a non-null value:

$$f(x) \neq 0 \; ; \; \text{where } x \neq 0 \tag{2}$$

That is, applying a DT to a non-null value will not nullify (erase, delete) that value, but may alter it. If a value is to be deleted, subtraction should be used. And the null value cannot be transformed:

$$f(0) = 0 \tag{3}$$

Another property is composition. DTs are functions, and thus compose like functions. If **f1** and **f2** are DTs, **f1•f2** denotes their composition. Function composition is not commutative (**f1•f2 ≠ f2•f1**) and is associative (**(f1•f2)•f3 = f1•(f2•f3)**).

Expressions that are formed by adding, subtracting, and transforming programs are *architectural meta-expressions* or simply *meta-expressions*.

Before proceeding further, I use the term "*structure*" to mean what are the parts and how are they connected? The structure of a cube, for example, is a solid bounded by six equal squares, where two adjacent faces meet at a right angle. The term "*property*" is an attribute that is given or is derivable from a structure. If **E** is the length of an edge (a given property), derivable properties of a cube are its surface area ($6*E^2$) and volume (E^3). The software analog: the structure of a program is its architectural meta-expression. Compilers prove properties of a program by analyzing its structure, such as the property of type correctness. In this paper, I focus solely on program structure. Now let's look at some applications of architectural metaprogramming.

3   Recent Advances in Program Refactoring

A *refactoring* is a transformation that changes the structure of a program, but not its behavior [20]. Classic examples include rename method and move a method from a sub-class to a superclass. Common *Integrated Development Environments (IDEs)*, such as Eclipse, Visual Studio, and IntelliJ, have built-in or plug-in refactoring tools. Discussed below is an interesting problem in program refactoring.

The use of components (e.g., frameworks and libraries) is common in contemporary software development. Components enable software to be built quickly and in a cost-effective way. The *Application Program Interface (API)* of a component is a set of Java interfaces and classes that are exported to application developers. Whenever an API changes, client code that invokes the API must also change. Such changes are performed manually and are disruptive events in program development. Programmers want an easy (push-button) and safe (behavior-preserving) way to update their applications when a component API changes [17][18].

Figure 4 illustrates an API change called "move method". An instance method **m** of a **home** class (Figure 4a) becomes a static method **m** of a **host** class (Figure 4b). The moved method takes an instance of the **home** class as an extra argument, and all calls to the old method are replaced with calls to the new method.

Figure 4 shows the essence of the problem: above the dashed lines is component code, and below is client code. When the API is refactored, the client code changes. As component developers do not have access to client code, the client programmer must manually update his/her own code.

This API change can be written as an architectural meta-expression. Let value **home.m** denote the **home** method **m()**, and let **host.m** denote the **host** method **m()**. Let μ be the DT that transforms **home.m** to **host.m**, and otherwise leaves all other primitive values unchanged. That is, μ**(home.m)=host.m** and for all **x≠home.m**: μ**(x)=x**. Let ϕ be the DT that renames all calls to **home.m** to calls to **host.m**, and otherwise leaves

```
(a)  class host {}

     class home {
        void m() {}
     }
     _  _  _  _  _
     class kcode {
        void y(){
           home h;
           h.m()
     }}}
     }
```

```
(b)  class host {
        static void m(home h)
        {}
     }

     class home {}
     _  _  _  _  _  _
     class kcode {
        void y'(){
           home h;
           host.m(h)
        }
     }
```

Fig. 4. Move Method

primitive values unchanged. That is, ϕ**(kcode.y)=kcode.y'** and for all primitives **x** that do not call **home.m**: ϕ**(x)=x**. The meta-expression that relates the updated program (P_{new}) to the original program (P_{old}) is:

$$P_{new} = \phi \bullet \mu (\ P_{old} \ ) = \mu \bullet \phi (\ P_{old} \ ) \qquad (4)$$

In this particular case, the order in which μ and ϕ are composed does not matter. The reason is that each transformation changes different code fragments (much like two pieces of aspect-oriented advice advising different join points [22]).

To see how computation (**4**) proceeds, let P_{old}**=home.m+kcode.y+..**:

```
  φ•μ( Pold )
= φ•μ( home.m + kcode.y + .. )        // substitution
= φ•μ(home.m) + φ•μ(kcode.y) + ..     // distribution
= φ(host.m) + φ(kcode.y) + ..         // evaluation of μ
= host.m + kcode.y' + ..              // evaluation of φ
= Pnew
```

Other API changes (refactorings) besides move method include: move field, delete method (which is usually done after a method is renamed or moved), change argument type (replace an argument type with its supertype), and replace method call (with another that is semantically equivalent and in the same class) [17]. My preliminary work suggests that these and other refactorings can be written as meta-expressions.

In a recent paper, Dig and Johnson explored how APIs evolve [18]. They manually analyzed the change logs, release notes and documentation of different versions of five medium to large systems (e.g., 50K to 2M LOC), including Eclipse, Struts, and JHotDraw. They discovered that over 80% of the API changes were due to refactorings. This means that a large fraction of API changes can be fully automated.

By 2020, programmers will use advanced IDEs that will "mark" API interfaces, classes, methods, and fields. The only way marked elements can change is by refactorings. When a new version of a component is released, the refactorings of its API are also released. These refactorings are applied automatically to the client code whenever a client installs a new version of a component, thereby avoiding the tedious and error prone changes that are now performed manually. In this way, the disruptive effects of updating component versions are minimized.

Underneath the covers, future IDEs will use architectural meta-expressions to perform these updates. Assume that DTs θ are sufficient to express API refactorings. Further assume that private edits to a component, which change component internals and are invisible to clients, are also modeled by transformations ε. Updating component $\mathbf{v_0}$ to version $\mathbf{v_1}$ is an interleaved sequence of refactorings and private edits, such as:

$$\mathbf{v_1} = \varepsilon_6 \bullet \varepsilon_5 \bullet \varepsilon_4 \bullet \theta_3 \bullet \varepsilon_3 \bullet \varepsilon_2 \bullet \theta_2 \bullet \theta_1 \bullet \varepsilon_1 (\mathbf{v_0}) \qquad (5)$$

The IDE will keep a history of these changes. The modifications $\underline{\theta}$ of $\mathbf{v_0}$ that may alter client code are the API refactorings, which is the projection of the changes of **(5)** with private edits removed:

$$\underline{\theta} = \theta_3 \bullet \theta_2 \bullet \theta_1 \qquad (6)$$

The metaprogramming function $\mathbf{U}$ automatically updates a client program $\mathbf{P_0}$ that uses $\mathbf{v_0}$ to a program $\mathbf{P_1}$ that uses $\mathbf{v_1}$, where $\mathbf{P_1} = \mathbf{U(P_0)}$:

$$\mathbf{U(x)} = \underline{\theta}(\mathbf{x} - \mathbf{v_0}) + \mathbf{v_1} \qquad (7)$$

To see a computation, let client program $\mathbf{P_0} = \mathbf{C} + \mathbf{v_0}$, where $\mathbf{C}$ is the client code to be updated. Applying $\mathbf{U}$ to $\mathbf{P_0}$ updates $\mathbf{P_0}$'s code (transforming $\mathbf{C}$ to $\underline{\theta}(\mathbf{C})$) and replaces $\mathbf{v_0}$ with $\mathbf{v_1}$. This is the essential idea behind [18].

```
U(P₀)
= θ( P₀ - V₀ ) + V₁              // substitution of U
= θ( C + V₀ - V₀ ) + V₁          // substitution of P₀
= θ( C ) + V₁                    // subtraction
= P₁
```

Note that $\mathbf{U}$ can be applied to any program $\mathbf{P_0}$, whose size can be arbitrarily large. One of the benefits of architectural metaprogramming is that its concepts scale to large programs.

Perspective. By 2020, IDEs will be *component evolution calculators*. They will allow programmers to edit components, and perhaps invisible to programmer actions, IDEs will create metaprogramming update functions like ʊ for distribution. When a client wants a new version of a component, s/he will download a metaprogramming function ʊ rather than the new version itself. The client's IDE will then apply ʊ to the client's code base, automatically and safely updating the client's program.[2] An interesting research problem is to generalize the above analysis to deal with refactorings that involve value additions and subtractions, and to develop in detail an algebra for refactorings in conjunction with a refactoring tool to show the connection between theory and practice.

4 Recent Advances in Program Synthesis

Declarative languages will be used to specify programs in 2020. Unlike past work that relied on formal logic specifications (and compilers to derive program implementations from such specifications), the languages I envision will be much simpler. They will exploit results from *Software Product Lines (SPLs)*, an area of research that focuses on designs for a family of systems and on automating system construction. A fundamental idea in SPL is using features to describe and differentiate programs within a family, where a *feature* is an increment in functionality [21][14].

Features are used in many engineering disciplines for product specification. At the Dell web site, customers configure a personal computer (i.e., a product in a Dell product line) by selecting optional hardware and software features listed on a web page [16]. Such pages are *Declarative Domain-Specific Languages (DDSLs)* for Dell products. Another example is BMW's web site to customize an automobile [11].

Software can be specified in the same way. Figure 5 shows an elementary DDSL for a product-line of Java programs. Called the *Graph Product Line (GPL)*, each program implements a unique combination of graph algorithms [25]. A particular program is specified by selecting a set of features.

Fig. 5. DDSL for the Graph Product Line

The program specified in Figure 5 (reading selected features from left to right) implements vertex numbering, strongly connected components, and cycle checking using a depth first search (**DFS**) on a weighted, directed graph. More generally, each

---

[2] There is a database transaction-like quality to this update. If any refactoring of θ fails, then the all changes are rolled back, and client-programmer intervention is needed to repair the program for subsequent ʊ application.

feature can be customized via parameters (much like GUI components have customizable property lists [2]), but the essential idea of declarative feature selections remains.

The compiler for the GPL DDSL outputs a meta-expression, shown below:

```
Number•StrongC•Cycle•DFS•Weighted(Directed)
```

As users select GPL features, terms are inserted into this expression. Evaluating the expression synthesizes the specified program. My students and I have built many examples of more realistic applications using this technology, ranging from customized or extensible database systems twenty years ago [3], to extensible Java preprocessors ten years ago [4], to web portlets [37] (which we'll consider later). We call this technology *Feature Oriented Programming (FOP)*, where features are either metaprogramming constants or functions [6]. A model of a product-line is an algebra: constants represent base programs (e.g., **Directed**), and functions add features (**Weighted**, **DFS**, etc.) to programs. Each domain has its own algebra, and different meta-expressions synthesize different programs of that domain (product-line). How are features expressed by architectural metaprogramming? This is the topic of the next subsections.

4.1 A Look Inside Features

If we peer inside implementations of FOP functions and constants, we find two ideas that have been popularized by *Aspect Oriented Programming (AOP)* [22]. (I will use the *ideas* of AOP, rather than their AspectJ semantics which has problems [26].) The first is introduction, also known as inter-type declarations. An *introduction* adds a new member to an existing class, or more generally adds a new class or package to a program. Introduction is metaprogramming addition.

The second idea is *advice*, which is the execution of additional code at points called join points. Although it is not obvious, advice is a distributive transformation (see [26] for an explanation, including examples of how complex pointcuts like **cflow** [22] are expressed transformationally). That is, applying advice **A** to a program **P** is the same as applying **A** to each component of **P** and summing the results. Advice or the act of advising is quite different from a refactoring even though both are transformations: refactoring is behavior preserving, whereas advise is behavior-extending. Neither AOP or FOP support subtraction.

Here's how introduction works. Start with a simple program **P** consisting of a single class **r** with field **b** (Figure 6a), and incrementally add or introduce method **foo** (Figure 6b), integer **i** (Figure 6c), and class **t** (Figure 6d). From a

```
class r {          class r {          class r {          class r {
   String b;          String b;          String b;          String b;
}      (a)            void foo()         void foo(){..}      void foo(){..}
                      {..}               int i;             int i;
                   }        (b)        }        (c)        }

                                                           class t {
                                                              String bar;
                                                              int cnt(){..}
                                                           }        (d)
```

Fig. 6. Incremental Development of Program **P**

metaprogramming viewpoint, the original program in Figure 5a is **P=r.b**. That is, program **P** consists of a single member **b** in class **r**. Introducing method **foo** adds another term to **P**'s meta-expression: (**P=r.b+r.foo**). Introducing field **i** adds yet another term (**P=r.b+r.foo+r.i**). And introducing class **t** adds even more terms (**P=r.b+r.foo+r.i+t.bar+t.cnt**). Evaluating the meta-expression for **P** in each figure synthesizes the listed program.

Now consider advice. *Join points* are events that occur during program execution, such as when a method is called, or when a method is executed, or when a field is updated [21]. Advice is a piece of code that is executed when designated join points occur. Although advice is usually given a dynamic interpretation (i.e., when an event occurs at run-time), it is also possible to give it a static metaprogramming interpretation "at this point in the program, insert this code" [26]. The latter interpretation is common for implementations of many aspect compilers, including the AspectJ compiler **ajc** [21].

Here's how advice works. Consider program **P** of Figure 7a. It consists of a single class **c** and an aspect with a single piece of advice. The advice extends each **set** method of **c** by printing "**hi**". A program that an aspect compiler synthesizes or weaves is shown in Figure 7b. A metaprogramming explanation of weaving is that an aspect compiler inhales the program's source, creates a meta-expression that sums all base code and introductions, and then applies advice. The meta-expression for program **P** in Figure 7a is:

$$P = hi(\ i + j + setI + setJ \ ) \qquad (8)$$

where values **i**, **j**, **setI**, and **setJ** correspond to the members of class **c**, and function **hi** is the advice. Evaluation of (**8**) proceeds incrementally. First **hi** distributes over each term:

$$P = hi(i) + hi(j) + hi(setI) + hi(setJ) \qquad (9)$$

and then each term is evaluated:

$$P = \ i \ + \ j \ + setI' + setJ' \qquad (10)$$

Some terms are fixed points (e.g., **hi(i)=i** and **hi(j)=j**, meaning that **hi** does not advise join points in **i** and **j**), while others transform values (**hi(setI)=setI'** and **hi(setJ)= setJ'**). Again, the view from an aspect compiler is to in-hale aspect files and base Java files, construct a meta-expression, and evaluate the expression to synthesize the specified program [26].

(a)
```
class c {
  int i,j;
  void setI( int x )
  { i=x; }
  void setJ( int x )
  { j=x; }
}

aspect asp {
  after(): execution(
     void c.set*(..))
     { print("hi"); }
}
```

(b)
```
class c {
  int i,j;
  void setI'( int x )
  { i=x; print("hi"); }
  void setJ'( int x )
  { j=x; print("hi"); }
}
```

Fig. 7. Compiling Advice

4.2 Architectural Metaprogramming Implementation of Features

A base program in FOP is a constant, which is a sum of introductions. An FOP function **F(x)** is a feature that advises or modifies (a_f) its input program **x** and introduces new terms (i_f). In other words, **F(x)** adds new members, classes, packages to an input program **x**, and integrates this new functionality by modifying or advising **x**. A general form of all FOP features **F** is:

$$F(x) = i_f + a_f(x)$$

Given a base program **B** and features **F** and **G**, their composition expands into architectural meta-expressions. The FOP expressions **B**, **F(B)**, and **G•F(B)** expand to:

$$B = b$$
$$F(B) = i_f + a_f(b)$$
$$G•F(B) = i_g + a_g(i_f + a_f(b)) = i_g + a_g(i_f) + a_g•a_f(b)$$

A program's code is synthesized by evaluating its meta-expression. This is how GenVoca [3] and AHEAD [6], two different implementations of FOP, work.

Perspective. By 2020, many narrow domains will be well-understood, and whose programs are prime candidates for automated construction from declarative specs. The complexity of these programs will be controlled by standardization, where programs will be specified declaratively using "standardized" features, much like personal computers are customized on Dell web pages. Programming languages will have constructs to define features and their compositions (e.g.[31][29]). Compilers will become *program calculators*: they will inhale source code, produce a meta-expression, perhaps even optimize the meta-expression [5], and evaluate the expression to synthesize the target program. Architectural metaprogramming will be at the core of this technology.

5   How Are Advice and Refactorings Related?

Program refactorings and advice are transformations. What does it mean to compose them? There is a lot of work on refactoring object-oriented code into aspects (e.g., [10][39]), but less work on refactoring programs that have *both* object-oriented code and aspect code (e.g.,[19][15]). Refactorings are not language constructs; they are transformations that are defined and implemented by tools that are "outside" of a target language. Thus, refactorings can modify both object-oriented code and aspect code. In contrast, advice only applies to constructs within a host language, i.e. object-oriented code and other aspect code, but not to refactorings.

To illustrate, let **P** be the program of Figure 7a. Applying the refactoring **rename(P,set*,SET*)** renames all lowercase **set** methods to uppercase **SET** methods, we obtain the program **P'** of Figure 8. Programs **P** and **P'** have the same behavior. The **rename** refactoring alters the Java source (by renaming **setI** to **SETI** and **setJ** to **SETJ**), and alters the advice declaration (by renaming **set*** to **SET***).

How can this be explained in terms of architectural metaprogramming? Recall differential operators in

```
class c {
  int i,j;
  void SETI(int x)
  {i=x;}
  void SETJ(int x)
  {j=x;}
}

aspect adv {
  after():
  execution
  (void c.SET*(..))
  { print("hi"); }
}
```

Fig. 8. Program **P'**

calculus: they transform expressions. The differential with respect to **x** of a summation is straightforward: every term is transformed:

$$\frac{\partial}{\partial x}(a+b) = \frac{\partial a}{\partial x} + \frac{\partial b}{\partial x}$$

rename is similar: it transforms each term of a meta-expression. Let β be a DT of **rename**, **i** and **j** be introductions, and **a** and **b** be advice. Beyond the distributivity of β over **+** and **-** in **(1)**, the β refactoring also distributes over advice application and composition:

$$\beta(a(i)) = \beta(a)(\beta(b)) \tag{11}$$

$$\beta(a \bullet b) = \beta(a) \bullet \beta(b) \tag{12}$$

A β transformation of expression **i+b•a(x)** is β**(i)**+β**(b)**•β**(a)**(β**(x)**). Mapping terms of an expression in this manner is called a *catamorphism* [27], a generalization of folds on lists in functional programming. Catamorphisms are grounded in *category theory*, the theory of mathematical structures and their relationships [32]. More later.

Here's how a meta-calculation proceeds. Given program **P** of Figure 7a, a compiler creates its meta-expression. The **rename** refactoring β is then applied to **P**; β distributes over each term of **P**, and then each term is evaluated: β**(hi)**=**HI**, β**(setI)**=**SETI**, and β**(setJ)**=**SETJ**. The terms β**(i)**=**i** and β**(j)**=**j** are fixed points. The result is the meta-expression for program **P'**:

```
β(P)
= β( hi( i + j + setI + setJ ) )              // substitution
= β(hi)( β(i) + β(j) + β(setI) + β(setJ) )     // distribution
= HI( i + j + SETI + SETJ )                    // evaluation
= P'                                                        (13)
```

Perspective. Refactorings are operators on meta-expressions that have higher precedence than advice. Interesting research problems are to determine if (a) all common refactorings can be expressed as meta-expressions, and (b) the exact relationship between refactorings and advice, and (c) to show under what circumstances the relationship is (or is not) a catamorphism. Catamorphisms are particularly simple mappings, and knowing when they can (or cannot) be applied may be very useful when building tools.

Note that refactorings, advice, and introductions modify the structure of a program's code, but they could also be used to express and modify the structure of grammars, makefiles, XML documents, and other non-code artifacts. We are now ready to make a conceptual leap to generalize architectural metaprogramming to non-code structures.

6 Recent Advances in Model-Driven Development

Model-Driven Development (MDD) is an emerging paradigm for software creation. It advocates the use of *Domain Specific Languages (DSLs)*, encourages the use of automation, and exploits data exchange standards [13][33]. An MDD model is written in a DSL to capture the details of a slice of a program's design. Several models are typically needed to specify a program completely. Program synthesis is the process of transforming high-level models into executables, which are also considered models [9].

There are many MDD technologies. The most well-known is OMG's *Model-Driven Architecture*, where models are defined in terms of UML and are manipulated by graph transformations [23]. Vanderbilt's *Model Integrated Computing* [35] and Tata's Mastercraft [24] are pioneering examples of MDD. More recently, other groups have offered their own MDD technologies (see [30] for a recent list).

MDD is an architectural metaprogramming paradigm. Models are values and transformations map models to models. To illustrate, consider two models: the Java source of a program and its bytecode. The transformation that maps Java source to Java bytecodes is `javac`, the Java compiler. If `javac` is a transformation, an interesting question to ask if it is distributive. That is, can each Java file be compiled separately from other files, and the bytecodes added? Does `javac(C+D)=javac(C)+javac(D)`? Unfortunately, the answer is no: `javac` is not distributive. I note that research by Ancona, et al. on separate class compilation may lead to a future version of `javac` that is distributive [1].

A more conventional example of MDD is PinkCreek. It is an MDD case study for synthesizing portlets, which are web components [37]. Transformations map an annotated state chart to a series of different platform-specific models. Figure 9 shows a graph where models are nodes and arrows are transformations; the most abstract model in a PinkCreek specification is a state chart (**sc**), and the most implementation-specific is Java source (**code**) and JSP code (**jsp**). The graph is created by a metaprogram that takes a state chart (**sc**) and applies transformations successively to derive each representation. (That is, a transformation maps an **sc** model to a **ctrl** model, another transformation maps a **ctrl** model to an **act_sk** model, etc.).

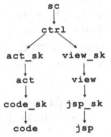

Fig. 9. PinkCreek Models

As FOP and MDD are both metaprogramming paradigms, how can they be combined? Recall that features extend the functionality of a program or a model. Let **S0** and **S1** be the source code representations of programs **P0** and **P1**. And let feature **F(x)** relate **S0** and **S1** by **S1=F(S0)**. Let **B0** and **B1** be the bytecode representations of **S0** and **S1**, and let **G(x)** be the bytecode feature that relates **B0** to **B1**, i.e., **B1=G(B0)**. These relationships are

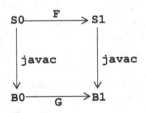

Fig. 10. Commuting Diagram

captured by the *commuting diagram* of Figure 10. It expresses a fundamental relationship in MDD between features (model-extension transformations) and derivations (model-conversion transformations) [37]. Bytecode **B1** can be synthesized from **S0** in two different ways: either derive **B0** from **S0** using `javac` and then apply feature **G**, or extend **S0** to **S1** by applying feature **F** and then derive **B1** using `javac`. Their equivalence is expressed compositionally as:

$$\textbf{javac} \bullet \textbf{F} = \textbf{G} \bullet \textbf{javac} \tag{14}$$

Another interesting point is the relationship between functions **F** and **G**. We know that **F** and **G** are features of the form: $\mathbf{F(x)} = \mathbf{i}_f + \mathbf{a}_f(\mathbf{x})$ and $\mathbf{G(x)} = \mathbf{i}_g + \mathbf{a}_g(\mathbf{x})$. In effect, **G** is a compiled version of **F**: both **F** and **G** advise their input programs **x** in equivalent ways (**F** advises source and **G** performs the corresponding advise in bytecodes) and both add equivalent introductions (**F** adds source members and **G** adds the corresponding members in bytecode). We have seen this correspondence before. The relationship between **F** and **G** appears to be a catamorphism: each source term of function **F** is mapped to a corresponding bytecode term of function **G**. Exploring this connection may be an interesting research problem.

Let's now return to commuting diagrams. An important property of commuting diagrams is that they can be pasted together. Given a model in the upper-left corner, we often want to compute the model in the lower right. Any path from the upper-left corner to the lower right produces the same result [32]. Three different paths are indicated in Figure 11.

To make this idea concrete, consider how features alter state charts in PinkCreek. In general, a feature extends a state chart by (a) adding new states, (b) adding new transitions, and (c) altering existing annotations. Figure 12a depicts a state chart of a base portlet. Figure 12b shows the result of a feature that adds a new state and transitions to Figure 12a.

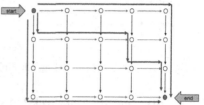

Fig. 11. Commuting Paths

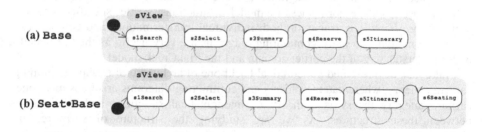

Fig. 12. State Chart Extensions

When a feature extends one representation, it may extend derived representations as well. In the case of PinkCreek, all of the models in Figure 9 may be modified when the state chart is extended. That is, if the state chart **sc** is extended, so too must its controller **ctrl**, and its action skeleton (**act_sk**), etc. (Figure 13a). PinkCreek has a metaprogram that translates a state chart feature into a feature of each lower-level representation; as a rule, the ability to translate features of one model to features of another is not always possible or practical. For PinkCreek, it was both possible and practical.

As features are composed, a multi-pleated commuting diagram is swept out (Figure 13b). Traversing this diagram synthesizes the representations of a target portlet. Synthesis begins at the root of the base diagram and ends at the target models which are produced by the last feature. Although all traversals produce the same results, not all traversals are equally efficient. Diagram traversal is an interesting optimization problem. Finding the cheapest traversal is equivalent to finding the most efficient metaprogram that will synthesize the target portlet. This is a form of *multi-stage programming* (i.e., writing programs that write other programs) and *multi-stage optimization* [36].

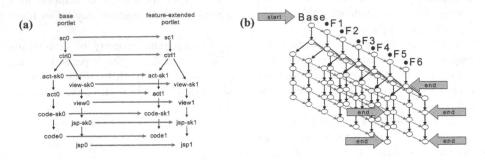

Fig. 13. PinkCreek Diagrams

Perspective. Initially PinkCreek tools did not satisfy the properties of commuting diagrams: synthesizing via different paths yielded different results. This exposed previously unrecognized errors in PinkCreek tools and specifications. The significance of commuting diagrams became immediately clear: they provided validity checks on the correctness of model abstractions, portlet specifications, and tools. They offered constraints on both individual transformations and compositions of transformations. In short, commuting diagrams are very useful as they provided a better understanding of the portlet domain and the PinkCreek model.

PinkCreek also revealed a theoretical backbone of architectural metaprogramming: category theory, where catamorphisms and commuting diagrams arise. As mentioned earlier, category theory is a theory of mathematical structures and relationships between these structures. As we are studying the structure of software, and mathematics is the science of structure, architectural metaprogramming may be a direct connection.

Although this connection is preliminary, I have already found that category theory unifies several previously disconnected results in metaprogramming and software design in a surprisingly simple and elegant way [8]. It points to an interesting and very different way of teaching and understanding software design and construction with an emphasis on science, and less on ad hoc techniques. Of course, much more work needs to be done to confirm this conjecture, but so far results are encouraging.

And finally, refactorings are not limited to the restructuring of source code; they apply to models and features as well (e.g., [34][38][40]), where the results of Section 3 and Section 5 should be directly applicable. Demonstrating this unity should be both an interesting and important research topic as it will further underscore the importance of architectural metaprogramming in software design and maintenance.

7 Conclusions

Just as the structure of matter is fundamental to chemistry and physics, so too is the structure of software fundamental to computer science. By structure, I mean what are modules and how do they compose? Today, the structure of software is not well-understood. Software design is an art form. As long as it remains so, our abilities to automate key tasks in program design, synthesis, and maintenance will be limited.

Recent work in program refactoring, program synthesis, and model-driven design are raising the level of abstraction in programming. Their individual successes are not accidental; I contend they focused on the essential complexities of software structure, and not on accidental complexities. Like other results, they are examples of a general programming paradigm that we are only now beginning to recognize. As is evident from the discussions in this paper, many details of architectural metaprogramming are not well understood and it is an open problem to nail them down precisely.

By 2020 the purview of software engineering, as before, will be to manage complexity. Embracing the ideas of architectural metaprogramming offers an appealing future: they will enable us to automate what is well-understood, to customize programs for performance, capability, or both, and to reduce maintenance and development costs, all on a principled basis. It will lead to higher-level programming languages, declarative languages for specifying programs in narrow domains, IDEs as program evolution calculators, and compilers as program calculators. Our understanding of programs, their representation and manipulation will be greatly expanded beyond code. But again, the grand prize is discovering the material that we will be teaching our future graduates and undergraduates that ties together these areas in an elegant way. An exciting future awaits us.

Acknowledgments. I gratefully acknowledge the helpful comments of S. Apel, O. Diaz, D. Dig, C. Kaestner, V. Kulkarni, C. Lengauer, R. Lopez-Herrejon, and S. Trujillo on earlier drafts of this paper.

References

[1] D. Ancona, F. Damiani, and S. Drossopoulou. "Polymorphic Bytecode: Compositional Compilation for Java-like Languages", *POPL 2005*.

[2] M. Antkiewicz and K. Czarnecki. "FeaturePlugin: Feature Modeling Plug-In for Eclipse", *OOPSLA Eclipse Technology eXchange (ETX) Workshop*, 2004.

[3] D. Batory. "Concepts for a Database System Compiler", *ACM PODS 1988*.

[4] D. Batory, B. Lofaso, and Y. Smaragdakis. "JTS: Tools for Implementing Domain-Specific Languages". *International Conference on Software Reuse*, 1998.

[5] D. Batory, G.Chen, E. Robertson, and T. Wang. "Design Wizards and Visual Programming Environments for GenVoca Generators", *IEEE TSE*, May 2000.

[6] D. Batory, J.N. Sarvela, and A. Rauschmayer. "Scaling Step-Wise Refinement", *IEEE TSE*, June 2004.

[7] D. Batory. "Multi-Level Models in Model-Driven Development, Product-Lines, and Metaprogramming", *IBM Systems Journal*, 45#3, 2006.

[8] D. Batory. "From Implementation to Theory in Product Synthesis", *POPL 2007* keynote.

[9] J. Bezivin. "From Object Composition to Model Transformation with the MDA", *TOOLS'USA*, August 2001.

[10] D. Binkley, et al. "Automated Refactoring of Object Oriented Code into Aspects", *ICSM 2005*.

[11] BMW. www.bmwusa.com

[12] F.P. Brookes. "No Silver bullet: Essence and Accidents of Software Engineering", *IEEE Computer*, April 1987.

[13] A. W. Brown, G. Booch, S. Iyengar, J. Rumbaugh, and B. Selic. "An MDA Manifesto", Chapter 11 in *Model-Driven Architecture Straight from the Masters*, D. S. Frankel and J. Parodi, Editors, Meghan-Kiffer Press, Tampa, FL, 2004.

[14] P. Clements and L. Northrup. *Software Product Lines: Practices and Patterns*, Addison-Wesley, 2001.

[15] L. Cole and P. Borba. "Deriving Refactorings for AspectJ", *AOSD 2005*.

[16] Dell Computers. www.dell.com

[17] D. Dig, C. Comertoglu, D. Marinov, and R. Johnson. "Automated Detection of Refactorings in Evolving Components", *ECOOP 2006*.

[18] D. Dig and R. Johnson. "How do APIs Evolve? A Story of Refactoring", *Journal of Software Maintenance and Evolution*, 18#2, 2006.

[19] S. Hanenberg, C. Oberschulte, and R. Unland. "Refactoring of Aspect-Oriented Software". *Net.ObjectDays 2003*.

[20] M. Fowler, K. Beck, J. Brant, W. Opdyke, and D. Roberts. *Refactoring: Improving the Design of Existing Code*, Addison-Wesley, 2000.

[21] K. Kang, et al. "Feature-Oriented Domain Analysis (FODA) Feasibility Study", Tech. Report CMU/SEI-90-TR-21.

[22] G. Kiczales, E. Hilsdale, J. Hugunin, M. Kirsten, J. Palm, and W.G. Griswold. "An overview of AspectJ", *ECOOP 2001*.

[23] A. Kleppe, J. Warmer, and W. Bast. *MDA Explained: The Model-Driven Architecture -- Practice and Promise*, Addison-Wesley, 2003.

[24] V. Kulkarni and S. Reddy. "Model-Driven Development of Enterprise Applications", in *UML Modeling Languages and Applications*, *Springer LNCS 3297, 2005.*

[25] R.E. Lopez-Herrejon and D. Batory. "A Standard Problem for Evaluating Product-Line Methodologies", *GCSE 2001*.

[26] R. Lopez-Herrejon, D. Batory, and C. Lengauer. "A Disciplined Approach to Aspect Composition", *PEPM 2006*.

[27] E. Meijer, M. Fokkinga, and R. Paterson. "Functional Programming with Bananas, Lenses, Envelopes, and Barbed Wire", *FPCA 1991*.

[28] M.P. Monteiro and J.M. Fernandes. "Towards a Catalog of Aspect-Oriented Refactorings", *AOSD 2005*.

[29] N. Nystrom, X. Qi, A.C. Myers. "J&: Nested Intersection for Scalable Software Composition", *OOPSLA 2006*.

[30] Object Management Group. www.omg.org/mda/committed-products.htm

[31] Odersky, M., et al. "An Overview of the Scala Programming Language". September 2004, scala.epfl.ch

[32] B. Pierce. *Basic Category Theory for Computer Scientists*, MIT Press, 1991.

[33] D.C. Schmidt. "Model-Driven Engineering". *IEEE Computer* 39(2), 2006.

[34] G. Sunyé, D. Pollet, Y. Le Traon, J-M. Jézéquel. "Refactoring UML Models". *Int Conf. UML*, LNCS 2185, Springer-Verlag 2001.

[35] J. Sztipanovits and G. Karsai. "Model Integrated Computing", *IEEE Computer*, April 1997.

[36] W. Taha and T. Sheard. "Multi-Stage Programming with Explicit Annotations", *PEPM 1997*.

[37] S. Trujillo, D. Batory, and O. Diaz. "Feature Oriented Model-Driven Development: A Case Study for Portlets", *ICSE 2007*.

[38] R. Van Der Straeten, V. Jonckers, and T. Mens. "Supporting Model Refactorings through Behaviour Inheritance Consistencies", *Int Conf. UML*, LNCS 3273, Springer-Verlag 2004.

[39] C. Zhang and H.-A. Jacobsen. "Resolving Feature Convolution in Middleware Systems", *OOPSLA 2004*.

[40] J. Zhang, Y. Lin, and J. Gray. "Generic and Domain-Specific Model Refactoring using a Model Transformation Engine", in *Model-driven Software Development*, (S. Beydeda, M. Book, and V. Gruhn, eds.), Springer 2005.

A Practical Escape and Effect Analysis for Building Lightweight Method Summaries*

Sigmund Cherem and Radu Rugina

Computer Science Department
Cornell University
Ithaca, NY 14853
{siggi,rugina}@cs.cornell.edu

Abstract. We present a unification-based, context-sensitive escape and effect analysis that infers lightweight method summaries describing heap effects. The analysis is parameterized on two values: k, indicating the heap depth beyond which objects escape; and b, a branching factor indicating the maximum number of fields per object that the analysis precisely tracks. Restricting these parameters to small values allows us to keep the method summaries lightweight and practical. Results collected from our implementation shows that the analysis scales well to large code bases such as the GNU Classpath libraries. They also show that summaries can help analysis clients approximate the effects of method calls, avoiding expensive inter-procedural computations, or imprecise worst-case assumptions.

1 Introduction

In the presence of method calls and heap allocation, program analyses must reason about the potential effects of invoking methods. When faced with this problem, typical analyses choose one of the two standard approaches: either perform an expensive inter-procedural analysis; or use a worst-case approximation of the possible method effects. The former affects the scalability and modularity of the analysis, whereas the latter can affect its precision. A middle ground is to summarize method behavior using effects [1] or other forms of method summaries, thus avoiding the costly inter-procedural computations or imprecise assumptions, at the expense of requiring method summaries to be provided from an external source. Summaries can be either supplied by a user and checked by the compiler; or computed automatically by a separate inference engine.

This paper proposes a practical inference algorithm that extracts lightweight method summaries (or signatures) to describe heap effects in Java programs. Our summaries serve as a foundation for other analyses, to approximate the effects of method calls. They can also be regarded as types; as such, they can be used to statically enforce a desired side-effect discipline, or for program understanding purposes.

This paper makes three contributions. First, it proposes lightweight method summaries in the form of *effect signatures* that concisely describe heap aliasing and heap access effects. Signatures provide information about objects being read or written, about returned objects, as well as about the aliasing effects of the method. Object are referred

---

* This work was supported in part by NSF grants CCF-0541217 and CNS-0406345.

S. Krishnamurthi and M. Odersky (Eds.): CC 2007, LNCS 4420, pp. 172–186, 2007.

to by their reachability from the parameters. Our signatures use k-limiting [2] to bound the heap depth in signatures. Objects beyond the k limit escape the k-bounded heap and are conflated into a $\top$ value denoting the rest of the heap. We distinguish between objects reachable through different fields, but we use a branching factor b to limit the number of outgoing fields per object. The key aspect of our approach is that the k and b parameters control the size of the signatures: small values of these parameters make the signatures lightweight. In our experience, small signatures are humanly readable, and can help programmers quickly understand the overall heap behavior of methods without exploring their code.

The second contribution is a flow-insensitive unification-based, context-sensitive analysis that infers method summaries for given values of parameters k and b. For each method, the analysis computes two signatures: a static signature, describing the effects of calling that method; and a virtual signature, describing the effects of calling the method, or any method that overrides it.

Third, the paper presents an evaluation of method signatures. We perform a case study of effect signatures for the entire GNU Classpath Java libraries version 0.92, and present signature statistics. We also perform case studies involving two dataflow analysis clients that use method signatures for the analysis of method calls. Our results indicate that both analyses benefit from using method summaries, but the benefits of using higher values of the parameters depends on the client.

The rest of the paper is organized as follows. Section 2 introduces the effect signatures. Section 3 presents our escape analysis algorithm. Section 4 presents experimental results. Finally, we discuss related work in Section 5 and conclude in Section 6.

2 Effect Signatures

The effect signature of a method describes the heap objects that the method accesses (i.e., reads or writes), and the aliases it might create. Method signatures use the notion of k-limiting [2] to bound potion of the heap that they accurately model. More precisely, objects reachable from static fields or through more than k field accesses from the method parameters are conflated together, and their access or alias effects are combined. We say that these objects escape the k-limited heap area of the current method.

This definition extends the traditional notion of escaped objects. Escape analyses commonly divide objects in three categories: a) those that never escape the current method's scope, e.g., objects unreachable outside the method; b) those that may escape the current method's scope but can be *captured* in the callers, e.g., returned objects; and c) those that may escape the current scope and are unrecoverable, e.g., objects stored in static fields. In our work, objects beyond the k-limit are also unrecoverable.

For clarity, we first discuss signatures that do not distinguish between different kinds of accesses (i.e., read vs. write), or between different object fields. The discussion about accesses and field-sensitivity follows afterward.

Consider a method m with parameters p_0, ..., p_n and return value r. The k-level effect signature of m uses at most $k + 1$ *attributes* for each parameter and for the return value, and is written as follows:

$$m : (\alpha_{0,0}, .., \alpha_{0,i_0}) \times ... \times (\alpha_{n,0}, .., \alpha_{n,i_n}) \rightarrow (\alpha_{r,0}, .., \alpha_{r,i_r})$$

Each attribute $\alpha_{i,j}$ is either $\bot$, $\top$, or a symbolic value. Bottom values $\bot$ correspond to parameters that have non-reference types (e.g., `void`, `int`, `char`, etc). Top values $\top$ correspond to objects that escape the k-limited heap. Symbolic values α describe abstract sets of objects (or regions). Different symbols refer to disjoint sets of objects. For each parameter p_j, the attributes in its sequence $\alpha_{j,0}, .., \alpha_{j,i_j}$ correspond to the accessed objects at depth 0, 1, .., i_j from p_j. If p_j has at most k attributes ($i_j < k$) and $\alpha_{j,i_j} \neq \top$, then the method does not access objects deeper that i_j levels from p_j. If p_j has $k + 1$ attributes, the last attribute must be $\top$, indicating that the method accesses objects reachable from p_j that are beyond the k limit. Multiple occurrences of the same attribute in the signature indicate aliasing effects. Below we give several examples to illustrate how method signatures capture different forms of effects.

Heap-escape effects. Consider $k = 1$. The following is the signature of a method that doesn't escape its first parameter to the heap, but escapes its second parameter, and returns an escaped reference:

$$m \; : \; \alpha \times \top \to \top$$

In general, if the first attribute of a parameter is a value $\alpha \neq \top$, then the parameter does not escape the k-limited area. In addition, if α doesn't occur elsewhere in the signature, the parameter is never store in a heap field.

Allocator methods. The following is the signature of a method that doesn't store its first parameter in the heap, and allocates and returns a fresh object. This is the typical signature of `toString` methods in Java:

$$\texttt{toString} \; : \; \alpha \to \beta$$

In general, if the first attribute of the returned value is a symbol that doesn't occur elsewhere in the signature, then the method behaves as an object allocator.

Returned parameters. Returned parameters are described using the same attribute for the parameter and the return value. For instance, method `append(int)` in class `StringBuffer` returns its parameter, without storing it into the heap:

$$\texttt{append} : \alpha \times \bot \to \alpha$$

Signatures can also express cases where the returned value is one among several parameters. For instance, method `max` in `java.math.BigDecimal` can return either of its two arguments. This behavior is described as follows:

$$\texttt{max} : \alpha \times \alpha \to \alpha$$

Heap accesses. Method signatures can indicate the portion of the heap that methods access. Consider the following methods:

$$m_1 : \alpha \to \bot$$
$$m_2 : (\alpha, \top) \to \bot$$

Neither method escapes its parameter. However, m_1 doesn't access objects other than its first parameter, whereas m_2 does.

Consider the heap effects of functions $set(o,v)$, that assigns v to the field f of object o; and $get(o)$ that retrieves the value of the same field. The 1-level signatures of these methods are:

$$set : (\alpha, \top) \times \top \rightarrow \bot$$
$$get : (\alpha, \top) \rightarrow \top$$

Neither method escapes the receiver object (the first parameter), but set escapes its second argument, and get returns an escaped reference. In contrast, 2-level signatures are more accurate and indicate where objects are loaded from or stored into:

$$set : (\alpha, \beta) \times \beta \rightarrow \bot$$
$$get : (\alpha, \beta) \rightarrow \beta$$

Here, α corresponds to the receiver object, and β to any objects that the fields of the receiver may reference during the execution of the method. The object loaded or stored is located one level deep from the receiver object.

In general, method signatures can describe the effects of methods that contain a combination of field load and store operations. For instance, the effects of m(x,y) with body "x.f = y.f; return x" is described by the following 2-level signature:

$$m : (\alpha, \gamma) \times (\beta, \gamma) \rightarrow (\alpha, \gamma)$$

Modeling read and write effects. In the signatures above, an attribute α or $\top$ indicates that the method accesses, i.e., reads or writes, the corresponding portion of the heap. We refine our representation by tagging with a label that indicates the kind of access:

- a write access "w" shows that an object field has been written;
- a read-field access "r" indicates that an object field has been read;
- a read-address access "a" shows that the reference of an object has been read.

Tags form a lattice where $a \le w$ and $a \le r$, since accessing a field requires reading its reference. An rw tag indicates the combination of r and w tags: $r \le rw$ and $w \le rw$. Tags are placed on all attributes, including $\top$, and are shown in superscripts. The signatures of methods set and get become:

$$set : (\alpha^w, \beta^a) \times \beta^a \rightarrow \bot$$
$$get : (\alpha^r, \beta^a) \rightarrow \beta^a$$

The signatures indicate that references to any of the objects described by β might be read, but their contents are not accessed.

Field sensitivity. We further refine signatures to describe the fields needed to reach objects in the signature. For example, the field-sensitive signature of set is:

$$set : (\alpha^w, f : \beta^a) \times \beta^a \rightarrow \bot$$

The signature says that the second argument might alias the field f of the receiver, but not any other field. When multiple fields are used, the signature lists each accessed field.

For example, a method *setFG* that receives two arguments and stores them in the f and g fields of the receiver object, would have the signature:

$$setFG : (\alpha^w, (f : \beta^a \mid g : \gamma^a)) \times \beta^a \times \gamma^a \rightarrow \bot$$

To maintain the signatures small we introduce a branching limit b, and restrict all attributes to have at most b different outgoing fields. When methods access more fields than the branching limit, fields are collapsed together, as in the field-insensitive case.

3 Signature Inference Algorithm

The goal of the k-level escape and effect analysis is to compute method signatures for all methods. We consider programs with the following syntax:

$$\begin{aligned}
\text{Locations:} \quad & loc ::= x \mid x.f \mid C.f \\
\text{Expressions:} \quad & e ::= loc \mid \texttt{null} \mid \texttt{new } C \mid m(x_0, .., x_n) \\
\text{Statements:} \quad & s ::= loc = e
\end{aligned}$$

Here, x ranges over variables, f over fields, C over classes, and m over methods. Variables include formal method parameters, denoted $p_0, .., p_n$. For virtual methods, p_0 is the reference to the receiver object. Expressions include static field accesses $C.f$ and instance field accesses $x.f$. To simplify the presentation, we assume that all expressions have reference types, and that methods always return a value. A throw statement "`throw x`" is represented as "`Exc.exc = x`" where `exc` is a static field of a special class `Exc`; catching an exception "`catch(Exception x)`" is represented as "`x = Exc.exc`"; and a return statement "`return x`" is modeled as an assignment to a special return variable: "`ret = x`". Arrays are modeled as a special field "`[]`".

The algorithm derives two signatures for each method m: a static signature $sig^S(m)$, that models a call to the method itself; and a virtual signature $sig^V(m)$ that models a virtual call that might be dispatched to the method or any of the methods that override it. This is motivated by the `invokespecial` bytecode instruction that statically calls a virtual method. The callee is determined statically using type information, even though the method is virtual and the call could have been dispatched. An important occurrence of this situation is the `<init>` method of `Object`, which is statically called after each object allocation. If one of the `<init>` methods escapes its receiver object, then `Object`'s `<init>` signature would be polluted and each object would escape right after allocation. The use of two signatures automatically solves this issue.

Figure 1 shows the k-level escape and effect analysis. The algorithm is formulated as a constraint-based analysis that uses unifications. The algorithm first performs an initialization, then analyzes each method by visiting each of its statements. Finally, it performs a context-sensitive instantiation of the callees' signatures into their callers.

Initially, each variable x is assigned a fresh attribute α representing the first attribute in its sequence. Each attribute has two pieces of information: the access tag (r, w, or a), and the maximum heap depth from any variable in the current scope. Subsequent attributes are generated *lazily*, as the analysis proceeds and determines that methods access deeper objects in the heap. Attributes are generated on-demand using a successor

Defintions:

$\bar{e}$ = first attribute of e

$sig(m)$ = signature of $m(p_1....p_n)$

$\overline{p_1} \times .. \times \overline{p_n} \to \overline{ret}$

$succ$ = lazy successor function

$$succ(\alpha_{[j]}, f) = \begin{cases} \alpha'_{[j+1]} & \text{if } \alpha_{[j]} \neq \top \\ & \text{and } j < k \\ \top & \text{otherwise} \end{cases}$$

Checking the branch limit:

If: $| \{f \mid hasSucc(\alpha_{[j]}, f)\} | > b$

Then: $unify(succ(\alpha_{[j]}, *), succ(\alpha_{[j]}, f))$

Initialization:

For each variable x:

$\bar{x} = \alpha_{[0]}$, fresh attribute $\alpha_{[0]}$ at depth 0

For each field access $x.f$:

$\overline{x.f} = succ(\bar{x}, f)$

For each static field $C.f$:

$\overline{C.f} = \top$

Set successor of $\top$:

$unify(\top, succ(\top, *))$

Recursive Unifications:

If: $unify(\alpha, \beta)$ and

($hasSucc(\alpha, f)$ or $hasSucc(\beta, f)$)

Then: $unify(succ(\alpha, f), succ(\beta, f))$

Intra-procedural constraints:

Build the static signature $sig^S(m)$:

For each assignment $loc = e$:

$unify(\overline{loc}, \bar{e})$ if $e \in \{x, x.f, C.f\}$

$a \in tag(\bar{x})$ if $e \in \{x\}$

$r \in tag(\bar{x})$ if $e \in \{x.f, m(x, ...)\}$

$r \in tag(\top)$ if $e \in \{C.f\}$

$w \in tag(\bar{x})$ if $loc \in \{x.f\}$

$w \in tag(\top)$ if $loc \in \{C.f\}$

Inter-procedural signature constraints:

For each static call $loc = m(y_0, .., y_n)$:

$sig^S(m) \leq \overline{y_0} \times ... \times \overline{y_n} \to \overline{loc}$

For each virtual call $loc = m(y_0, .., y_n)$:

$sig^V(m) \leq \overline{y_0} \times ... \times \overline{y_n} \to \overline{loc}$

For each method $m : sig^S(m) \leq sig^V(m)$

If m overrides m' : $sig^V(m) \leq sig^V(m')$

Signature embedding:

$\alpha_0 \times .. \times \alpha_n \to \alpha_r \leq \alpha'_0 \times .. \times \alpha'_n \to \alpha'_r$

If there exists μ such that:

$\mu(\top) = \top$

$\mu(\alpha_i) = \alpha'_i$, $\forall i = 0..n, r$

$succ(\alpha, f) = \beta \Rightarrow succ(\mu(\alpha), f) = \mu(\beta)$

$tag(\alpha) \leq tag(\mu(\alpha))$

Fig. 1. The k-level escape and effect analysis. An expression e has an attribute sequence starting with attribute $\bar{e}$. Successors in the sequence are obtained lazily with function $succ()$.

function $succ$. Given an attribute $\alpha_{[j]}$ at depth j, and a field f, function $succ$ returns the successor attribute for that field if one exists. Otherwise, it creates a fresh successor $\alpha'_{[j+1]}$ at depth $j + 1$. The successor function returns the $\top$ value when the maximum depth $j = k$ has been reached; and collapses all successors when the branching limit b is reached. A special field "*" denotes that all fields have been collapsed.

When the analysis unifies two attributes, it merges their access tags, and takes the maximum heap depth. Unifications are recursive, so that unifying two attributes requires unifying each of their corresponding successors. To ensure laziness, this is done only if at least one of them has a successor. As usual, unifications can be implemented efficiently using union-find structures.

After initialization, the algorithm performs an intra-procedural computation of static method signatures. For each assignment, the analysis unifies the attributes of the expressions in the assignment. It also sets the appropriate access tags, according to the semantics of assignments, as shown in the top right corner of Figure 1.

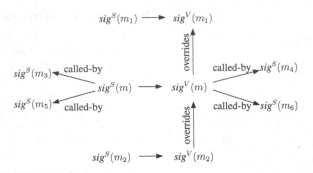

Fig. 2. Dependences between static and virtual method signatures for a method m

Finally, the analysis runs the inter-procedural part of the algorithm. The analysis imposes two kinds of inter-procedural signature constraints: call-site and overriding constraints. We use a notion of signature embedding (or subtyping) to describe the fact that the effects in a signature are reflected in another signature. We write $sig \le sig'$ to denote that signature sig is embedded in sig'. Signature embedding is defined in the lower right part in Figure 1. With this definition, the analysis requires that: 1) each static signature of a method must be embedded in the virtual signature of that method; 2) the virtual signature of a method must be embedded in the virtual signature of the method it directly overrides, if any; and 3) at each call site, the appropriate signature of the callee must be embedded into the call site signature. Hence, the analysis uses the overriding relations to determine possible targets at each call. The analysis is context-sensitive: it instantiates the signature of the callee at each call site via embedding.

Inter-procedural signature constraints are graphically illustrated in Figure 2. In the presence of recursive functions, signature constraints become circular and require a fixed-point-computation. The analysis uses a worklist algorithm to solve the constraints. Initially, all methods are added to the worklist. At each step, the algorithm removes a method m from the worklist and enforces the embedding constraints corresponding to the incoming edges to m in Figure 2. If the signature of m changes, then the analysis adds to the worklist the signatures of all methods on the outgoing edges from m.

Treatment of recursive structures. With the analysis presented so far, objects belonging to cyclic structures always escape the k-limited heap, and objects in recursive structures typically escape, too. We briefly sketch an extension that improves the analysis precision in such cases. The idea is to regard the escape signatures as graphs where nodes are attributes, and edges model the successor relations. Using this conceptual representation, signatures in the standard algorithm are k-bounded DAGs. In the extended algorithm, they are k-bounded cyclic graphs. This is done by changing the meaning of depth: the depth of each attribute is the depth in the spanning tree of the graph. The algorithm is changed so that, after the *succ* or *unify* functions are applied, the depths of *all* attributes are recomputed; those beyond the k limit are conflated into $\top$. This extension allows the analysis to treat all elements of a recursive structure such as a list as non-escaping, by representing them using a single non-top attribute having a self loop.

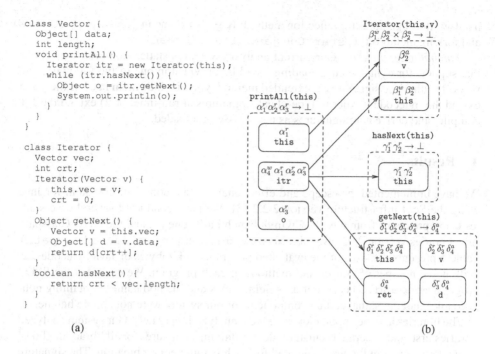

```
class Vector {
  Object[] data;
  int length;
  void printAll() {
    Iterator itr = new Iterator(this);
    while (itr.hasNext()) {
      Object o = itr.getNext();
      System.out.println(o);
    }
  }
}

class Iterator {
  Vector vec;
  int crt;
  Iterator(Vector v) {
    this.vec = v;
    crt = 0;
  }
  Object getNext() {
    Vector v = this.vec;
    Object[] d = v.data;
    return d[crt++];
  }
  boolean hasNext() {
    return crt < vec.length;
  }
}
```

(a)   (b)

Fig. 3. Escape and effect analysis with $k = 4$, $b = 0$: a) example program; and b) analysis results for each method. The call to `System.out.println()` is omitted; this method reads the content of the object passed in.

Example. Figure 3 shows an example of inter-procedural k-level effect analysis. This example uses a `Vector` class and an `Iterator` for vectors. The `Vector` class has a method `printAll()` that uses an `Iterator` to print all of the elements in the vector. The right part of the figure shows the analysis result for $k = 4$ and $b = 0$ for methods `printAll`, `getNext`, `hasNext`, and for the constructor `Iterator`. For each method, the dashed box groups the variables of that method. The arrows show the inter-procedural constraints at the call sites to `getNext`, `hasNext`, and `Iterator`. The escape attributes of each variable are shown above the variable. Method signatures are shown above each method's box.

The limit of $k = 4$ allows the analysis to precisely identify the accessed objects. For instance, the 4-level signature of `getNext` identifies that the returned object is an object at depth 3 from the receiver; and that no object beyond that level is accessed.

Java Features. We briefly discuss several other Java features.
Interface, abstract, static, and native methods. Interface and abstract methods only have a virtual signature, since they cannot be called statically. Similarly, static methods only have a static signature. For native methods, we manually wrote signatures to model their effects.

Threads and calls by reflection. All objects passed to child threads, or passed as arguments to calls by reflection are marked as escaped. This is done by providing hand-written signatures for reflection methods (e.g. forName in java.lang.Class) and forking methods (i.e. start0 in java.lang.Thread).

Dynamic class loading. Our current analysis system is static. However, we believe that support for dynamic class loading could be provided in one of the following two ways: 1) either use signatures as extended method types, include them in class files, and extend the bytecode verifier to type-check signatures at run-time; or 2) extend the JIT compiler and derive new signatures as new classes get loaded.

4 Results

We have implemented the escape and effect analysis in a compilation system for Java using the Soot infrastructure version 2.2.2 [3]. We have conducted several case studies using programs from the SPECjvm98 benchmark suite [4] and the GNU Classpath Java libraries version 0.92 (available at: www.gnu.org/software/classpath). Table 1 presents the sizes of the evaluated programs in kilobytes of Java bytecodes, as well as the number of classes and methods in each program. We excluded the SPEC program mpegaudio because it uses field names and method names containing non-printable characters, that certain components of our system were not able to handle.

The libraries and the application code were analyzed separately. Our system analyzed libraries first, and generated signature files containing signatures for all library methods. A separate signature file was generated for each parameter combination. The signature files are in text format; they are humanly readable and can be manually edited [1]. Next, when analyzing an application, the system first loaded signatures from the appropriate signature file. Our tool automatically detected when the application changed library method signatures via overriding. This was the case for a few methods in the SPEC test harness that extended classes in java.io or java.awt. To preserve soundness, we have manually edited the violating signatures (13 in total) and reanalyzed the libraries. No violations were then reported with the new signatures.

The remaining of this section presents three case studies: a study of library methods and two analysis clients. The signatures in these studies use values of k between 1 to 4, and values of b of $0, 1, 2, 5,$ and 15. The extension for cyclic and recursive structures discussed in Section 3 has only been used in the first study; in the other two studies it was disabled because it did not impact the analysis clients.

4.1 Case Study 1: Library Methods

The first case study evaluates the analysis of the GNU Classpath Java libraries and presents statistics regarding the method effects in these libraries. In this experiment we used a Dual Xeon 3 Ghz machine with 4Gb of memory, running Linux.

Analysis cost. Table 2 presents the analysis times for the entire GNU Classpath libraries, for different values of k and b. These results demonstrate the scalability of our approach: the analysis can analyze a code base containing more than 50K methods and 16 Mb of Java bytecodes in 1 minute or less. For example, for $k = 3$ and $b = 5$, the

---

[1] The signature files can be browsed online at: http://www.cs.cornell.edu/projects/frex/sigs

Table 1. Application sizes

Program	Size(Kb)	Classes	Methods
compress	68	12	44
jess	319	151	690
raytrace	110	25	176
db	67	3	34
javac	579	176	1190
mtrt	110	26	180
jack	180	56	316
Total SPECjvm98	1433	473	2851
GNU Classpath v.092	16815	6586	54436

Table 2. Analysis times (in seconds) for the GNU Classpath libraries

$b \backslash k$	1	2	3	4
0	23	25	25	26
1	25	27	28	32
2	26	28	35	39
5	33	35	37	43
15	34	41	66	280

analysis takes less than 40 seconds. In comparison, the time needed by Soot just to load the class files from disk and build the intermediate representation is about 6 minutes, an order of magnitude larger. Memory consumption is also a concern when performing whole-program analysis on a very large code base. Loading the intermediate representation requires about 900Mb of memory. The memory needed by our analysis ranged from 100Mb to 300Mb, for different values of the parameters.

Signature information. To better understand the escape behavior of methods in the Java libraries, we have collected statistics about reference parameters and returned values in library methods. Reference parameters can be classified in four categories: escaped, stored, returned, and borrowed. Escaped parameters are reachable from static fields, thrown exceptions, or objects beyond the k-limit. Stored parameters are reachable through one or more field dereferences (within the k-limit) from another parameter. All of the other parameters are borrowed. If a reference is passed into a borrowed parameter of a method, then the method does not create additional copies of that reference.

Return values are divided in five groups: escaped, stored, loaded, parameter, and fresh. Stored return values are objects that, besides being returned, are also reachable from a parameter's field. Loaded return values are objects that were reachable from a parameter's field even before executing the method. Write effects play a key role in distinguishing loaded values from stored values: if an object is represented by an attribute with only read effects, all of the object's fields may be loaded but are never stored. Fresh returned values denote new objects returned by allocator methods.

Table 3 shows the distribution of reference parameters and return values among all signatures generated for the GNU library. The following summarizes our findings:

- A large fraction (roughly 69%) of the method parameters are just borrowed;
- An escape analysis with $k \geq 2$ can identify that about 6% of the parameters are being stored in the field of another parameter;
- Few of the parameters (1%) are returned, and few of the returned objects 4% come from the parameters;
- A large fraction of methods, 42%, are allocator methods that return fresh objects. An additional 14% of the returned objects are loaded from a parameter field;
- Signatures improve for higher values of k and b. However, increasing values of these parameters yield diminishing returns. Signatures can be further improved using the more precise treatment of cycles and recursive structures.

Table 3. Distribution of parameters and return values in static signatures

			Parameter values				Returned values				
k	b	model cycles	Escaped	Stored	Returned	Borrowed	Escaped	Stored	Loaded	Returned param.	Fresh
1	0	no	30.7%	0%	0.9%	68.4%	53.8%	0%	0%	4.3%	41.9%
2	2	no	24.3%	5.9%	0.9%	68.9%	39.3%	0.7%	13.6%	4.3%	42.1%
3	5	no	23.2%	6.9%	0.9%	69.0%	36.8%	1.1%	15.5%	4.3%	42.3%
4	15	no	22.3%	7.5%	1.0%	69.2%	35.4%	1.4%	16.2%	4.4%	42.6%
4	15	yes	17.9%	11.8%	1.0%	69.3%	33.9%	2.3%	16.8%	4.4%	42.6%

4.2   Case Study 2: Variable Uniqueness Analysis

The second case study evaluates method summaries in the context of a dataflow analysis client aimed at identifying unique variables. A variable is unique if it holds the only live reference to the object it points to. The uniqueness information is used by a compiler to provide compile-time memory management for Java programs, by automatically inserting *free* statements when the program updates a unique variable. In this study, method summaries are used to improve the analysis precision at method calls.

The uniqueness analysis is formulated as a forward dataflow analysis. At each program point, the analysis computes a partition of variables, i.e., a set of disjoint sets of variables. A heap object referenced by a variable in a set can be referenced only by other variables in the same set. When a set contains a single variable, that variable is unique. At each allocation site $x = new()$, the analysis creates a new partition $\{x\}$. The transfer functions remove variables when they are updated; move them to other sets when they are copied; or kill entire sets when variable references are stored into the heap.

In the absence of method signatures, method calls are also treated conservatively: variable sets are killed when a reference in the set is passed as an argument or returned from a method. When method summaries are available, the analysis of method calls is enhanced in three ways. First, calls to allocator method are treated as allocation sites. Second, a set is not killed when a variable in the set is passed as an argument to a method, but the method signature indicates that the corresponding parameter is just borrowed. Finally, the analysis models returned parameters as assignments in the caller.

Evaluation.   We ran two versions of the uniqueness analysis, with and without method summaries, and compared the amount of memory freed using these analyses. We also compared these memory savings to those obtained from a sophisticated inter-procedural shape analysis that we previously developed [5]. For a fair comparison, we used the same machine as in our previous work, a 2Ghz Pentium with 1Gb of memory.

When using worst-case assumptions for method calls, the uniqueness analysis took 2 seconds for all the the benchmarks together. The compiler inserted 86 frees, allowing the deallocation of 4% of the total memory. When using the method summaries of $k = 1$ and $b = 0$ to model method calls, the analysis took 3 seconds, inserted 710 free statements, and enabled the deallocation of 36% of the total memory. In comparison, shape analysis [5] is able to reclaim up to 54% of the memory, but it is significantly more expensive, requiring a total of 11 minutes for the analysis of all of the benchmarks. Table 4 shows a breakdown of the memory savings for each benchmark, using each of

Table 4. Case Study 2: Maximum memory usage with no GC, and total analysis times

Program	Memory (Mb)			Savings (%)		Shape
	Total	Summaries		Summaries		analysis
	allocated	No	Yes	No	Yes	savings[5]
compress	111	111	111	0%	0%	78%
jess	305	305	246	0%	19%	19%
raytrace	161	138	32	14%	80%	81%
db	81	81	37	0%	54%	86%
javac	240	238	230	1%	4%	14%
mtrt	170	147	41	13%	75%	77%
jack	313	313	257	0%	17%	24%
Average				4%	36%	54%
Total analysis time		2sec	3sec			11 min

Table 5. Case Study 3: Additional redundant loads for the SPECjvm98 programs

$b\backslash k$	1	2	3	4
0	6%	6%	7%	7%
1	7%	11%	13%	13%
2	8%	11%	13%	13%
5	8%	11%	14%	14%
15	8%	11%	14%	14%

the three analyses. For some applications, such as *db* and *jess*, the additional saving when using summaries are due to the ability of recognizing allocator methods. We also experimented with larger values $k > 1$ and $b > 0$, but although the compiler added a few more frees, the memory usage of the transformed programs was unchanged.

In summary, the uniqueness analysis with method summaries runs much faster than a full-blown inter-procedural shape analysis; it is more precise compared to using worst-case assumptions; and higher values of k and b do not bring more benefits.

4.3   Case Study 3: Redundant Loads

The third study is a dataflow analysis aimed at identifying redundant loads. We ran this analysis with and without using method summaries, and compared the total number of identified redundant loads.

The analysis is a forward dataflow analysis that computes a set of available loads at each program point. The analysis is similar to the standard available expressions analysis and uses set intersection as the merge operator. A load statement $x = y.f$ is redundant if $y.f$ is available before the statement.

At method calls, the analysis uses the method signatures to determine the fields that the callees might update. A method updates field f if the signature of that method contains an attribute with write effects and outgoing edge f or "*". The analysis preserves a load $x.f$ if it determines that the callee doesn't update field f.

Evaluation. Table 5 shows the analysis results for the SPECjvm98 benchmarks. For each value of k and b, the table shows the number of additional redundant loads that the analysis has identified, as a percentage of the number of redundant loads identified when using worst-case assumptions at method calls. The results indicate an increase of up to 14% more redundant loads. Unlike in the previous case study, higher values of k and b lead to performance improvements in the client analysis. However, there seems to be no additional improvement beyond $k = 3$ and $b = 5$. For this experiment we used the same machine as in the previous experiment. The analysis time for any parameter combination took less than 2 seconds per benchmark.

Table 6. Comparison of related pointer and escape analyses. Columns indicate: flow-sensitivity (FS); context-sensitivity (CS); unification-based analyses (Unif); the k and b limits; whether method summaries are computed; and the largest application analyzed (only for Java analyses). Notes: [1] context-insensitive within an SCC; [2] object-sensitive; [3] estimated bound.

Algorithm	FS	CS	Unif	k	b	Method Summaries	Largest Java app. analyzed Name	Size(Mb)
Choi et. al. [8]	✓	✓		∞	∞	✓	Trans	0.5
Whaley, Rinard [9]	✓	✓		∞	∞	✓	Pbob	0.3
Blanchet [10]		✓		∞	0	✓	Jess	0.4
Gay, Steensgaard [11]		✓		1	∞		Marmot	1.5^3
Bogda, Hoelzle [12]	✓	✓		2	∞	✓	Javac	0.6
Ruf [13]	✓[1]	✓		∞	∞	✓	Marmot	1.5^3
O'Callahan [14]	✓	✓		∞	∞	✓	Ladybug	0.4
Cherem, Rugina [15]	✓	✓		∞	∞	✓	Javac	0.6
Whaley, Lam [16]	✓			∞	∞		Gruntspud	0.7
Milanova et al. [17]	✓[2]			∞	∞		Soot-1.beta.4	1.1
Sridharan,Bodík [18]	✓			∞	∞		Sablecc-j	2.4
Wilson, Lam [19]	✓	✓		∞	∞	✓	—	—
Liang, Harrold [20]	✓	✓		∞	∞	✓	—	—
Fähndrich et al. [21]	✓	✓		∞	∞		—	—
Lattner,Adve [22]	✓[1]	✓		∞	∞	✓	—	—
This paper		✓	✓	any	any	✓	Classpath v0.92	16.3

5   Related Work

Type and effect systems. Type and effect systems have been originally proposed in the seminal work of Gifford and Lucassen on type and effect systems for mostly functional languages [1]. Effect annotations for Java have been proposed in several systems, including JML [6], a specification language that allows specifying pure methods, and assignable locations that a method can mutate; or AliasJava [7], a system that supports an annotation lent that indicates non-escaping method parameters. Our effect signatures are richer and cover a larger set of effects compared to these systems. In addition to read/write effects, our signatures can describe method allocator effects, aliasing effects in the shallow heap, or returned parameters. Furthermore, our work focuses on the efficient static inference of such effects, rather than on type-checking effect annotations.

Escape and pointer analysis. Escape and pointer analyses has been an active area of research for many years. A large number of algorithms have been proposed in the past two decades. Table 6 summarizes a relevant subset of these algorithms and classifies them according to their features, shown in the columns of the table. The distinctive feature of our algorithm is that it is parameterized on the values of parameters k and b. These values can be tuned to trade precision for efficiency, and vice-versa.

Most analyses use infinite depth and field branching ($k = b = \infty$). Exceptions include the analysis of Gay and Steensgaard [11] where objects escape when they are stored in the heap, i.e. $k = 1$; the analysis of Bodga and Hoelzle [12], with $k = 2$; and the analysis of Blanchet [10] which identifies objects by their heap depth, hence $b = 0$. In essence, our parameterized escape analysis generalizes all of these analyses.

Escape analyses have been traditionally used to identify objects that do not escape their method or thread scopes, thus enabling stack allocation or synchronization elimination optimizations [11,9,12,10]. Pointer analyses have been mainly concerned with building points-to sets, or resolving alias queries [21,16,17,18]. Other pointer analyses have been used to summarize method effects [22,15,23]. Our work focuses on this last use of pointer analysis. Therefore, the ability of the analysis to compute and build procedure summaries becomes an important aspect, as effects can be expressed more naturally using summaries. In existing algorithms, method summaries are points-to graphs [20,13,22,15]; type representations of points-to graphs [14]; or pairs of input-output points-to graphs, in the case of flow-sensitive analyses [9,19,23]. Pointer analyses that do not compute method summaries require an additional MOD analysis to translate the points-to set information into side-effect information for each method [17]. In contrast to all of the existing analyses that compute method summaries, our analysis has the ability to control the sizes of the summaries, by tuning the values of k and b. For small values of k and b, the analysis becomes scalable and efficient, and signatures become lightweight and humanly readable.

Although all analyses in Table 6 exhibit a certain degree of context-sensitivity, some use restricted forms. Some analyses treat recursive cycles in a context-insensitive manner to avoid fixed-point computations for recursive procedures [13,22]. For large code bases such as the Java libraries that have large recursive cycles, large portions of the code will end up being analyzed in a context-insensitive manner. Object-sensitive analyses [17] use another restricted form where calling contexts distinguish only the receiver object. Our analysis uses the general, unrestricted notion of context-sensitivity, and uses a context-sensitive heap abstraction.

As shown in the last column of Table 6, our case study on the GNU Classpath libraries involves a whole-program code base larger than those experimented with in previous escape or pointer analysis studies. This demonstrates the scalability of our escape analysis using lightweight summaries.

6   Conclusions

We have proposed lightweight method signatures to summarize heap aliasing and heap access effects. We also have presented a very efficient unification-based, context-sensitive algorithm to derive such signatures. We have demonstrated the scalability of signature inference a large code base, and shown that computed summaries can help analysis clients to approximate the effects of methods calls and avoid worst-case assumptions.

References

1. Lucassen, J.M., Gifford, D.K.: Polymorphic effect systems. In: Proceedings of the Symposium on the Principles of Programming Languages. (1988)
2. Jones, N., Muchnick, S.: Flow analysis and optimization of Lisp-like structures. In: Conference Record of the Symposium on the Principles of Programming Languages, San Antonio, TX (1979)
3. Vallee-Rai, R., Hendren, L., Sundaresan, V., Lam, P., Gagnon, E., Co, P.: Soot - a Java optimization framework. In: CASCON '99, Toronto, CA (1999)

4. Uniejewski, J.: SPEC Benchmark Suite: Designed for today's advanced systems. SPEC Newsletter Volume 1, Issue 1, SPEC (1989)
5. Cherem, S., Rugina, R.: Compile-time deallocation of individual objects. In: Proceedings of the International Symposium on Memory Management, Ottawa, Canada (2006)
6. Burdy, L., Cheon, Y., Cok, D., Ernst, M., Kiniry, J., Leavens, G., Leino, R., Poll, E.: An overview of JML tools and applications. International Journal on Software Tools for Technology Transfer 7(3) (2005) 212–232
7. Aldrich, J., Kostadinov, V., Chambers, C.: Alias annotations for program understanding. In: Proceedings of the Conference on Object-Oriented Programming Systems, Languages and Applications, Seattle, WA (2002)
8. Choi, J.D., Gupta, M., Serrano, M.J., Sreedhar, V.C., Midkiff, S.P.: Stack allocation and synchronization optimizations for java using escape analysis. ACM Trans. Program. Lang. Syst. 25(6) (2003) 876–910
9. Whaley, J., Rinard, M.: Compositional pointer and escape analysis for Java programs. In: Proceedings of the Conference on Object-Oriented Programming Systems, Languages and Applications, Denver, CO (1999)
10. Blanchet, B.: Escape analysis for Java: Theory and practice. ACM Transactions on Programming Languages and Systems 25(6) (2003) 713–775
11. Gay, D., Steensgaard, B.: Fast escape analysis and stack allocation for object-based programs. In: Proceedings of the International Conference on Compiler Construction, Berlin, Germany (2000)
12. Bogda, J., Hoelzle, U.: Removing unnecessary synchronization in Java. In: Proceedings of the Conference on Object-Oriented Programming Systems, Languages and Applications, Denver, CO (1999)
13. Ruf, E.: Effective synchronization removal for Java. In: Proceedings of the Conference on Program Language Design and Implementation, Vancouver, Canada (2000)
14. O'Callahan, R.: Generalized Aliasing as a Basis for Program Analysis Tools. PhD thesis, School of Computer Science, Carnegie Mellon Univ. (2001)
15. Cherem, S., Rugina, R.: Region analysis and transformation for Java programs. In: Proceedings of the International Symposium on Memory Management, Vancouver, Canada (2004)
16. Whaley, J., Lam, M.: Cloning-based context-sensitive pointer alias analysis using binary decision diagrams. In: Proceedings of the Conference on Program Language Design and Implementation. (2004)
17. Milanova, A., Rountev, A., Ryder, B.: Parameterized object sensitivity for points-to analysis for Java. ACM Transactions Softw. Eng. Methodol. 14(1) (2005) 1–41
18. Sridharan, M., Bodík, R.: Refinement-based context-sensitive points-to analysis for java. In: Proceedings of the Conference on Program Language Design and Implementation. (2006)
19. Wilson, R., Lam, M.: Efficient context-sensitive pointer analysis for C programs. In: Proceedings of the Conference on Program Language Design and Implementation. (1995)
20. Liang, D., Harrold, M.: Efficient points-to analysis for whole-program analysis. In: Proceedings of the Symposium on the Foundations of Software Engineering, Toulouse,France (1999)
21. Fähndrich, M., Rehof, J., Das, M.: Scalable context-sensitive flow analysis using instantiation constraints. In: Proceedings of the Conference on Program Language Design and Implementation, Vancouver, Canada (2000)
22. Lattner, C., Adve, V.: Data Structure Analysis: An Efficient Context-Sensitive Heap Analysis. Tech. Report UIUCDCS-R-2003-2340, Computer Science Dept., Univ. of Illinois at Urbana-Champaign (2003)
23. Salcianu, A., Rinard, M.: Purity and side effect analysis for Java programs. In: Proceedings of the Conference on Verification, Model Checking and Abstract Interpretation. (2005)

Layout Transformations for Heap Objects Using Static Access Patterns*

Jinseong Jeon, Keoncheol Shin, and Hwansoo Han

Division of Computer Science
Korea Advanced Institute of Science and Technology (KAIST)
Daejeon 305-701 Republic of Korea
{jinseong.jeon,keoncheol.shin}@arcs.kaist.ac.kr, hshan@cs.kaist.ac.kr

Abstract. As the amount of data used by programs increases due to the growth of hardware storage capacity and computing power, efficient memory usage becomes a key factor for performance. Since modern applications heavily use structures allocated in the heap, this paper proposes an efficient structure layout based on static analyses. Unlike most of the previous work, our approach is an entirely static transformation of programs. We extract access patterns from source programs and represent them with *regular expressions*. Repetitive accesses are usually important pieces of information for locality optimizations. The expressive power of regular expressions is appropriate to represent those repetitive accesses along with various access patterns according to the control flow of programs. By interpreting statically obtained access patterns, we choose suitable structures for pool allocation and reorganize field layouts of the chosen structures. To verify the effect of our static optimization, we implement our analyses and optimizations with the CIL compiler. Our experiments with the Olden benchmarks demonstrate that layout transformations for heap objects based on our static access pattern analysis improve cache locality by 38% and performance by 24%.

1 Introduction

Efficient memory usage is getting more important as more programs try to deal with large and complex data sets. Researchers investigated many ways to improve the efficiency of memory management, including additional hardware, new architectures, and compiler optimizations. Compiler optimizations are more attractive than other methods, since compilers can transform application codes to have more memory-friendly behaviors without any additional costs but a longer compile time spent in static analyses. Several compiler optimizations for memory management attempt to attain better locality by modifying application codes. Segregating the heap according to the lifetime of objects [1] or the pointing shapes of data structures [2], for instance, is studied. Region-based memory management [3], array regrouping [4, 5], and field layout restructuring [6–8] are

---

* This work was supported by grant No. R01-2006-000-11196-0 from the Basic Research Program of the Korea Science & Engineering Foundation.

S. Krishnamurthi and M. Odersky (Eds.): CC 2007, LNCS 4420, pp. 187–201, 2007.

other optimizations investigated by researchers. Some techniques use compile-time evaluated properties of programs by applying data structure analysis [2] or region inference [9]. Other techniques, on the other hand, rely on profiling for necessary information.

Previous studies on optimizations using memory access patterns are usually profile-based, since it is difficult to analyze memory access behaviors at compile-time. Profiling, however, is sensitive to inputs and execution environments sometimes. Hence profile-based optimizations can be limited in their usages. On the contrary, our goal is to predict memory access patterns through static analysis. In this paper, we propose a novel method to represent memory access patterns as *regular expressions*. This method is a completely compile-time process. Once we obtain memory access patterns in the forms of regular expressions, we use those pieces of information to guide heap layout transformations based on *pool allocation* and *field layout restructuring*.

The common essence of pool allocation and field layout restructuring is to enhance data locality by modifying the heap layout of programs. To achieve better data locality, both techniques find data that are simultaneously referred and collocate them with one another. Granularity is the only difference; the former deals with instances of structures, but the latter focuses on fields within structures. Our pool allocation scheme is similar to the pool allocation by Lattner and Adve [2] in that both use custom memory allocation routines for certain data structures. The difference is how to choose target structures for pool allocation; they use an expensive pointer analysis to find close relationships among structures, while we use an inexpensive pattern analysis to find heavily accessed ones. Our earlier work [8] used profiling to find memory access sequences of programs. In this paper, we propose a regular expression technique to make the whole optimizing procedure static.

Regular expressions are simple yet expressive enough to capture important access patterns for locality optimizations. Affinity relations among fields or objects are mostly determined by frequently executed portions of programs such as loops. The *Kleene Closure*[1] [10] in regular expression is intuitively appropriate to represent repetition. Considering other features commonly found in C-like imperative languages, regular expressions are indeed adequate for denoting the memory access patterns of programs. Not only can we abstract repetitive accesses with *closure* but also consecutive instructions with *concatenation* and conditional branches with *alternation*. Moreover, interpreting regular expressions is straightforward, thanks to their conciseness.

This paper makes the following contributions:

- We propose a novel method to represent the memory access patterns of programs with regular expressions.
- We present new analyses to select structures for pool allocation and to estimate their field affinity relations by interpreting memory access patterns represented as regular expressions.

---

[1] We use the term *closure* for the rest of this paper.

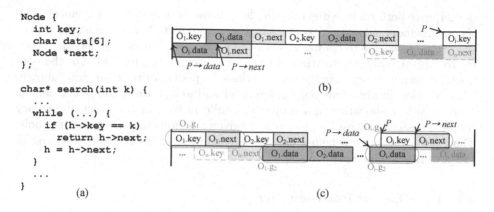

```
Node {
  int key;
  char data[6];
  Node *next;
};

char* search(int k) {
  ...
  while (...) {
    if (h->key == k)
      return h->next;
    h = h->next;
  }
  ...
}
        (a)
```

(b)

(c)

Fig. 1. (a) Motivating example, (b) structure layout with pool allocation, (c) structure layout after field layout restructuring [8]

– We evaluate the performance impact of our static scheme with the compiler implementation of our analyses and heap layout transformations.

The rest of this paper is organized as follows. Section 2 briefly introduces pool allocation and field layout restructuring. Calculating memory access patterns with regular expressions is detailed in Sect. 3. Selecting structures for pool allocation and estimating field affinity relations are discussed in Sect. 4. Section 5 shows our experimental environments and evaluations. Finally, Sect. 6 contrasts our work with prior studies and Sect. 7 concludes this paper.

2   Heap Layout Transformations

Before we discuss how to extract access patterns at compile-time, this section describes two heap layout transformations. Pool allocation [2] and field layout restructuring [8] are main transformations which use our static access patterns. Detailed descriptions on how to use our static access patterns for two transformations will be presented later in Sect. 4.

2.1   Pool Allocation

When objects are individually managed by `malloc` and `free`, compilers cannot predict exact addresses of dynamically allocated objects. This lack of layout information causes many compiler techniques (*e.g.*, field layout restructuring, software prefetching, *etc.*) to be either less effective or not exploitable [2]. Pool allocation [2, 8] is an effective technique that provides compilers with layout information and leads to better data locality as well. Figure 1(b) shows a structure layout when objects are allocated in a pool.

Collocating closely related objects with one another improves data locality by the effect of prefetching in the cache memory. In addition to that, pool allocation can improve performance due to a simpler scheme for memory management. The general memory allocation routines in the standard C library consume lots of execution cycles due to complex free-list management. For every allocation, they try to find an available fraction of memory searching the free-list. On the contrary, custom memory management routines for pool allocation are quite simple. They reserve chunks of memory beforehand and assign a fraction of the chunks for each object allocation in a simple and uniform way. In the event of memory releases, custom free routine just restore given fractions to corresponding pools. Thus, pool allocation schemes execute less number of instructions resulting in the performance increase.

2.2   Field Layout Restructuring

Considering the example code shown in Fig. 1(a), we notice that *key* and *next* fields are referred every loop iteration whereas *data* field is referred just once when the function `search` finds the node whose `key` matches with the argument k. According to this reference behavior, it is expected that grouping *key* and *next* fields as shown in Fig. 1(c) has an advantage over the original pool layout as in Fig. 1(b) in terms of data locality and performance. Based on this observation, we proposed a field layout restructuring scheme in our previous work [8]. Because the *key* and *next* fields are frequently accessed in the loop, they are collocated together in a group. The *data* fields are shaped into another group and placed apart from the *key* and *next* group. The drawbacks of field layout restructuring in Fig. 1(c) are extra run-time instructions to compute correct field offsets from the base pointers of objects. Although extra instructions are not necessary for the first group, the rest of groups require extra run-time calculations. Nevertheless, compiler optimization and pool alignment are able to make the overhead lower.

3   Regular Expressions for Access Patterns

Our specific goal is to establish a fully automatic compile-time framework for field layout restructuring with pool allocation. Such framework needs to find structures whose instances are intensively used and to estimate adequate field layouts for those structures. Then the framework finally transforms the heap layout into the locality-enhanced layout as shown in Fig. 1(c). In order to design the compile-time framework, we have to obtain memory access patterns from the semantics of programs. Moreover, the memory access patterns should imply both repetitive accesses and field affinity relations. Considering the empirical knowledge that the repetitive small parts of programs dominate the most of data usage, we notice that field affinity relations will be heavily affected by frequently executed parts of programs such as loops. *Regular expressions* can naturally represent repetitions with *closures*, which make regular expressions suitable for the abstraction of memory access patterns. Besides the repetition (*closure*), regular expressions can capture the access patterns in sequential instructions with *concatenation* and conditional branches with *alternation*.

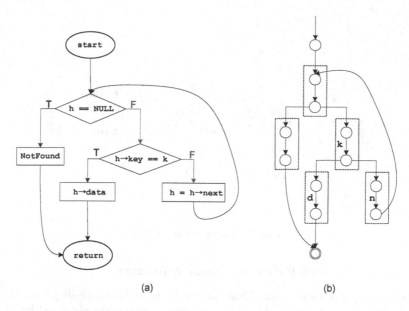

Fig. 2. (a) Control-flow graph of the motivating example, (b) converted automaton

3.1 Conversion of CFGs into Automata

Access patterns of programs are determined by their control flow and data access instructions. When we want to obtain field access patterns, we can use the sequence of referred field names. The sequence, however, can be too long and we need to statically abstract the sequence somehow. The control-flow information obtained from the *control-flow graph* (CFG) plays a critical role in reducing the sequence of field names. Observing that automata and regular expressions are equivalent, we find a novel method to capture access patterns with regular expressions. By converting CFGs into automata with access sequences labeled on edges, we can express access patterns with automata. We then exploit an automata reduction technique to summarize access patterns as regular expressions.

Figure 2(a) depicts the CFG of the motivating example and Fig. 2(b) depicts the automaton[2] converted from Fig. 2(a). Each instruction is converted to its own start state and end state. An edge is added between the two states and labeled with the access pattern of the instruction. In order to preserve control-flow information, we connect the end state to the start states of its successors, labeling the edges with empty strings. Finally, we link the start state of a function to a corresponding start point, and end points to the accepting state of the function, labeling the edges with empty strings too. Consequent automaton as shown in Fig. 2(b) encompasses all the possible behaviors of a function, since it mimics the CFG of the function without loss of control-flow information.

---

[2] For convenience, we use an initial letter of each field for the rest of this paper.

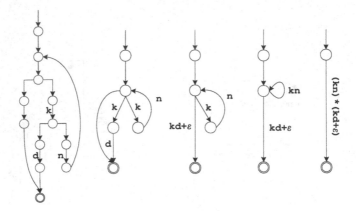

Fig. 3. Automata reduction

3.2   Access Pattern Extraction from Automata

Extracting regular expressions from automata is an instance of path problems [11, 12]. Regular expressions for access patterns are simply obtained by using a state elimination technique (Chap. 3.2.2 of [10]). Figure 3 shows the progress of automata reduction. The order of state elimination is crucial for compilers to extract understandable patterns from automata. First of all, we remove the states which have outgoing edges labeled with empty strings and no incoming back-edges. Because these states represent the instructions unrelated with field accesses or straightforward control-flow information, removing them first helps automata more concise. The remaining steps follow the *weak topological order* (WTO) that combines hierarchical ordering and topological ordering [13]. To make closures correctly enclose loops, we need to postpone the elimination of the states that have incoming back-edges, since those states are the heads of components (usually the heads of loops). The elimination order among the heads of components follows the *recursive strategy* that is also introduced in [13]. Not to prematurely evaluate outer components before the analyses of inner components stabilize, the heads of components should be eliminated from the inner-most one to the outer-most one. The excluded states from the criteria mentioned above are erased in topological order.

The second automaton in Fig. 3 depicts the status after removing all the states which have outgoing edges labeled with empty strings and no incoming back-edges. The third and fourth automata show progressive changes, eliminating the rest of states except for the one that has an incoming back-edge. In the last automaton, the field access pattern of the motivating example is abstracted as $(kn)^*(kd + \varepsilon)$. This pattern implies all the possible behaviors of the function **search** as follows:

- $(kn)^*kd$: the function successfully finds the specific key.
- $(kn)^*$: the search of the matching key failed, or the first *while* condition check fails due to the null-valued head of the linked list.

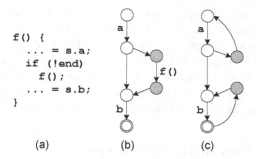

```
f() {
    ... = s.a;
    if (!end)
        f();
    ... = s.b;
}
```

(a)   (b)   (c)

Fig. 4. (a) Example code for self recursive function, (b) automaton after intra-procedural pattern analysis, (c) automaton after inter-procedural pattern analysis

3.3   Extension to Inter-procedural Patterns

Since the CFG in Fig. 2(a) has just intra-procedural information, the access pattern extracted from the corresponding automaton includes the reference behavior of the function body only. To gain accurate field affinity relations over the entire execution, access patterns should cover the semantics of the whole programs as well. Thus, function call relations are also important. Unless programs have mutually recursive calls, extending our scheme to inter-procedural access patterns is straightforward. Unfortunately, we cannot handle mutual recursion yet. The following description only deals with normal and self recursive calls.

To obtain inter-procedural patterns, we visit functions in reverse topological order of a call graph. When we meet a call site while building an automaton for a function, we label the corresponding edge with the name of callee. We can guarantee that access patterns for normal call sites are already completed, since we are visiting in reverse topological order of the call graph. For such cases, we just replace function names with access patterns of callees. As for self recursions, consider the example code in Fig. 4(a). The function f has a recursive call to itself. Once we calculate the intra-procedural access pattern of the code, we will have the automaton shown in Fig. 4(b) that has the function name on the edge representing the call site. Obviously, we do not have the access patterns for the function. For such recursive call sites, we connect the state before the call site to the start state of the function and connect the accepting state of the function to the state after the call site. Then we eliminate the edge representing the call site. Figure 4(c) depicts the consequent automaton.

Although the method described above can resolve self recursive functions well, obtained patterns through that solution are not precise enough to express the access patterns of self recursive functions. Let the access pattern of the function in Fig. 4(a) be F. The precise access pattern, F can be described with the following grammar:

$$F \rightarrow ab \mid aFb$$

This grammar is represented as $a^i b^i$ $(i > 0)$. This pattern is one of the typical examples that cannot be expressed by regular expressions. In other words, an exact way to represent the access patterns for recursive cases requires *Context-free Grammar*. Nevertheless, regular expressions have enough evidences to understand the reference behaviors of programs. For example, the automaton in Fig. 4(c) implies the regular expression a^*abb^*. We can, however, infer a very helpful knowledge that a and b are accessed frequently but separately. We only lose the information that a and b are accessed at the same number of times as $a^i b^i$ can imply. This may not be an important fact for our optimization.

4   Interpretation of Regular Expressions

This section explains how we interpret regular expressions for access patterns. We use regular expressions to identify beneficial structures for pool allocation and to estimate affinity relations among the fields of chosen structures. In the following subsections, we introduce previous work and a profiled-based method, and then describe our static methods.

4.1   Structure Selection for Pool Allocation

Lattner and Adve [2] proposed a structure selecting algorithm for their automatic pool allocation framework. They find data structures whose instances have distinct behaviors, and then segregate the instances into separate memory pools. According to their experimental results, most pools are used in a type-consistent style [2]. From this observation, our pool allocation uses a "one structure per pool" policy. We simply focus on how to choose structures that are intensively used in programs. Those structures are easily identified by investigating regular expressions for structure access patterns. The structures in closures of regular expressions are what we want to identify as intensively used ones.

A structure access pattern is obtained by substituting field names in a field access pattern with the structure names to which the fields belong. As for the motivating example in Fig. 1(a), structure access pattern $(N \cdot N)^*(N \cdot N + \varepsilon)$ (N denotes the structure Node) is obtained from the corresponding field access pattern $(kn)^*(kd+\varepsilon)$. Since the structure Node is the only structure that appears in the closure, it becomes a candidate for pool allocation. Lastly, we accept the only structures that are frequently allocated with dynamic memory allocation routines. We can obtain allocation patterns for candidate structures by labeling automata with their allocation sites. As we did in structure selection, we regard the structures in closures as frequently allocated ones.

4.2   Field Affinity Estimation

One way to analyze field affinity relations is counting co-occurrences within a window sliding over a field access sequence. The counted number is called *neighbor affinity probability* (NAP) [7]. Figure 5 depicts the progress of profile-based affinity estimation. *Temporal relationship graph* (TRG) [14] is a weighted graph where its nodes represent fields and the weights of its edges represent

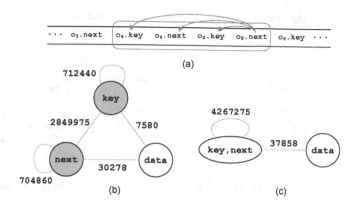

Fig. 5. (a) Profiled memory access sequence and a sliding window to calculate NAP, (b) initial STRG, (c) STRG after grouping *key* and *next* fields

NAPs between fields. Since one field can be accessed consecutively, we extend TRG to have self-edges and name it STRG. Figure 5(a) shows the concept of NAP calculation using a sliding window over a profiled field access sequence. An initial STRG after profiling the motivating example is shown in Fig. 5(b). Since the NAP between *key* and *next* fields is larger than the sum of their own self-affinities, we choose two fields as a group. After grouping, the resulting STRG is shown in Fig. 5(c). The edges are merged and the weights are modified to encompass the previous relationships. Until the STRG does not change, we repeat the following procedure: finding a beneficial grouping and merging fields. Each node in the final STRG becomes a group in a field layout restructuring scheme. The groups in final STRG are placed in decreasing order of the weights of self-edges. In Fig. 5(c), we cannot find a profitable grouping any more. As a result, {*key*, *next*} and {*data*} are placed in the heap as shown in Fig. 1(c).

Statically obtained field access patterns imply the abstract relationship between fields, but not presented with numerical values. To overcome the gap between realistic values and abstract relationships, we devise a symbolic approach. Instead of NAP, we label edges of STRG with closure signs to indicate how often two fields are accessed together. Consider the example in Fig. 6, assuming a program that performs list generation, parity check, and random search in turn. The regular expression that represents the access pattern of the program is shown in the top of the figure. Based on this regular expression, we construct a symbolic STRG as shown in Fig. 6(a) where the weights of the edges are denoted with closure signs.

Note that the access patterns which reside within doubly nested closures are denoted with double closure signs to distinguish nested levels. For example, imagine that the **search** function is invoked repeatedly. The pattern for this case is $((kn)^*(kd + \varepsilon))^*$. We get this by enclosing the pattern of the function with an outer closure. From that pattern, we label the edge between *key* and *next*

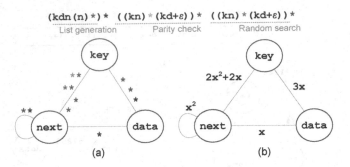

Fig. 6. (a) STRG with closure signs, (b) STRG with a closure variable

fields with one double closure and another single closure. The former represents the presence of two fields in the inner-most closure. The latter represents that the *next* field appears at the end of the inner-most closure and meets the *key* field at the very following access. Similarly, we label the edge between *key* and *data* fields with one single closure. If more than two fields are concatenated within a closure (*e.g.*, $(kdn)^*$), we label with closure signs all the edges of all possible combinations of two consecutive fields within the closure (as if we see $(kd)^*(dn)^*(nk)^*$).

After building symbolic STRGs, we regard all closure signs as the same variable as shown in Fig. 6(b). Since it is next to impossible to predict the number of loop iteration (function invocation) at compile-time, we assume loops (functions) are iterated (invoked) at the same number of times. Finally, we evaluate the affine equations by assigning the fairly large value (100) to the closure variable. 10, 100, and 1000 make the same field layouts in our evaluations. The rest of estimating procedure is the same as profile-based estimation depicted in Fig. 5.

5   Experimental Evaluation

5.1   Implementation

We implement our framework based on the CIL framework [15], which includes access pattern analysis, structure selection analysis, field affinity analysis, and layout transformation. We assume that most programs access fields by explicit field names, since users cannot ensure the memory layouts generated by compilers. Under this assumption, we transform explicit field names to field references on modified field layouts. For some field references we add extra instructions to calculate field offset as described in [8]. Memory management routines such as `malloc` and `free` calls are transformed into custom memory management routines using pool allocation [2,8]. Programs used in our evaluations do not have mutually recursive calls. Therefore, our framework can obtain inter-procedural patterns without any effort to handle such cases.

Table 1. Times spent in analysis and compilation

Program	SLOC	Structure Selection	Field Affinity	Code Transform	Total	GCC
chomp	378	0.021	0.006	0.003	0.030	0.212
ft	926	0.050	0.014	0.010	0.074	0.298
health	474	0.024	0.004	0.002	0.030	0.202
mst	408	0.031	0.004	0.002	0.037	0.195
perimeter	345	0.012	0.012	0.001	0.025	0.197
treeadd	154	0.002	0.000	0.000	0.002	0.120
tsp	433	0.011	0.004	0.002	0.017	0.201
voronoi	975	0.048	0.004	0.003	0.055	0.295

One limitation in our framework is that we cannot recognize custom memory management routines already used by original programs. In addition, it handles the only structures that are allocated in a type-aware fashion. If our framework cannot recognize dynamic allocations for certain structures due to lack of type information, the structures will be discarded by the structure selection analysis. *Health* in the Olden suite [16] has its own allocators, which lose type information and cause both the structure selection analysis and the transformer not to identify beneficial structures. For such cases, we feed the structure selection analysis with user-given hints which consist of target structures and corresponding custom allocators. The CIL is extended to accept user-given hints for our experiments.

5.2   Experimental Environment

Our evaluations are performed on a Redhat 9.0 Linux PC equipped with a 2.6GHz Pentium4 processor. This machine contains 8KB L1D cache (64byte cache line, 4-way set associative), 512KB L2 cache (64byte cache line, 8-way set associative), and 1.7GB main memory. All the benchmarks are compiled with GCC 3.2.2 at -O3 optimization level. We use the Cachegrind from the Valgrind's Tool suite (ver. 3.1.0) [17] to simulate cache behaviors and to measure cache misses using the same cache configuration as the machine on which we evaluate execution times. We measure the number of cache misses at both levels of cache in order to estimate locality improvements in the cache memory hierarchy. We measure execution times to evaluate the effect of layout transformations on performance by using the UNIX `time` command. All the reported execution times are the minimum elapsed time out of ten runs. To confirm the effect of our static mechanism, we examine programs with two different size inputs.

Some of the Olden suite, "chomp" from the McGill benchmark suite [18], and "ft" from the Ptrdist suite [19] are used in our evaluations. Some benchmarks in those suites do not use dynamic structures at all and some are not compiled with the CIL. Those benchmarks are excluded from our experiments. Table 1 shows source lines of code (SLOC) [20] and analysis times for each program. As shown in the table, additional times spent in our analyses and conversion are small enough for all cases.

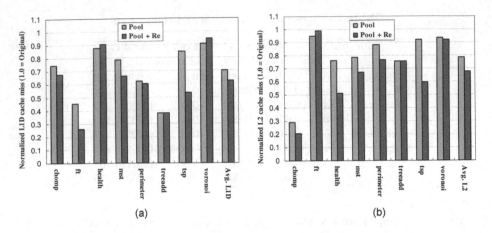

Fig. 7. Normalized numbers of misses in (a) L1D and (b) L2 caches

5.3 Improvements in Cache Locality

Figure 7 shows normalized cache misses in L1D and L2. The numbers are averages of two different size inputs. *Pool* and *Pool + Re* denote the effect of pool allocation alone and field layout restructuring with pool allocation, respectively.

In our evaluations using data intensive benchmarks, pool allocation is significantly effective. Compared with original programs, its miss reductions are roughly 30% for L1D and 22% for L2 on average. These miss reductions are due to better locality by gathering instances of certain structures in the same pools.

Under pool allocation, field layout restructuring can be an auxiliary method to reduce cache misses more. Compared with original programs, its miss reductions are 38% for L1D and 32% for L2 on average. In four cases (*chomp, mst, perimeter,* and *tsp*), it is quite beneficial to miss reductions in both cache levels. For the particular case (*treeadd*), the field affinity analysis choose an inefficient layout, which makes more cache misses. But, the miss increases are very marginal. In the remaining three cases, cache misses in either L1D or L2 are reduced more than pool allocation alone.

There are some cases in which cache misses in either L1D or L2 increase. The miss increases in one cache are usually canceled out by the reductions in the other level cache. For *ft* and *health*, miss reductions in one cache are influential enough to eliminate the effect of increased cache misses in the other level. For *voronoi*, however, the miss increase in one cache is not canceled out due to relatively small improvements of the other level cache.

5.4 Improvements in Performance

Table 2 shows execution times and dynamic instruction counts of benchmarks. The column labeled with *Original* provides base results from original programs. *Pool* and *Pool + Re* columns show the impact of pool allocation alone and

Table 2. Execution times and dynamic instruction counts

Program	Input Parameters	Original exec (sec)	Original #instr ($\times 10^9$)	Normalized (1.0 = Original) Pool exec	Normalized (1.0 = Original) Pool #instr	Normalized (1.0 = Original) Pool + Re exec	Normalized (1.0 = Original) Pool + Re #instr
chomp	7,8	7.44	2.28	0.59	1.34	0.47	1.34
	6,10	18.05	3.77	0.55	1.43	0.50	1.43
ft	$10^3, 2 \times 10^5$	8.25	1.78	0.83	0.97	0.73	0.97
	$10^3, 3 \times 10^5$	19.40	3.13	0.87	0.97	0.79	0.97
health	11, 50, 1, 1	56.24	40.59	0.78	0.75	0.70	0.81
	11, 60, 1, 1	86.05	49.69	0.71	0.76	0.63	0.81
mst	5000	19.23	19.12	0.84	0.82	0.83	0.83
	9000	65.73	62.08	0.82	0.82	0.82	0.84
perimeter	12	7.18	10.85	0.78	0.77	0.84	0.81
	13	17.11	25.59	0.76	0.74	0.84	0.78
treeadd	24	2.52	4.60	0.48	0.44	0.55	0.44
	26	10.17	18.39	0.48	0.44	0.55	0.44
tsp	10^6	9.92	15.33	0.96	0.99	0.97	1.02
	2×10^6	20.44	31.68	0.96	0.99	0.97	1.02
voronoi	10^6	5.22	7.53	0.98	0.99	0.99	1.00
	2×10^6	11.03	15.81	0.99	0.99	0.99	1.00
Avg. % improved				22.64%	11.24%	24.04%	9.41%

field layout restructuring with pool allocation, respectively. The results of layout transformations are normalized with original programs.

As a result of the enhancement of cache locality, the performance of programs also improves. Compared with original programs, execution times of pool allocation are reduced by 23% on average. This substantial improvements in performance are due to not only the remarkable miss reductions of the caches, but also the reductions in the number of instructions executed in custom memory management routines using pools. As shown in the table, dynamic instruction counts of pool allocation are reduced by 11% on average. These results are due to simpler internal structures for memory management and removal of many custom `malloc` and `free` calls.

As shown in the *Pool + Re* column, the performance of transformed programs with the field layout restructuring improves less than the corresponding cache performance. This result is caused by the overhead of run-time address calculations, which is not negligible for some benchmarks. Although we can have no doubt that our affinity analysis is beneficial to enhance cache behavior, field affinity relations are not dominant factors to determine the ideal field layout for real executions. We guess that the overhead of field offset calculations should have been considered as importantly as field affinity relations. Taking run-time overhead into field layout selection is another direction of future work. Nevertheless, there are three cases (*chomp*, *ft*, and *health*) where the performance improvements are quite sizable. These results are occurred when the benefits gained from enhancing cache locality overwhelm the overhead of run-time address calculations.

6   Related Work

Rabbah and Palem [7] suggest a field clustering technique that consecutively puts the same fields from numerous structure instances by employing customized allocation routines. After clustering the instances, they place the fields in vertically aligned layouts. Their layouts have no overhead of run-time field offset calculation, however, require extra padding space to be inserted between fields to make constant offsets for all fields. These useless padding sometimes incurs the waste of memory usage and causes more cache misses.

Our previous work [8] proposes a field layout restructuring scheme that combines the benefits of previous works and relieves the problems of Rabbah and Palem's scheme [7]. We compact fields by eliminating useless padding. This condensation demands extra run-time instructions for some fields accesses. Due to pool alignment and field grouping, however, we can eliminate or reduce the overhead of run-time offset calculations.

Shen et al. [4] develop a frequency-based affinity analysis for array regrouping. Their approach is similar to the work of Chilimbi et al. [6] in that both are based on data access frequencies. They enrich their analysis by designing a context-sensitive inter-procedural analysis. They implement both static estimation and lightweight profiling of the execution frequency, and compare them with each other. According to their experiments, it is a fairly safe to assume that all the counts of loops and function calls are the same.

Lattner and Adve [2] devise an automatic pool allocation, which segregates pointer-based data structure instances in C and C++ programs into separate memory pools. Based on a context-sensitive pointer analysis and the escape property for data structures, they determine which structures are beneficial to pool allocation. As shown in our experimental results, pool allocation improves program performance due to locality enhancement.

Java enables researchers to apply dynamic analyses [21, 22], since it is inherently performed on a run-time system. Dynamic analyses can obtain very accurate information in that they take run-time behaviors into account. This advantage leads run-time optimizations to better performance if their overheads are sufficiently relieved.

7   Conclusion

We present a novel method to represent memory access patterns with regular expressions. Using statically obtained access patterns, we select structures for pool allocation and estimate field affinity relations for field layout restructuring. These analyses and both layout transformations are integrated into our framework based on the CIL. Our evaluation shows that the cache misses for L1D and L2 are reduced by 38% and 32%, respectively. As a result, performance improvement is 24% on average. Statically analyzed access patterns are useful not only for layout transformation but also for the compiler techniques that attempt to optimize memory management of data intensive programs. We believe our access pattern analysis will find profitable usages in many compiler optimizations.

References

1. Seidl, M.L., Zorn, B.G.: Segregating heap objects by reference behavior and lifetime. In: ASPLOS-VIII. (1998) 12–23
2. Lattner, C., Adve, V.: Automatic pool allocation: improving performance by controlling data structure layout in the heap. In: PLDI '05. (2005) 129–142
3. Cherem, S., Rugina, R.: Region analysis and transformation for java programs. In: ISMM '04: International Symposium on Memory Management. (2004) 85–96
4. Shen, X., Gao, Y., Ding, C., Archambault, R.: Lightweight reference affinity analysis. In: ICS '05: International Conference on Supercomputing. (2005) 131–140
5. Zhong, Y., Orlovich, M., Shen, X., Ding, C.: Array regrouping and structure splitting using whole-program reference affinity. In: PLDI '04. (2004) 255–266
6. Chilimbi, T.M., Davidson, B., Larus, J.R.: Cache-conscious structure definition. In: PLDI '99. (1999) 13–24
7. Rabbah, R.M., Palem, K.V.: Data remapping for design space optimization of embedded memory systems. ACM TECS **2**(2) (2003) 186–218
8. Shin, K., Kim, J., Kim, S., Han, H.: Restructuring field layouts for embedded memory systems. In: DATE '06: Design, Automation and Test in Europe. (2006) 937–942
9. Tofte, M., Birkedal, L.: A region inference algorithm. ACM TOPLAS **20**(4) (1998) 724–767
10. Hopcroft, J.E., Motwani, R., Ullman, J.D.: Introduction to automata theory, languages, and computation, 2nd edition. Addison-Wesley (2001)
11. Tarjan, R.E.: A unified approach to path problems. J. ACM **28**(3) (1981) 577–593
12. Tarjan, R.E.: Fast algorithms for solving path problems. J. ACM **28**(3) (1981) 594–614
13. Bourdoncle, F.: Efficient chaotic iteration strategies with widenings. In: FMPA '93: Formal Methods in Programming and their Applications. (1993) 128–141
14. Gloy, N., Smith, M.D.: Procedure placement using temporal-ordering information. ACM TOPLAS **21**(5) (1999) 977–1027
15. Necula, G.C., McPeak, S., Rahul, S.P., Weimer, W.: CIL: Intermediate language and tools for analysis and transformation of c programs. In: CC '02. (2002) 213–228
16. Rogers, A., Carlisle, M.C., Reppy, J.H., Hendren, L.J.: Supporting dynamic data structures on distributed-memory machines. ACM TOPLAS **17**(2) (1995) 233–263
17. : Valgrind. (http://valgrind.org/)
18. : McGill benchmark suite. (http://llvm.org/)
19. Austin, T.M., Breach, S.E., Sohi, G.S.: Efficient detection of all pointer and array access errors. ACM SIGPLAN Notices **29**(6) (1994) 290–301
20. Wheeler, D.A.: SLOCcount. (http://www.dwheeler.com/sloccount/)
21. Guyer, S.Z., McKinley, K.S.: Finding your cronies: static analysis for dynamic object colocation. In: OOPSLA '04. (2004) 237–250
22. Huang, X., Blackburn, S.M., McKinley, K.S., Moss, J.E.B., Wang, Z., Cheng, P.: The garbage collection advantage: improving program locality. In: OOPSLA '04. (2004) 69–80

A New Elimination-Based Data Flow Analysis Framework Using Annotated Decomposition Trees

Bernhard Scholz[1] and Johann Blieberger[2]

[1] The University of Sydney
[2] Technische Universität Wien

Abstract. We introduce a new framework for elimination-based data flow analysis. We present a simple algorithm and a delayed algorithm that exhibit a worst-case complexity of $\mathcal{O}(n^2)$ and $\tilde{\mathcal{O}}(m)$. The algorithms use a new compact data structure for representing reducible flow graphs called *Annotated Decomposition Trees*. This data structure extends a binary tree to represent flowgraph information, dominance relation of flowgraphs, and the topological order of nodes. The construction of the annotated decomposition trees runs in $\mathcal{O}(n + m)$. Experiments were conducted with reducible flowgraphs of the SPEC2000 benchmark suite.

1 Introduction

Elimination-based approaches [19] are used for data flow analysis problems [17, 18, 15, 5, 3, 4] that cannot be solved with iterative approaches [12, 8]. There exist other applications for elimination methods, which go beyond the area of program analysis [24]. For solving data flow analysis problems there are two families of elimination-based approaches: algebraic methods and methods using path expressions.

Algebraic elimination methods [1, 9, 6, 21] consist of three steps: (1) reducing the flowgraph to a single node, (2) eliminating variables in the data flow equations by substitution, and (3) back-propagating the solution to other nodes. Algebraic elimination methods require two algebraic operations for a set of equations: *substitution* and *loop-breaking*. The substitution transformation is the replacement of the occurrence of a variable by its term whereas loop-breaking eliminates the occurrence of a variable on the right-hand side. Though not very efficient, Gaussian elimination is a generic algebraic elimination method to solve data flow equations in cubic time [16].

Path expressions were introduced in [24] to solve data flow equations. The flowgraph is seen as a deterministic finite state automata [10] whose language consists of all paths emanating from the start node to a node. The language is represented as a regular expression whose alphabet is the edge-set of the flowgraph. To find the data flow solution of a node, a path homomorphism is applied to the path expression. The operators $\cdot$, $\cup$, and $*$ of the regular expressions are re-interpreted. An elimination method using path expressions comprises two steps: (1) the computation of path expressions for all nodes in the flowgraph, and (2) the application of the path homomorphism. An inefficient algorithm for converting flowgraph to path expressions is described in [10] and runs in $\mathcal{O}(n^3)$.

In this paper we present a new path expression algorithm using the decomposition properties of reducible flowgraphs. The contribution of our work is threefold:

S. Krishnamurthi and M. Odersky (Eds.): CC 2007, LNCS 4420, pp. 202–217, 2007.

- a new representation of reducible flowgraphs called *Annotated Decomposition Trees* that combines control flow information, dominance relation, and topological order,
- an algorithm for computing annotated decomposition trees in linear time,
- an elimination framework based on annotated decomposition trees that computes path expressions.

The paper is organized as follows. In Section 2 we describe the basic notions required to present our approach. In Section 3 we outline the idea behind elimination-based methods using path expressions and show a motivating example. In Section 4 we present the construction of annotated decomposition trees for reducible flowgraphs. In Section 5 we show a simple and a delayed algorithm for computing path expressions. In Section 6 we present the results of our experiment. Related work is surveyed in Section 7. We draw our conclusions in Section 8.

2 Background

Flowgraph and Path Expressions. A *flowgraph* is a directed graph $G(V, E, r)$ where V is the set of nodes and E is the set of edges. We refer to n as the number of nodes and m as the number of edges. A flowgraph is trivial if there is a single node in V. Edge $u \to v$ has *source* u and *destination* v. Vertex r is a distinguished *root node* (aka. start node). A path π is a sequence of edges $\langle (v_1 \to v_2), (v_2 \to v_3), \ldots, (v_{k-1} \to v_k) \rangle$ such that two consecutive edges $(v_i \to v_{i+1}) \in E$ and $(v_{i+1} \to v_{i+2}) \in E$ share the same node v_{i+1}. The empty path is denoted by ε. In a flowgraph all nodes are reachable, i.e., there is a path from r to every other node in V.

Definition 1. *The path set Paths(u, v) is the set of all paths from u to v in the flowgraph.*

In a regular expression, ε denotes the empty string, $\emptyset$ denotes the empty set, $\cup$ denotes set union, $\cdot$ denotes concatenation, and $*$ denotes reflexive, transitive closure under concatenation. Thus each regular expression R over Σ represents a set $\sigma(R)$ of strings over an alphabet Σ defined as:

1. $\sigma(\varepsilon) = \{\varepsilon\}; \sigma(\emptyset) = \emptyset; \sigma(a) = \{a\}$ for $a \in \Sigma$.
2. $\sigma(R_1 \cup R_2) = \sigma(R_1) \cup \sigma(R_2) = \{w \mid w \in \sigma(R_1) \text{ or } w \in \sigma(R_2)\};$
3. $\sigma(R_1 \cdot R_2) = \sigma(R_1) \cdot \sigma(R_2) = \{w_1 w_2 \mid w_1 \in \sigma(R_1) \text{ and } w_2 \in \sigma(R_2)\};$
4. $\sigma(R^*) = \bigcup_{k=0}^{\infty} \sigma(R)^k$, where $\sigma(R)^0 = \{\varepsilon\}$ and $\sigma(R)^i = \sigma(R)^{i-1} \cdot \sigma(R)$.

For the algorithms in this paper we implicitly use simplifications for the regular expression operators: $[\varepsilon \cdot R] = R$, $[R \cdot \varepsilon] = R$, $[\emptyset \cdot R] = \emptyset$, $[R \cdot \emptyset] = \emptyset$, $[\emptyset \cup R] = R$, $[R \cup \emptyset] = R$, $[\emptyset^*] = \varepsilon$, and $[\varepsilon^*] = \varepsilon$.

Definition 2. *A path expression $P(u, v)$ is a regular expression over E whose language $\sigma(P(u, v))$ is the path set Paths(u, v).*

A node u *dominates* a node v if all paths from r to v include node u. All nodes u that dominate v are also called *dominators* of v. The immediate dominator u of a node v is a *dominator* of v that does not dominate any other dominator of v and u is not v.

The immediate dominator of node v is written as $idom(v)$. The immediate dominators of nodes form a tree called a *dominator tree*.

A *back edge* in a flowgraph is an edge whose destination dominates its source. A flowgraph is *reducible* if the set of edges E can be partitioned into disjoint sets E_F and E_B where E_F is the set of *forward edges* and E_B is the set of back edges. The set of forward edges must form a directed acyclic graph. A graph which is not reducible is called *irreducible*. Reducible flowgraphs (RFG) have the property that for each loop there exists a single entry point.

Binary Leaf Trees. A *binary leaf tree*[1] $T(V, E, r)$ is a rooted binary tree whose inner nodes always have two children. Set V is the set of nodes, E is the set of edges and r is the root node of the tree. The left child of a node x is denoted by $l(x)$ and the right child as $r(x)$. The parent node of a node x is denoted by $p(x)$. A path in the tree is a sequence of nodes $\langle v_1, v_2, \ldots, v_k \rangle$ for which v_i is the parent of v_{i+1} for all i, $1 \leq i < k$.

Data Flow Analysis. A monotone data flow analysis problem [8] is a tuple DFAP($L, \wedge,$ F, c, G, M), where L is a bounded semi-lattice with meet operation $\wedge$, $F \subseteq L \rightarrow L$ is a monotone function space associated with L, $c \in L$ are the "data flow facts" associated with start node r, $G(V, E, r)$ is a flowgraph, and $M : E \rightarrow F$ is a map from G's edges to data flow functions. We extend function M to map a path $\pi = \langle (u_1 \rightarrow u_2), \ldots, (u_{k-1} \rightarrow u_k) \rangle$ to a function of F.

$$M(\pi) = \begin{cases} M(u_{k-1} \rightarrow u_k) \circ \ldots \circ M(u_1 \rightarrow u_2), & \text{if } \pi \neq \varepsilon \\ \iota, & \text{otherwise} \end{cases} \quad (1)$$

where ι is the identity function.

3   Motivation

In program analysis we compute a value for each node in the flowgraph. This value is called the meet-over-all-paths solution. It is the solution of applying the meet operator for the analysis result of all paths from the root node to a given node in the program[2].

Definition 3. *The meet-over-all-path (MOP) solution is defined for a node $u \in V$ as*

$$MOP(u) = \bigwedge_{\pi \in Paths(r,u)} M(\pi)(c) \quad (2)$$

where c is the initial data flow value associated with the root node.

Elimination methods directly compute the MOP solution. They solve the set of local data flow equations by either using substitution and elimination (aka. Gaussian Elimination) or by employing a path homomorphism [24]. In this work we focus on the latter approach. Path expressions represent path sets that are mapped into the function

---

[1] Binary leaf trees are sometimes also called *extended binary trees* [13].
[2] For backward problems we are interested in the set of reverse paths from the end node to a given node.

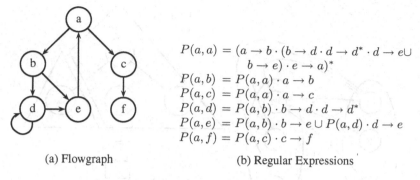

(a) Flowgraph

$$P(a,a) = (a \rightarrow b \cdot (b \rightarrow d \cdot d \rightarrow d^* \cdot d \rightarrow e \cup$$
$$b \rightarrow e) \cdot e \rightarrow a)^*$$
$$P(a,b) = P(a,a) \cdot a \rightarrow b$$
$$P(a,c) = P(a,a) \cdot a \rightarrow c$$
$$P(a,d) = P(a,b) \cdot b \rightarrow d \cdot d \rightarrow d^*$$
$$P(a,e) = P(a,b) \cdot b \rightarrow e \cup P(a,d) \cdot d \rightarrow e$$
$$P(a,f) = P(a,c) \cdot c \rightarrow f$$

(b) Regular Expressions

Fig. 1. Running Example

space of the data flow problem. This mapping is defined by reinterpreting the $\cup$, $\cdot$, and $*$ operators used to construct regular expressions as shown in [23]. The central idea of elimination methods is that MOP is computed as:

$$MOP(u) = \bigwedge_{\pi \in Paths(r,u)} M(\pi)(c) = M(P(r,u))(c), \tag{3}$$

where $P(r,u)$ is the path expression for path set $Paths(r,u)$. The mapping function is extended with the following operators of the regular expressions

$$M(P_1 \cdot P_2) = M(P_2) \circ M(P_1)$$
$$M(P_1 \cup P_2) = M(P_1) \wedge M(P_2)$$
$$M(P^*) = M(P)^*$$
$$M(\varepsilon) = \iota$$

The operation $M(P_2) \circ M(P_1)$ is the function composition and $M(P)^*$ is a fixpoint operation. For simple data-flow analysis problems the fixpoint operation is quite often the identity function [19].

The complexity of elimination methods using path expressions depends on the path expression size. Consider the example depicted in Figure 1. Assume we want to solve a data flow analysis problem for the flowgraph given in Figure 1(a). An elimination method using path expressions computes a path expression as given in Figure 1(b). Then, mapping function M is applied to path expression $P(r,u)$. To improve the performance of such an approach, expressions are reused (such as $P(a,a)$ in the running example). Without reuse of sub-expressions the memory complexity grows exponentially with the size of the flowgraph [10].

4   Annotated Decomposition Trees

For the elimination framework we introduce a new data structure called an Annotated Decomposition Tree (ADT) that recursively splits the reducible flowgraph into intervals. An interval is a subgraph of the flowgraph and has the following properties: (1)

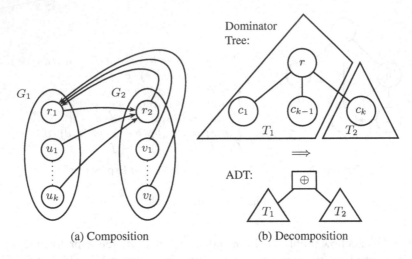

(a) Composition   (b) Decomposition

Fig. 2. Composition and Decomposition of Reducible Flowgraphs

every interval has a single entry node, and (2) the single-entry node of the interval dominates all nodes of the interval.

The ADT is a binary leaf tree. An inner node in the ADT represents a composition operation that composes two disjoint intervals G_1 and G_2. The leaves of the tree represent trivial intervals consisting of a single node in the flowgraph[3]. The composition operation is a generalisation of work published in [25, 26, 11].

Definition 4. *Let $G_1(V_1, E_1, r_1)$ and $G_2(V_2, E_2, r_2)$ be flowgraphs such that V_1 and V_2 are disjoint sets. The composition $G_1 \oplus_{(F,B)} G_2$ is defined as*

$$(V_1 \cup V_2, E_1 \cup E_2 \cup (F \times \{r_2\}) \cup (B \times \{r_1\}), r_1)$$

where $F \subseteq V_1$ and $B \subseteq V_2$ denote the sources of the forward and backward edges. Node r_1 becomes the new single-entry node of the composed interval.

The composition of two intervals G_1 and G_2 is depicted in Figure 2(a). The single-entry nodes of the intervals are denoted by r_1 and r_2. The edge set $F \times \{r_2\}$ connects a subset of nodes in G_1 to r_2. The edge set $B \times \{r_1\}$ connects a subset of nodes in G_2 to r_1.

By Definition 4, root node r_1 dominates all nodes of G_1 and G_2 because every node in the composed interval can only be reached via r_1. The same holds for r_2, i.e., r_2 dominates all nodes in G_2. This implies that the nodes of G_1 form a sub-tree in the dominator tree with r_1 as a root-vertex of the sub-tree, and single-entry node r_2 is immediately dominated by r_1.

The forward edges of a reducible flow graph form a directed acyclic graph imposing a topological order $<$ such that for all edges $(u, v) \in E_F$, $u < v$ holds. Since the single-entry node of an interval dominates all nodes in the interval, the single-entry node of the

---

[3] Because ADTs are binary leaf trees, there are $n - 1$ inner nodes where n is the num. of leaves.

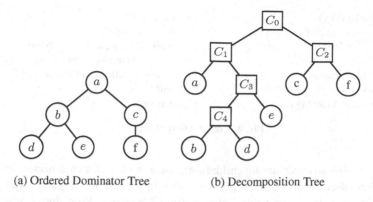

(a) Ordered Dominator Tree   (b) Decomposition Tree

Fig. 3. Dominator and Decomposition Tree of Example

interval is smaller than the nodes in the interval with respect to the topological order. The composition implies that $r_1 < r_2$. Given a composition $G_1 \oplus G_2$, the inequality

$$\forall u \in V_1 : \forall v \in V_2 : r_1 \leq u < r_2 \leq v \tag{4}$$

holds. Assume a total order R of nodes in the flowgraph $[u_1, \ldots, u_n]$ such that for $(u_i, u_j) \in E_F, i < j$. An interval decomposition of the flowgraph partitions the ordered nodes into two parts. Vertex r_1 has index 1 and all the nodes between 1 and $r_2 - 1$ belong to the interval G_1. The nodes from r_2 to n belong to G_2. By recursively applying the decomposition for ordered nodes, we have a range representation of the tree. For example a possible total order for the flowgraph in Figure 1(a) is $[a, b, d, e, c, f]$. The first composition of the ADT splits the ordered nodes in two halves, i.e., $[[a, b, d, e], [c, f]]$. By recursively splitting intervals, we obtain $[[[a], [[b, d], e]], [c, f]]$ representing the intervals of the flowgraph.

In the following we deal with the problem of finding an ADT for a given flowgraph. Because there might be several possible topological orders of a flowgraph, we can have several ADTs for a single flowgraph. However, for a given topological order of a flowgraph there exists a single ADT. The ADT is constructed by using the dominator tree and a given topological order.

We observe that the root node r_2 is immediately dominated by r_1 and therefore is a child of r_1 in the dominator tree. Assume that the children $c_1, \ldots, c_{k-1}, c_k$ of node r_1 in the dominator tree are ordered by the topological order, i.e., $c_i < c_j$. Vertex r_2 is the child c_k (cf. Equation 4) and the nodes of G_2 are nodes which are dominated by r_2. A simple decomposition scheme of the ordered dominator tree (as illustrated in Figure 2(b)) allows the construction of the ADT. Interval G_1 is the result of the decomposition of the dominator tree without subtree c_k. Interval G_2 is the result of the decomposition of subtree c_k.

The decomposition of the dominator tree results in a simple algorithm for constructing an ADT: (1) order the children of the dominator tree with respect to topological order of the nodes and (2) recursively traverse the ordered dominator tree and construct the ADT. The algorithm for constructing the decomposition tree is shown in Figure 4.

CONSTRUCTADT()
1   **for** $i \leftarrow |V| \ldots 2$ **do**
2        $u \leftarrow order(i)$
3        $v \leftarrow idom(u)$
4   PUSH u *onto* s_v
5   **endfor**
6   **return** TRAVERSE(r)

TRAVERSE (u)
1    $x \leftarrow$ LEAF(u)
2   **while** *stack* s_u *is not empty* **do**
3        $v \leftarrow$ POP *node from* s_u
4        $x \leftarrow$ NODE(x, TRAVERSE(v))
5   **endwhile**
6   **return** x

Fig. 4. Construction of the ADT

For constructing an order among children we use a stack s_u for each node u in the flowgraph. Procedure *ConstructADT* pushes nodes in reverse topological order onto the stack of its immediate dominator. Before calling *Traverse* in Procedure *ConstructADT*, the stack of a node contains all its children in reverse topological order. The element on top of the stack is the right-most child of the node and the bottom element of the stack is the left-most child of the node. The stack allows us to partition the graph as illustrated in Figure 2(b).

The construction of the ADT is performed in function *Traverse*. Function *Leaf* with parameter u creates a new leaf in the decomposition tree where u is a node of the flowgraph. Function *Node* creates an inner node with a left and right child. The construction is performed recursively beginning with the root node of the dominator tree. Inside the loop the children of node u are popped from the stack in reverse topological order and for each child a decomposition operation is created. The function *Traverse* pops exactly $n - 1$ elements from the node stacks. We have n function calls of *Traverse*. Thus, the space and time complexity of function *Traverse* is $\mathcal{O}(n)$.

For the running exampe the dominator tree is shown in Figure 3(a). The children of the nodes are ordered with respect to the topological order. The first composition is the cut between node a and c because c is the right-most children with respect to the topological order. The resulting two dominator trees are recursively cut and each cut represents an inner node in the ADT. The resulting decomposition tree is depicted in Figure 3(b).

So far, we have not discussed how to determine the forward and backward edges of a composition. To compute F- and B-sets we traverse the set of edges and associate each edge to a composition in the ADT. The edge is associated to the composition node in the ADT that is the nearest common ancestor of leaves u and v. An edge is an element of set F if it is a forward edge, otherwise it is element of set B. Set F is empty for leaf nodes in the ADT. The algorithm in Figure 5(a) annotates the decomposition tree with sets F and B. It exhibits a complexity of $\mathcal{O}(n + m)$ by using the efficient nearest common ancestor algorithms [7, 2] with a complexity of $\mathcal{O}(1)$ for a single NCA query.

The F- and B-sets are given in Figure 5(b). For example, consider edge $a \rightarrow c$. The nearest common ancestor of leaves a and c is the extended composition C_0 in the decomposition Tree of Figure 3(b). Vertex a is smaller then node c in the topological order. Therefore, the edge is a forward edge and stored in F_{C_0}. Because the target of an edge is inherently defined by the composition, i.e. either node r_1 or node r_2 depending whether it is a forward or backward edge, we only add the source of an edge to F or B. This means, that for edge $a \rightarrow c$ node a is added to F_{C_0}.

COMPUTEFBSETS (ADT)

1   **for** *all* $u \rightarrow v \in E$ **do**
2     $x \leftarrow \text{NCA}(ADT, u, v)$
3   **if** $u \rightarrow v \in E_B$ **then**
4       $B_x \leftarrow B_x \cup \{u\}$
5   **else**
6       $F_x \leftarrow F_x \cup \{u\}$
7   **endif**
8   **endfor**

u	F_u	B_u
C_0	$\{a\}$	$\{\}$
C_1	$\{a\}$	$\{e\}$
C_2	$\{c\}$	$\{\}$
C_3	$\{b, d\}$	$\{\}$
C_4	$\{b\}$	$\{\}$
a	n/a	$\{\}$
b	n/a	$\{\}$
c	n/a	$\{\}$
d	n/a	$\{d\}$
e	n/a	$\{\}$
f	n/a	$\{\}$

(a) Algorithm   (b) F- and B-sets

Fig. 5. Algorithm and Example for Computing F- and B-Sets

5   Path Expressions

We compute path expressions for nodes using the annotated decomposition tree of a reducible flowgraph as the underlying data structure. Path expressions are computed by an inductive scheme. For the inductive step we construct path expressions by using the properties of the composition (see Def. 4).

Theorem 1. *If* $G(V, E, r)$ *is a trivial flowgraph, then*

$$P(r,r) = \begin{cases} (r \rightarrow r)^*, & \text{if } (r \rightarrow r) \in E, \\ \varepsilon, & \text{otherwise.} \end{cases} \tag{5}$$

Otherwise the flowgraph is composed and $G(V, E, r) = G_1(V_1, E_1, r_1) \oplus_{(F,B)} G_2(V_2, E_2, r_2)$. *For given path expressions* $P_1(r_1, u)$ *of* G_1 *(for all* $u \in V_1$*) and given path expressions* $P_2(r_2, v)$ *of* G_2 *(for all* $v \in V_2$*), the path expressions of the composed flowgraph are:*

$$\forall u \in V_1 : P(r, u) = L \cdot P_1(r_1, u) \tag{6}$$
$$\forall v \in V_2 : P(r, v) = R \cdot P_2(r_2, v) \tag{7}$$

where[4]

$$X = \bigcup_{u \in F} P_1(r_1, u) \cdot (u \rightarrow r_2) \tag{8}$$

$$Y = \bigcup_{v \in B} P_2(r_2, v) \cdot (v \rightarrow r_1) \tag{9}$$

$$L = [X \cdot Y]^* \tag{10}$$
$$R = L \cdot X \tag{11}$$

Proof. See Appendix.

---

[4] $\bigcup_{x \in X} f(x)$ is the empty set if set X is empty.

COMPUTEPATHEXPR (w)
1   **if** w *is not a leaf* **then**
2   COMPUTEPATHEXPR$(l(w))$
3   COMPUTEPATHEXPR$(r(w))$
4       $X \leftarrow \bigcup_{u \in F_w}[\text{EVAL}(u) \cdot u \to r_2]$
5       $Y \leftarrow \bigcup_{v \in B_w}[\text{EVAL}(v) \cdot v \to r_1]$
6       $L \leftarrow [X \cdot Y]^*$
7       $R \leftarrow L \cdot X$
8       $z \leftarrow l(w)$
9   **if** z *is a leaf and* $z \to z \in E$ **then**
10          $L \leftarrow L \cdot (z \to z)^*$
11   **endif**
12      $z \leftarrow r(w)$
13   **if** z *is a leaf and* $z \to z \in E$ **then**
14          $R \leftarrow R \cdot (z \to z)^*$
15   **endif**
16   LNK_UPD$(w, r(w), L)$
17   LNK_UPD$(w, l(w), R)$
18 **endif**

LNK_UPD (x, y, v)
1   $p(y) \leftarrow x$
2   $R_y \leftarrow v$

EVAL (x)
1   **if** $p(x) \neq p(p(x))$ **then**
2       $R_x \leftarrow [\text{EVAL}(p(x)) \cdot R_x]$
3       $p(x) \leftarrow p(p(x))$
4   **endifreturn** R_x

MAIN $()$
1   $adt \leftarrow$ CONSTRUCTADT$()$
2   COMPUTEFBSETS(adt)
3   COMPUTEPATHEXPR(adt)
4   **if** G *is not trivial* **then**
5   **for** $u \in V$ **do**
6           $P(r, u) \leftarrow$ EVAL(u)
7   **endfor**
8   **else**
9       $P(r, r) \leftarrow \begin{cases} (r \to r)^*, & \text{if } (r \to r) \in E, \\ \varepsilon, & \text{otherwise.} \end{cases}$
10 **endif**

Fig. 6. Computing Path Expressions: Delayed Algorithm

Simple Algorithm: A simple algorithm traverses the ADT in bottom-up fashion and updates the path expressions for nodes in G_1 and G_2 according to Theorem 1. The complexity of the simple algorithm is $\mathcal{O}(n^2)$ because in the worst case $\mathcal{O}(n)$ updates are performed for a node in the ADT and there are $\mathcal{O}(n)$ nodes in the ADT.

Delayed Algorithm: A more efficient algorithm does not update the path expressions of all nodes in the intervals G_1 and G_2. Only the nodes in F and B of a composition are updated and the update of the remaining nodes is deferred to a later stage.

The construction of path expressions implies that a path expression of node u in the flowgraph is a sequence of L and R prefixes followed by either ε or $(u \to u)^*$. We store the path expressions L and R at the left and right child of an inner node in the ADT and the path expression ε or $(u \to u)^*$ at the leaves. Then, a path from the root of the ADT to node u defines the path expression[5] by mapping the nodes of the path to their path expressions. This observation enables the usage of a path compression scheme [22] to implement the delayed update.

In Figure 6 we outline the algorithm for constructing path expressions with a delayed update. The LNK_UPD operation assigns a path expression to a node in the ADT and constructs the tree for path compression. The EVAL operation queries the sequence of L and R prefixes for a node of the flowgraph. The complexity of the algorithm is bounded by the number of composition nodes in the decomposition tree (i.e. $n - 1$) and the

---

[5] Without loss of generality we store ε in the root of the ADT.

number of leaves (i.e. n). With a simple path compression scheme the delayed update is bounded by $\mathcal{O}(m \log n)$ (as outlined in Figure 6). A more sophisticated path compression algorithm with $\mathcal{O}(m\alpha(m,n))$ introduced in [22] improves the upper bound of the overall algorithm. However, in practice the sophisticated path compression scheme will not be superior to the simple path compression scheme due to small problem sizes [14].

6 Experimental Results

We have implemented the simple and the delayed algorithm in C and measured the performance of the algorithms on a 2.6GhZ AMD computer. We also implemented Sreedhar's algorithm [21] and compared its performance to the simple and the delayed algorithm. As a benchmark we used the SPEC2000 benchmark suite. The flowgraphs were generated by the GCC compiler. In this experiment we are interested in the following numbers: (1) the execution time to construct ADTs for SPEC2000, (2) the speed-ups of the simple and delayed algorithm vs. Sreedhar's algorithm, and (3) the reduction of the number of $\cdot$, $\cup$ and $*$ operators by using the delayed algorithm.

The results of the experiment are shown in Table 1. The execution times for constructing the ADT and computing the path expressions are given in columns t_{adt} and t_c. Note that all time measurements are in microseconds. The construction of ADTs is fast but it takes longer than computing path expressions. The computation of ADTs requires four steps: (1) compute topological order, (2) compute dominator tree, (3) perform the pre-processing step for NCAs, and (4) construct the ADT using the dominator tree, topological order, and NCA relation. Hence, the execution time to construct ADTs

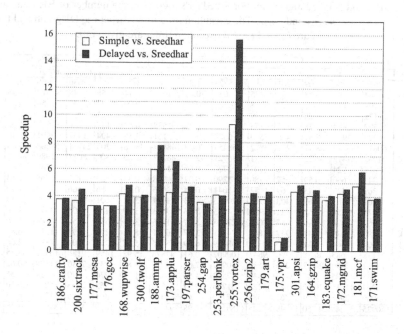

Fig. 7. Speed-Ups: Simple and Delayed Algorithm vs. Sreedhar

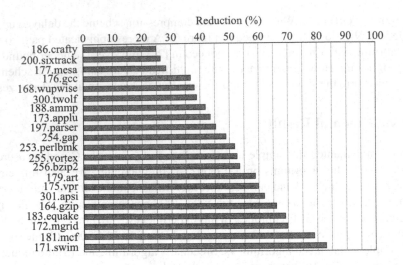

Fig. 8. Reductions of Operations (%) between 0% and 100%. Benchmarks achieving better reductions are listed first.

Table 1. Results of the simple and delayed ADT algorithm, and results of Sreedhar's algorithm. Columns n and m are the number of nodes and edges in the flowgraph. Column t_{ADT} is the execution time to construct the ADT. n_*, $n_\cup$, and $n_.$ are the number of regular expression operators and t_c is the execution time to compute path expressions. Note that the n_* and $n_\cup$ are identical for the simple and delayed algorithm. For Sreedhar's algorithm the number of E1, E2a, and E2b reductions are n_{E1}, n_{E2a}, and n_{E2b}. The execution time to construct the DJ-graph and the time to perform the reductions are t_{dj} and t_r. All execution times are given in μs.

	Problemsize			Simple Algo				Delayed Algo		Sreedhar's Algo				
Bnchm.	n	m	t_{adt}	n_*	$n_\cup$	$n_.$	t_c	$n_.$	t_c	n_{E1}	n_{E2a}	n_{E2b}	t_{dj}	t_r
gzip	1639	2369	2.09	201	613	5723	1.27	3500	1.23	199	636	966	5.36	7.25
wupwise	444	657	0.78	58	175	3031	0.72	1010	0.44	58	148	317	1.58	3.89
swim	109	158	0.16	27	28	280	0.09	223	0.09	27	30	56	0.43	0.39
mgrid	179	269	0.26	51	49	628	0.16	408	0.16	51	46	111	0.64	0.74
applu	590	899	0.78	172	153	3958	0.72	1538	0.52	172	156	567	1.93	4.33
vpr	4227	5973	5.51	498	1509	16672	3.54	9161	3.15	494	1437	2991	13.75	21.57
gcc	60818	96156	88.47	3412	33822	468454	90.28	148878	49.38	3303	24761	58003	203.85	863.93
mesa	21981	31418	32.22	1330	9171	196921	42.15	48257	16.20	1300	8071	17989	72.61	245.83
art	615	924	0.87	130	205	2720	0.68	1462	0.55	125	213	505	2.06	4.61
mcf	449	660	0.59	57	180	1290	0.34	968	0.37	57	173	265	1.53	1.79
equake	309	423	0.43	67	73	1041	0.24	676	0.25	66	66	232	1.10	1.66
crafty	6161	9563	7.69	403	3107	70633	14.13	14941	5.34	401	2359	6619	20.40	183.23
ammp	3773	5754	6.53	431	1725	24543	5.03	9013	3.09	427	1408	3390	12.30	28.53
parser	4967	7428	6.90	655	2099	27705	5.37	11056	3.84	652	1756	3584	16.16	30.65
sixtrack	6998	10576	15.41	947	2844	74721	13.57	16941	5.61	293	694	1619	6.83	13.07
perlbmk	6904	10464	9.11	265	3529	33429	6.89	15495	5.28	254	3004	4892	22.68	46.98
gap	21178	31685	26.78	1490	9847	109902	20.61	47878	15.98	1459	9188	16587	68.75	123.09
vortex	18633	27490	24.82	236	9539	80959	17.02	37950	13.86	235	7630	11138	60.62	96.50
bzip2	1648	2495	2.07	277	642	7563	1.56	3619	1.30	276	590	1024	5.35	9.99
twolf	7294	11216	10.39	875	3227	51216	9.27	17397	5.74	863	2763	5845	23.76	70.05
apsi	2009	2968	2.64	367	688	7782	1.64	4413	1.53	364	696	1257	6.45	9.79
Total	170925	259545	244.50	11949	83225	1189171	235.28	394784	133.91	11076	65825	137957	548.15	1767.87

has the same magnitude as computing path expressions with the simple algorithm. The delayed algorithm has a significantly smaller runtime and is approx. 1.8 times faster than the simple algorithm.

We compared the runtime of our algorithms[6] with the runtime of a C++/STL implementation of Sreedhar's eager algorithm. For the comparison we measured the time to construct the DJ-graphs (Column t_{dj}) and the reduction phase (t_r). However, we did not measure the propagation phase which is a simple traversal over the dominator tree. The speed-ups of the simple and delayed algorithm vs. Sreedhar's algorithm are shown for each Spec2000 benchmark in Figure 7. The speed-ups vary depending on the size of the flowgraphs. For small flowgraphs the execution time of the simple and delayed algorithm is of the same magnitude. For large flowgraphs the execution time diverges by up to a factor of 9.3 and 15.6, respectively.

The delayed algorithm has significantly smaller path expressions. The delayed algorithm reduces the number of regular expression operators by 38.1%. We attribute the more compact path expressions to the re-use of regular expressions. Though the number of $*$ and $\cup$ operators is the same for both algorithms, the number of $\cdot$ operators is reduced by a factor of three. This substantial reduction is due to reusing the same L and R sub-sequences. The reductions for all benchmarks are shown in Figure 8. The reductions vary between 24.8% (best case) and 83.0% (worst case) depending on how many sub-sequences of L and R prefixes can be reused. Larger flowgraphs have a greater potential for reuse of sub-path expressions.

7   Discussion and Related Work

Besides Gaussian elimination with order $\mathcal{O}(n^3)$ complexity, there are five elimination algorithms known in literature: (1) *Allen-Cocke interval analysis* [1], (2) *Hecht-Ullman $T_1 - T_2$ analysis* [9], (3) *Graham-Wegman analysis* [6], (4) *Sreedhar-Gao-Lee DJ graph based analysis* [21], (5) *Tarjan interval analysis* [23], (see [19] for a comparison of the first four algorithms). Algorithms (1) to (4) are algebraic elimination-based algorithms using substitution and loop-breaking. Only (5) is an elimination-based approach using path expressions. Note the approach introduced in [20] is marginally related to elimination-based algorithms because this approach detects standard structured control-flow patterns, such as "if-then-else", "begin-end", or "while-do", which is not our concern.

Allen-Cocke interval analysis establishes a natural partition of the variables and a variable order on each of a sequence of systems that, when used to order the equations, results in a highly structured coefficient matrix facilitating the equation-reduction process. Hecht-Ullman $T_1 - T_2$ analysis, Tarjan interval analysis, and Graham-Wegman analysis avoid repeated calculations of common substitution sequences in the equations by delaying certain computations. Sreedhar-Gao-Lee DJ graph based analysis employs structural information of the so-called DJ graph, a union of the CFG and its dominator tree, to find efficient substitution sequences.

Hecht-Ullman $T_1 - T_2$ analysis uses a nondeterministic substitution order for terms in the equations; the substitutions are recorded in a height-balanced $2 - 3$ tree to take

---

[6] Our algorithms are highly-tuned C-algorithms.

advantage of possible common factors in subsequent calculations. Tarjan interval analysis establishes a linear variable order and eliminates variables from the system of equations in that order, delaying some calculations; a path compressed tree is used to remember sequences of reduced equations for these delayed calculations. Graham-Wegman analysis establishes an order of substitutions for each term in the system that avoids duplication of common substitution sequence calculations. It uses a transformed version of the original flowgraph to remember previous substitutions. By delaying computations, Sreedhar-Gao-Lee DJ graph based analysis can be made more efficient. In contrast to Tarjan interval analysis, the Sreedhar-Gao-Lee algorithm employs simple path compression on the dominator tree.

Among the known elimination algorithms the best in terms of worst-case complexity is Tarjan's interval analysis algorithm, which balances the path compressed tree in a preprocessing operation. This algorithm has a runtime of $\mathcal{O}(m \log m)$ employing a simple path compression scheme. By using a sophisticated data structure for path compression a better upper bound of $\mathcal{O}(m\alpha(m, n))$ can be achieved. However, the simple path compression scheme will outperform the sophisticated one for typical problem sizes in program analysis.

Our algorithm is based on structural information of the decomposition tree. Thus it is more similar to the Sreedhar-Gao-Lee algorithm than to the other algorithms. It uses simple path compression employed on the decomposition tree to remember sequences of reduced equations for delayed calculations. It is, however, easy to use Tarjan's preprocessing operation and a separate data structure to achieve a more efficient version of our algorithm.

8   Conclusion

In this paper we introduced a new framework for elimination-based data flow analysis using path expressions. Elimination-based frameworks are used for program analysis problems [17, 18, 15, 5, 3, 4] that cannot be solved with iterative solvers. The framework uses a new data structure called annotated decomposition trees (ADTs) that comprises topological order, dominance relation, and the control flow. We presented a simple algorithm and a delayed algorithm that employed annotated decomposition trees as a data structure. The worst-case complexities of both algorithms are $\mathcal{O}(n^2)$ and $\tilde{\mathcal{O}}(m)$.

We conducted experiments with the SPEC2000 benchmark suite. The delayed algorithm runs 1.8 times faster than the simple algorithm and has 38.1% of the operators in comparison with the simple algorithm.

Acknowledgement

We would like to thank Bernd Burgstaller, Shirley Goldrei, and Wei-ying Ho for their useful comments and for proof-reading the manuscript. This work has been partially supported by the ARC Discovery Project Grant "Compilation Techniques for Embedded Systems" under Contract DP 0560190.

References

1. F. E. Allen and J. Cocke. A program data flow analysis procedure. *Comm. ACM*, 19(3):137–147, 1976.
2. M. Bender and M. Farach-Colton. The lca problem revisited. In *Proc. of Latin American Theoretical Informatics*, pages 88–94, 2000.
3. J. Blieberger. Data-flow frameworks for worst-case execution time analysis. *Real-Time Syst.*, 22(3):183–227, 2002.
4. R. Bodik, R. Gupta, and M. L. Soffa. Complete removal of redundant computations. In *Proc. of PLDI*, pages 1–14, 1998.
5. T. Fahringer and B. Scholz. A Unified Symbolic Evaluation Framework for Parallelizing Compilers. *IEEE TPDS*, 11(11), November 2000.
6. S. L. Graham and M. Wegman. Fast and usually linear algorithm for global flow analysis. *J. ACM*, 23(1):172–202, 1976.
7. D. Harel and R. Tarjan. Fast algorithms for finding nearest common ancestors. *Siam J. Comput.*, 13(2):338–355, May 1984.
8. M. S. Hecht. *Flow Analysis of Computer Programs*. Elsevier North-Holland, New York, 1 edition, 1977.
9. M. S. Hecht and J. D. Ullman. A simple algorithm for global data flow analysis problems. *SIAM J. Comput.*, 4(4):519–532, 1977.
10. J. E. Hopcroft, R. Motwani, and J. D. Ullman. Introduction to automata theory, languages, and computation, 2nd edition. *SIGACT News*, 32(1):60–65, 2001.
11. R. Joshi, U. Khedker, V. Kakade, and M. Trivedi. Some interesting results about applications of graphs in compilers. *CSI J.*, 31(4), 2002.
12. G. A. Kildall. A unified approach to global program optimization. In *Proc. of Symposium on Principles of Programming Languages*, pages 194–206. ACM, ACM Press, 1973.
13. D. E. Knuth. *Fundamental Algorithms*, volume 1 of *The Art of Computer Programming*. Addison-Wesley, Reading, Mass., third edition, 1997.
14. T. Lengauer and R. E. Tarjan. A fast algorithm for finding dominators in a flowgraph. *ACM Trans. Program. Lang. Syst.*, 1(1):121–141, 1979.
15. E. Mehofer and B. Scholz. A Novel Probabilistic Data Flow Framework. In *Proc. of CC*, pages 37 – 51, Genova, Italy, April 2001. Springer.
16. M. C. Paull. *Algorithm design: a recursion transformation framework*. Wiley-Interscience, New York, NY, USA, 1988.
17. G. Ramalingam. Data flow frequency analysis. In *Proc. of PLDI*, pages 267–277, New York, NY, USA, 1996. ACM Press.
18. T. Robschink and G. Snelting. Efficient path conditions in dependence graphs. In *Proc. of ICSE '02*, pages 478–488, New York, NY, USA, 2002. ACM Press.
19. B. G. Ryder and M. C. Paull. Elimination algorithms for data flow analysis. *ACM Computing Surveys*, 18(3):277–315, Sept. 1986.
20. M. Sharir. Structural analysis: A new approach to flow analysis in optimizing compilers. *Computer Languages*, 5:141–153, 1980.
21. V. C. Sreedhar, G. R. Gao, and Y.-F. Lee. A new framework for elimination-based data flow analysis using DJ graphs. *ACM TOPLAS*, 20(2):388–435, 1998.
22. R. Tarjan. Applications of path compression on balanced trees. *J. of the ACM*, 26(4):690–715, Oct. 1979.
23. R. E. Tarjan. Fast algorithms for solving path problems. *J. ACM*, 28(3):594–614, 1981.
24. R. E. Tarjan. A unified approach to path programs. *J. ACM.*, 28(3):577–593, 1981.
25. O. Vernet and L. Markenzon. Maximal reducible flowgraphs. Technical Report RT029/DE9, D. de Engenharia de Sistemas, Instituto Militar de Engenharia, Rio de Janeiro, Brasil, 1998.
26. O. Vernet and L. Markenzon. Solving problems for maximal reducible flowgraphs. *Disc. Appl. Math.*, 136:341–348, 2004.

A Appendix

Definition 5. *Path $a = \langle (u_1, u_2), \ldots, (u_{k-1}, u_k) \rangle$ is connectable to path $b = \langle (v_1, v_2), \ldots, (v_{l-1}, v_l) \rangle$ if u_k is equal to v_1.*

Definition 6

$$A \cdot B = \begin{cases} \bigcup_{a \in A} \bigcup_{b \in B} a \cdot b, & \text{if } a \text{ is connectable to } b \\ \emptyset, & \text{otherwise} \end{cases} \tag{12}$$

Proof (Proof of Theorem 1). Proof by structural induction over the ADT. Each subtree in the ADT represents a sub-flowgraph of the flowgraph.
Inductive Hypothesis: $\forall u \in V : \sigma(P(r, u)) = Paths(r, u)$
Basis: Both cases are trivially true by Proposition of Theorem 1.
Induction Step: The composition operation $\oplus_{(F,B)}$ (cf. Figure 2 and Def. 4) allows us to break the paths of the composition into segments, as suggested in Figure 9. Note that r_1 becomes r after the composition. Path set $Paths(r, r)$ is depicted in Figure 9(a). A path in $Paths(r, r)$ starts in r and uses a path in G_1 as a sub-path to reach a node $u \in F$. From node $u \in F$ there exists an edge to node r_2 by Def. 4. From node r_2 a path in G_2 is used as a sub-path to reach a node $v \in B$. By Def. 4 there exists an edge from $v \in B$ to r. Since a path may consist of several cycles we express the path set $Paths(r, r)$ as

$$Paths(r, r) = \bigcup_{i \geq 0} \left[\bigcup_{u \in F} \bigcup_{v \in B} Paths(r, u) \cdot \{\langle u \to r_2 \rangle\} \cdot Paths(r_2, v) \cdot \{\langle v \to r \rangle\} \right]^i \tag{13}$$

where the inner term describes for a concrete $u \in F$ and $v \in B$ all possible simple cycles. Note that if set B is empty, the path set $Paths(r, r)$ becomes ε because the inner term reduces to an empty set and Kleene's closure of the empty set yields ε, i.e. $\emptyset^0 = \varepsilon$. A node $u \in V_1$ is described by path set $Paths(r, r)$ concatenated by path set $Paths(r_1, u)$ that is a path in G_1 as illustrated in Figure 9(b). Therefore,

$$\forall u \in V_1 : Paths(r, u) = Paths(r, r) \cdot Paths(r_1, u). \tag{14}$$

As depicted in Figure 9(c), a node $v \in V_2$ can be described by the concatenation of a path from r to r_2 and a path in G_2 from r_2 to node v:

$$\forall v \in V_2 : Paths(r, v) = Paths(r, r) \cdot Paths(r, r_2) \cdot Paths(r_2, v) \tag{15}$$

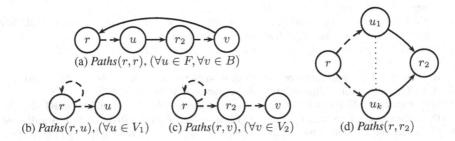

(a) $Paths(r, r)$, $(\forall u \in F, \forall v \in B)$

(b) $Paths(r, u)$, $(\forall u \in V_1)$ (c) $Paths(r, v)$, $(\forall v \in V_2)$ (d) $Paths(r, r_2)$

Fig. 9. Piecewise description of path sets: dotted lines are paths; solid lines are edges

The paths of path set $Paths(r, r_2)$ are depicted in Figure 9(d). The possible paths from $Paths(r_1, u)$ to r_2 are merged:

$$Paths(r, r_2) = \bigcup_{u \in F} Paths(r_1, u) \cdot \{\langle u, r_2 \rangle\} \tag{16}$$

It can be shown by an indirect argument (using Def. 4) that all paths from r to $u \in V_1$ are contained in set $Paths(r, u)$ of Equation 14 and that all paths from r to $v \in V_2$ are contained in set $Paths(r, v)$ of Equation 15. By using the inductive hypothesis we transform Equation 13 to the following path expression:

$$Paths(r, r) = \bigcup_{i \geq 0} \left[\left(\bigcup_{u \in F} \sigma(P_1(r_1, u) \cdot (u \to r_2)) \right) \cdot \left(\bigcup_{v \in B} \sigma(P_2(r_2, v) \cdot (v \to r_1)) \right) \right]^i \tag{17}$$

$$= \sigma([X \cdot Y]^*) = \sigma(L) \tag{18}$$

Equations 14 and 15 are transformed as

$$\forall u \in V_1 : Paths(r, u) = \sigma(L) \cdot \sigma(P_1(r_1, u)) = \sigma(L \cdot P_1(r_1, u)) \tag{19}$$

$$\forall v \in V_2 : Paths(r, v) = \sigma(L) \cdot \sigma(X) \cdot \sigma(P_2(r_2, v)) = \sigma(R \cdot P_2(r_2, u)) \tag{20}$$

where $Paths(r, r_2) = \bigcup_{u \in F} \sigma(P_1(r_1, u) \cdot (u \to r_2)) = \sigma(X)$.

A Declarative Framework for Analysis and Optimization

Henry Falconer, Paul H.J. Kelly, David M. Ingram, Michael R. Mellor,
Tony Field, and Olav Beckmann

Department of Computing, Imperial College London
180 Queen's Gate, London SW7 2BZ, U.K.
p.kelly@imperial.ac.uk

Abstract. DeepWeaver-1 is a tool supporting cross-cutting program analysis and transformation components, called "weaves". Like an aspect, a DeepWeaver weave consists of a query part, and a part which may modify code. DeepWeaver's query language is based on Prolog, and provides access to data-flow and control-flow reachability analyses. DeepWeaver provides a declarative way to access the internal structure of methods, and supports cross-cutting weaves which operate on code blocks from different parts of the codebase simultaneously. DeepWeaver operates at the level of bytecode, but offers predicates to extract structured control flow constructs. This paper motivates the design, and demonstrates some of its power, using a sequence of examples including performance profiling and domain-specific performance optimisations for database access and remote method invocation.

Introduction. Aspect-oriented programming tools, such as AspectJ [12], can be used to implement performance optimizations. However, tools like AspectJ are too weak, both to perform interesting optimizing transformations, and to capture the conditions for their validity. Similar problems arise when using AspectJ for static program analysis, e.g. to check usage rules for library code, or to detect software defects. For many, this is a consequence of deliberate simplicity in the aspect language design. This paper presents a prototype system which is powerful enough to express complex analyses (and transformations) - yet, like an aspect weaver, retains a declarative style by which some simplicity can be retained. The tool is motivated and illustrated using a series of examples, including intra-method performance profiling, and domain-specific optimizations for database access and remote method invocation.

Example. We begin with a very simple motivating example, a domain-specific performance optimisation for Java code that uses the JDBC (Java Database Connectivity) library. Consider this Java fragment:

```
ResultSet staff = statement.executeQuery("SELECT * FROM employees");
ResultSet clients = statement.executeQuery("SELECT * FROM customers");
... complex and messy code that uses clients but not staff ...
```

S. Krishnamurthi and M. Odersky (Eds.): CC 2007, LNCS 4420, pp. 218–232, 2007.

The first "executeQuery" call is redundant since its result set "staff" is never used. With DeepWeaver-1, we can write a weave that eliminates such redundant calls; see Figure 1.

The query part of the weave is a subset of ISO Prolog, with a rich set of built-in predicates to query properties of Java bytecode. When the query succeeds, the value bound to the weave's parameters (in this case "ExecCall") are passed to the Java action.

```
weave removeSelect(CodeBlock ExecCall):
  method("ResultSet Statement.executeQuery(String)", ExecMethod),
  call(ExecMethod, _, ExecCall, _),
  assignment(Result, ExecCall, _),
  \+ reaching_def(Result, _, _).
{
  System.out.print("Removing redundant SELECT at ");
  System.out.println(ExecCall.method);
  ExecCall.remove();
}
```

Fig. 1. A complete DeepWeaver-1 weave to locate and remove "executeQuery" calls whose results could never be used. The Java action is triggered for each instance of the Prolog variable "ExecCall" for which the query succeeds. The \+ operator is Prolog's "not", and in this example it succeeds if no match for the "reaching_def" predicate can be found.

How it works: The first step in Figure 1 is to find "ExecMethod", the body of the "executeQuery" method. Then we find a call to this method, "ExecCall". Then we find the assignment of "ExecCall"s return value to a variable "Result". Finally, we check that no *reaching definition* for "Result" can be found - that is, that the value returned by the "executeQuery" call is not used. Note that the SQL query string (`String`) cannot induce side effects, so the transformation is always valid, provided no exceptions are thrown.

1   Contributions

This paper introduces the DeepWeaver-1 language design, and illustrates its power using selected examples. The key contributions offered include:

- JoinPoints are `CodeBlocks`: the query part of a weave binds the weave parameters to `CodeBlocks`, which are contiguous regions of bytecode. The action part of the weave can then operate on these `CodeBlocks`, removing, modifying or replacing them. We show that this simple idea is remarkably effective.

- Structured control flow is rendered as predicates, which yield `CodeBlocks`. Thus, we operate on a low-level intermediate representation, yet can analyse code in structured, source-code terms - independently of source code details.
- Actions can operate on `CodeBlocks` from different parts of the codebase – thus, weaves can be truly "cross-cutting". The parameters bound by an action's query may refer to `CodeBlocks` gathered from disparate parts of the codebase.
- DeepWeaver-1's "interjections" provide a way for an action to inline advice before, after, around or instead of any `CodeBlock`. Interjections provide typed templates which can be bound to free variables at the context of use. Interjections can, furthermore, be specialised by replacing placeholder method calls.
- We introduce, motivate and demonstrate these concepts by means of a series of example applications. We conclude with a critical evaluation of the success of the work.

2   Background

Our primary motivation has been to build performance optimisation tools, in particular tools which embody domain-specific performance optimisation expertise. We have found AspectJ a remarkably valuable tool for building extensible profilers. We have also explored "domain-specific optimisation components" - which apply performance optimizations automatically. Our experience has been extremely positive: using AOP techniques has the potential to reduce dramatically the complexity of such software. It has also been frustrating; our requirements stretch the capabilities of conventional aspect languages. This paper reports on our first attempt to build a tool that does what we want.

We are not the first to explore these ideas. AspectJ extensions such as tracematch [4] and dataflow pointcut [15] cover some of the same ground. Meanwhile quite a number of tools have used Prolog or Datalog to query the codebase [9,13,18]. We review these and other work from the literature, and contrast them to DeepWeaver-1, in Section 5.

3   The Design of a Deeper Weaver

Program Representation. A key feature of our design is our decision to operate on a low-level intermediate representation (our implementation is built on SOOT [17]). A common alternative is to work with the abstract syntax tree (AST), and many successful tools do this [19,7,6,8]. This supports transformation by pattern-matching and tree rewriting very easily. However, our experience has been that more complex and interesting transformations are not easily expressed this way. Some support for this view will, we believe, be provided by examples presented later in this paper.

```
weave loopWithNoYield(CodeBlock Loop):
  method("* Thread.yield()", YieldMethod),
  loop(Loop),
  searchForCall(Loop, Loop, YieldMethod, TargetIfFound),
  null(TargetIfFound).

{
  System.out.print("Found a loop not broken by a yield() call in ");
  System.out.println(Loop.method);
}
```

Fig. 2. This weave finds loops which are not broken by a call to the `yield` method (as might be required in a non-pre-emptive threading context). The `loop` predicate matches all loops, whether arising from Java's `while`, `do..while` or `for` constructions. The `searchForCall` predicate finds the targets of all calls to the specified method between two points, and yields null if a path with no call exists.

Predicates Capture Control Structure. An AST makes it easy to match structured control-flow constructs such as loops. However, you need a rule for each loop type (or perhaps introduce a hierarchy of node subtypes). Using Prolog (or Datalog) predicates to characterise loops accounts for this rather neatly. For example, in Figure 2, the predicate `loop` matches all control-flow cycles.

CodeBlocks. DeepWeaver predicates are used to identify program constructs, which can then be operated on in the Java action part of the weave. This is done using `CodeBlocks`. A `CodeBlock` is a contiguous, non-empty sequence of bytecode.

Since Java only has structured control-flow, control flow constructs can be represented faithfully as `CodeBlocks`.

To avoid the confusion caused by stack instructions, `CodeBlocks` are represented using the SOOT "Jimple" intermediate representation [17]. For many common uses of DeepWeaver, the programmer need not be concerned with details of the SOOT representation, and we discourage programmers from operating at that level.

In the Java part of a weave, the programmer has access to the `CodeBlocks` passed in from the Prolog query part. We have imposed no limit to the possible transformations that can be applied. However, there are common operators which are "safe", in that they cannot yield invalid bytecode control flow when applied to well-formed `CodeBlocks`[1]. These include `cb.remove()`, `cb.interject-Before()` and `cb.interjectAfter()`. As we shall see in the next section, these allow code to be inserted at any specified point.

---

[1] In the current implementation, we do have some predicates that can create non-well-formed `CodeBlocks` (such as the LHS of an assignment).

```
aspect counters
{ // table of counter variable ids for each method
  static Hashtable counterLocals = new Hashtable();

  // first, a weave to add a counter variable to all methods
  weave addCounterVariable(SootMethod Method):
    method("* *(..)", Method).
  {
    DeepWeaverClass targetClass = DeepWeaverClass.classFromMethod(Method);
    Local myCounter = targetClass.insertLocalIntoMethod(Method,
                                                     IntType.v());
    counterLocals.put(Method, myCounter);
  }
  // now, a template for the code to insert
  interjection incrementCounter(int counter) {
    counter += 1;
  }
  // Insert the code at each access to an object of class C
  weave countAccesses(CodeBlock Access):
    assignment(Access, Rhs, Assignment), type(Access, "C").
  {
    InterjectionPrototype incCode
      = Interjection.getInterjectionByName("counters.incrementCounter")
                  .makePrototype();
    // Create one-element parameter list for interjection
    List params = new ArrayList();
    Local myCounter = (Local)counterLocals.get(Access.method);
    params.add(myCounter);

    // Insert the parameterised interjection
    Access.interjectBefore(incCode, params);
} }
```

Fig. 3. This aspect consists of two weaves, applied one after the other. The first adds a counter variable to each method. The second inserts code to increment the counter wherever an object of class C is updated. The interjection is a template whose bytecode is inserted at each insertion point. It is parameterised with the id of the counter variable.

Interjections. Interjections are templates for code that is to be inserted. A simple example is shown in Figure 3. The body of the interjection is copied directly at the specified location. Thus, in this example, it is the context's copy of the counter variable that is incremented. We discuss type safety of interjection parameters in Section 4.3.

Structure of a DeepWeaver Aspect. A DeepWeaver aspect consists of a sequence of weaves, together with definitions of interjections, helper predicates, and helper methods in Java. Each weave consists of a Prolog "query" part, followed by a Java "action" part.

```
aspect placeholders {
  interjection maybeCall() {
    if (Math.random() < 0.5) {
      Interjection.PLACEHOLDER_METHOD_FT(0);
    } else {
      System.out.println("Call omitted to reduce load");
  } }
  weave chickenOut(SootMethod Method, CodeBlock Target,
                   CodeBlock Location, List Params ):
    method("static void C.*()", Method),
    call(Method, Target, Location, Params).
  {
    InterjectionPrototype ip
      = Interjection.getInterjectionByName("placeholders.maybeCall")
                    .makePrototype();
    ip.replaceMethodCall(0, null, Method, Params);
    Location.replace(ip, Params);
} }
```

Fig. 4. This example shows the use of an interjection placeholder method. This weave rewrites calls to (static, void, parameterless) calls of class C, so they are omitted randomly. The method being called, **Method**, is substituted into the interjection.

The action part of a weave is executed once for each successful match of the query part.

Weave Composition. Weaves are applied to the target program in the sequence they appear in the aspect. Each weave is applied across the whole codebase, before the next begins.

Actions change the codebase. To avoid chaos, updates to the codebase are not executed immediately, during execution of the action. Instead, the implementation defers changes until all query matching has been completed. Thus, queries always apply to a consistent, static view of the codebase — and CodeBlocks always refer to what they were bound to.

Note that interjections provide a mechanism for "code quoting". However, it is substitution *into* quoted code that is often tricky in metaprogramming systems. Figure 4 shows our current solution. The interjection calls a special static method, Interjection.PLACEHOLDER_METHOD_FT(0). We replace this with the method we need to call using "ip.replaceMethodCall(0, null, Method, Params)". Each placeholder is numbered, from zero.

4   Evaluation

To evaluate the effectiveness of the DeepWeaver-1 design, we present two example optimisations that we have developed. In section 4.3 we review the results of these case studies.

```
predicate columnUsed(CodeBlock Target, CodeBlock Column):
 // Find program points where Target is used
 reaching_def(Target, Use, false),

 // Check that use is subject of a "get"
 call("* ResultSet.get*(String)", Use, Location, ColumnArgs),
 encloses(Location, Use),

 // Get parameter value, i.e. column name
 member(ColumnArg, ColumnArgs),
 local_constant_def(ColumnArg, Column).
}
```

Fig. 5. To rewrite the "select" query to specify the columns needed, we need to track down which columns will be accessed. We need to trace all possible control paths, and find where the ResultSet is used. Each use involves a "get" method, whose parameter is the name of the column being accessed. We need to collect all these names. It may be that the ResultSet escapes (by being returned, or passed as a parameter) — in which case we give up. **Reaching_def**'s third parameter reflects whether the definition escapes from the current method; set to **"false"** ensures the predicate fails if we are unable to track down all the uses.

```
weave refineSelectQuery(CodeBlock QueryString, List Columns):
 // Find JDBC execute() call site
 method("ResultSet Statement.executeQuery(String)", ExecMeth),
 call(ExecMeth, _, ExecCall, QueryStringLocal),

 // Find variable to which result is assigned
 assignment(Target, ExecCall, _),

 // Find the query string (from the method's constant pool)
 member(QSLocal, QueryStringLocal),
 local_constant_def(QSLocal, QueryString),

 // Collect set of Column strings used to access the ResultSet
 findall( Column, columnUsed(Target, Column), Columns ).
{
 // (Assume for brevity that it is a SELECT * and Columns is not empty)

 // Create new query String from list of Columns to select
 // (definition omitted for brevity)
 String newQuery = makeNewQuery(QueryString, Columns);

 // Replace existing string constant with new query string
 QueryString.replaceValue(StringConstant.v(newQuery));
}
```

Fig. 6. A weave to implement the "select *" optimisation. We use Prolog's "findall" to collect all the columns accessed, using the predicate in Figure 5.

4.1   The "Select *" Optimisation

Many common tutorial introductions to using the Java Database Connectivity (JDBC) library begin with code like this:

```
ResultSet r = s.execute("select * from employee");
while ( r.next() ) {
  String col1 = r.getString("Name");   // Get column 1
}
```

This is inefficient; we found, for example, that with a 10-column table, it is about twice as fast to select just the one column that is being used:

```
ResultSet r = s.execute("select Name from employee");
while ( r.next() ) {
  String col1 = r.getString("Name");   // Get column 1
}
```

To implement this in DeepWeaver-1, we need to find the columns being accessed, as illustrated in Figure 5. The DeepWeaver predicate to do this collects the set of parameters of get methods applied to the result set returned by the call to the execute method. Figure 6 shows how this is used to rewrite the original query to specify the columns needed.

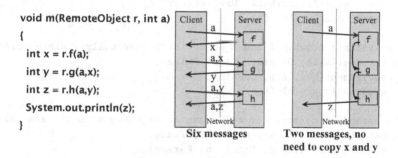

Fig. 7. A sequence of three method calls on a remote object "r" results in three call-return round-trip network transactions. Furthermore, parameter "a" is transferred several times, and also results "x" and "y" are returned unnecessarily. The aggregated implementation suffers fewer network latencies and transfers less data.

4.2   The RMI Aggregation Optimisation

Java's Remote Method Invocation (RMI) mechanism is convenient but if used carelessly results in unnecessary communication. Figure 7 illustrates the potential value of aggregating RMI calls. We have built several implementations of this optimisation [21]. Correctness issues for the optimisation are quite subtle; a formal analysis is given in [2].

Consider an RMI call A, followed by some intervening code, then a second
RMI call B. Our approach to RMI aggregation is to consider whether RMI call
A can be relocated so that it can be combined with the later call, RMI B.

```
predicate isAggregatableRMIPair(CodeBlock CallA, CodeBlock CallB,
                      List ParamA, List ParamB, CodeBlock ResultOfA):
// A and B are distinct RMI calls, and A precedes B:
call(RemoteMethodA, RemoteObjectA, CallA, ParamA),
type(RemoteObjectA, "java.rmi.Remote"),
precedes(CallA, CallB), CallA \= CallB,
call(RemoteMethodB, RemoteObjectB, CallB, ParamB),
type(RemoteObjectB, "java.rmi.Remote"),
dominates(A,B), post_dominates(B,A),

// If A or B is in a loop they're both in the same one:
forall ( loop(Loop),
  ( ( encloses(Loop, CallA), encloses(Loop, CallB)
    ); // OR
    ( \+ encloses(Loop, CallA), \+ encloses(Loop, CallB)
  ) ) ),
// A's result is not used before B
assignment(ResultOfA, CallA, _),
\+ ( reaching_def(ResultOfA, UseOfResult, _),
  precedes(UseOfResult, CallB)
),
// Assignments between A and B do not have externally-visible effects:
\+ ( between(CallA, OnPath, CallB, false),
     assignment(Lhs, Rhs, OnPath),
     externally_visible(Lhs)
),
// No method or constructor calls can occur between call A and call B:
\+ ( between(CallA, Location, CallB, false),
     call(Method, Target, Location, Params),
     \+ side_effect_free_method(Method) ).
```

Fig. 8. A predicate to test the validity of RMI aggregation

RMI Aggregation validity conditions. The conditions under which this is
valid are encoded in Figure 8. In summary, this states:

- **A and B are distinct RMI calls, and A precedes B.**
- **All paths to B go through A**, that is, "dominates(A,B)")
- **All paths from A go through B** ("post_dominates(B,A)")
- **If A or B is in a loop they're both in the same one.**
  Note that the forall predicate succeeds when all instances of Loop satisfy
  the condition. In Prolog, ";" is logical "or"; recall that \+ is "not").
- **A's result is not used before B**

- **Assignments on paths between A and B do not have externally-visible effects.** This is necessary for two reasons: firstly, another thread might observe changes to externally-visible objects out-of-order relative to the state of the remote server. Secondly, if call A throws an exception, the intervening code will already have been executed — so we must ensure it has no effects visible in or beyond the exception handler.

  The "false" parameter to `between` ensures we find all assignments `OnPath` that *might* be reached. The definition of "`externally_visible`" could be very sophisticated; a simple implementation would check that the LHS is a local variable with no escaping uses prior to call B.

- **No method or constructor calls can occur between call A and call B – apart from those known to be side-effect free.** This is required because DeepWeaver's analysis is currently not inter-procedural. In our prototype implementation we treat simple String operations as side-effect free in order to allow aggregation in the presence of simple code to prepare string parameters.

This example has been simplified for presentation purposes. In particular we have only considered the case where A returns a result but B does not.

RMI Aggregation Implementation. The conditions for validity of the RMI aggregation optimisation, listed above, can easily be assembled to form a Deep-Weaver predicate for the query part of the weave:

```
isAggregatableRMIPair(CallA, CallB, ParamA, ParamB,
                      ResultA, ResultB)
```

The action part of the weave is sketched in Figure 9. The code required to do this is somewhat involved. First we delete call A. We need to identify any parameters common to the two calls, and to check for where the result from call A is used as a parameter to call B. We then need to construct the body and formal parameter list for the aggregate call, which is inserted into the server class (if the target object's type is actually an interface, we need to insert the code into all classes that implement it). Finally, we need to construct the actual parameter list for the call to this new method, which replaces call B.

4.3   Evaluation: Discussion

Performance: Weave-Time. The time taken to apply a weave to a codebase depends, of course, on the weave itself. To evaluate this, we created an artificial benchmark generator creating simple candidates for the RMI aggregation optimisation. Applying the RMI aggregation weave to 100 such classes takes less than 20 seconds.

It is quite possible to write predicates which are extremely inefficient (for example, queries involving all control flow paths in a method). Although this has not yet proven a serious concern, the worst-case behaviour could be very poor.

```
weave rmiResultForwarding(
              CodeBlock CallA,  CodeBlock CallB,
              List ParamA, List ParamB,
              CodeBlock ResultA,  CodeBlock ResultB )
  isAggregatableRMIPair(CallA, CallB, ParamA, ParamB, ResultA, ResultB).
{
       ...Remove call A.
       ...Create new server method, to implement the aggregated call.
       ...Insert it into each potential callee class.
       ...Replace call B with call to the new aggregated method.
}
```

Fig. 9. Outline of implementation of RMI aggregation. The implementation is too complicated to include here, mainly due to the necessary manipulation of parameter lists for the new aggregated method.

Performance: Execution Time. There is no performance overhead for code inserted using interjections (for example in Figure 3 where interjected code increments a counter). The bytecode is inlined directly. The performance imporvement that can be achieved by changing the code base obviously depend on the nature of the transformations specified by the Deepweaver actions. For example, we have found that the "Select *" optimisation can easily yield a factor of two reduction in query execution time (MS SQL Server, using one column from a 10 column table). The value of the RMI aggregation optimisation depends on the network performance, and the amount of redundant data movement that can be avoided. The performance improvements of the optimisation were evaluated in our earlier work, which used a run-time framework with higher overheads [21].

The Query Language and Program Model. DeepWeaver's design centres on the use of Prolog predicates to identify `CodeBlocks` within a low-level three-address-code IR. Many interesting applications are expressed quite naturally this way. Some are difficult. For example, a transformation that interchanges a pair of nested loops: this is easy to express as rewriting in an abstract syntax tree. With DeepWeaver the loop (excluding its body) is not a contiguous block.

Queries are not always easy to write or to understand. We are developing idioms for common situations, and aim to support them with more built-in operators – for example to express regular expressions over paths [11].

The separation between query and action parts can sometimes be awkward, since some queries need to use Java (for example to query a software configuration description). Also, actions commonly need to issue followup queries.

A key design decision was whether to build our own Prolog engine. The alternative would be to export the code factbase into an external Prolog engine, or to implement the Prolog primitives as calls from Prolog to Java. We made this decision in order to retain control over query execution, and we plan to explore query optimisation. The disadvantage is that our Prolog implementation is partial, and there would be advantages in exploring the use of the full power of Prolog, perhaps including constraint Prolog.

As it stands our Prolog implementation is very restrictive; we lack terms, higher-order and non-declarative features.

The Action Language. DeepWeaver resembles AspectJ (and is built as a pure extension of the AspectBench compiler for AspectJ [3]). In AspectJ, the Java "advice" is inserted at the selected joinpoint. In DeepWeaver, we don't have a joinpoint - we have a set of bindings for the query predicate's parameters. This is passed to the Java action part, which is executed *at weave time.*

This gives us considerable expressive power, which we need for complex examples like RMI aggregation. However it makes some tasks much more difficult and more prone to error. A key area for enhancement is to introduce a more refined type system that distinguishes different kinds of CodeBlock – essentially we need to expose SOOT's Jimple IR more explicitly.

The Interjection Mechanism. DeepWeaver's interjections provide a means to create a bytecode template that can be parameterised and then inserted into the codebase. A key weakness is that we cannot check that actual parameter types match formal parameter types. Note also that interjections are naturally used in a polymorphic way – this is what we need, for example, in the RMI aggregation example, where the type of the aggregated method depends on the type of the original methods. We also need to take care with exceptions: if interjected code might throw an exception, the host code must be able to handle it.

Another weakness is that only interjections can be used as prototypes - we commonly wish to move or duplicate CodeBlocks. To handle this we need to account for a CodeBlock's free variables and ensure inserted code's variables are bound properly.

5   Related Work

Query Languages for Code. DataLog, a similarly restricted, declarative form of Prolog, has been adopted by several projects. JQuery [20] and CodeQuest [9] use it to query the Eclipse [16] IDE's abstract syntax tree. CrocoPat [5] uses it for design pattern recovery and metrics. Bddbddb [13] is closer to our work in operating at the bytecode level, and supports intra- and inter-procedural dataflow analyses. CrocoPat and bddbddb include substantial query optimisation.

Transformation and Rewriting. AspectJ [12] provides a join point model for matching points in Java code, at which new code will be inserted before and/or after. A code matching query is restricted, for comprehensibility reasons, to various predefined code points (e.g. method call) but allows flexibility in identifier and type matching. Aspicere [1] tries to work around the restrictions in the joinpoint model when applied to C using a Prolog-like query language.

Many IDEs support refactoring program transformations initiated by the user. JunGL [18] is an interesting refactoring scripting language, quite comparable to DeepWeaver-1, that uses Datalog queries embedded within an ML-based language.

TXL [6] and Stratego [19] are very general and powerful tools for source-code transformation. They both provide a mechanism to specifying grammars, pattern matching and rewriting. Stratego supports strategies to control rewrite order, and dynamic rules for context sensitive rewrites.

Establishing the soundness of optimizing program transformations is an issue that we have not dealt with formally in this paper. Soundness has been addressed in other contexts, however, for example Rhodium [14], which is a domain-specific language for specifying program analysis and transformation in the context of a C-like intermediate language.

6   Conclusions and Further Work

DeepWeaver-1 is a prototype tool which shows considerable promise:

- It provides a delivery vehicle for domain-specific performance optimisation components. DeepWeaver aspects package together a declarative statement of the conditions for validity of an optimisation (the "query part"), with the implementation of the transformation (the "action part").
- DeepWeaver-1's low-level IR, and the role of `CodeBlocks` as the focus for queries, works remarkably well when combined with the power of a Prolog-like query language. Prolog predicates allow structured control flow to be captured where it is needed, whilst also supporting control-flow and data-flow–based reasoning. These are often useful for characterising the validity of optimisations.
- We have demonstrated the power of the approach using a small number of application examples.

There remain many challenges in developing these ideas. We plan two major directions for further work:

1. Enhancing the query language. We need to clarify the rendering of the IR in the query language, and refine the type system. We also need to support user-definable data-flow analyses in an elegant and expressive way (bddbddb [13] is promising in this regard). Similarly, and likely by this means, we need to handle inter-procedural analysis. Key to these is query optimisation. We may also extend the query language conceptually to handle `CodeBlocks` with holes, free variables, and to represent "slices" of dependent instructions.
2. Enhancing the static safety and expressiveness of the action language. Our goal is to attain a statically-verifiable guarantee that a weave cannot generate a "broken" codebase: basic safety properties such as stack balance, name clashes, initialised and bound variables (see, for example, SafeGen [10]). Central to this is to support type-checked parameterisation of interjections, and to check that the free variables of cloned `CodeBlocks` are bound to variables of the right type when they are interjected.

Acknowledgments. This work was supported by the EPSRC SPOCS grant (EP/E002412), EPSRC PhD studentships, and by an IBM Faculty Award.

References

1. Bram Adams and Tom Tourwé. Aspect orientation for C: Express yourself. In *AOSD SPLAT Workshop*, 2005.
2. Alexander Ahern and Nobuko Yoshida. Formalising Java RMI with explicit code mobility. In *OOPSLA '05: Proceedings of the 20th annual ACM SIGPLAN conference on Object oriented programming, systems, languages, and applications*, pages 403–422, New York, NY, USA, 2005. ACM Press.
3. Chris Allan, Pavel Avgustinov, Aske Simon Christensen, Bruno Dufour, Christopher Goard, Laurie Hendren, Sascha Kuzins, Jennifer Lhoťk, Ondrej Lhoťk, Oege de Moor, Damien Sereni, Ganesh Sittampalam, Julian Tibble, and Clark Verbrugge. ABC the AspectBench compiler for AspectJ: A workbench for aspect-oriented programming language and compilers research. In *OOPSLA '05: Companion to the 20th annual ACM SIGPLAN conference on Object-oriented programming, systems, languages, and applications*, pages 88–89, New York, NY, USA, 2005. ACM Press.
4. Chris Allan, Pavel Avgustinov, Aske Simon Christensen, Laurie Hendren, Sascha Kuzins, Ondrej Lhoták, Oege de Moor, Damien Sereni, Ganesh Sittampalam, and Julian Tibble. Adding trace matching with free variables to AspectJ. In *OOPSLA '05: Proceedings of the 20th annual ACM SIGPLAN conference on Object oriented programming, systems, languages, and applications*, pages 345–364, New York, NY, USA, 2005. ACM Press.
5. Dirk Beyer and Claus Lewerentz. CrocoPat: Efficient pattern analysis in object-oriented programs. In *Proceedings of the 11th IEEE International Workshop on Program Comprehension (IWPC 2003, Portland, OR, May 10-11)*, pages 294–295. IEEE Computer Society Press, Los Alamitos (CA), 2003.
6. James R. Cordy, Charles D. Halpern-Hamu, and Eric Promislow. TXL: a rapid prototyping system for programming language dialects. *Computer Languages*, 16(1):97–107, 1991.
7. Kei Davis and Daniel J. Quinlan. Rose: An optimizing transformation system for C++ array-class libraries. In *ECOOP '98: Workshop on Object-Oriented Technology*, pages 452–453, London, UK, 1998. Springer-Verlag.
8. Dawson R. Engler. Incorporating application semantics and control into compilation. In *USENIX Conference on Domain-Specific Languages (DSL'97)*, pages 103–118. USENIX, 1997.
9. Elnar Hajiyev, Mathieu Verbaere, and Oege de Moor. Codequest: Scalable source code queries with datalog. In Dave Thomas, editor, *ECOOP'06: Proceedings of the 20th European Conference on Object-Oriented Programming*, volume 4067 of *Lecture Notes in Computer Science*, pages 2–27, Berlin, Germany, 2006. Springer.
10. Shan Shan Huang, David Zook, and Yannis Smaragdakis. Statically safe program generation with SafeGen. In *GPCE*, pages 309–326, 2005.
11. David Lacey, Neil Jones, Eric Van Wyk, and Carl Christian Frederikson. Proving correctness of compiler optimizations by temporal logic. *Higher-Order and Symbolic Computation*, 17(2), 2004.
12. Ramnivas Laddad. *AspectJ in Action: Practical Aspect-Oriented Programming*. Manning Publications Co., Greenwich, CT, USA, 2003.

13. Monica S. Lam, John Whaley, V. Benjamin Livshits, Michael C. Martin, Dzintars Avots, Michael Carbin, and Christopher Unkel. Context-sensitive program analysis as database queries. In *PODS '05: Proceedings of the twenty-fourth ACM SIGMOD-SIGACT-SIGART symposium on Principles of database systems*, pages 1–12, New York, NY, USA, 2005. ACM Press.

14. Sorin Lerner, Todd Millstein, Erika Rice, and Craig Chambers. Automated soundness proofs for dataflow analyses and transformations via local rules. In *POPL 2005: Proceedings of the 32nd ACM SIGPLAN-SIGACT symposium on Principles of programming languages*, pages 364–377, New York, NY, USA, 2005. ACM Press.

15. Hidehiko Masuhara and Kazunori Kawauchi. Dataflow pointcut in aspect-oriented programming. In *The First Asian Symposium on Programming Languages and Systems (APLAS'03)*, volume 2895 of *Lecture Notes in Computer Science*, pages 105–121. Spinger-Verlag, November 2003.

16. The Eclipse Foundation Inc. The Eclipse extensible development platform.

17. Raja Vallée-Rai, Laurie Hendren, Vijay Sundaresan, Patrick Lam, Etienne Gagnon, and Phong Co. SOOT - a Java optimization framework. In *Proceedings of CASCON 1999*, pages 125–135, 1999.

18. Mathieu Verbaere, Ran Ettinger, and Oege de Moor. JunGL: a scripting language for refactoring. In *ICSE '06: Proceeding of the 28th international conference on Software engineering*, pages 172–181, New York, NY, USA, 2006. ACM Press.

19. Eelco Visser. Program transformation with Stratego/XT: Rules, strategies, tools, and systems in StrategoXT-0.9. In C. Lengauer et al., editors, *Domain-Specific Program Generation*, volume 3016 of *Lecture Notes in Computer Science*, pages 216–238. Springer-Verlag, June 2004.

20. Kris De Volder. Jquery: A generic code browser with a declarative configuration language. In Pascal Van Hentenryck, editor, *PADL '06: Eighth International Symposium on Practical Aspects of Declarative Languages*, volume 3819 of *Lecture Notes in Computer Science*, pages 88–102. Springer, 2006.

21. Kwok Cheung Yeung and Paul H. J. Kelly. Optimising Java RMI programs by communication restructuring. In *Proceedings of the ACM/IFIP/USENIX International Middleware Conference 2003, Rio De Janeiro, Brazil, 16–20 June 2003*, LNCS, June 2003.

Author Index

Lecture Notes in Computer Science

For information about Vols. 1–4305

please contact your bookseller or Springer

Vol. 4354: M. Hanus (Ed.), Practical Aspects of Declarative Languages. X, 335 pages. 2006.

Vol. 4353: T. Schwentick, D. Suciu (Eds.), Database Theory – ICDT 2007. XI, 419 pages. 2006.

Vol. 4352: T.-J. Cham, J. Cai, C. Dorai, D. Rajan, T.-S. Chua, L.-T. Chia (Eds.), Advances in Multimedia Modeling, Part II. XVIII, 743 pages. 2006.

Vol. 4351: T.-J. Cham, J. Cai, C. Dorai, D. Rajan, T.-S. Chua, L.-T. Chia (Eds.), Advances in Multimedia Modeling, Part I. XIX, 797 pages. 2006.

Vol. 4349: B. Cook, A. Podelski (Eds.), Verification, Model Checking, and Abstract Interpretation. XI, 395 pages. 2007.

Vol. 4348: S.T. Taft, R.A. Duff, R.L. Brukardt, E. Ploedereder, P. Leroy (Eds.), Ada 2005 Reference Manual. XXII, 765 pages. 2006.

Vol. 4347: J. Lopez (Ed.), Critical Information Infrastructures Security. X, 286 pages. 2006.

Vol. 4346: L. Brim, B. Haverkort, M. Leucker, J. van de Pol (Eds.), Formal Methods: Applications and Technology. X, 363 pages. 2007.

Vol. 4345: N. Maglaveras, I. Chouvarda, V. Koutkias, R. Brause (Eds.), Biological and Medical Data Analysis. XIII, 496 pages. 2006. (Sublibrary LNBI).

Vol. 4344: V. Gruhn, F. Oquendo (Eds.), Software Architecture. X, 245 pages. 2006.

Vol. 4342: H. de Swart, E. Orłowska, G. Schmidt, M. Roubens (Eds.), Theory and Applications of Relational Structures as Knowledge Instruments II. X, 373 pages. 2006. (Sublibrary LNAI).

Vol. 4341: P.Q. Nguyen (Ed.), Progress in Cryptology - VIETCRYPT 2006. XI, 385 pages. 2006.

Vol. 4340: R. Prodan, T. Fahringer, Grid Computing. XXIII, 317 pages. 2007.

Vol. 4339: E. Ayguadé, G. Baumgartner, J. Ramanujam, P. Sadayappan (Eds.), Languages and Compilers for Parallel Computing. XI, 476 pages. 2006.

Vol. 4338: P. Kalra, S. Peleg (Eds.), Computer Vision, Graphics and Image Processing. XV, 965 pages. 2006.

Vol. 4337: S. Arun-Kumar, N. Garg (Eds.), FSTTCS 2006: Foundations of Software Technology and Theoretical Computer Science. XIII, 430 pages. 2006.

Vol. 4335: S.A. Brueckner, S. Hassas, M. Jelasity, D. Yamins (Eds.), Engineering Self-Organising Systems. XII, 212 pages. 2007. (Sublibrary LNAI).

Vol. 4334: B. Beckert, R. Hähnle, P.H. Schmitt (Eds.), Verification of Object-Oriented Software. XXIX, 658 pages. 2007. (Sublibrary LNAI).

Vol. 4333: U. Reimer, D. Karagiannis (Eds.), Practical Aspects of Knowledge Management. XII, 338 pages. 2006. (Sublibrary LNAI).

Vol. 4332: A. Bagchi, V. Atluri (Eds.), Information Systems Security. XV, 382 pages. 2006.

Vol. 4331: G. Min, B. Di Martino, L.T. Yang, M. Guo, G. Ruenger (Eds.), Frontiers of High Performance Computing and Networking – ISPA 2006 Workshops. XXXVII, 1141 pages. 2006.

Vol. 4330: M. Guo, L.T. Yang, B. Di Martino, H.P. Zima, J. Dongarra, F. Tang (Eds.), Parallel and Distributed Processing and Applications. XVIII, 953 pages. 2006.

Vol. 4329: R. Barua, T. Lange (Eds.), Progress in Cryptology - INDOCRYPT 2006. X, 454 pages. 2006.

Vol. 4328: D. Penkler, M. Reitenspiess, F. Tam (Eds.), Service Availability. X, 289 pages. 2006.

Vol. 4327: M. Baldoni, U. Endriss (Eds.), Declarative Agent Languages and Technologies IV. VIII, 257 pages. 2006. (Sublibrary LNAI).

Vol. 4326: S. Göbel, R. Malkewitz, I. Iurgel (Eds.), Technologies for Interactive Digital Storytelling and Entertainment. X, 384 pages. 2006.

Vol. 4325: J. Cao, I. Stojmenovic, X. Jia, S.K. Das (Eds.), Mobile Ad-hoc and Sensor Networks. XIX, 887 pages. 2006.

Vol. 4323: G. Doherty, A. Blandford (Eds.), Interactive Systems. XI, 269 pages. 2007.

Vol. 4322: F. Kordon, J. Sztipanovits (Eds.), Reliable Systems on Unreliable Networked Platforms. XIV, 317 pages. 2007.

Vol. 4320: R. Gotzhein, R. Reed (Eds.), System Analysis and Modeling: Language Profiles. X, 229 pages. 2006.

Vol. 4319: L.-W. Chang, W.-N. Lie (Eds.), Advances in Image and Video Technology. XXVI, 1347 pages. 2006.

Vol. 4318: H. Lipmaa, M. Yung, D. Lin (Eds.), Information Security and Cryptology. XI, 305 pages. 2006.

Vol. 4317: S.K. Madria, K.T. Claypool, R. Kannan, P. Uppuluri, M.M. Gore (Eds.), Distributed Computing and Internet Technology. XIX, 466 pages. 2006.

Vol. 4316: M.M. Dalkilic, S. Kim, J. Yang (Eds.), Data Mining and Bioinformatics. VIII, 197 pages. 2006. (Sublibrary LNBI).

Vol. 4314: C. Freksa, M. Kohlhase, K. Schill (Eds.), KI 2006: Advances in Artificial Intelligence. XII, 458 pages. 2007. (Sublibrary LNAI).

Vol. 4313: T. Margaria, B. Steffen (Eds.), Leveraging Applications of Formal Methods. IX, 197 pages. 2006.

Vol. 4312: S. Sugimoto, J. Hunter, A. Rauber, A. Morishima (Eds.), Digital Libraries: Achievements, Challenges and Opportunities. XVIII, 571 pages. 2006.

Vol. 4311: K. Cho, P. Jacquet (Eds.), Technologies for Advanced Heterogeneous Networks II. XI, 253 pages. 2006.

Vol. 4310: T. Boyanov, S. Dimova, K. Georgiev, G. Nikolov (Eds.), Numerical Methods and Applications. XIII, 715 pages. 2007.

Vol. 4309: P. Inverardi, M. Jazayeri (Eds.), Software Engineering Education in the Modern Age. VIII, 207 pages. 2006.

Vol. 4308: S. Chaudhuri, S.R. Das, H.S. Paul, S. Tirthapura (Eds.), Distributed Computing and Networking. XIX, 608 pages. 2006.

Vol. 4307: P. Ning, S. Qing, N. Li (Eds.), Information and Communications Security. XIV, 558 pages. 2006.

Vol. 4306: Y. Avrithis, Y. Kompatsiaris, S. Staab, N.E. O'Connor (Eds.), Semantic Multimedia. XII, 241 pages. 2006.